STUDIES IN THE ACQUISITION OF ANAPHORA
VOLUME I

STUDIES IN THEORETICAL PSYCHOLINGUISTICS

STUDIES IN THE ACQUISITION OF ANAPHORA

Volume I
Defining the Constraints

Edited by

BARBARA LUST

Cornell University, Ithaca, U.S.A.

D. REIDEL PUBLISHING COMPANY

A MEMBER OF THE KLUWER ACADEMIC PUBLISHERS GROUP

DORDRECHT / BOSTON / LANCASTER / TOKYO

Library of Congress Cataloging-in-Publication Data

CIP

Studies in the acquisition of anaphora.

    (Studies in theoretical psycholinguistics)
    Bibliography: p.
    Includes index.
    Contents: v.1. Defining the constraints
    1. Anaphora   (Linguistics) 2. Language   acquisition. 3.
Generative grammar. I. Lust, Barbara, 1941–   II. Series.
P299.A5S78 1986   415   86–3226
ISBN 90–277–2121–1 (v.1)
ISBN 90–277–2122–X (pbk. : v.1)

Published by D. Reidel Publishing Company.
P.O. Box 17, 3300 AA Dordrecht, Holland.

Sold and distributed in the U.S.A. and Canada
by Kluwer Academic Publishers,
190 Old Derby Street, Hingham, MA 02043, U.S.A.

In all other countries, sold and distributed
by Kluwer Academic Publishers Group,
P.O. Box 322, 3300 AH Dordrecht, Holland.

2-0487-250 ts

TABLE OF CONTENTS

PREFACE

This book is addressed to a central area of current linguistics and psycholinguistics: anaphora. It is a collection of independent studies by individuals who are currently working on problems in this area. The book includes two independent volumes. The major focus of these volumes is a psycholinguistic problem: the first language acquisition of anaphora. The volumes are intended to provide a basic reference source for the study of this one central, critical area of language competence. They combine results from the interdisciplinary study this area has attracted in recent years.

Each of the studies collected here is intended to be readable independently of the others. Thus a theoretical linguist or psycholinguist may each use this book only in part.

Two basic assumptions underlie this collection of studies. (1) Significant psycholinguistic study of the problem of first language acquisition requires *a basis in linguistic theory*. We look to linguistic theory (a) for the formulation of testable hypotheses which are coherent with a general theoretical model of language competence, and which, by empirical confirmation or disconfirmation, will have consequences which can be integrated in a general theory of language and of mind. This is because we pursue explanation of the problem of first language acquisition, not merely description. (b) We also look to linguistic theory for precision in the description of language stimuli and language behavior in empirical studies. This is in order to promote replicability and interpretability of empirical results.

(2) Significant advance in the study of the nature of human language and of the human competence for language can and must be made by *empirical study of language behavior*. Although major advances in this study have been made recently by deductive theory construction alone, an essential and irreplaceable test of such theory of the mind must include empirical test of its empirical predictions. Under the assumption that such theoretical study can and must have empirical consequences, we hold procedures for this empirical test to the same rigor of experimental method as any science.

The studies in volume one fall into *three parts*. Part A collects several *theoretical studies* on the nature of anaphora. These provide a general introduction and definition of the linguistic domain of anaphora, and pursue several theoretical issues which are currently critical to the linguistic study of this area. Part B collects several *experimental studies* which have produced empirical results in the study of various aspects of the acquisition of anaphora. These studies cover each of the basic types of anaphora. Each seeks empirical evidence on the precise nature of the principles and constraints which the child brings to bear in acquiring the grammar of anaphora in first language. The *commentary* (Part C) critically considers certain experimental studies reported in this volume and relates their results to other work in the fields of linguistics and psycholinguistics.

The *introduction* to this first volume attempts to summarize and formulate the basic issues which motivate the study of anaphora and to give an overview, summarizing major results across individual experimental studies of first language acquisition of anaphora and evaluating their significance. It relates these results to others from other laboratories not represented in this volume and argues that evidence from empirical work to date supports the existence of certain linguistically significant principles and constraints which the child brings to bear on the language acquisition process and which thus appear to be included in the human competence for natural language. It assesses the nature of these constraints in terms of their linguistic specificity.

Volume two is focussed on the interaction of these internal constraints with experience of language data. Any comprehensive model of first language acquisition must confront this interaction which clearly provides the grist of the real facts of first language acquisition of a specific language. More specifically, however, it is only through precise study of the effects of such experience, both theoretically and empirically, that one can confirm the precise nature of the internal constraints themselves. Thus Volume II includes initial theoretical study of relevant aspects of learnability theory. In addition it includes examples of study of the interaction of the constraints on anaphora with the parser itself, i.e., with that component of language knowledge which mediates between incoming data and the internal representation of language knowledge. It also includes examples of empirical study of second language acquisition of anaphora (after the experience of a first language), and study of acquisition of anaphora under experience through hearing loss. It also addresses basic issues of methodology which must be confronted in the attempt to measure grammatical competence through the dark mirror of the basic empirical data, i.e., child language performance.

All of the work represented here is motivated by the major intellectual problem which Noam Chomsky has formulated: how is it possible that a child acquires a first language under the deprived stimulus conditions available; what characteristics of the human mind insure this acquisition; to what degree can we both formulate these characteristics with scientific precision and empirically validate them? A component of the work represented here calls on recent linguistic work in the theory of "Government and Binding" (GB) which is currently being developed by Chomsky and scholars working in his theoretical framework. This theory has formulated precise principles for the study of anaphora, viz., a set of "Binding principles." We have made an effort in the chapters collected here to extract basic and deep principles from this theory in such a way that each will be readable by both linguists and non-linguists without previous extensive familiarity with all of the details of the subtle, complex and fast-developing theory of GB. Necessarily, the chapters vary in the degree to which they have succeeded in this task.

The experimental studies reported in this first volume, and in the second, include several from our laboratory here at Cornell, but also several from other laboratories working independently on related problems (e.g., the laboratory of Tom Roeper and his students at the University of Massachusetts, Amherst, that of Guy Carden and collaborators at University of British Columbia as well as the Piagetian laboratory initiated by Hermine Sinclair in Geneva, Switzerland). We present this range in the belief that sound empirical results must replicate under differing theoretical points of view given comparability in experimental method.

Finally, most of the research in this book deals with anaphora in English, although we seek to identify deep, 'universal' principles of acquisition. Cross-linguistic study is currently making major advances in the theoretical study of anaphora in Universal Grammar; and extensive cross-linguistic experimental study of acquisition of anaphora is now becoming available. We restrict ourselves to the study of English in order to provide groundwork, an assessment of what is firmly kown in English, as a base for comparison that will be necessary to interpretation of forthcoming results of cross-linguistic studies.

The first volume and the second would never have been possible without the scientific exchange among individual scholars represented here who chose to share their results bearing on similar problems, in the trust that the truth lies in converging evidence from independent scholars. The volumes would also not have been possible without the silent collaboration of other scholars not directly represented here. James Gair provided constant theoretical analysis and critical inquiry on the nature of the results reflected here, and invaluable support. John Bowers and Wayne Harbert each provided linguistic analyses of individual manuscripts and critical support throughout. Louis Mangione provided consistent theoretical exchange on critical issues. Hermine Sinclair provided basic education in the area of developmental psycholinguistics as a science and continual intellectual exchange on issues and data. Lila Gleitman provided critical feedback on several studies and issues and tireless, invaluable support. Guy Carden provided detailed critical analysis of research methodology and results. D. T. Langendoen shared and taught linguistic inquiry. Marion Potts provided invaluable support. Ken Wexler and Tom Roeper provided invaluable intellectual provocation and editorial advice.

Research in our laboratory represented in this volume owes deeply to the discipline, consistency, insight and commitment of several irreplaceable research assistants and associates: YuChin Chien, Suzanne Flynn, Terri Clifford, and Michiko Edwards. Assistance in data analyses was critically provided by Shirley Hsu and Ling Wu as well as by, very fundamentally, YuChin Chien.

Manuscript preparation would not have been possible without the tireless skillful support of Vicki Griffin. She, with the assistance of Shawn Lovelace and Kay Stickane, conquered the word processor and manuscript production with incomparable skill.

Our research represented in this volume was supported by grants from NSF #BNS 7825115, 8318983, and 8206328 and by smaller grants for individual studies from the Cornell University College of Human Ecology College Grants Committee. Two institutions provided support which was critical to the completion of this work: Cornell University Department of Human Development and Family Studies, and MIT Department of Linguistics and Philosophy.

Ithaca, New York   BARBARA LUST
July 1985

INTRODUCTION

BARBARA LUST

INTRODUCTION

CONTENTS

B. Lust (ed.), Studies in the Acquisition of Anaphora, Vol. I, 3–103.
© 1986 by D. Reidel Publishing Company.

I. GENERAL INTRODUCTION

This introduction has five sections. The *first section* reviews the basic tenets of the research paradigm inspired by the theory of Universal Grammar. It defines the focal concern of all the studies in this volume, *anaphora*, establishing a vocabulary which is general enough to extend to both linguistic and psycholinguistic study. It attempts to motivate the interdisciplinary study of anaphora which has inspired the collection of papers in this volume.

The *second section* of this introduction briefly reviews more specific linguistic concepts and issues which are necessary to the study of anaphora (either theoretical or empirical), referring the reader to sources in this volume and in the field for detail. The *third section* formulates questions which motivate current study of first language acquisition of anaphora with regard to these concepts. The *fourth section* provides a brief review of certain critical results from the empirical studies of first language acquisition of anaphora which are reported by contributors to this book, setting these in the context of other studies in the field. The *fifth section* draws tentative conclusions for the initiation of a theory of first language acquisition of anaphora and derives implications of these results for linguistic theory of UG. It sketches directions for future research.

1. THEORY OF UNIVERSAL GRAMMAR (UG)

The theory of Universal Grammar (UG) attempts to provide a "system of principles, conditions and rules that are elements or properties of all human languages, not merely by accident, but by necessity ..." (Chomsky, 1975, 29). In doing so it attempts to articulate fundamental principles and parameters "that sharply restrict the class of attainable grammars and narrowly constrain their form" (Chomsky, 1981a, 3−4). At the same time, "UG is taken to be a characterization of the child's pre-linguistic initial state" (Chomsky, 1981a, 7). In this sense, it is "an element of shared biological endowment" (Chomsky, 1981a, 8). Through its dual nature, UG comprises both a linguistic theory and a theory of one component of the human cognitive competence for language (Chomsky, 1975, 29).

1.1 The Fundamental Prediction of the Theory of UG for Acquisition: Constraint

The fundamental prediction of the theory of UG is that possible human languages are *constrained* in form. This entails that first language acquisition is *constrained* by the existence of UG as a component of the language faculty.

1.1.1 Definition of Constraint

The dual nature of the theory of UG requires that the term "constraint" is used in two senses. In one sense, determined by linguistic theory, specific constraints exist on grammars. In another sense, with regard to acquisition, we speak of constraint on first language acquisition; i.e., constraint on the mapping from Primary Linguistic Data (PLD) to the theory of the adult language. The mediation of UG between PLD and attained grammar restricts the infinite number of possible false leads which would be provided by random induction from unguided experience of surface data. While constraints on grammar will help to explain why first language acquisition is constrained, these two senses of the term "constraint" are not equivalent.

The introductory papers in this volume, which study the linguistic theory of anaphora, pursue the definition of the first sense of 'constraint,' i.e., the definition of principles which determine the possible grammars for anaphora in human language. The later papers, which are psycholinguistic studies of the first language acquisition of anaphora, seek evidence of the second sense of constraint, i.e., constraint on first language acquisition. All of the studies, and the commentary (Part C), are concerned with the match and mismatch between these two sets of results on the two dimensions of the term 'constraint.'

First language acquisition is predicted to be constrained by UG in two different ways.

1.1.2 *Constraint by Structure-Dependence*

First, UG predicts that children's early hypotheses about language will
be 'structure-dependent.' 'Structure-dependence' in this case means that
experienced language data will be analyzed in terms of an abstract
representation of sentence stimuli. Early hypotheses about possible
grammatical components are "defined on sentences of words analyzed
into abstract phrases. The phrases are 'abstract' in the sense that neither
their boundaries nor their categories (noun phrase, verb phrase, etc.)
need be physically marked. Sentences do not appear with brackets,
intonation boundaries regularly marking phrases, subscripts identifying
the type of phrase or anything of the sort" (Chomsky, 1975, 32). These
structure-dependent hypotheses are contrasted with 'structure-independent' hypotheses which for example "involve only analysis into words"
and properties like "earliest ("leftmost") defined on word sequences"
(32). It has been proposed that the component of human cognition whch
is specialized for language acquisition (UG) "contains the instruction:
construct a structure-dependent rule, ignoring all structure-independent
rules. The principle of structure-dependence is not learned, but forms
part of the conditions for language learning" (33).

1.1.3 *Constraint by Principles and Parameters*

Second, the principles and parameters of UG also determine constraint
on possible grammars. For example, the empty category principle
(ECP), i.e., the principle that 'an empty category must be governed,' as
in Chomsky, 1981a, which has been postulated as a component of UG,
will rule out an infinite set of grammars wherein empty categories are
not governed. Similarly, the 'Binding Principles' (Chomsky, 1981a) (See
II.2. below) will rule out an infinite set of grammars which do not obey
these principles. Parameters determine, of all possible structure-dependent analyses of data, which dimensions of language organization are
critical for grammar construction.

Thus, UG proposes that there is a significant deductive component to
first language acquisition. This is determined by the application of
biologically determined principles and parameters to the structure-
dependent experience of primary language data.

2. ANAPHORA

2.1 *Definition*

Wasow, this volume, provides a general definition of *anaphora* and introduction to the grammatical theory surrounding it. For the purposes of the studies in this book, anaphora may be defined generally as the relation between a 'proform' (called an 'anaphor') and another term (called an 'antecedent'), wherein the interpretation of the anaphor is in some way determined by the interpretation of the antecedent. Sentences 1 and 2 represent such relations with two types of proforms, 1 a lexically realized pronoun, 2 a null NP. In current literature in the field, a null NP is posited (represented as Ø in our notation in this volume) under the following conditions. We assume that in keeping with the 'Extended Projection Principle', a null NP is present whenever a thematic argument is assigned by the verb but the corresponding argument position contains no lexical material; and (b) "a sentence must always contain an empty category as subject if no overt subject is present . . ." (cf. Chomsky, 1982, 197; see also Jacobson, 1982.) In 1 and 2 we interpret the referent of the proform as John through anaphoric relation of the proform to the antecedent. In each case, we say that the interpretation of the proform (*he* or Ø) is in some way 'determined' by the interpretation of the antecedent, *John.*

(1)   *John$_i$* returned home late after *he$_{i,j}$* worked at the office
(2)   *John$_i$* returned home after Ø$_i$ working at the office

The term 'antecedent' is used to refer to the NP to which the anaphor is related, whether it precedes the anaphor (as in 1 or 2) or follows it, as in 3 and 4. We term the former (1 and 2), *forward anaphora* and the latter (3 and 4), *backward anaphora.*

(3)   After *he$_{i,j}$* worked at the office *John$_i$* returned home
(4)   After Ø$_i$ working at the office, *John$_i$* returned home

Coindexing is used in these examples to indicate that the indexed terms are related in an anaphora relation. In the examples above these terms may be said to involve intended coreference. In each case, the reference of the proform shares the reference of the antecedent, indicated by '*i*.' In these examples, the pronoun, but not the null also allows a possible alternative referent, other than the one of the NP antecedent in the sentence, thus allowing a second interpretation for the pronoun (specified as '*j*').

Although relations of anaphora may involve VP and sentential anaphors, as in 5 and 6 respectively, the studies in this volume restrict their inquiry mainly to NP anaphora.

(5)   John *returned home late* after Mary *did*
(6)   Sam said that *John would return late* and Suzy said *it* too

It has been argued that similar principles may constrain VP and NP anaphora (Bresnan, 1978) but extensive comparative psycholinguistic work on these does not yet exist.

Although the term 'anaphora' is also used to refer to certain relations in discourse e.g., 7, the studies in this volume mainly restrict their attention to intrasentential anaphora.

(7)   *John* left home. *He* skipped town.

The term 'anaphor' is often used in this volume and in the field in a more general sense than in certain current studies, which attribute a more restricted meaning to the term. (See for example, Freidin, this volume, Chomsky, 1981a, 1982). We use the term 'BT-anaphor' for the more restricted use of this term which is derived from Chomsky's current 'Binding Theory' (see section II.2. below).

We will use the term, *anaphor type* to differentiate whether a lexical pronoun as in 1 or 3, or a reflexive pronoun (e.g., 'himself'), or a null as in 2 or 4, is involved as anaphor. We will use it to differentiate classes of null anaphors also (see II.2.).

2.2 *Grammatical Centrality of Anaphora*

During the last decade of research, *anaphora* has emerged as central to natural language, and to the formulation of UG. Its productivity may be linked to the recursive properties of natural language since complex sentence formation in all languages inherently involves redundancy reduction, and therefore provides a domain for possible anaphora. Anaphora relates to widely varying aspects of language structure. For example, movement rules like question formation, and rules of quantifier scope are argued to cohere with the anaphora relations of a language (cf. Wasow, this volume 107—122; Chomsky, 1981a, 1982; Koster, 1978, 1981; May, 1981).

As discussed by several papers in this volume (e.g., Wasow, Freidin, Reinhart, van Riemsdijk, and Carden respectively), intrasentential anaphora consults a set of fundamental grammatical factors including sentence configuration (e.g., c-command) and other properties of syntactic domain (e.g., presence or absence of tense; category of constituent; argument structure of verb.) In particular, see Friedin in this volume on this issue. The grammatical factors which anaphora consults are argued to be basic to some, perhaps all, grammatical modules in UG.

2.3 Anaphor Types

The grammar of anaphora differentiates the distribution of anaphor types and their interpretation in terms of the specifics of their syntactic domain.

2.3.1 Lexically Realized NP

Recent research has proposed general principles which both relate and differentiate lexically realized pronouns like *he*, reflexive anaphoric pronouns, like *himself*, and nouns like *names*.

Names and lexical pronouns share certain restrictions.[3] For example, each of the following sets of constructions (8 to 10, 11 to 12, and 13 to 14) are ruled out with either pronouns or names. (The asterisk here refers to ungrammaticality with the particular coindexing represented.) See Lasnik, 1976 on this issue.

(8)   *$John_i$ worships him_i
(9)   *$John_i$ worships $John_i$
(10) *He_i worships $John_i$

(11) *He_i is happy whenever $John_i$ comes to town
(12) *$John_i$ is happy whenever $John_i$ comes to town

(13) *$John_i$ was happy to hear about him_i
(14) *$John_i$ was happy to hear about $John_i$

At the same time, names and lexical pronouns are also differentiated as can be seen by the contrast between 15 and 16.

(15) *$John_i$ said $John_i$ was happy
(16) $John_i$ said he_i was happy

Pronouns and reflexives are also differentiated. As can be seen in 17, the reflexive pronoun 'himself' provides a complement to a lexical pronoun 'he/him' (e.g., 8) in certain contexts. See also 18 vs. 13.

(17) $John_i$ worships $himself_i$
(18) $John_i$ was happy to hear about $himself_i$

This complementation is not complete, however, as 19 and 20 show. See Huang, 1982, Harbert, 1983, Bouchard, 1982 on these issues.

(19) $John_i$ gathered his belongings around $him_{i,j}$
(20) $John_i$ gathered his belongings around $himself_i$

2.3.2   Null NP

Null NP's (sometimes referred to as 'empty categories' (ec)) have been argued in recent research to be differentiated among themselves just as the "overt" (i.e., lexically realized) nominal categories are. In addition, some null NP's have reflexes like full lexically realized NPs (e.g., names) in several ways. For example, in 21, the null NP and the pronoun *him* cannot be coindexed just as the name and the pronoun cannot in 8.

(21)   *The man_i who Mary thinks $\emptyset_i$ worships him_i is here

Similarly, the pronoun *he* and the null anaphor in 22 cannot be coindexed just as the pronoun and the name cannot be in 10.

(22)   *Who_i does he_i think Mary worships $\emptyset_i$

Both the linguistic and psycholinguistic research represented in this volume is critically concerned with discovering general principles which apply across different lexically realized anaphors and across both these and null anaphors. At the same time they are concerned with discovering principles which differentiate these sets.[4]

2.4   Core and Periphery in the Grammar of Anaphora

The grammar of anaphora interacts fundamentally with pragmatic components in language knowledge. For example, pronouns are often used with only deictic or discourse referents, e.g., 7 above. In English, reflexive pronouns differ from lexical pronouns by generally requiring sentence antecedents and forbidding deictic or discourse antecedents, as suggested by a comparison of 23 and 24.[5] (The asterisk in this case refers to non well-formed discourse.)

(23) *Who loves $John_i$? $John_i$ loves $himself_i$
(24) Who loves $John_i$? $John_i$ loves him_i

In English, null anaphors typically require sentence internal antecedents, although this is not the case in all languages and is not always true in English. Current linguistic study of anaphora is centrally concerned with specification of the lines between grammatical and pragmatic determinants of anaphora, both in terms of differentiation between anaphor types and in terms of the range of the grammatical constraints on anaphora. Reinhart's chapter in this volume is centrally concerned with this issue, as is Wasow's more generally. Several of the psycholinguistic studies of acquisition in this volume specifically vary both pragmatic and grammatical factors in test of their interaction.

3. FORMULATING THE ACQUISITION QUESTIONS

3.1 Learnability of Anaphora

With regard to anaphora, the critical question we must ask is: how does the child come to know the grammar of anaphora? That is, how does it come to allow determination of all possible anaphora options, e.g., 1–7, 17–20, 24 above; but eschew impossible anaphora e.g., 8–14, 21–22, 23 above, in closely related structures. Given that the range of possible well-formed and non-well-formed utterances form infinite classes, what principles does the child use to determine these classes? What is the nature of these principles? To what degree are they inductively and/or deductively determined? In what way are they constrained? In what way do they constrain acquisition?

3.2 First Language Acquisition of Anaphora

Anaphora provides a critical focus for study of first language acquisition for several reasons. (1) Because anaphors mainly do not have independent reference, they require computation i.e., determination of their relation to their antecedent. Their interpretation cannot be determined solely by properties of the stimulus (i.e., the anaphor) per se. This point is particularly salient where the anaphor is a null NP. In this case, distinct from lexical pronouns, for example, there is no sensory information in the stimulus at all. In fact, in one sense, "there is no stimulus at all" other than one projected as a result of computation of an anaphora relation. Because anaphora so clearly reflects computational knowledge which is not stimulus-dependent, its study allows us to evaluate what general principles children may bring to bear *from within* on the language acquisition process. Its study thus allows evaluation of a possible deductive component in first language acquisition. In particular, to the degree that anaphora clearly must consult specific *grammatical factors* in its computation, we can explicitly evaluate this computation for evidence of reference to these. (2) Anaphora also provides a critical domain for the study of *interaction of the language faculty with other cognitive faculties*. As we have seen above, the grammar of anaphora interacts fundamentally with pragmatics. In addition, pragmatic factors (e.g., discourse context) often seem to be able to override grammatical factors in determining possible anaphora (cf. Wasow, this volume, Reinhart, this volume, McCray, 1980; Hammerton, 1970). If children bring structure-dependent principles to bear on acquisition of anaphora, they must do this in spite of the fact that pragmatic context can and often does override such principles (thus appearing to offer an alternative for them). Such results would corroborate the proposed modular role of the principles of UG; i.e., it would suggest they are distinct from the principles of other cognitive competence which provide pragmatic reasoning. (See Osherson and Wasow 1976 in this regard.)[6]

(3) The data to which the child is exposed are to a certain degree intractable with regard to grammatical factors in anaphora. For example, although the role of the configurational structure of *c-command* in the grammar of anaphora is supported by a wide array of data (see II.1.2 and 3 below), other data do not support it. (For example, see Wasow, this volume; Carden, this volume; Kuno, to appear. See also Freidin, this volume, for evidence of specification of grammatical factors beyond c-command which account for anaphora data.) A similar problem arises in the case of examples like 19 and 20 above. Here general principles for differentiating anaphor types are not obvious from the syntactic domain in which the anaphors occur. In addition, adult coreference judgments are often unsteady on critical examples of anaphora. If, in spite of this data divergence, children bring systematic structure-dependence to bear on acquisition of anaphora, this will suggest that the basis for this is not simple induction from the data.

In the case of anaphora we can be quite certain that neither negative evidence about what is not well-formed, nor explicit tutorial presentation of what is well formed is available to the child. It is difficult even to conceive what form negative evidence would take regarding null anaphors. In addition, studies of the 'baby talk register' BTR (Gleitman et al., 1984 for example), have shown that complex sentence structures which involve anaphora (e.g., coordinate and subordinate sentences) are infrequent in the BTR (although certain forms of null anaphors do occur, e.g., those in imperatives and questions). Pronouns in the BTR are often substituted for by names. These facts would assure that the child must acquire a theory of anaphora on the basis of primary linguistic data which are, for the most part, outside of the constrained BTR.

4. PROBLEMS WHICH ARISE IN EMPIRICAL ACQUISITION STUDY

4.1 *Language Development vs. Grammar Development*

The empirical investigation of constraint on first language acquisition requires that we give up the 'convenient idealization' that language acquisition is 'instantaneous,' which is often made in theory construction of UG. By definition, the initial state (S_0) involves absence of knowledge of the language to be acquired. *A priori* no cutoff of the 'initial state' can be simply assumed. In addition, as is well known, the behavioral data of child language, i.e., both comprehension and production data, are not in accord with this idealization. Child language appears impoverished and differs at different ages. The empirical studies in this volume and in the field of psycholinguistics thus typically investigate language of children from 2—7 or more years of age.[7]

The fact that language acquisition is not instantaneous does not mean that the properties of UG necessarily change with time. It does not invalidate a possible close link between the theory of UG and the study of first language acquisition. It may only mean that the acquisition function from the PLD to the complete grammar of the specific language being acquired, under the constraint of a constant UG, takes time.[8]

In addition, in interpreting the child language data, it should be noted that the mere fact that child language differs at different ages does not necessarily mean that this child language directly evidences developing knowledge of even specific language grammars. It would be possible to hold a version of an instantaneous model of first language acquisition if this impoverished and changing behavioral data resulted from deficits on other cognitive components only, e.g., memory, or certain task performance abilities, while grammatical competence for the specific language involved was already complete. In this case these other deficits would act as a kind of filter on the *use* of language competence. (This view is implied for example by some recent work in the field, see Goodluck to appear, Lasnik and Crain, to appear.)

In general, this latter view, if supported, would push the occurrence of language acquisition back in time to a yet undefined point. It must, however, be tested empirically. In such test, the issue of task-related performance deficits can be evaluated through seeking converging evidence across different tasks, as in several of the papers in this volume. The issue of independent memory development is not as easily assessed, since it is well known that memory cannot easily be evaluated independently of 'content' of material remembered. For example, it is well known that the same memory capacity provides different results for memory of a list of unrelated nonsense items and for an equally long list of items conducive to some structural organization. It is thus difficult to separate an ability to structure language material (e.g., by a grammar) from an ability which is linked to memory capacity alone. However, experimental manipulation of sentence structure and length can approach this issue.[9]

The collection of papers in this volume assumes both that study of first language data is necessary to the study of UG, and that experimental design must be concerned with the isolation of grammatical from non-grammatical factors in characterizing the child's language knowledge.

II. *LINGUISTIC BACKGROUND*

The articles by Wasow, Reinhart and Freidin and commentarial articles by van Riemsdijk and Carden in this volume provide review and discussion of issues critical to the current linguistic and psycholinguistic study of anaphora, and references to further current work. The article by Wasow provides a general summary of the basic issues in the study of anaphora, with historical perspective. The articles by Reinhart and Carden focus on issues which include the proper representation of the interaction between pragmatics and grammar in anaphora; and, more specifically, the interaction between general principles of linearity and dominance in the grammar of anaphora. Freidin's article reviews and criticises specific issues related to the differentiation of anaphor types in terms of the current Binding Theory (BT) (Chomsky, 1981a, 1982).

The next subsections of this introduction briefly review the basic concepts and issues which underly these linguistic studies and which are necessary to the characterization of well-formed anaphora, and its acquisition: i.e., 'precede and command;' 'Binding Theory' and 'Pragmatics and Grammar.'

1. PRECEDE AND COMMAND

"Precede" and "command" fundamentally characterize syntactic domains in which anaphora holds. They have been defined as two "dimensions of tree structure," i.e., "two kinds of . . . relation" which are reflected in phrase structure representation (Langacker, 1969, 169). They were argued early (by Langacker) to provide two 'primacy' relations for the grammar of anaphora which could significantly simplify the statement of constraints on well-formed anaphora.[10] (See Koster, 1978, 1981 for recent discussion of the relation of these primacy relations to 'locality principles,' i.e., "principles that aim at narrowing the 'space' in which linguistic rules apply.") They were specifically stated for English pronoun anaphora but Langacker speculated that they might be applicable to other languages and argued that the notion 'command' in particular could be extended to other aspects of grammar, e.g., null anaphora in infinitival complements.

Since their initial formulation by Langacker, the proper definition of 'command' and the role of each of the primacy relations in the grammar has been the subject of much study. The concepts of 'precede' and 'command' have also guided much recent first language acquisition research, including that represented in several of the experimental papers in this volume. Carden (319–357 in this volume) sketches linguistic issues relevant to these primary relations regarding pronouns in English and formulates related psycholinguistic issues regarding first language acquisition. (See also Reinhart, 1983, 34–57, 1976 and 1981 for basic formulation of these issues; and Wasow, 1979). The article by Freidin assesses the generalizability of the notion 'command' in current BT. The article by Reinhart argues that the 'core' and the 'periphery' of the grammar of anaphora can be defined in part by the degree to which types of anaphora are determined by command (see 123–150, this volume).

1.1 *Precede*

The relation 'precede' characterizes a relation between units in terms of their linear order. It typically characterizes the case where an antecedent occurs before an anaphor in the linear string of the sentence. Issues concerning the relation 'precede' have mainly concerned pronoun anaphora.

1.1.1 *Basic Data. Forward Pronouns: Frequency*

Pronouns may precede or follow their antecedents in English, as seen in 1 and 3 above. Although forward pronouns (which follow their antecedents) are predominant in both spoken and written English, this bidirectionality has been true of English since at least 11th century Old English. Oshima (1980), shows the existence of backward pronoun anaphora in Blickling Homilies CXLIXIX in 25.

(25)   pa *he* pis gecweden hæfde, pa astah *ure Drihten* on heofenas
        (when *he* had said this, *our Lord* ascended into heaven)

It is still not clear under what conditions of use backward pronominalization occurs (see Reinhart, this volume; Warburton and Prabhu 1972, Bickerton 1975, Kuno 1972a, b, 1975 and to appear and Bolinger, 1977 for examples of attempts to characterize these conditions). However, it has been argued that backward pronominalization use cannot be explained solely by the discourse context in which it appears, i.e., that it is not explained as really *forward* from discourse context (Carden, 1982). For example, in his analysis of examples of backward pronouns in a sample of spontaneous speech, Carden found that 93% were not predictable from preceding discourse; while in a sample of written examples, 51% were not.

1.2 *Command*

The notion of *command* critically refers to the dimension of dominance and to constituent structure in configurational representation of sentences.

For the purposes of the papers in this volume, the version of command termed 'c-command' may be assumed. Reinhart's (1983a, 18) simplified definition in 26 is sufficient in most cases.

(26)   Node A c(constituent)-commands node B if the branching node most immediately dominating A also dominates B.

In 27 for example, the term A is said to 'c-command' the term B because the first branching node (x) above A also dominates the term B. Specific linguistic proposals differ in various specifications of x or of its relation to A (see Saito, 1984 for a useful review).

(27)

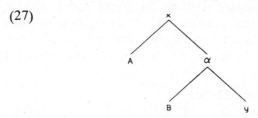

The relation of c-command is said to define the syntactic domain of a given node as follows:

(28)   the domain of a node A consists of all and only the nodes c-commanded by A

                                        (Reinhart, 1983a, 19)

The relation of command is independent of the relation of linear precedence, i.e., nodes which are c-commanded by A may either precede or follow A equivalently.[11]

1.2.1 Basic Data

In general, neither pronouns nor other anaphors may c-command their antecedent; and antecedents may not be c-commanded by their anaphors, as in 29 or 30 for example.

(29)   *He likes John's hat
(30)   *Ø to leave early for John's vacation home was what he was trying to do.

In general, some anaphor types must be c-commanded by their antecedents within some established domain while others must not be, as in 31 and 32 respectively, where the domain is the sentence.

(31)   *John*ᵢ liked *himself*ᵢ
(32)   **John*ᵢ like *him*ᵢ

1.3 Relation Between Precede and Command in Constraints

1.3.1 Command vs. Precede

Reinhart (1976, 1983a) argued on the basis of a range of data that the linear relation of precedence may be otiose in the statement of grammatical constraint on anaphora. The critical domain for determining well-formed antecedent-anaphor relations, she argued, may involve only c-command. She argued that examples like 33 in which the pronoun does not precede, but does command the name, show that forward pronouns, like backward ones in 10 or 11, may be blocked by c-command.[12]

(33)   *Near *Dan*ᵢ *he*ᵢ saw a snake

1.3.2 Confounding of Precede and Command in English

The reason that backward pronouns appear more restricted in English, Reinhart suggested, may be that in a right branching language, like English, there will be "a large correlation between the domains defined by 'precede-and-command' and by 'c-command'" (1983, 47). In right branching languages, what precedes will often also command. Not only will the subject normally c-command the constituents of the VP (given that the language is SVO), but the subject of a main clause will normally c-command complements which are adjoined under S or VP, as in the schematized configuration of a right branching subordinate clause in 34.

(34)

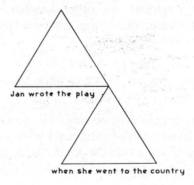

If there is a grammatical constraint against pronouns or other anaphor types c-commanding their antecedents (or against antecedents being c-commanded by anaphors) it follows that backward pronouns like 10 and 11 and forward ones like 33, would be ungrammatical, and it also follows that relations of 'precede' would appear unmarked in the English language.

2. BINDING THEORY

2.0 *Binding Theory: Differentiation of Anaphor Type*

Definition of constraint on anaphora must distinguish anaphor types since "The distribution of coindexed NP differs according to NP-type" (Freidin, this volume).

2.0.1 *Binding Principles*

In recent linguistic theory, an attempt has been made to formulate and systematize fundamental principles which characterize and constrain "relations of anaphors, pronouns, names and variables to possible antecedents" (Chomsky, 1981a, 6). This Binding Theory (BT), which is proposed to constitute one module of a general theory of UG, concerns itself not only with lexical pronouns, but with the whole set of nominal categories, both lexically overt and null, which may enter into anaphoric relations. The principles are intended to apply not only to English anaphora but to anaphora across all possible languages. Freidin's chapter (this volume) studies the definition of these principles, proceeding from Chomsky, 1981, 1982.

The proposed Binding Principles (BP) are three.

(35)   A. An anaphor must be locally bound
(36)   B. A pronoun must be locally free
(37)   C. An *r* expression must be free

In the statement of these principles, three nominal categories are assumed. (1) 'Anaphors' (in this case 'BT-anaphors') include reflexives and reciprocals (like 'himself' and 'each other'). (2) 'Pronouns' include the lexical pronouns, e.g., 'he,' 'she.' (3) '*r* expressions' consist of names (as in 9 or 10 above), or variables as in the empty category in 38.

(38)   Who did you see Ø?
        (for which *x*, you saw *x*)

A term '*x*' is said to be 'bound' by another term, '*y*', if *x* is c-
commanded by *y*, and coindexed with *y*. A term is said to be 'free,' if it
is not so c-commanded and coindexed. The definition of what constitutes locality in 37 is currently under study (see Freidin's chapter this
volume, Harbert 1983, and Huang 1982 for example). In general, 'local'
has been taken to refer to "in its governing category" where the
governing category of *x* is taken to be ... "the minimal S or NP
containing the term *x* and a governor of *x*" (Chomsky, 1982, 20). In
general a 'governor' may include lexical heads of phrases which take *x*
as complement, and also certain non-argument antecedents which bind
an anaphor, usually COMP (cf. Saito, 1984; Lasnik and Saito, 1984;
Chomsky, 1981a). As Freidin (this volume) argues, however, the definition of 'local' may differ across principles A and B.

Principles A—C have been found to account for a wide array of data.
For example, they account for the fact that pronouns and anaphors are
typically in complementary distribution, as in 8 and 17, and 18 and 13,
for example. They account for why certain types of null anaphors
appear to behave like NP as in 21 and 22 above. They account for a
range of constraints in examples like 8—14. While principle A accounts
for the well-formedness of 17 and 18 for example, principle B accounts
for why 8 and 13 are ill-formed. Principle C accounts for the illformedness of 9—12 and 14 or 29 and 30.

2.0.2   *Typology of Empty Categories*

The BP above do not distinguish empty categories from overt categories. In more recent work (Chomsky 1982), it has been theorized that
if the binding principles A and B are correct, then the abstract features
'anaphoric' and 'pronominal' which distinguish overt nominal categories
will also distinguish empty categories. If so, then just as these features
distinguish BT *anaphors* like reflexives (+an −pron), lexical pronouns
(−an +pron), and names (−an −pron) they should distinguish a
typology of empty categories, as in Table I. 'Pronominals' then (+Pron)
define a general class regardless of phonetic content of anaphor type.
They "are elements containing the features person, gender, number
and possible CASE, and an optional phonological matrix, excluding

elements identified as nonpronominal lexical items (e.g., 'John')"
(Chomsky, 1982, 20). BT "anaphors" (+an) also define a general class.
They are defined as having the basic property that they "may fail to
denote" in themselves, thus requiring a grammatical antecedent. "A pure
anaphor is one that always fails to denote but is, in effect, interpreted as
a variable assigned a value by virtue of its relation to its antecedent"
(83).

TABLE I

Features		Lexical Category	Empty Category	EC Example
+an	−pron	himself/each other	NP-trace	*John* is likely *t* to win
−an	+pron	he	pro	*pro* parla (he is speaking) (Italian)[a]
+an	+pron	——	PRO	*John* tried *PRO* to go
−an	−pron	name	variable	*Who* did you see *t*?

[a] Such null arguments in tensed sentences are allowed in 'pro drop languages' (Rizzi, 1983, Chomsky, 1982).

Various combinations of the two features (+/− pronominal) and (+/−
anaphor) thus exhaustively describe both the lexically overt and empty
anaphor types.[13]

According to this theory, expressions (whether lexical or null) are
first assigned to nominal categories by the feature system above; then
the BT and other principles apply. Current linguistic studies are
concerned with the issue of whether the features actually characterize
the ec themselves or are a reflex of the grammatical position of the
ec. (See Freidin, this volume; and Brody, 1984 for discussion. See
Bouchard, 1982, Montalbetti, 1984, and Bowers 1982 for studies
of principles underlying typology of lexical and empty anaphoric
categories.)

2.1 *BT and Command*

The BT is formulated in terms of the notion c-command, as this notion
crucially defines 'bound' and 'free'; and thus distinguishes principles A
and (B and C). (The BT also involves c-command more indirectly in
that the definition of 'government' which may be critical to the definition
of 'local' in the explication of these principles, may include c-command
as a "necessary condition" for its definition, as in Saito, 1984 for
example).

2.2 BT and Linear Precedence

Linear precedence is not involved in the statement of the BP. Principle C rules out 33 and 29 or 30 equivalently.

2.3 BT Summary

The BT essentially incorporates in the grammar the revisions which were suggested by Reinhart in 1976 (II.1.3 above) with regard to the primacy constraints on anaphora. It further specifies the role of c-command in the differentiation of the distribution and interpretation of anaphor types. It extends the range of these principles across not only pronouns, and lexically overt elements, but also across empty categories. It thus widely extends the range of grammatical constraint on anaphora, at the same time as it simplifies the statement of constraints on anaphora.

2.4 BT and Control Theory

A separate module of UG, viz., 'control theory', has been proposed to account for the interpretation of the null anaphor referred to as PRO in Table I. PRO, like a pronoun, may be construed as having an antecedent from long distance and it does not require a unique antecedent (i.e., it may have a split antecedent). It does not require a c-commanding antecedent, as in 39; although it may have one, as in 40 (cf. Chomsky, 1981a, 78).

(39)   We feel that PRO_i learning to cooperate is important for $their_i$ development

(40) $John_i$ tried PRO_i to go

Like a BT anaphor, PRO in examples like 40 above is obligatorily construed with its sentence antecedent. On the other hand, some occurrences of PRO involve arbitrary pragmatic control:

(41)   PRO winning the war was the primary preoccupation of the time

Because it is proposed to have properties both of pronominals and anaphors, PRO is proposed to occur only in 'ungoverned' positions, thus consistent with BT.

As can be seen from the examples above, although c-command is not required for all occurrences of PRO, neither is linear precedence. The proper linguistic representation for "control" of PRO critically involves the lexicon as well as both structural and pragmatic factors. Its proper representation and its relation to BT are currently central to linguistic inquiry (see for example, Chomsky, 1981a, b; Bresnan, 1982a, b; Mohanan, 1983; Koster, 1984; Williams, 1980; and van Riemsdijk and Williams, to appear, in this regard).

3. PRAGMATICS AND GRAMMAR

3.1 *Precede and Command*

Precede and *command* can be differentiated in terms of their relation to a grammatical core of language knowledge. Since command is defined over configurational structure which is involved in the geometric representation of abstract sentence structure, it may be assumed to be essential to "structure dependence" of UG. Syntactic domains defined in terms of command cannot be inductively derived from surface data in any obvious way.

Precede, on the other hand, is not a strictly grammatical relation. Although grammars crucially must make reference to linearity, a relation of precedence itself is easily provided by general cognition. Syntactic domains established in terms of precedence can easily be induced from surface analyses of linguistic or non-linguistic data.

3.2 *Linearity in Language*

Because language exists in real time (either in production or in comprehension) it critically involves relations of linear order between language units. These linear relations may be represented either as temporal 'before-after' relations as in spoken language, or equivalently as 'left-right' relations in the literal or geometric representation of these temporal relations.

Linearity crucially determines language well-formedness. For example, at the level of syntax, most languages are characterized by an unmarked 'word order.' In addition, certain syntactic rules may critically consult linear order. It has been claimed, for example, that 'Wh-movement' rules (e.g., question formation), universally move the "Wh-word" to the front of a sentence (i.e., backward) rather than to the end of a sentence (i.e., forward).

3.3 Linearity and UG

We have seen above that certain proposals for definition of principles of UG (which concern anaphora (i.e., BT)) do not involve 'precedence.' While there is no issue as to whether linearity is essential to natural language, it remains possible that UG itself never determines *specific* relations of precedence. The order-free property of BT may represent a fundamental property of the principles of UG.

It is possible that current study of the theory of Universal Grammar will show that Universal Grammar itself may not involve statements of specific linear order.[14] In this case, specific linear orders will be set for each specific language only when general a-directional principles of grammar organization which are determined by parameters of UG are interpreted in terms of specific language data which occur in real time.

3.4 Pronoun Precedence and UG

3.4.1 Pronoun Precedence

There are several areas of anaphora data which have been argued to show that linear relations of precedence must be incorporated into grammar, possibly into the module of UG concerned with anaphora. See Carden (this volume), Mohanan, 1981, Langacker, 1969, Kuno, to appear, for examples of such arguments. These data all involve pronoun anaphora. We suggest below that to date none of these observations require that linear precedence of pronouns actually reflects a principle of UG, although the issue deserves further study.

3.4.1.1 Pronoun Precedence: Language Typology

In discussion of the relationship between pronouns and antecedents, it has been claimed that in a number of languages an antecedent must always *precede* a pronoun to which it is related. This constraint may be stated as in 42:

(42)   Within a sentence, a preceding pronoun cannot be coindexed
        with a following NP.

The proposed constraint in 42 is often referred to as a "precedence
constraint." That is, in these languages, only if a pronoun follows an
antecedent NP can it be interpreted coreferentially with an NP. Some of
the languages for which this claim has been made include Chinese (Tai,
1973), Japanese (Nakai, 1976), Tamil (Veluppillai, 1981), Malayalam
(Mohanan, 1981, 1982a, b), and Arabic (Gary and Gamal-Eldin,
1982). These languages are claimed to differ from languages like
English, which optionally allow both forward and backward pronoun
coindexing depending on configuration.

The claim in 42 asserts an exclusively linear principle which grammatically constrains pronoun coindexing regardless of configurational
relations (e.g., c-command) between antecedent and pronoun. Tai states
for example:

(43)   "Unlike English, Chinese doesn't allow backward pronomi-
        nalization under any condition, . . . even if two referential
        noun phrases are in the relationship of command" (1973,
        661).

Mohanan similarly states, of Malayalam.

(44)   "Whatever may be the c-command relation between pro-
        nouns and antecedents, all and only those versions of a
        sentence in which the pronoun follows the antecedent are
        grammatical. . . ." (1982b, 165).

3.4.1.2 *The Facts*

Subsequent study of pronouns has shown that the claim in 42 is not
supported for all languages cited above. As Oshima (pc), Huang (1982)
and Whitman (1982) suggest, for example, Japanese speakers frequently
accept backward anaphoric pronouns in cases like those in 45 and 46.

(45)   *Kare*$_{i,j}$ no   tuma wa *Masayuki*$_i$ o dekiai site iru.
        he   poss wife   Masayuki   doting on is

        (*His*$_{i,j}$ wife is doting on *Masayuki*$_i$)

(46)   *Soko*$_{i,j}$ kara John ga yatte kita *tokoro*$_i$.
        there   from John   came   place

        (*The place*$_i$ that John came from *there*$_{i,j}$)

(Huang 1982, 393 attributes 46 to Kuno 1973). (See Kuno, to appear for further Japanese examples.)

Similarly, in Chinese (Huang, 1982; Mangione pc) backward pronouns are required in the case of resumptive pronouns in relative clauses such as 47 and are allowed in certain other conditions, including 48.

(47)   wǒ gěi $tā_i$ mǎi shū-de $nèige$ $rén_i$ ...
       I   give (s)he buy book-rel that-M person

       (The person I gave a book to . . .)

(48)   bùguǎn $tā_i$ de máma   xǐ-bu-xǐhuān, $Zhangsan_i$ dōu
       regardless   he   de mother   like-not-like   Zhangsan   all

       děi   lái
       must come

       (Whether his$_i$ mother likes it or not, Zhangsan$_i$ has to come)

In addition, subsequent study in each of these languages has shown that there are cases where forward pronouns are blocked, e.g., 49 and 50 in Japanese (Oshima, in preparation, p. 7 and pc)

(49)   Watasi$_i$ wa $Taroo_j$ no $kare_{i*,j*}$ ni taisuru
       I   Taroo Poss he   toward

       kasin   o ayabunda
       overconfidence   feared

       (I feared $Taroo$'s$_j$ overconfidence in $him_{j*,k}$)

(50) $Masayuki_i$ no   soba de $kare_{i*}$ ga hebi   o mituketa
       Masayuki Poss near at he   snake   found

       (Near $Masayuki_i$, he$_{i*}$ found a snake)

In Chinese, Huang, 1982 and Mangione pc argue that examples like 51 are blocked:

(51)   Wǒ bù   xǐhuān $Zhangsan_i$ dùi $tā_{i*}$ de tàidu
       I   not like   Zhangsan   to   he   de attitude

       (I don't like Zhangsan's$_i$ attitude toward him$_{j,i*}$)

See Lust, Gair and Mangione (in preparation) for a study of the structural conditions under which backward pronouns are allowed, and forward pronouns blocked, in several of the languages concerned in 3.4.1.1.

3.4.1.3 *The Problem*

It may be that further study will show that backward pronouns do occur in some cases in all of the languages such as cited in 3.4.1.1. However, it is possible on the other hand that some languages will show a complete restriction on backward pronouns without exception. Egyptian Collo- quial Arabic may be such an example. For example, 52 is ruled out by native speakers. In EC Arabic, however, forward pronouns as in 53 are also ruled out as are backward null anaphors in structures like 54.

(52)   lamma saaf   *huwwa$_i$* il-lahma ʔakal   *ik-kalb$_{i*}$* il-ʔakl
        when saw(-he) he   the meat ate(-he) the-dog the-food

        (When he$_{i*j}$ saw the meat, the dog$_i$ ate the food)

(53)   lamma xallaS   maHammad$_i$ il-Gada raaH
        when finished(-he) Mohammad the-lunch went(-he)

        huwwa$_{i*}$ mišwaar
        he   walk

        (When Mohammad$_i$ finished lunch, he$_{i*j}$ went for a walk)

(54)   lamma naTT Ø$_i$ naTTa ʔakal   il-ʔird$_{i*}$ il-mooza
        when jumped(-he)jump ate(-he) the monkey the banana

        (When Ø$_{i*j}$ jumped, the monkey$_i$ ate the banana)

This more complete range of data suggests that the accurate description of the constraint on anaphora in EC Arabic must be deeper than a simple precedence constraint on pronouns such as in 42. In Arabic, as in other languages, a complete study of the anaphora systems of a language will be required before a pronoun precedence principle can be defended as the correct grammatical formulation of the constraint observed in examples like 52. (See Fisher, 1985 for example for such study in Khmer, Mohanan 1982a, b for Malayalam, Huang, 1984 for Chinese, Kuno, to appear, and Oshima, 1979 and in preparation, for Japanese.)

3.4.1.4 *Pronoun Precedence: Coordinate Structures*

It has also been argued that English itself may require a grammatical principle like 42. For example, it has long been recognized that coordinate structures in English are distinguished from other structures in that pronoun precedence is required in conditions like 55 and 56 (see Langacker, 1969 for example). (See also Carden, this volume.)

(55)   Penelope cursed *Peter*$_i$ and slandered *him*$_{i,j}$
        Penelope cursed *him*$_{i*,j}$ and slandered *Peter*$_i$

(56)   Sally adored *bagels*$_i$ and devoured *them*$_{i,j}$
        Sally adored *them*$_{i*,j}$ and devoured *bagels*$_i$

3.4.1.5 *The Facts*

The English pronoun precedence requirement in 3.4.1.4 does not hold in all cases of coordination. It is restricted to cases of coordination which involve parallel structure, as 57 and 58 show.

(57)   John had seen *him*$_{i,j}$ and *the thief*$_i$ knew it and ran
(58)   Mary was praising *her*$_{i,j}$ work and *Sarah*$_i$ was embarrassed

3.4.1.6 *The Problem*

Huang has suggested that the full range of coordination data in English are consistent with a possibility that "the precedence principle should be restricted to a universal theory of discourse, and need not be assumed in sentence grammar" (1982, 400). The fact that the precedence facts are restricted to parallel structures (where, as Langacker had suggested, "relations of dominance are in effect neutralized" (172)) is consistent with this proposal, since these do not have, and may not need, a specifically syntactic account. See Williams 1977, 1978, Gundel 1980, Goodall 1984 for initial studies of this problem.

3.4.1.7 *Pronoun Precedence: PP's Inside VP*

Another area of English data which has been argued to require linear order precedence for its grammatical description involves structures like 59–62. (See Carden, this volume, and Kuno, to appear.)

(59)   I spoke to *Ben*$_i$ in *his*$_{i,j}$ office
(60)   *I spoke to *him*$_i$ in *Ben's*$_i$ office

(61)   I spoke to *Sarah$_i$* about *her$_{i,j}$* problem
(62) ?/*I spoke about *her$_{i,j}$* problem to *Sarah$_j$*

3.4.1.8 *The Facts*

The requirement for linear precedence in these examples is not a general one in these structures, as 63–65 suggest.

(63)   I spoke to *her$_{i,j}$* mother about *Sarah's$_i$* health
(64)   I gave to *his$_{i,j}$* brother all *John's$_i$* belongings
(65)   I offered to tell *his$_{i,j}$* wife all about *John's$_i$* success

3.4.1.9 *The Problem*

3.4.1.8 shows that a simple principle of pronoun precedence also cannot account for the full range of structures covered in this English domain. Since these structures also involve parallelism (of PP), it is possible that further work on these structures will need to involve precedence at a non-syntactic level similar to the coordinate structure case.

3.4.1.10 *Pronoun Precedence: The Basis for an Alternative Explanation*

The frequency of forward pronouns both in English and across languages and the putative nonexistence of languages which have only backward pronouns may reflect basic and universal facts about pronominalization. These facts are not necessarily inconsistent with BT. For example, if pronouns are 'free in their governing category' as stipulated by principle B of binding theory, this means they are "free" to be anteceded from outside their governing category. A set of potential antecedents will be available from any preceding discourse. This preceding discourse will always be available to any particular utterance. Succeeding discourse is not. The universal possibility for forward pronouns in natural language in this case could be a reflex of a structural property of grammar (i.e., principle B of BT), together with a *precedence* principle of general cognition and discourse structure. It will not be due to a *grammatical* principle of precedence for pronouns.

An explanation for why pronouns in English and in other languages clearly occur more frequently in a forward direction (even when the language allows backward pronouns) may involve similar factors. In this case, since pronouns clearly can and do occur either forward or backward in certain domains, this clearly cannot reflect an autonomous grammatical constraint. It therefore *must* reflect a pragmatic constraint. That this preference for forward pronouns is not grammatically determined is supported by the fact that the preference appears to hold for pronouns in natural languages regardless of basic structural differences across languages, e.g., whether languages are right branching like English or Arabic, or left branching like Japanese or Sinhalese.

In addition, lexical pronouns are the only anaphor type for which a unique principle of linear precedence has been claimed to exist in the grammar. Lexical pronouns have specific semantic features, the amount and nature of these differing from language to language. In English (for example, *he, she, they*), these involve only person, gender, and number. In Japanese they involve a larger set, e.g., *kare* (he) is not used to refer to a superior and when used, e.g., by a young woman, 'kare' may refer to a 'boyfriend'; *boku* (I) may carry the features of superior male speaker. Pronouns may integrate more fully with pragmatic systems (e.g., discourse principles of precedence) than other anaphor types do, because of this fact, which makes them more like 'names.'

Note that these observations do not imply that grammatical factors are not relevant to pronouns — only that pragmatic factors may intersect with these to a greater degree than with other anaphor types. On the contrary, principle B of Binding Theory licenses this integration with pragmatics for pronouns (as they must be free in their governing category); just as they license it for names (they must be free everywhere).[15]

3.5 *Pragmatics and Grammar: Reinhart's Proposal*

Reinhart recently (e.g., 123—150, this volume) has proposed a specification of the division of pragmatic and grammatical principles in the knowledge of anaphora. She argues that the center of the grammar of anaphora should be restricted to syntactically bound domains, i.e., domains involving c-command. With regard to pronoun interpretation, this means that only bound variable interpretations of pronouns are grammatically determined. All other pronoun interpretation, she argues, can be pragmatically determined. Strict linear (non structure-dependent) precedence and other non grammatical factors would thus be expected to affect only non-bound-variable pronoun interpretation. Under this proposal, all the precedence effects in the examples in II.3.4 above must be pragmatically determined, since they do not involve pronouns which are c-commanded by their antecedent.

If confirmed, this proposal would have profound consequences on the theory of anaphora. For example, it determines a distinction between anaphoric construal, i.e., the linking of linguistic terms (antecedent and anaphor) by the grammatical operation of 'coindexing', and the judgment of 'intended coreference' between them. The former applies in the case of bound variable interpretations of pronouns; the latter applies in the case of other (non-bound) interpretation of pronouns. (This distinction within the nature of anaphora is related to an earlier distinction between 'construal' and 'coreference' in the work of Hust and Brame (1976), and to current inquiry into the nature of binding (Higginbotham, 1980, 1983), as well as to current inquiry into the statement of grammatical constraint with regard to coreference (Lasnik, 1976, 1981 and Bowers, 1982).

Reinhart's proposal also unifies pronouns and null anaphors in the core of grammar in terms of their syntactic domain, i.e., c-command, not in terms of their phonetic form. In addition, the property of "plus or minus c-command" not only differentiates anaphor types as in current BT, but differentiates whether a language phenomenon is grammatically or pragmatically accounted for.

The Reinhart proposal also has profound consequences for revisions of current BT, since it has the consequence of omitting principle C from the grammar and conflating A and B. Reinhart proposes a pragmatic principle of communication to account for the principle C facts, and certain principle B facts, viz., a pragmatic communicative strategy approximated in 66. (See Reinhart's 29, this volume.)

(66)   If a certain structure allows bound anaphora interpretation, then a speaker should use the bound anaphora form (e.g., reflexive) if (s)he intends coreference; otherwise the hearer assumes that noncoreference must be intended

By this strategy, for example, 67 and 68 could be ruled out without consulting grammar. Each allows an alternative form with a reflexive which the speaker did not take.

(67)   *John saw him
(68)   *He wants John to go

The Reinhart proposal is currently under study linguistically.[16]

III. REFINING THE QUESTIONS OF FIRST LANGUAGE ACQUISITION

The linguistic issues raised above correlate with issues of first language acquisition.

1. LINEAR PRECEDENCE IN FIRST LANGUAGE ACQUISITION OF ANAPHORA

In previous research, it has been proposed that "children shift from a linearly based approach to coreference to a structurally based approach" (Roeper, this volume).

Tavakolian had made this proposal on the basis of experimental study of first language acquisition: "Children's initial use of precedence relationships in structurally analyzing a string and in determining the antecedent of a proform indicates that precedence relations are incorporated into a grammar earlier than hierarchical relationships" (1977).

Solan has formalized this proposal more recently (1983). For Solan, "... the general restriction at early stages is "$Pro_i \ldots NP_i$ is impossible." (By 'Pro' Solan intends *pronoun* here). This proposal forms the basis for a developmental model of acquisition of anaphora, and for a theory of grammatical constraint on pronominal anaphora, which Solan terms the BAR (Backward Anaphora Restriction). Under this constraint, all structural restrictions on pronominal anaphora are developmentally acquired, and they concern only backward anaphora; forward pronouns are not structure-dependent and are completely free. The child's initial hypotheses are incorrectly based on precedence alone: "... once the child knows that his language has anaphora, he will assume that forward anaphora is the only possibility" (91). In addition, the child's subsequent grammar is constructed around a grammar which critically involves precedence. It treats backward pronouns and forward pronouns completely differently, one as a grammatical phenomenon, one not.

Ingram and Shaw (1981), and Taylor-Browne (1983) have made a related proposal (of unique, non structure-dependent *precedence* at initial levels of acquisition of anaphora) on the basis of their experimental data. Carden (this volume) argues for their proposal on the basis of a linguistic theory of anaphora which involves a "precede and command" version of the relevant linguistic constraint. Unlike Solan, Carden proposes that a structure-dependent constraint *is* eventually acquired for forward pronouns, but he argues that it is acquired only after the constraints on backward pronouns are acquired. These in turn develop only after a purely linear non-structure-dependent principle of precedence.

A priori, the proposal of an initial non-structure-dependent principle of precedence is a feasible one. On purely theoretical grounds, Chomsky reasons so. He considers that if the theory of Universal Grammar adequately "describes" the "shared biological endowment" which makes it possible for humans to acquire language, and "explains" how this acquisition is possible, then the "primitive basis" for this theory "must meet a condition of epistemological priority . . . That is . . . we want the primitives to be concepts that can plausibly be assumed to provide a preliminary prelinguistic analysis of a reasonable selection of presented data, that is, to provide the primary linguistic data that are mapped by the language faculty to a grammar . . . ." Considering this, Chomsky proposes, "It would . . . be reasonable to suppose that such concepts as "precedes" . . . enter into the primitive basis . . ." of the theory of UG. Perhaps such notions "can be directly applied to linguistically unanalyzed data" (Chomsky, 1981a, 10).

Intuitively, a linear precedence basis to the first language acquisition of anaphora would appear to be motivated if the basis of first language acquisition were determined by computational 'processing' efficiency, where processing involved language in real time. Intuitively, computational mechanisms that offend linear sequence relations, by involving a 'back up,' would appear to be more complex than those that do not. (See Berwick and Weinberg 1984 for an initial attempt to deal with this issue formally, and Berwick and Wexler to appear on these issues.)

If the concept 'precedence' uniquely determines children's early hypotheses about anaphora, however, several negative consequences follow for both the general theory of first language acquisition and for the theory of UG. The concept 'precedes' does not in itself independently determine grammatically well-formed anaphora, as is suggested by the BT principles reviewed above and by data such as 3, 4, 57, 58 or 63–65 above for English. Thus, if the child formulates its first hypotheses about possible anaphora in the language it is acquiring solely in terms of a linear 'precedence' principle, its grammar will be incorrect in principle, according to this theory, and according to this language. A qualitative restructuring will be required.

It is a priori possible that the path of first language acquisition does involve such major qualitative restructuring. To the degree that it does

so, however, (i) this weakens the explanatory force of the theory of UG
as a theory of first language acquisition (i.e., one which significantly
explains how knowledge of language is attained because it *constrains*
first language acquisition) and (ii) pushes back in time the major
question for acquisition of the adult language without necessarily
helping to explain it. The critical issue of acquisition is no less severe
with this restructuring: i.e., what causes the eventual 'qualitative shift'
from the primitive a-linguistic theory to the grammatical theory? Indeed,
an initial "precedence only" principle may exacerbate the acquisition
problem because we now have to explain not only how the child
eventually acquires the correct grammar for its language but how it
comes to undo/unlearn the false hypotheses it has held. If a 'boot-
strapping' theory (see Pinker, 1984 for discussion) can be developed for
the primitive concepts at issue, and can explicate how the a-linguistic
concepts fortuitously integrate with related concepts in the adult
grammar, then the second problem may begin to be resolved. If a
'maturation' theory of acquisition (Borer and Wexler, to appear) is
supported, this may also help to resolve the second problem. We know
of no such proposal for the domain of anaphora, however. In addition,
the first issue remains in any case. To the degree that such primitive
a-linguistic concepts can and do 'explain' early stages of first language
acquisition, the fundamental empirical thrust of the theory of UG, viz.,
to explain how first language acquisition is possible (with 'speed' and
'apparent felicity'), is obviated.

In addition, if the concept 'precedence' significantly and singly
determines children's early hypotheses about anaphora, this would
predict that the child's language differs from the adult's not only in that
it will omit a range of possible anaphora (e.g., the backward anaphora in
the examples above), but also in that it will allow certain ungrammatical
anaphora, e.g., 33 above. This problem will be particularly severe in
languages which widely require and/or allow backward anaphora in
certain structures, e.g., Chinese as in 49, 50 and 72 (Huang's examples
127 and 129, 1982, p. 373); and which more widely block forward
anaphora.

(72) a. $\emptyset_i$ súirán   méiyǒu kōng, *Zhangsan*$_i$ háishì lái   -le
         though no   time   Zhangsan still   come -ASP

(Though he$_i$ had no time, Zhangsan$_i$ came nevertheless)

b. *súirán *Zhangsan*$_i$ méiyǒu kōng, $\emptyset_i$ háishì lái-le

Restrictions which limit the size of the range of possible anaphora in child language do not critically offend basic principles of learnability theory. On the basis of positive evidence alone, the child can extend this range. The proposed existence of ungrammatical language, however, such as predicted by a non-structure-dependent precedence principle, does pose a problem for learnability theory. In the absence of negative evidence, some other explanation must be sought for how the child learns to overcome these errors.

There are several additional problems with a proposal for the developmental primacy of an autonomous principle of 'precedence.' (1) It implies that children apply distinctly different principles to pronouns and non-pronoun anaphor types, e.g., empty categories or reflexive pronouns. This is not consistent with current linguistic theory which in principle subsumes all of these anaphor types under 'binding theory' and argues that all consult principles of grammatical structure, specifically, c-command. Although it remains possible that the precedence proposal is empirically true for child language, in spite of its inconsistency with this current theory, if it were true, this would raise a particular problem for the theory of acquisition of anaphora. Namely, if children have access to grammatical (structure-dependent) principles for non-pronouns, e.g., null NP's or empty categories, why then do they withhold these principles from pronouns in particular, excluding this class? On the other hand, if children do not apply structural principles to null anaphora either, then it is not clear how and why they would apply a linear precedence requirement to stimuli which do not exist, like null anaphors. (2) Solan's proposal of the precedence principle in particular claims that both children and adults apply distinct different principles to forward and backward pronouns. It claims that with development, children consult grammatical structure for backward pronouns but do not do so for forward pronouns. There is no known support for such a qualitative linguistic differentiation of forward and backward pronouns in the linguistic study of pronoun anaphora, although there are arguments against it (cf. Reinhart, 1976, 1983a, this volume; Lasnik, 1976). Again this does not deny the empirical possibility for the phenomenon in first language acquisition. Again, however, if children and adults can access grammatical structure for backward pronouns, why should they restrict it from application to forward pronouns? (Carden's proposal avoids this problem since it acknowledges eventual 'late' acquisition of "blocked forward" pronouns.) (3) Solan claims that an initial hypothesis of strict and autonomous precedence by the child is consistent with some version of UG: "This is consistent with a theory of acquisition that claims that the acquisition process is constrained by linguistic universals" . . . "A child learning a language such as Japanese . . . will not have to modify his hypothesis about the restriction of BA since . . . there is a total ban against backward anaphora for non-null pronouns" (86). In addition, "universally there are no restrictions prohibiting forward anaphora" (91). The facts Solan cites for Japanese backward pronouns are not correct, as seen above (II.3.4.1 and 2). Thus if the child entertains the "precedence-only" stage of the BAR, it will entertain mistaken hypotheses for Japanese, as well as for English. Even if the facts were correct for Japanese pronouns, however, and/or if they *are* correct for other languages, if the child established a linear precedence constraint on the basis of observed forward pronoun order in a language, it would be establishing a principle which is incorrect for other (e.g., null) anaphor types and anaphora relations in language, as we noted above. (It should be noted that this would be a particular problem for Japanese since lexical third person pronouns like 'kare' are marked and restricted in use. For example, they have only entered the language recently (e.g., with the current generation), and are rarely used by children at all.)

1.1 *Clarifying the Acquisition Issue vis-à-vis Linearity*

It is necessary to distinguish *linearity*, which refers to a dimension of organization along which items may be related, and *precedence*, which refers to a specific linear relation between items. The relation of *precedence* describes a nonsymmetric, irreflexive, relation of one term to another in a linear string. Sensitivity to *linearity* cannot be at issue for a language learner, although its relation to UG is, as discussed above (II.3.2 and II.3.3).

Most proposals that children begin first language acquisition with a linearity-based theory propose, more precisely, that children bring a hypothesis of 'precedence' to bear on first anaphora and that this hypothesis is independent of structure. A specific principle of non-structure-dependent *precedence*, not one of *linearity*, is at issue.

The distinction between *precedence* and *linearity* has been confused in the literature to date. For example, Solan states that there appears to be no known language wherein only backward pronouns are allowed and forward disallowed. Solan concludes from this that "this constitutes strong evidence for the relevance of linear order" (64). What Solan appears to intend is that this fact appears to evidence the relevance of 'precedence.' As Lasnik and Crain (to appear) show, for example, if linear order defined a parameter of language variation (e.g., like 'head direction' or 'branching direction') one would expect precisely the reverse case. That is, languages should vary in possible order constraints (yielding both forward and backward constraints equivalently on pronouns).

Note also that the concept 'precedes' must clearly be available to even very young children from principles of general cognition. Although there are general restrictions on the young child's conception of time (e.g., Piaget and Inhelder, 1973) and general restrictions on the mapping of temporal relations to linguistic expressions (e.g., Ferreiro, 1971, Amidon and Carey, 1972), these restrictions would not deny that the child can access very basic principles of linear order, such as those required by the principle 'an antecedent must precede an anaphor.' In addition, although the structure of discourse is still not well studied in first language acquisition, it might be assumed that even the very young child to some degree accesses a principle of temporal sequence in organizing early discourse. For example, 'mention a topic before discussing it.' The acquisition issue of concern here is not whether the young child has access to such primitive principles of temporal sequence as involved in 'precedence,' but whether it uses such notions *exclusively* to organize its early hypotheses about well-formed anaphora in the language it is acquiring, that is, exclusively of specifically linguistic structure-dependent principles.

2. REFINING THE ISSUES OF BT IN FIRST LANGUAGE ACQUISITION

With regard to BT (see II.2 above and Freidin's article in this volume), we must first evaluate evidence for fundamental principles which underlie BT. Sensitivity to *configuration,* such as defined by c-command, is essential to application of binding principles, e.g., it is necessary to distinguish 'bound' and 'free' in principles A and B, and C, and/or to determine distribution of various lexical and null anaphor types. If children do not have or do not apply a sensitivity to configurational structure, the principles of BT will be rendered otiose. If in acquisition of anaphora, children are forming hypotheses of *precedence* in the absence of structure-dependence, then this precedence principle obviates BT. Thus testing the question of precedence discussed above is fundamental to testing the relevance of BT to a characterization of children's early hypotheses about anaphora.

In addition, essential questions for the study of anaphora must be the following: Do children's early hypotheses for differentiating anaphor types function in terms of nominal categories defined in terms of phonetic shape, as in Principles A, B, or C, which refer to lexically overt pronouns, anaphors (e.g., reflexives) and *r* expressions (e.g., names). Or do they evidence general principles which generalize over phonetic shapes of anaphors? In particular, do children generalize principles over both null and phonetically realized nominal anaphor types? What initial differentiation is there between lexical anaphors (e.g., BT-anaphors like reflexive pronouns) and lexical pronouns, and between various types of null anaphors? What evidence is there for differentiation of bound and free anaphora? If this differentiation is made by children at early stages of acquisition, what informs this differentiation? Is it made in terms of (phonetic form of) nominal category or in terms of configurational domain, e.g., c-command? Is it made in terms of a more general distinction between pragmatics and grammar?

Particular issues arise with regard to 'control' structures. Do children integrate the anaphora in these structures into a general theory of anaphora and/or differentiate them from other structures which are determined by BT. To what degree do properties of the lexicon support or substitute for structural properties in acquisition of control? (See Pinker, 1984 for initial study of these latter issues.)

2.1 *Relations among the Binding Principles (BP) in First Language Acquisition*

If BT principles A, B and C (section II.2 above and Freidin's article in this volume) constitute a component of UG, then we may predict that these principles constrain children's hypotheses about the form of the grammar they are acquiring.

2.1.1 *Relation of Principles A and B*

Within the BT itself, as discussed in II.2 above, there is no reason to predict that one of these principles may hold in the absence of the other.

In fact, since these principles are defined as complements of each other, it would be predicted on theoretical grounds that if one principle (A or B) is evidenced, the other must be also.

2.1.2 *Learnability Theory and BP*

It has recently been proposed that there may be motivation for evidence in acquisition of binding principle A (i.e., 'an anaphor must be locally bound') before principle B (i.e., 'a pronoun must be locally free'), on the basis of learnability theory. This hypothesis is based on a general "principle of minimal falsifiability" (PMF) whereby it is hypothesized that children's first hypotheses are the most restrictive ones, i.e., those that are 'the most easily disconfirmed' (Williams, 1981, 29–30). An approach to this theory has been developed in particular by Berwick, who develops a related 'subset property' in learnability theory (Berwick, 1982). This property formally and procedurally captures the learnability requirement that initial hypotheses in acquisition are intrinsically ordered. Basically "the acquisition procedure always guesses a subset language if possible, that is, the smaller language that is also compatible with the positive evidence encountered so far" (Berwick, 1982, 276). The subset property is argued to be "a necessary condition for positive-only acquisition" (277), i.e., acquisition in which the child is not negatively corrected. Berwick tentatively applies this learnability principle to principle A and B of the BT for anaphora. He notes, ". . . the set of surface structures (now interpreted in an extended sense to include coindexing) where pronominals can appear is larger than the set of surface structures in which pure anaphors appear" (300). Therefore one could hypothesize:

(73)   . . . The tightest assumption is that an NP is *bound* in its Minimal Governing category, hence the default assumption should be that an NP is an anaphor" (Berwick, 1982, 300).

According to this hypothesis, principle A might then be predicted to have priority in children's earliest hypotheses regarding anaphora.

There are several theoretical problems with the application of the subset property to acquisition of anaphora. See Manzini and Wexler (to appear) for analyses of these issues. As Berwick notes, the analysis in 73 above "is not forced . . . since in fact pronominals and pure anaphors are in nearly complementary distribution" (301). Thus, although the domains of the two principles may sometimes overlap, the domains are for the most part not in an inclusion relation, but in a complementation relation. Overcoming the assumption that NPs are BT-anaphors will thus not involve negative evidence any less than overcoming the assumption that anaphors are pronouns, i.e., unbound. In addition, principles A and B are complementary principles of grammar. Although their domains (i.e., the language data they allow) may sometimes overlap, the grammatical principles themselves do not overlap. Thus if children formulate hypotheses in terms of the extensive domain of their language, they will be mistaken in relating these facts to their grammar in a principled way. In addition, if children mistakenly assume a pronoun is a BT-anaphor this would mean that they not only do not understand something about pronouns, but that they also do not understand something about BT-anaphors since they believe pronouns can be included as anaphors. This error could not be based on the hypothesis that principle A always holds since they would not have principle A in the absence of a well-formed category 'BT-anaphor' on which the principle is based

2.1.3 Linguistic Theory and BP

Freidin (this volume) also makes a prediction for differential relation between principles A and B in acquisition; but on linguistic grounds. See Freidin's examples 41 and 53 (151−188, this volume) for revised statements of principles A and B in accord with a revised differential definition of their domains. As Freidin hypothesizes, if these domains across principles A and B are different, "we might expect to find differences in the acquisition of the S-paradigms for pronouns and anaphors" (151−188). On the other hand, if principles A and B are hypothesized by the child to have complementary domains, at least at initial stages of acquisition, we might expect complementary and coherent evidence of both principles A and B, at least within the S-paradigm Freidin describes.

3. PRAGMATICS AND GRAMMAR OF ANAPHORA

As Reinhart discusses (123-150, this volume), her proposal of a principled distinction of pragmatic coreference in free anaphora from grammatically determined construal of bound anaphora (II.3.5), predicts that acquisition patterns for free and bound anaphora may differ distinctly. While structural sensitivity may be evidenced for bound anaphora in acquisition, there is no reason to expect such for free anaphora, e.g., for definite pronoun interpretation in non-c-commanding environments. Pragmatic context effects should be salient on pronoun interpretation. If linear precedence is a strictly pragmatic principle derived from cognition outside of grammatical competence, then it should apply to lexical pronouns but not to bound anaphors, either lexical or null. Pragmatic effects should also be particularly salient on the particular pronoun-antecedent relations covered by principle C, since in Reinhart's theory, this principle C constraint is pragmatically accomplished. In fact, principle C effects may be expected to develop with development of speaker-hearer communicative competence.

IV. EVIDENCE FROM THE LANGUAGE ACQUISITION DATA

The experimental studies in this volume begin to address the issues raised above. (1) They investigate evidence for a 'Directionality constraint' in first language acquisition of anaphora in English, and evaluate its nature. They investigate evidence for the role of an autonomous non structure-dependent linear precedence principle in defining this constraint. (See in particular the papers by Lust and Clifford, Lust et al., and Carden) (2) The studies provide evidence on the differentiation of anaphor types in terms of their interpretation (whether bound or free) and on their distribution, in first language acquisition. They evaluate anaphor type both in terms of phonetic form, and in terms of syntactic domain. (See in particular the articles by Roeper, Lust et al., Sherman and Lust and van Riemsdijk) These results have implications for the role of the BT in first language acquisition. In addition, the studies provide information on the role of the lexicon in control relations for anaphora, and on the interaction of lexical and syntactic domain factors in determining these relations. (See Sherman and Lust). (3) Finally, they allow tentative initial conclusions on the interaction of pragmatic and grammatical factors in the determination of anaphora in first language acquisition.

We will sketch critical results on these issues below, briefly setting results of the studies in this volume into the context of previous results available from literature in the field where possible. We refer the reader to the individual studies and references cited for details.

1. DIRECTIONALITY EFFECT

Numerous studies of first language acquisition of English have now documented what may be characterized as a *directionality constraint* on anaphora in early child language. The constraint may be formulated as in (74).

> (74)   In first language acquisition of anaphora in English, the anaphor should follow, not precede, the antecedent

Empirical evidence for the directionality constraint in 74 has been provided by several different measures on several different experimental tasks. The evidence has been gathered on different types of anaphors (both pronoun and null anaphors) and on several different types of structures. It has accumulated from several different laboratories (see also Tavakolian, 1977, 1978a; and Solan, 1977, 1983. See Carden, this volume for report of further replication of this effect.)

Constraint. The directionality effect has been formulated as a 'constraint' in 74, because it results in a restriction on first language acquisition. The child does not take all the options available in the adult grammar equivalently. To a significant degree, one option of antecedent and pronoun order is taken (forward); the other is not (the backward order).

We first review the evidence for the directionality constraint in first language acquisition of English (IV.1.1—1.3). We then consider several proposals on the nature of this constraint (1.4). We consider a proposal that the directionality constraint may be spurious (1.4.1). We then show that the data suggest that the constraint cannot be simply due to the structure of the stimulus sentences independent of anaphora direction (1.4.2). We then consider (1.4.3) ostensible support for the claim that the observed directionality constraint is based strictly on linear precedence alone and is non structure-dependent. We review additional data provided in this volume (Lust and Clifford) which is critically inconsistent with the claim that strict non-structure-dependent precedence is the source of the directionality effect observed in children's language. We acknowledge proposed counterevidence to these results (1.4.4) and summarize (1.4.5) conclusions and questions on the nature of the directionality effect.

1.1 Children's Production: Elicited Imitation Data

In previous studies, children have been found to imitate sentences with forward pronouns such as in 75, significantly more successfully than sentences with backward pronouns such as in 76. (See Lust, Chien and Flynn, to appear for study of this elicited imitation task as a measure of grammatical competence.)

(75) a. *Tommy* ran fast because *he* heard a lion
     b. *Jenna* drank some juice while *she* was having lunch

(76) a. Because *he* heard a lion, *Tommy* ran fast
     b. While *she* was having lunch, *Jenna* drank some juice

In Lust (1981) 24 young children (2,6—3,5 years,months; mean age 3.0) who were grouped by MLU imitated sentences such as 75 with forward pronouns significantly better than sentences such as 76 with backward pronouns. Means correct were .61 and .21 respectively on a score range of 0—2. (See figure 1.) The factor of *Directionality* thus significantly modified imitation success rate. In this same study, 45 older children (age 3,6—5,7 mean age 4.4), who were grouped by age into 6-month age groups, also imitated the sentences with forward pronouns significantly better than those with backward. (Means correct were 1.77

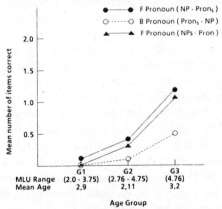

Fig. 1. Forward and Backward Pronouns: Development of Correct Imitation in a group of young children (Lust, 1980).

and 1.18 respectively.) *Directionality* thus also significantly modified the imitation success rate in the older children, although the overall imitation ability of the older children was higher for all of these sentences than for the younger children. (See figure 2.)

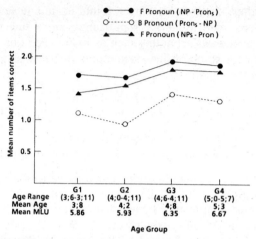

Fig. 2. Forward and Backward Pronouns: Development of Correct Imitation in a group of older children (Lust, 1980).

Analyses of imitation errors in this study (where 'error' means any significant change in the model sentence) confirm that pronominalization direction is involved in these imitation success rates.[17] 44% of imitations of sentences with backward pronouns involved a change in anaphora (antecedent and/or anaphor) in the young group; 28% in the old group did. These changes included: (i) reversal of backward pronoun to forward pronoun; (ii) use of two pronouns, or two nulls, eliminating the nominal antecedent altogether; (iii) use of two nouns, eliminating the pronoun. These errors are rare or nonexistent among errors in imitation of sentences with forward pronouns.

In addition, when children in this study were administered sentences with a redundant NP as in 77 or 78 which allowed forward or backward pronouns, they frequently spontaneously pronominalized these (54% of younger children, 47% of older children). 100% of these spontaneous pronominalizations were in a forward direction, even if backward pronominalization was allowed, as in 78.

(77)   *Jane* was sad because *Jane* dropped the ice cream
(78)   Because *Sam* was thirsty, *Sam* drank some soda

A subsequent, more extensive study (Lust, Loveland and Kornet, 1980), confirmed these prior results as Figure 3 shows.

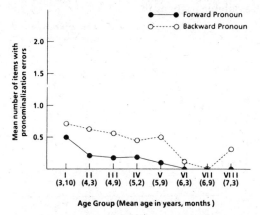

Fig. 3. Amount of Pronominalization Error on Imitation of Forward and Backward Pronouns (Lust, Loveland and Kornet, 1980).

1.2 *Children's Comprehension*

Act Out Task Test of Comprehension. A number of different studies have also evidenced a Directionality effect on comprehension of pronouns in first language acquisition.

The Lust, Loveland and Kornet study (1980) tested the same group of 82 Ss (3,5–7,5 in age) on a set of sentences like 79 and 80 below in a comprehension test using 'act-out' procedures. These sentences resemble 75 and 76 in all aspects of structure except that lexically they involved discrete 'act-outable' predicates relative to a restricted set of dolls and props which were made available to the child for the task. (See Lust, Chien, and Flynn, to appear, for discussion of experimental methodology involved in this task).

(79)   *Oscar* bumped the wall when *he* found the penny
(80)   When *he* closed the box, *Cookie Monster* lay down

The results of the comprehension task also showed effects of a *Directionality* factor. Figure 4 shows that Ss were correct significantly more often on sentences like 79 with forward pronouns than on those with backward pronouns like 80. (Means correct were 1.82 vs. 1.32 overall respectively.) (In this study, Ss were scored correct on sentences like 79 and 80 if they either chose the doll named in the sentence to interpret the anaphor or one of the other dolls (from an available set of 3) which were available to them.)[18]

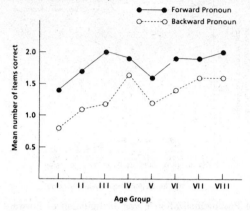

_Fig. 4. Development of Correct Comprehension of Sentences with Forward and Backward Pronouns (Lust, Loveland and Kornet, 1980).

More specifically, these act-out task results showed, as Figure 5 displays, that significantly more coreference judgments with the name in the sentence were computed if the pronoun followed the name (as in 79) (mean coreference judgments on scale of 0–2 was 1.83) than if it

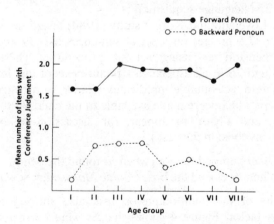

Fig. 5. Amount of Coreference Judgments in Interpretation of Forward and Backward Pronouns (Lust, Loveland and Kornet, 1980).

preceded it (as in 80) (mean coreference judgment .49). Ss thus not only were more successful at comprehending sentences with forward pronouns than with backward but they computed an anaphoric relation with a pronoun significantly more frequently if it was forward than if it was backward.

In another experiment using an act-out task, Tavakolian 1977 also found a directionality constraint on coreference computation with pronouns. This study involved a group of 24 Ss (3,0−5,6 in three age groups of 8 Ss each).[19] In each of a different set of structures exemplified in 81 through 84 below, Tavakolian found that significantly more coreference judgments with a name in the sentence were computed for the forward pronouns (97% and 99% for 81 and 82 respectively) than for the backward (33.3% in both 83 and 84).

(81)   *The sheep* tells *the duck* for *him* to jump over the horse
(82)   *The sheep* tells *the duck* that *he* should jump over the horse
(83)   *For him* to kiss *the lion* would make *the duck* happy
(84)   That *he* kissed *the lion* made *the duck* happy

In a more recent experiment, Solan 1983 (experiment 4, p. 139) tested the comprehension of 36 Ss 5−7 years of age in 3 groups of 12 Ss each on one sentence of each of the types exemplified in 85−88 (with forward pronouns). Solan used an act-out task similar to Tavakolian's.

(85)   *The horse* told *the sheep* that *he* would run around
(86)   *The horse* hit *the sheep* after *he* ran around
(87)   *The horse* hit *the sheep* in *his* yard
(88)   *The horse* hit *the sheep* after *his* run

The same subjects were tested on sentences like 89 and 90 below (experiment 2, p. 122), with backward pronouns.

(89)   After *he* ran around, *the horse* hit *the sheep*
(90)   After *his* run, *the horse* hit *the sheep*

Although the children in this study were older, Solan's results showed (like Tavakolian's, and similar to Lust, Loveland, and Kornet's) that 94% of the Ss provided coreferential responses between the pronoun and the name in the sentence on forward sentences like 85−88. Only 47% provided them for sentences with backward pronouns like 89 and 90.

Question Task Test of Comprehension. In an early experiment, Carol
Chomsky (1969, 104–111) tested comprehension of 40 children, aged
5,0 to 10 years on a series of sentences which varied in pronoun
direction. Chomsky used a different comprehension task, which asked
the child questions like "Who got the candy?" after a sentence like 91.
(There were 5 sentences with forward pronouns and 5 with backward
pronouns where coreference was possible with a sentence antecedent.)

(91)   After *he* got the candy, *Mickey* left
(92)   Before *he* went out, *Pluto* took a nap
(93)   *Pluto* thinks *he* knows everything
(94)   *Mickey* yawned when *he* sat down

All the sentences referred to two figures, "Mickey Mouse" and "Pluto
Pup," which stood before the child. Results showed that all but 4 of the
40 Ss chose coreference with the name in the sentences more often on
forward than on backward pronouns, Four Ss never gave coreference
judgments at all on the backward sentences.

1.2.1 *The Nature of Comprehension Test Data: Noncoreference*
Judgments

Depression of coreference judgments on backward anaphora, compared
to forward replicates across all studies which test comprehension. In
some studies, which score errors independently of coreference (see
Notes 18 and 19), this depression is complemented by a higher number
of errors on backward anaphora. Errors may involve, for example,
acting out one clause only, or forgetting lexical items necessary to
computation of the grammatical relations of the complete complex
sentence stimulus. The Directionality effect is also complemented by
an increase in noncoreference judgments on backward anaphors over
forward anaphors, i.e., choice of a doll made available in the environment but not mentioned in the sentence. However, in the act-out task,
the unmarked situation, all other things being equal, seems to be for the
subject not to generate the additional cognitive load of a second referent
if possible. Thus in some studies there is very little noncoreference
judgment, regardless of grammatical structure of the stimulus sentences.
This has been the case in numerous studies where the child has been
pretrained to use one or two dolls equivalently for act-out. This was the
case for example in the studies reported in articles 6, 7 and 8 in this

volume, or in preceding studies like Lust, Loveland and Kornet, 1980. In the comprehension test of 101 Ss aged 3,11 to 7,11 on sentences with null anaphors and pronouns which is reported in article 7 of this volume, only 12% of responses showed noncoreference judgments, 2% on forward, 10% on backward, even though the pronoun involved in the stimulus sentences, being free, allowed such reference to an external antecedent in either case.

Some studies using an act out task, from some labs, do get a high amount of noncoreference judgment in this task, particularly on backward anaphora, e.g., Tavakolian, 1977, Solan, 1983. Although the reasons for this difference across application of the act-out task remain to be confirmed, several factors of task design suggest themselves.[20] Further study is necessary on the possible effects of such methodological differences across comprehension studies on assessment of grammatical competence. The point we make here is simply the following: the directionality effect is reflected in several different behavioral measures in comprehension tasks. Basically it is represented in modulation of amount of coreference judgment between forward and backward pronoun directions. Complementary differences in amount of noncoreference judgments are possible but not necessary complements to this main effect. (See Padilla Rivera 1985 for a more extensive study relative to this issue.)

1.3 *Generalization of the Directionality Effect Across Anaphor Types*

The directionality effect is not limited to sentences with pronouns. It also has been observed on sentences which involve a null anaphor like 95 and 96 below. Tavakolian 1977 found a pattern of results on these sentences which was similar to that on sentences with pronouns like 81–84 above. That is, children gave a significantly greater amount of coreference judgments on the forward cases like 95 than on backward like 96. (These sentences were tested on the same children who were tested on pronouns.)

(95)   *The sheep* tells *the duck* Ø to jump over the horse
(96)   Ø to kiss *the lion* would make *the duck* happy

In this case, 25% of responses were coreferent with a following antecedent in 96, while 96% were coreferent with a preceding NP in sentences like 95.

Similarly, in the study reported in article 7 of this volume, 101 Ss, mean age 5,6, were tested on both imitation and comprehension of sentences like 97—100 below, half of which involved pronouns like 97 and 98 with tensed complement clauses, and half of which involved null subjects in nontensed complement clauses like 99 and 100.

(97)   *Fozzie* tickled *Kermit Frog* when *he* dropped the car
(98)   When *he* dropped the tissue, *Kermit* rubbed *Scooter*
(99)   *Scooter* squeezed *Fozzie* when Ø dropping the tissue
(100) When Ø hitting the block, *Scooter* kicked *Fozzie Bear*

In imitation, this study provided evidence of the same type of errors on both backward nulls and backward pronouns (e.g., reversal of anaphora direction, dropping of NP to create two null subjects, use of two pronoun subjects, or dropping of anaphor to create two redundant NP subjects). In results of the comprehension task in this study, children were found to comprehend forward nulls like 99 significantly more successfully (mean .52 on a range of 0—2) than backward like 100 (mean .33). More particularly, children assigned coreference judgments with subject significantly more often on forward (.60) than on backward (.46) nulls, as they did on pronouns.

The 'directionality effect' is thus not linked to the lexical pronoun, an anaphor type which is phonetically realized, but applies to anaphora more generally. It applies to null anaphors also, where pronouns and nulls are tested in related structures.

1.3.1 *Coordinate Structures*

Other research in the field using production data has suggested that the directionality constraint is also not linked only to subordinate structures. It also holds on acquisition of coordinate structures with null arguments of various types (cf. Lust, 1974, 1977, 1981; Lust and Mervis, 1980). For example, children find it significantly easier to imitate structures like 101 than 102 and structures like 101 appear earlier in natural speech than 102.

(101)   Push the truck and Ø the car
(102)   Push Ø and pull the truck

1.4 *The Nature of the Directionality Effeect*

The results reviewed above suggest that the Directionality Constraint is not linked to specific tasks or modes of language use, e.g., production or comprehension. It is therefore not based merely on a simple 'processing constraint' which requires production of an antecedent before a pronoun, since there is no reason why such a production constraint should affect sentence comprehension. Rather, to the degree that both production (elicited imitation and natural speech) and comprehension (act out) tasks involve computation of anaphora, the results appear to reflect a fundamental constraint on children's computation of anaphora. The fact that the directionality effect is observed on a range of subordinate and coordinate structures suggests the generality of this effect in the child's grammar.

The results above also suggest that the directionality constraint cannot be merely a generalization from stimulus frequency, as it would be for example, if the child, exposed to the frequency facts on pronouns (e.g., II.1.1.1 above) simply was stimulus-conditioned by these frequency facts. If the child were simply being conditioned on frequency of phonetically realized anaphors, there would be no reason for this to be generalized to null anaphors, which involve no stimulus at all, or to generalize over both subordinate and coordinate structures.

It might be argued that if children treat overt null anaphors like pronouns, e.g., implicitly expanding them to pronouns, they then may apply the directionality constraint to them on the basis of some version of "stimulus generalization" from frequency of pronoun use. If this is the case, however, then the children are obviously not stimulus-dependent in the first place (since nulls are processed as completely as pronouns) so there would be no reason why they should become stimulus-dependent for the distribution of either pronoun or null anaphors. We will review evidence below also which shows that although children do assign a pronoun interpretation to null anaphors in certain cases, this pronoun assignment appears to be structure-dependent.

These results do not resolve the critical ambiguity involved in the phenomenon of observed unmarked pronoun precedence in English, or in English acquisition (cf. II.1.3.2 above). They suggest that children have established a principle which determines precedence for anaphora. Because of the grammatical structure of English, however, the results do not disambiguate whether this principle could have been set by

children's sensitivity to the configurational (right branching) facts of the
language they are acquiring, or whether the principle is simply one
based exclusively on induction from the surface facts which frequently
display linear precedence of pronouns.

1.4.1. *Lasnik and Crain's Proposal on the Directionality Effect*

Lasnik and Crain (L & C) (to appear) have argued against the existence
of a precedence principle in first language acquisition. They suggest that
imitation errors wherein children convert backward to forward pronouns
must mean that the children 'understand' backward pronouns. L & C
compare the conversion children make in these cases to adult translation from French to English. They argue that one wouldn't want to claim
in the case of such a translation that the person doing the translating
doesn't know French. Thus one shouldn't conclude from this change on
the imitation stimulus that the children who make this "translation"
don't "have access to rules allowing backward anaphora." If this line of
reasoning were valid it could suggest that the directionality constraint
was spurious in children's production. (L & C do not do so.)

With regard to comprehension task results, Lasnik and Crain suggest
that "children know that pronouns don't need linguistic antecedents;"
and that they "can refer to unmentioned objects present in the experimental work space" . . . this "may in fact be the preferred interpretation
for many children" of backward pronouns. This would explain why 14/
24 of Tavakolian's Ss interpreted the backward pronoun consistently by
an external referent when they did not apply coreference with the following name. If this suggestion were correct, the ostensible constraint
against backward anaphora in the comprehension data could reflect
merely the fact that children prefer a coreferential reading for an anaphor
and antecedent in forward anaphora, but a noncoreferential reading in
backward anaphora. Backward pronouns thus in a sense would not be
anaphoric at all. Thus, there would be no actual constraint on "directionality of anaphora" in comprehension.

A preference for deictic interpretation of backward pronouns when
the situation allows it and a facility for production of both forward and
backward pronouns cannot explain the data set which constitutes the
directionality effect reviewed above, for the following reasons.

(i) L & C's explanation for the imitation data (i.e., children really do have grammatical competence for backward pronouns and thus frequently reverse pronoun order) and their explanation for the comprehension data (i.e., children prefer deictic interpretation of backward pronouns) raise an issue. If children can assign backward anaphora grammatically as in imitation data, then why do they not do so in comprehension?

(ii) L & C suggest that this inconsistency can be resolved by the fact that there are external referents present in the comprehension task, but not in the imitation task; and when there are external referents, the preferred interpretation of a backward pronoun shifts from anaphoric to non-anaphoric. With regard to L & C's interpretation of the comprehension data, the suggestion is most certainly true that children know that pronouns do not need sentence-internal antecedents. This is evidenced, for example, by a high deictic use of pronouns in early child speech, long before overt anaphoric use (cf. Clifford, 1984). It has also been confirmed that children like adults, are more sensitive to pragmatic context in the case of backward pronouns than in the case of forward, e.g., Lust, Loveland and Kornet, 1980; and Lust et al. this volume. The evidence does not support the claim that noncoreference is a preferred interpretation when external referents are available however. (a) Notice in IV.1.2 that coreference, not noncoreference, is the preferred interpretation across a wide array of studies using the act-out task in spite of an available reference set. The percentage of children using the same doll for a coreference response to backward pronouns in a domain allowing free anaphora increases with age in this task, e.g., as in the study in Lust et al. this volume. But the low percentage of responses using an external doll does not change significantly with age (1%–5%). Also in earlier studies like Carol Chomsky 1969 (in a comprehension task based on questions), the predominant responses were coreferent to a doll named in the sentence, although the child always had other referents in front of them. In addition, we saw above that the directionality effect on children's comprehension generalized to null anaphors. Although there might be some motivation for a deictic interpretation of backward pronouns, there is none for backward nulls, since nulls in English do not generally in themselves involve deixis.

On the imitation task, in addition, experimentation has shown that even where a pragmatic lead is made available to a child before a model sentence as in 103 and 104 below, children still produce the forward pronouns significantly more easily than the backward (Lust, Loveland,

& Kornet, 1980). This suggests that the directionality effects in imitation
are also independent of the presence or absence of external referents.

(103)   This is a story about *Ernie*. When *he* sat down *Ernie* turned
        around.
(104)   This is a story about *Ernie*. When *Ernie* sat down *he* turned
        around.

(iii) L & C's proposed explanations for both the imitation and
comprehension data, even if they are provocative, do not account
for the full set of data, e.g., difference in amount of errors between
forward and backward pronouns in both comprehension and imitation
tasks. For example, there are more incorrect responses to backward
pronouns in the comprehension task, even when correctness would have
allowed either a coreferent or a noncoreferent response, and several
referents are available. This suggests that the directionality effects are
independent of possible noncoreferent judgments.

With regard to L & C's interpretation of production data, the full set
of results we reviewed above suggests that children do not have full
competence for backward anaphora, even though some children some
of the time do make the imitation error of pronoun reversal. For
example, imitations with pronoun reversal errors often also include
errors (changes) in the grammatical structure of the stimulus sentence,
e.g., from subordination in 76a to coordination (as in "Tommy heard a
lion and he ran fast"). In addition, when children fail imitation of
backward anaphora, all of their errors do not include pronoun reversal.
Not only the anaphora reversal error but the whole set of errors which
apply to backward anaphora must be explained. In addition, failure at
backward pronoun imitation was paralleled by a significantly greater
failure to successfully comprehend backward pronouns than forward.
As reported above, this matched set of imitation and comprehension
deficits constitutes the directionality effect and must be explained. A
uniform explanation is merited.

(iv) Consider that it were true that in imitation children do have
competence for backward anaphora production but in comprehension,
although they have the competence for backward, they prefer coreference on forward and noncoreference on backward. Even if so, this
would not answer the question of the nature of the directionality effect,
nor deny that one exists. The questions would still have to be answered:
why in imitation do children not produce backward anaphora as freely

as they do the forward if they have equal facility for it? Why in comprehension do they not assign coreference judgments on backward pronouns/nulls when they show they have the competence to do so on forward, and *do* do so on forward?

The complete set of evidence suggests then that the directionality effect in comprehension data cannot be explained by a preference for noncoreference judgments on backward anaphora, and that the directionality effects in imitation are not spurious because they are not subsumed under the pronoun reversal error. However, if the children do not have the full grammatical competence for backward pronouns, as suggested by their production and comprehension deficits reviewed above, then how do they accomplish the mapping from the stimulus sentence with the backward pronoun to their own imitation productions? Specifically, how do they accomplish the assignment of the following antecedent to the preceding pronoun in order to reverse pronoun direction in this error?[21] This may be explained only by a study of the nature of elicited imitation itself (cf. Lust, Chien and Flynn, to appear), and by further analysis of anaphora (cf. IV.3.3).

With Lasnik and Crain, we argue below that the acquisition data do not support a directionality principle which determines *precedence* solely in terms of linear ordering of antecedent and anaphor. However, we suggest that the full range of acquisition data do confirm a different type of directionality effect which remains to be explained.

Several factors must be considered in the explanation of this constraint.

1.4.2 *Relation to Sentence Structure: Pre- and Post-Posed Clauses*

As can be seen in the examples above, sentences tested with backward anaphora often have preposed clauses, e.g. 76, while sentences with forward anaphora have postposed clauses, e.g., 75. Postposed right branching clauses like 75 are the unmarked form for English (see Fodor, Bever and Garrett, 1974 for summary of experimental evidence on this claim). Given this fact, it would be possible that the directionality effects that have been observed in first language acquisition of anaphora would be explained by this structural difference, rather than by the directionality of anaphora per se.

This difference in subordinate clause position, and in direction of embedding has been shown not to explain the anaphora directionality effect. The directionality preference for forward pronouns, for example, has been found also in sentences like 105, which have preposed subordinate clauses (which would have allowed backward pronouns) but have forward pronouns. The imitation of these sentences is significantly better than imitation of similar sentences (with preposed subordinate clauses) with backward pronouns, e.g., 76.

(105)   Because *Jenna* saw a mouse *she* ran away

As can be seen in Figures 1 and 2, children generally do imitate left branching structures, with preposed clauses, with more difficulty than they do right branching structures with postposed clauses. However, the difference in imitation success between sentences with variation in both embedding direction and anaphora direction (e.g., 75 vs 76) is significantly greater than the difference between sentences which vary just in embedding direction, without varying in anaphora direction (e.g., 75 vs 105). This shows that while there is an effect due to embedding direction and while children do recognize the preposed clause order as more marked, the anaphora directionality effect (i.e., the constraint in 74), is independent of this effect (cf. Lust, 1981). (Article 7 in this volume replicates these results on a different set of sentences with a different set of children.)

1.4.3 *Linear Dependence or Structure Dependence*

Tavakolian's (1977) explanation for the observed directionality constraint was that children eliminate 'command' from the adult grammatical principles, and function on the basis of 'linear precedence' alone. Children must *acquire* reference to the 'command' component of constraint on anaphora. In sentences like 83 and 84, the anaphor precedes the antecedent, but does not command it, and so the adult grammar which is formulated in terms of command as in II.1.2 above, "will not mark them as noncoreferential" (1977, 150−1). Children, however, do treat these as noncoreferential, suggesting that they ignore command, and attend to precedence.

On the basis of the stimulus sentences Tavakolian tested, however, this conclusion is not a necessary one. The sentential subjects in the stimulus sentences, e.g., 83, are clearly marked structures in English. They are outside the simple application of X-bar theory, which constrains phrase structure according to UG. For example, this theory does not provide the NP → S structure which these sentences involve. Tavakolian herself suggests that in these sentences in fact "it is not clear whether children analyzed the first clause as a simplex sentence conjoined to the second clause." If so, she speculates, "then children are not ignoring command relationships in formulating" their anaphora rule. This is because "hierarchical relations were never established among the elements so that the notion of command could be incorporated into the rule" (153). If this were correct, then precedence relations may be used by children for antecedent-anaphor relations in the case where no hierarchical structure is available to establish locality conditions between antecedent and anaphor. In this case, anaphora cannot be established linguistically. (See II.3.4 above for a possible linguistic basis to this proposal.)

Results in IV.1.4.2 may also appear to support the claim that the child is not associating configuration with linearity relations between antecedent and anaphor. These results suggest that even when the child has the option to use backward pronoun anaphora, because the backward pronoun would be in a subordinate clause, children do not take this option. These results also do not unambiguously confirm that children are attending *only* to linearity, however. Although these results do suggest that the directionality effect is to some degree independent of specific structures in which antecedent and anaphor occur, this could reflect a directionality constraint on early child language, no matter how that constraint was determined. In fact, in these results, Ss were found to be sensitive to preposing and postposing of subordinate clauses at the same time that they did not modulate anaphora direction. This suggests that in these data children do not modulate anaphora direction in these structures (where directionality of anaphora is optional) *in spite* of structural sensitivity, not *because of* lack of structural sensitivity.

1.4.3.1 Blocked Forward Anaphora: The 3-D Study

A critical test of the nature of the forward directionality constraint in first language acquisition must involve a test of whether children block forward pronouns when the unmarked configurational structure of English is modified, and in particular, when it is modified in such a way that forward anaphora is obligatorily blocked grammatically (by command).

In English, sentences like 107 reflect such a condition. If the forward directionality constraint in English acquisition is linked to the right branching configuration of English, then the forward directionality constraint may be interrupted when this configuration is interrupted. Unlike unmarked configurations, in 107 the pronoun c-commands the name although it follows it. In 108 the pronoun is c-commanded by the name although it precedes it.

(107)   *Under *Oscar the Grouch$_i$*, *he$_i$* bounced the ball
(108)   Under *him$_{i,j}$*, *Oscar the Grouch$_i$* bounced the ball

The accepted adult judgment which grounds the linguistic literature is that anaphora in 107 is blocked, while in 108 it is allowed (cf. II.1 above).

If children apply principles of linear precedence which are determined solely by the linear surface relations between anaphor and antecedent in the string and which are non structure-dependent, then they should demonstrate forward directionality effects on these sentences just as on the sentences in the studies reviewed above, which structurally allow forward anaphora because they do not involve c-commanding anaphors (IV.1.1−1.2).[22] If on the other hand, the forward directionality effect is set by configurational facts of English which involve c-command, and is not set simply by surface facts of linear precedence, then one might predict that children should significantly modulate the forward directionality constraint on sentences like 107. In particular, on these sentences forward anaphora may be treated as backward anaphora usually is, i.e., it should be significantly blocked in production and/or comprehension.

Article 6 of this volume (see also Lust and Clifford, 1982) reports results of a study which explicitly tested this hypothesis. In addition, this study explicitly tested two different factors which are usually associated with anaphora directionality and which may provide confounding factors. One was *Distance* between name and anaphor. For example, if children did modify anaphora judgments in sentences like 107 above, it could be argued that the critical factor was the reduced distance between name and pronoun in these sentences. In fact, if children's hypotheses are primarily affected by surface facts relevant to the acoustic stimulus, then Ss might be expected to modulate anaphora judgments in terms of surface distance between name and anaphor.

There has been some suggestion in the literature that distance between name and anaphor may modulate anaphora judgments in first language acquisition. (See C. Chomsky, 1969, Chipman and Gerard, to appear; Read and Chou Hare, 1977; Cohen Sherman, 1983, to appear.) Read and Chou Hare 1977, for example, show results which suggest that increased closeness between name and anaphor (e.g., 109 compared to 110) results in increased coreference judgments. The Read and Chou Hare sentences varied both *distance* and *depth* of embedding (i.e. number of phrase nodes), however, in sentences like 109 and 110. Thus their distance comparison was confounded. (Note too that this increased coreference is the opposite result of what would be predicted if children consult configuration on sentences like 107.)

(109)   Cookie Monster made *Oscar* wash *himself*
(110)   Cookie Monster made *Ernie* draw a picture of *himself*

The study reported in article 6 experimentally varied *depth* of embedding of the preceding term (name or pronoun) independently of *distance*. Children did continue to imitate sentences with forward pronouns, e.g., 107, significantly better than those with backward, e.g., 108, as children had in previous studies; (and as they did in this study on a set of sentences with subordinate clauses). However, imitation success was significantly depressed on both backward and forward pronouns. There were more anaphora errors on these sentences (31% of items) than on those sentences with subordinate clauses (12% of items) and the nature of imitation errors revealed that children frequently adjusted both the command relations of the stimulus sentence and the directionality of anaphora together.

In addition, comprehension task results in Lust and Clifford, this volume, showed that children gave an equivalent number of coreference and noncoreference judgments on this task overall. These results differ markedly from results of previous studies where anaphora was optionally allowed. There children normally give a much higher percentage of coreference than noncoreference judgments, cf., IV.1.2. In addition, children gave as many noncoreference judgments on forward as on backward anaphora. This result also differs markedly from previous studies where noncoreference judgments are often higher on backward than on forward anaphora, cf., IV.1.2. Finally, children gave a significantly higher number of coreference judgments on backward than on forward pronouns in this study, a result which also differs markedly from results of previous studies where higher coreference judgments are related to forward anaphora.

In addition, children here in this study showed a higher percentage of a different type of response on these sentences. Many responses in the article 6 study involved the children using themselves, not the antecedent of the sentence, to interpret the pronoun. This reponse was accentuated on forward pronouns. (For example in a sentence like "Under Ernie's foot, he put the penny" children would have themselves, not Ernie put the penny under Ernie's foot.)

The results of this study then confirmed that when c-command configuration of the stimulus sentence is reversed in English, as it was in the stimulus sentences in this Chapter 6 study, relations of precedence are no longer privileged.

The results from the study reported in article 6 confirm results from previous study. Lust, Loveland and Kornet (1980) had tested children (3,5–7,5 years) (82 Ss) (5,6 mean age) on sentences with both forward and backward pronouns which did not allow coreference because of c-command restrictions, as in 107 and 111, as well as on sentences which optionally allowed coreference (e.g., 79 and 80 above). Children in this study, as in the study reported in article 6 in this volume imitated the forward pronouns in sentences like 107 significantly better than the backward pronouns in sentences like 111 (like 79 and 80). At the same time, they blocked coreference judgments on both forward and backward pronouns in sentences like 107 and 111 significantly from earliest ages tested.

(111)   *He* turned around when *Snuffles* found the penny

1.4.3.2 *Modulation of Anaphora Interpretation with Direction of Embedding*

The study reported in Lust et al. in this volume provides further evidence that children consult configuration, not only linearity in anaphora. In this study, position of complement sentence containing an anaphor, i.e., whether it precedes or follows the main clause, was found to determine children's choice of antecedent to a significant degree. Results showed that for sentences like 112, with postposed subordinate clauses, the main clause subject is preferred antecedent for a complement subject anaphor. When complement clauses are preposed as in 113, however, the object is preferred antecedent.

(112)   *Fozzie* tickled *Kermit Frog,* when *he* dropped the car
(113)   When *he* dropped the tissue, *Kermit* rubbed *Scooter*

In fact, the forward directionality effect is negated by structure-dependence in this case, since there are as many (or more) object choices for antecedents on backward anaphors like 113 as there are subject choices on forward anaphors like 112 (*see* Lust et al., figure 6). (This would suggest that the forward directionality effect in first language acquisition may be linked to the sentence subject antecedent in English.)

A related result favoring object antecedents in left branching structures was independently found in a study of anaphora in preposed complements by Solan (his experiment 2, 1983). Sentences like 114 were given by Solan in a comprehension test to 36 Ss, aged 5—7.

(114)   After *he* ran around, *the horse* hit *the sheep*

While subject antecedence was assigned only 12% of the time, object antecedent was assigned 24% of the time on such sentences. Although Solan's sample's mean age is older than that reported in Lust et al., this volume, this effect is most marked in 5 year olds (youngest group tested).

The results in IV.1.4.3 then confirm that determination of ante-cedent-anaphor relations is significantly dependent on structure, not simply on linear precedence in first language acquisition of English.

1.4.4 *Alternative Proposals on the Blocked Forward Pronoun Effect*

1.4.4.1 *The Proposal by Carden, et al.*

Carden (319–357 in this volume) argues that the evidence from the study reported in Lust and Clifford of this volume does not disprove the claim that children acquiring English begin with a strictly linear non structure-dependent principle in anaphora. Carden's argument has two parts. (1) In the case of a sentence like 107, many responses involved the child *not* choosing Oscar to perform the action, but also not choosing Big Bird or Ernie from the reference set. Rather as mentioned above, children often chose themselves as referent of the subject pronoun and themselves performed the action. Carden suggests that this behavior is ambiguous as to whether the child may have *intended* the NP sentence antecedent to be the agent of the main clause. Whereas other behaviors involving choice of another doll (e.g. Ernie) are unambiguously indicators of noncoreferential judgments in this task on a sentence like 107, such 'use of self as agent' behaviors are not. Carden thus proposes a reanalysis of data such that these responses are either eliminated or interpreted as if they were intended to be coreferential. (2) Carden also reports results of other research from another laboratory which uses a different methodology, viz., a question test of comprehension (which is like the test used by Carol Chomsky 1969). In this test the child is simply asked "who bounced the ball" after a sentence like 107. This research reports results wherein children generally answer "Oscar the Grouch" to a sentence like this, especially in the case of forward pronouns (Ingram and Shaw, 1981). These results, the authors suggest, show that the forward directionality constraint is being applied by children independently of the structural configuration which characterizes the syntactic domain between antecedent and anaphor. Such results would thus support an exclusively linear non structure-dependent principle of pronoun precedence, in contrast to the results of Lust and Clifford, this volume.

Carden's proposal raises interesting issues concerning the possibility for different results on different tasks designed to measure the same aspects of grammatical competence in acquisition. The reader is referred to Carden's article for details concerning this issue. However, several points must be kept in mind regarding the comparison of Carden's results to those reported in Lust and Clifford in this volume.

(i) Carden is correct that behaviors on the act-out task which involve the child performing a predicate action do not unambiguously rule out the possibility that the child actually intended the doll named in the sentence to be doing the action. This is because the act out task of course requires the children themselves to perform the actions with the dolls in all cases. However, the basic facts remain to be explained. (a) Why are there so many more examples of this type of "self as agent" behavior in this particular study, and not in other studies using different sentence structures, e.g., Lust et al. this volume (where only 4% use of self behaviors are observed)? (b) why are there significantly more such behaviors within this study in Lust and Clifford on forward pronouns than on backward?

(ii) When children chose themselves as main clause subject they were distinctly *not* choosing the doll named in the sentence as antecedent, although they clearly can and do do so in other situations. Indeed in other studies, use of the named doll is their unmarked response. Thus if the "self as agent subject" response simply intended coreference, it is not clear why children didn't simply use the doll named as coreferent as they clearly can and do in other situations. The "self as agent subject" responses empirically cannot simply be *assumed* to reflect coreference; and they *are* empirically an example of *non*coreference with the doll named. In fact, use of an external doll not mentioned in the sentence has been argued to be cognitively more complex in the act out task than use of a doll mentioned (*see* Padilla Rivera, 1985). In this case, there would be more reason to suspect that a child's 'use of self' behavior in the task was an attempt to substitute for a noncoreference rather than for a coreference behavior.

In fact, 'use of self as agent' behaviors cannot be simply assumed to reflect either coreference or noncoreference judgments without further empirical evidence. This primitive "self as agent" response is frequently observed in tests of early child language comprehension, cf. Dale, 1976, p. 123; fn. 1; Chapman, 1978; Shatz, 1978; Ferreiro, 1971; and may be a non-linguistic strategy in response to a linguistic stimulus which taxes the child's grammatical competence. For this reason, the study in Lust and Clifford separated these behaviors from other behaviors in its scoring and analyses of coreference and noncoreference judgments.

These self-behaviors cannot be 'eliminated' from the data however as Carden (this volume) proposes. Empirically post-hoc elimination of data is not valid. No statistical analyses of significant differences are possible without estimate of the total variance in the data to which these responses contribute. Theoretically, these responses themselves consti- tute data, they constitute one option the child took as opposed to others it was capable of, and it did so selectively, significantly more in certain grammatical conditions than in others.

(iii) Even if all "use of self as subject" responses were scored as indicating intended coreference, there still would be no directionality effect significantly favoring forward coreference over backward corefer- ence in these data. (See details in Lust and Clifford.)

(iv) Moreover, consider that children may have simply preferred coreference on forward pronouns more than backward in the Lust and Clifford sentences, just as in the structures tested in previous studies. If this were true, it would not explain the other aspects of the data, e.g., a greater percent of noncoreference judgments overall in this study and as many clear noncoreference as coreference judgments overall. These behaviors, independent of "use of self as agent" behaviors, suggest that children were treating the forward pronouns differently in this study, in fact treating them like backward pronouns in general.

(v) The question task used by studies cited by Carden (e.g., Ingram and Shaw, 1981) involve different task demands than the elaborated act out task. The behaviors in the question task (e.g., Chomsky, 1969, Ingram and Shaw, 1981) do not display syntactic encoding to the degree that the act out task does. Because they do not, the question task results must be interpreted as ambiguous as to how much syntactic computation was actually involved in the response. In particular, the question task demands are conducive to the one response which repeats the name of the doll named in the stimulus sentence (which would be scored as a coreference response). This response accounts for the majority of the data in this question task, but accounts for a lesser proportion of data in the act out task, possibly because the act out task allows more and subtler options for child behavior in response to the task. The question task used by Ingram and Shaw (reported by Carden, this volume) produces a higher amount of coreference judgments on structures on which other tasks show less coreference. For example, on sentences with backward pronouns which optionally allow coreference, children in Lust, Loveland and Kornet (1980) (aged 3,5−7,5) who were tested in an act-out task show 24% coreference judgment; and Solan (1978, 1983) (with Ss aged 5,6−7,7) shows only 36% coreference judgment in an act-out task, even though the group is older. Carden (this volume) reports Ingram and Shaw to have found 53% coreference with a 3,0 to 7,11 group using the question task. (Note, that such comparisons of percent across different empirical studies can only be suggestive. No test of statistical significance of difference between such percents is possible without quantitative evaluation of score variance within each population, and of size and nature of population, as well as assessment of population sampling, method and design factors across each of the studies.) These results suggest to us that if certain syntactic factors are at issue (perhaps those related to configuration), a more sensitive task than the question task (i.e., one that allows more options for child response) may be necessary for measurement of grammatical competence.

In any case, the logical structure of the task comparison raised by

Carden in this volume is the following. Of two tasks (the elaborated actout and the question task), both provide evidence of certain effects (e.g., the directionality constraint replicates over both). However, one, the act out task, picks up an additional factor which the question task does not. In this case, the additional effects of the act out task must be accounted for. On logical grounds, the fact that a less sensitive task does not evidence them cannot in itself invalidate these results.

The comprehension task comparisons are currently being studied further (see Carden, this volume, for example and Lust, Chien, and Gray, in preparation. See also Lasnik and Crain (to appear) for reference to other independent forthcoming work on comprehension test methodologies).

(vi) In addition, these issues of methodology do not concern the data reported in 1.4.3.2.

(vii) Interacting factors (e.g., *Depth*) exist.

1.4.4.2. *The Proposal by Solan 1983*

Solan has suggested (1983, 87) that children's sensitivity to a constraint against anaphora in sentences like 107 (which was demonstrated in the study reported in Lust and Clifford in this volume) shows Ss' "recognition that the BAR applies at the level of logical form in the grammar, but shows nothing about directionality." (Solan's claim suggests that in logical form the preposed PP of 107 is interpreted by representation in its unmarked postposed form, with a backward pronoun. (See Carden this volume for a related proposal).) The proposal that the constraint involved in sentences like 107 reflects a constraint which holds at logical form is an interesting and significant one. However, this proposal clearly does not in itself 'explain' the acquisition data observed, and does not deny the significance of the findings with regard to the nature of children's constraint on directionality, for the following reasons. (i) Critically, even if the relevant constraint involved in sentences like 107 did hold exclusively at logical form, the data showing that children block coreference on these forms from early ages would still document that children can systematically relate the forward pronoun in the S-structure of the stimulus sentence to the backward pronoun of the proposed logical form. Therefore Ss must not be applying a simple linear precedence constraint (e.g., Step 1 of Solan's BAR) to surface anaphora data and they can and do relate backward pronouns to these S-structures. In addition, the structure of logical form would not predict the data in 1.4.3.2 in which the forward directionality constraint appears to be significantly linked to subject position. (ii) While it has been argued on linguistic grounds that certain binding constraints appear to apply at logical form, it has also been argued that these constraints must *also* apply at S-structure (cf. Chomsky 1981). There are problems still to be resolved in these theoretical proposals. As R. Freidin (this volume, 178 ff.) has observed, the application of binding constraints at logical form has been motivated by sentences like 115. Here in S-structure the pronoun does not c-command the antecedent. In logical form it does. If the constraint applies at LF, this would block coreference as the sentence does.

(115)   *Which book about *which pianist$_i$* did *she$_i$* read?
        (for which pianist y) (for which book x) [she read [x about y]]

As Williams points out, however, (class lecture) a sentence like 116 should also allow coreference because in its logical form, the pronoun does not c-command the antecedent, while in surface structure it does. However, the sentence does not allow coreference, suggesting that the relevant constraint must apply at S-structure.

(116)   **She$_i$* still likes every man that *Mary$_i$* loved
        (Every x, x a man that Mary loved, she still likes)

In general these proposals rest on speculative proposals for the proper representation of the S-structure and logical form of the sentences involved. (See Freidin, this volume, for further discussion of this issue of level of representation of the binding constraints.)

1.4.5 *Conclusions and Questions on the Nature of the Directionality Constraint*

The above review (1.4) of an initial set of experimental studies of first language acquisition suggests then that surface precedence alone, exclusive of structure, does not exclusively determine anaphora domains for children even at early stages of first language acquisition. The evidence suggests that syntactic domain for children involves a sensitivity to basic properties of the unmarked grammar of the language they are acquiring (viz., properties related to command in the language), and to configuration of specific sentences in which antecedent and anaphor appear.

These results suggest (in accord with the linguistic theory reviewed in II.2) that the observed directionality constraint on anaphora in first language acquisition of English may be a *reflex* of basic properties of the grammatical structure of English.

1.4.5.1 *Linearity and Branching Direction*

Certain aspects of the data reviewed above suggest that the structure-dependence of children's application of the forward directionality constraint in acquisition may be determined by the right branching direction of English which determines that command in English usually is recursively rightward (i.e., the commanded term is usually to the right of the commanding term). (We leave aside for the moment the separate issue of which type of "command" is most critical.) (i) The study reported in Lust and Clifford, this volume, showed that in children's imitation, increased *depth* both increased children's ability to handle structures, and accentuated the forward directionality constraint. Depth in this study was represented by right branching embedding within recursive prepositional phrases. Also in imitation errors in this study, children's movement of preposed prepositional phrases to a postposed right branching structure was linked to anaphora direction in these phrases, as children generally changed this direction to forward when they changed the branching direction to rightward. (ii) In other studies in this volume (e.g., Lust et al.) children's imitation data showed that children's imitation of right branching (i.e., postposed) subordinate clauses was significantly superior to their imitation of left branching (preposed) subordinate clauses. (iii) The comprehension test data showed that branching direction significantly modulated choice of antecedent in anaphora interpretation of subordinate clause anaphors and even broke the forward directionality constraint in cases (1.4.3.2). They suggested that the directionality effects in English acquisition may be particularly linked to subject. As has been observed (e.g., Reinhart, 1976), in a right branching language the subject commands most other materials (whether these are within a VP or within adverbial subordinate clause positions).

1.4.5.2 *Branching Direction Parameter*

Reinhart (this volume) raises several issues on the specification of this branching direction variable. She notes for example that not all aspects of English command are rightward. Possessive NP's and adjective phrases for example, like 117 involve left branching in English:

(117)   John's mother's favorite aunt . . .

We have suggested elsewhere (e.g., Lust, 1983 and in preparation; Lust and Mangione, 1983; Lust, Mangione and Chien, 1984b; Lust and Chien, 1984), that these facts require definition of a 'principal branching direction' parameter (i.e., 'PBD'), one which specifies a principled subset of branching structures as critical to the grammar of a language, and to initial hypotheses in first language acquisition. Several other parameter formalizations are also possible, e.g., 'head direction' (Chomsky, 1981a).

1.4.5.3 *Branching Direction Parameter and the Binding Theory*

If this proposal is correct, this raises the issue of the relation of such structure-dependence to the binding theory of UG. BT consults 'command' within a language regardless of general parametric principles of embedding in a grammar such as captured by the notion of a PBD. Reinhart (this volume) speculates that "If the PBD principle is correct, this means that the child makes no use at all, at the relevant stage, of the BP, but rather operates by an altogether independent parameter." This conclusion does not appear to us to be a necessary one. There is nothing intrinsically contradictory between the PBD and the BP. In fact, since both are defined with regard to 'command' relations they may be intrinsically related. While one (PBD) describes a parameter of grammatical organization, the other (Binding Principles) describes a set of principles which apply within a specific language grammar. The domain of the first is grammar. The domain of the second is specific sentences. The data above suggest that the child may be sensitive to both of these dimensions and may attempt to integrate them.

2. BINDING THEORY IN FIRST LANGUAGE ACQUISITION

Below we briefly sketch the outlines of initial results of acquisition studies in this volume which bear on BP in first language acquisition of

English, relating them to research in the field, and to results in IV.1. Current work in progress pursues these issues in more detail (see Manzini and Wexler, in preparation, Wexler and Chien, to appear, Roeper and Williams, to appear, Padilla Rivera, 1985, Jakubowicz, 1984, for example.)

2.1 *Prerequisites for Binding Theory.*

The results reviewed above in IV.1. suggest that acquisition of anaphora evidences the essential prerequisite for the Binding Theory, viz., structure-dependence. Consistent with the basic principles of Binding Theory (e.g., II.2 above), acquisition facts suggest that the child's establishment of linearity in antecedent-anaphor relations may be in part a reflex of configurational facts in syntactic domains for anaphora.

2.1.1 *C-Command*

We saw above (II.2.1) that c-command provides the foundation of the Binding principles (see Freidin, this volume).

Several experimental studies in the field have argued that the child's structure-dependence in determination of domains for anaphora may consult some version of command, including c-command. For example, Solan (1981), using a version of the act-out test of comprehension finds children's coreference judgments between name and pronoun to differ in sentences like 118 and 119 below. He reports that Ss find significantly less coreference in 119 which Solan argues involves c-command by the pronoun of the name than in 118 which does not involve such c-command relation (36Ss, 5.2—8.5 years, months; 12 Ss in each of 3 groups).

(118)   The horse hit him after the sheep's run
(119)   The horse hit him in the sheep's yard

Similarly, Goodluck, 1981, using a version of the act-out task similar to Solan's, argues that children assign less coreference between object NP and null anaphor in 121 than in 120 (30 Ss, 4—6 year olds, 10 of each age). Goodluck argues that the syntactic domain of the object ('the girl') antecedent and anaphor (∅) in 120 and 121 is differentiated by command relations between them. In 120 but not in 121, the object may c-command the (Ø), and c-command determines control of the null anaphor.[23]

(120)   *The boy* hits *the girl* after Ø jumping over the fence
(121)   *The boy* is hit by *the girl* after Ø jumping over the fence

The study reported in Lust and Clifford, this volume, (94 Ss, 3.5—7.11) involved c-command in the design of its stimulus sentences. Thus evidence for structural sensitivity in the results of that study may also be taken as evidence of children's sensitivity to c-command. The results of this study replicated previous study (Lust, Loveland, and Kornet, 1980, 82 Ss, 3.5 to 7.5, 10—11 in each of 8 age groups) where stimulus sentences also involved c-commanding pronouns.

Each of the results listed above, if taken individually, would allow alternative explanations and are based on relatively small samples at the critical youngest ages. The studies vary in their definition of 'command' and no experimental study has yet systematically varied different types of command (opposing 'c-command' to 'S-command' and to 'k-command,' or to the various definitions of command reviewed in Saito 1984 for example). However, the set of results taken as a whole are suggestive that children may be sensitive to some version of command and that they may consult this structural property in determining antecedent-anaphor relations.[24]

2.1.2   *Beyond C-Command*

Several of the results above show that children are not only consulting the command relations between antecedent and anaphor. For example, the results of the study in chapter 6 of this volume showed that when normal English c-command relations were reversed as in 108, children did not simply reverse the anaphora relations they normally assign to sentences, i.e., now assigning backward anaphora primarily. That is, they did not simply reverse their behavior on these sentences from their behavior in structures with unmarked right branching c-command relations like "*John* saw a snake when *he* walked out." Rather, results evidenced a continued attempt by the children to apply a forward directionality constraint even in sentences with reversed c-command, although this attempt was clearly modulated. Children treated sentences like 108 as they treated other backward pronouns, i.e., with depressed performance and depressed coreference judgment.

In addition, evidence reviewed above has shown that in several instances of complex sentences with adjunct clauses, (particularly with right branching temporal adverbial clauses), children primarily chose matrix subject as antecedent. This result may be related to c-command (since the subject c-commands all that follows in these sentences). However, it cannot be due to c-command alone, since in some cases, where the effect has been found, both subject and object c-command the adjunct (e.g., Cohen Sherman, 1983 and Chapter 8 this volume), as in 122.

(122)   *Ernie* tells *Big Bird* that *he* will pat the tissue

In addition, when subordinate clauses were preposed (section IV.1.4.3.2 above), children significantly shifted to choice of object as antecedent for anaphors. This cannot be explained by c-command alone, since in these cases neither main clause subject nor object c-commands the preposed subordinate clause anaphor (cf. Note 22).

Given that the directionality constraint shows evidence of structure-dependence (IV.1. above) and given that children do show general evidence of sensitivity to command (IV.2.1.1 above), these results may suggest that children are not simply responding to the immediately given structure of the stimulus sentence (which reflects c-command), but are also consulting general principles relevant to the grammar they are constructing, as suggested in IV.1.4.5.

2.1.3 *Relations Among Anaphor Types: Empty and Phonetically Realized*

Several studies in this volume and in the field suggest that young children easily establish an equivalence between empty categories and phonetically realized ones.

2.1.3.1 *Initial Hypotheses Regarding Empty Categories (ec)*

Two studies in this volume suggest that in certain domains children's early hypotheses attribute pronominal features to a null NP. (i) Roeper's study (Article 5 in this volume) reports that results of pilot data from an experimental study suggest that children (9 Ss 5—7 years of age, 22 Ss 8—10 years of age) may interpret the null nominal categories in sentences like both 123 and 124 as a pronominal (i.e., as small 'pro' in current BT; see II.2. above and van Riemsdijk, article 9 this volume, for discussion of this issue).

(123)   *Who* thinks *he* wears a hat?
(124)   *Who* does *he* think Ø wears a hat?

.   That is, in a picture choice test of comprehension of both of these sentence types, Roeper reports that children frequently chose a picture of a person identified as "doing the thinking" to interpret both the null anaphor and the pronoun subject of the predicate 'wears a hat.' If children were representing the null in 124 as a bound variable (cf. II.2.0.2), they should have blocked coreference between the c-commanding and preceding NP (*he*) and this Wh-trace. Rather, Roeper's subjects appear to have assimilated this empty category to a pronoun, thus allowing free coreference with an NP antecedent. (See Roeper, Rooth, Mallis and Akiyama, in preparation, for further study of this issue.) In Roeper's study then, an empty category which is a variable in BT, having features '−anaphor −pronominal' is treated '−anaphor, +pronominal.'

(2) The study in Lust et al., in this volume, reported that children (101 Ss, age 3,2−7,9) significantly often converted the null anaphor in a sentence like 125 to a pronoun, usually tensing the sentence accordingly, in an imitation task. They also allowed pragmatic lead to modulate the interpretation of this anaphor in a comprehension task. These converging production and comprehension results suggested that children's initial hypothesis concerning the empty category of a sentence like 125 is to assimilate it to a lexical pronoun.

(125)   Johnny washed the table when Ø drinking juice
(126)   Johnny washed the table when he was drinking juice

In this study, then, an empty category which is presumably a PRO, i.e., it has the features '+anaphor +pronominal' in BT (cf. II.2.0.2), is treated as '−anaphor, +pronominal.'

The two studies above show children treating an empty category as '+pronominal' in certain environments, regardless of whether or not it has BT-anaphoric features in adult grammar.

2.1.3.2 *Relation Between Null Anaphors and Lexical Pronouns*

Other studies have confirmed that children appear to conflate null anaphors and lexically realized pronouns. This effect seems to be dependent on the structure in which these anaphor types appear. Whether the child assimilates the null to the pronoun or the pronoun to the null appears to be also dependent on this structural domain.

2.1.3.2.1 *Coordinate Structures.* Tavakolian (1977, 142) tested 24 Ss (3,0—5,6) on comprehension of conjoined sentences which involved either a null or a pronoun subject, e.g., 127 and 128. The fact that children treated null and pronoun similarly in spite of the pronoun being free and the null being bound in this context suggests to Tavakolian that "the same rules are operating in the determination of antecedents in both cases" (143).

(127) The duck jumps over the horse and Ø stands on the rabbit
(128) The duck jumps over the fence and he stands on the rabbit

Recently Cohen Sherman (1983) also tested children (36 Ss, 3,0—7,11) in 3 age groups on comprehension and imitation of coordinate sentences with both null anaphors and pronouns in sentences like 129 and 130.

(129) The Mommy hugs the Daddy and Ø pats the dog
(130) Daddy hugs the boy and he closes the door

Cohen Sherman, like Tavakolian, found a nonsignificant difference in comprehension success across these two types and also found that children chose the subject significantly more often than object for both the null and the pronoun. Critically, in the Cohen Sherman imitation study, most anaphor type conversions in children's imitations of these structures are from pronoun to null, not from null to pronoun (49% compared to 6%). In the Tavakolian results above, also, the null is the basis for generalization in coordinate structures.

Both of the above studies thus suggest that the child is establishing a kind of "equivalence" between the null anaphor and the pronoun in subject position of the coordinate structure. In the case of these studies, the child is assigning a reading which appears to be the 'bound' one, to the pronoun (i.e., the reading determined by the c-commanding antecedent, the subject of the coordinate VP). This is opposite to the result in the studies above with temporal adjuncts (IV.2.1.3.1) where the child was found to assign a free reading to a null.

2.1.3.2.2 *Embedded S Complements.* Cohen Sherman (1983; *see also* Sherman and Lust, this volume) also tested 72 Ss (mean age 5,5) on two types of embedded complements, one with a nontensed complement like 131; one with a tensed complement like 132.

(131)   The turtle (promises/tells) the monkey Ø to drop the penny
(132)   Ernie (promises/tells) the monkey that he will drop the penny

She found that children in imitation often changed complement type and anaphor type (22% of errors). Most of these conversions involved change of sentential (132), to surface VP (131), complements. In comprehension, pragmatic effects were resisted in accord with the .bound nature of the null anaphor in 131. Again, as in the coordinate structures, children take the null anaphor, not the pronoun, as the unmarked case.

2.1.3.3   *Summary of Relations Between Anaphor Types*

Children's conversion of anaphors is thus not general and independent of structure. The reason why children systematically generalize nulls to pronouns in certain domains as in temporal adverbial adjunct clauses (2.1.3.1) may be related to the child's initial hypothesis that null subjects are governed in these adjunct sentence domains where there is no immediately c-commanding antecedent which binds the null. Subjects in this case, since they are assumed to be governed, should have case, and thus be lexically realized. Thus the child positions a pronoun in the place of the null subject. The Wh-questions in which Roeper (this volume) also found a pronoun interpretation of a null subject are also sentence domains where the child may assume the null argument to be governed.

In embedded VP's either like 129 or like 131, however, children may not make this initial hypothesis that the null subject is governed and must have case, possibly because these null anaphors have immediately c-commanding antecedents. In these structures the child does not form the hypothesis that the null is a pronominal since these null categories are bound in a minimal S domain.

2.2.2 Evidence for the Binding Principles in First Language Acquisition of English

The BP differentiate anaphor types (II.2). Experimental evidence is not yet available to confirm at what age the Binding Principles (II.2 above) are first available to children in first language acquisition. Several studies suggest such evidence by 5—7 years of age (e.g., Deutsch and Koster 1982 for Dutch; Padilla Rivera 1985 for Spanish; Jakubowicz 1984 and Wexler and Chien, to appear for English); but controlled studies of large samples of younger children are not yet available.

Otsu 1981 argues on the basis of an experimental study that "once the child masters *each other,* *himself,* *him,* and the English complementation system, he always honors BT." Otsu tested 60s from 3,1 to 7,1 on a series of tasks, measuring both sentence syntax and BP, and involving reflexives and pronouns, like 133 and 134 below.

(133)   The hippo remembered that the monkey tickled him
(134)   The hippo remembered that the monkey tickled himself

Otsu's hypothesis is confirmed at older ages by the data he reports. Otsu's 6 and 7-year olds showed 75 percent and 92 percent (respectively) success on both the syntax of these stimulus sentences and the interpretation of the Binding Principles. Otsu's data do not appear to confirm this claim at younger ages, however. For example, with pronouns like 'him', e.g., 133 (where principle B of the BP is at issue), of 36 Ss who passed the syntax test, as many Ss fail the Binding theory test as pass it (18 each). (See Otsu's figure 5.5, p. 181.) Most of the Ss who fail pronouns are younger than 6—7 years. In addition, Ostu's (1981) results on a test of comprehension on sentences like 133 and 134 above are inconsistent with the proposal that children's initial hypothesis is that proforms are BT anaphors. Otsu's group of 60 Ss (ages 3—7 years) included 12 three-year-olds. 31% of these three-year-olds interpreted the reflexive like a pronoun by choosing a nonlocal antecedent i.e., main clause subject rather than complement clause subject, while 14% interpreted the pronoun as a reflexive. These results suggest that young children may confuse lexical pronoun and the BT-anaphor (reflexive) pronoun in early use. However, if one form is the unmarked assumption, the pronoun is. Also, in testing these Ss for their imitation of sentences like 133 and 134 above, only one three-year-old correctly imitated either type of sentences and the one child who did, imitated the pronoun but not the reflexive correctly. Although these data suggest a disconfirmation of Otsu's hypothesis at younger ages, theoretical and methodological issues involved in test of children's 'knowledge of the syntax of complementation' may be involved in this result.

2.2.2.1 *Relations Between Principles A and B (Reflexives and Lexical Pronouns)*

Jakubowicz (1984) has experimentally tested the prediction made by Berwick in 73. This is the prediction that children's first language acquisition of anaphora is guided by the initial hypothesis that various anaphor types are locally bound. By this hypothesis, children are predicted to mistakenly treat lexical pronouns (which by principle B may not be locally bound) as 'BT anaphors' e.g. to treat pronouns, (e.g., 'he' or 'him') as reflexives (e.g., 'himself'). Jakubowicz tested children's comprehension of sentences which included 135 and 136 below.

(135)   John said that Peter washed him
(136)   John said that Peter washed himself

In a preliminary study consisting of seven 3-year-olds, ten 4 year olds and eleven 5 years olds, Jakubowicz reports that "when errors appear they concern pronouns only and in most cases they consist of binding the pronoun in its governing category as if it were an anaphor" (167). That is, in a sentence like 135, children have "Peter" wash himself, as they do in 136. (In a follow up study, Jakubowicz argues that linear distance between name and anaphor type does not account for these results.)

A similar result had been previously reported for Dutch acquisition by Deutsch and Koster (1981) for sentences like 137 with a pronoun in object position.[25]

(137)   De vader van Pieter wast hem
        (The father of Peter washes him)

These results require replication with larger samples of subjects, particularly at younger ages. (See Wexler and Chien, to appear).

2.2.2.2 *An Alternative View*

If they replicate, however, the results of the studies in 2.2.2.1 (which have argued that children's initial hypothesis regarding various anaphor types is that these are BT-anaphors (e.g., reflexive pronouns)) have a possible different explanation. Namely, children may be consulting locality conditions for the proform, where locality conditions are determined by the configurational domain in which the anaphor appears. These locality conditions are independent of the nominal category of the proform. Possible distinctions the child may recognize in nominal category (e.g., reflexive vs. pronoun) may be overriden where these share a like domain. The configurations in ´ the examples in 135—137 involve either a reflexive pronoun or a lexical pronoun in a position which is c-commanded by the main clause subject in a clausal domain. If children respond to this locality and if this locality condition is a stronger principle for the child than the morphological differentiation of lexical items then the child may assign a 'bound' reading to pronouns in this condition whether or not they are morphologically marked as reflexives.

This alternative explanation would mean that the results in 2.2.2.1 are not solely due to any particular hypothesis about particular classes of nominal categories defined in terms of their phonetic shape (e.g., reflexive pronoun (BT-anaphor) "himself" vs. lexical pronoun "him") but involve a structure-dependent hypothesis which consults configuration to determine anaphor type.

This hypothesis would be consistent with several independent results from studies in this volume and reviewed above: (1) the general structure-dependence of the child's anaphor determination (reported in IV.1 and IV.2.1.1 above); (2) the evidence that phonetic form of anaphor appears to be overridden by structural domain in certain cases (IV.2.1.3).

If this explanation of the IV.2.2.2 results were correct, it would also explain why the proposal in 73 is not supported by several independent aspects of child language. (1) In natural speech the pronoun is clearly acquired before the reflexive in English. The pronoun is used first clearly in a deictic manner. For example, Clifford (1984) studied natural speech samples of 16 children from 2.0 to 3.0 (years, months) in age from mean length of utterance ranging from 2.36 to 3.39. She found that all subjects use personal pronouns across the sample from 2% to 50% of utterances; but only 3 Ss use reflexive at all, and this in only 1% of utterances with pronouns. (2) A study by Potts et al. (1979) tested the reflexive in a cloze type procedure. Here, many 4-year-olds decomposed the reflexive in a frame like "He can dress — (himself)" to 'hisself.'

(Otsu, 1981 also reports productivity of this created form in an imitation task involving reflexives and pronouns.) This result suggests, as Potts has noted, that the reflexive may undergo development as a lexical item during the early years of acquisition (1979).

The results above would suggest that research questions on the acquisition of anaphor types and the principles of their differentiation may more productively ask − "what are the principles of structure-dependence which determine locality for children at early stages of acquisition," rather than solely − "which nominal categories ground children's early hypothesis about anaphora." Given the language-specific nature of the morphological forms which constitute nominal categories across languages, it would make sense that these must be learned. They would not provide the bases for initial hypotheses thus.

More recent work by Padilla Rivera (1985) begins to significantly resolve the issues raised by this alternative proposal. Padilla Rivera has shown that young native Spanish-speaking Ss (80 Ss from 3,0 to 9,11) made an early distinction in comprehension between the Spanish reflexive pronoun and the lexical pronoun in direct object position of simple sentences like 138 and 139.

(138)   La hormiguita se cepilla detrás de la zanahoria
         The ant-(dim) self brushes behind the carrot

(139)   La rana la cepilla delante del helicóptero
         The frog (third person singular) combs in front of the helicopter

In accord with the results in 2.2.2.1, Padilla Rivera also found that there was significantly more correct comprehension of the reflexive than of the lexical pronoun in this domain, and 50% group success rate was only attained on these structures for the first time in the 7 year age group. However, even the youngest Ss distinguished the pronoun and the reflexive by giving significantly more coreference judgments on sentences with reflexives than on those with pronouns, and by giving significantly more disjoint reference judgments on sentences with lexical pronouns than on those with reflexives.

Critically, however, Padilla Rivera also tested these same Ss on sentences with pronoun and reflexives in PP adjuncts like 140 and 141. These PP domains in Spanish, even more consistently than in English (see II.2 above), provide a marked domain for the language learner.

Both pronouns and reflexives occur here. This PP domain is a binding domain for pronouns, since the pronoun is free in this domain, but not for reflexives, since the reflexive must continue to be bound by main clause subject in these cases.

(140) La tortuga empuja la pelota al lado de sí misma
The turtle pushes the ball on side of herself

(141) La pantera patea el avioncito detrás de ella
The panther kicks the plane-(dim) behind her

Padilla Rivera found that Ss conflate the reflexive and the pronoun in this domain, assimilating the reflexive to the pronoun. Ss gave significantly more disjoint reference responses to reflexives in the PP than in the S domain, and significantly fewer coreference with subject responses. Especially in the first two age groups, Ss treat the reflexive similarly to the pronoun here. These results confirm, as suggested above, that children's initial hypotheses regarding the binding principles are not formulated solely in terms of the nominal category (i.e., lexical pronoun, or reflexive pronoun), but in terms of the domain in which these nominal categories appear. In accord with the other results reviewed in this volume, children's hypotheses regarding anaphora are once again seen to be constrained; they are "too tight" in a sense. The child assumes that the constituent in which the proform appears is a binding domain, and must learn to override this assumption, i.e., to modulate it, for the reflexive in the PP. Children's assimilation of the reflexive to the lexical pronoun is structure-dependent. It does not occur in the sentence domain, but mainly in the PP domain. Here there is no c-commanding antecedent within the domain for the reflexive; and thus the reflexive is treated as the pronoun, i.e., as free in this PP domain. Children thus apply general principles of structure-dependence over both BT-anaphors and lexical pronouns. The Spanish children's assimilation of anaphor types to the free pronominal form, rather than to the reflexive (in the marked PP domain), is coherent with English results in article 7 of this volume (see IV.2.1.3 above). Finally, as Padilla Rivera argues, these results suggest that children assume that the locality conditions, i.e., the relevant syntactic domains, are the same for principles A and B. Not only is the sentence a binding domain for both principles, but so is the PP. (See II.2 above and Freidin's chapter this volume for a proposal that another outcome was possible.) (See Padilla

Rivera 1985 for related results on anaphora in Spanish complex sentences with subjunctive complements.)

3. PRAGMATICS AND GRAMMAR IN ACQUISITION OF ANAPHORA

Study of the profound issues raised by Reinhart's proposal (e.g., this volume) (see II.3 and III.3 above) has barely begun. However, several experimental results from studies in this volume, and others in the field to which they are related, do provide initial data on these issues.

3.1 *Effects of Pragmatic Context on Interpretation of Anaphora*

3.1.1 *Pronoun Anaphora*

Several experimental studies have varied presence or absence of pragmatic context in order to assess the interaction of this factor with structural factors in children's computation of pronoun anaphora. For example, Lust, Loveland and Kornet (1980) tested the effects of adding a pragmatic lead to sentences with pronouns which were blocked configurationally from coreference in adult grammar: e.g., 142 and 143.

(142)   *He* turned around when *Snuffles* found the penny
(143)   In *Snuffles'* mouth, *he* put a candy

The pragmatic lead in these cases involved preceding each sentence with, "Now I am going to tell you a little story about . . ." the doll named in the sentence (e.g., *Snuffles*). As reported above (e.g., IV.1.4.3), when no pragmatic context was given, Ss showed significantly reduced coreference judgment in interpretation of these sentences, from earliest ages tested (3 years) to the oldest (7 years); suggesting that structural factors were consulted. However, when the pragmatic lead was given, young children significantly increased coreference judgment on these sentences, incorrectly attributing coreference to the pronouns to a significantly higher degree in both cases. This effect of pragmatic context appears not to decrease significantly until 6 or 7 years. (See Figures 7 through 10 in Lust, Loveland and Kornet, 1980, p. 383.)

A similar set of effects is apparent with analysis of the results of the C. Chomsky (1969) question test of children's interpretation of pronoun anaphora. Five of the sentences C. Chomsky tested on a group of 40 Ss (5,0 to 10,0 years), were of the following type, resembling 142 above.

(144)   *He* was glad that *Mickey* got the candy
(145)   *He* didn't know why *Pluto* felt so sad

Of the 40 Ss C. Chomsky tested, five of them (most of the nine 5-year-olds in the group) sometimes attributed coreferential readings to the pronouns with the following name. However, all the subjects except one assign noncoreference more often than coreference on the set 'of 5 sentences with structures like these. Even the young children assign coreference on this sentence type significantly less than they do on the forward sentences (although no statistical tests are applied to the data). The observed occurrence of some coreferential responses on sentences like 144 or 145 appears clearly linked to the semantic or pragmatic context of the item. For example, the highest amount of coreference (5 of 9 Ss) occurs in the sentence 144 above; where there is a clear semantic/pragmatic link between the clauses independent of their anaphora. The lowest amount of coreference (1 of 9 Ss) occurs on sentences like 145, where content of the lexicon would encourage noncoreference. Although the issue deserves further study, the results suggest that in neutral conditions the child blocks coreference on backward pronouns where configuration constrains against anaphora, but that the young child will allow the semantics or pragmatics of the sentence to override these structural constraints. Thus although the C. Chomsky results are sometimes interpreted as showing that "children at age 5 regularly interpret sentences like (the above) to mean" that the name corefers with the pronoun" (Read and Chou Hare, 1979, 99), a close inspection of the data does not support this general conclusion.

Notice, that it is precisely such cases of pronoun antecedent relations on which linguists have found adult judgment to waver with sufficient pragmatic context (e.g., Wasow, Reinhart, this volume). Such effects of pragmatic context on pronoun interpretation would be predicted if principle C is in essence not a grammatical principle, as suggested by Reinhart, and/or if pronoun interpretation interacts in modular fashion with pragmatic context as suggested in II.3 above.

3.1.2 *Pronominal Anaphora*

Reinhart's suggestion that pragmatic coindexing and grammatical binding are distinct would allow that pragmatic coindexing could develop in complete separation from grammatical development, and thus could be developmentally primary. The facts reviewed above, which show that children con⌐ult grammatical configuration in computation of anaphora when no pragmatic context is available, are not consistent with a developmental primacy of pragmatic coindexing over grammatical development, if this means that only pragmatic coindexing should be available to young children.

A few studies assess the range of the pragmatic effects more specifically. These are not limited only to pronoun anaphors. The results of the study reported in article 7 of this volume, for example, suggest that sensitivity to pragmatic context extends over not only pronouns but over null anaphors in related sentences. This shows that pragmatic context may effect anaphora regardless of phonetic form of anaphor and that in cases it may effect both optional and obligatory anaphora as it does in the study in the articles by Roeper and Lust et al. (See also IV.2.1.3 above.) As argued above, however, it is possible that the children conflated pronouns and nulls in these cases to 'pronominals;' and pronominals in general reflect a sensitivity to pragmatic factors.

3.1.3 Bound Null Anaphors

In addition, children's modulation of computation of anaphora with pragmatic sensitivity is not independent of the structure in which the antecedent and anaphor appear, as might be expected if pragmatic coindexing were independent and developmentally primary. For example, Cohen Sherman (1983) (see Sherman and Lust this volume) showed that the null anaphor in coordinate sentences like 146 and the null anaphor (PRO) in sentences like 147 resisted the effects of pragmatic context that comparable sentences with a pronoun in an embedded sentence like 148 did show.

(146)   The turtle tickles the skunk and Ø bumps the car
(147)   The turtle tells the monkey Ø to drop the penny
(148)   Oscar tells Big Bird that he will drop the block

Since both 146 and 147 involve 'bound' anaphors in that they are obligatorily coindexed with c-commanding antecedents, these results suggest that sensitivity to pragmatic context, even in early stages of acquisition, is determined by the configurational properties of the domain in which the antecedent and anaphor appear. (See Lust, Mangione and Chien, 1984a, b for initial test of a similar hypothesis in Chinese acquisition.)

3.2 *Bound and Free Anaphora as a Grammar-Pragmatics Distinction*

The above results are in accord with Reinhart's (and the general BT) proposal that distinction between 'bound' and 'free' anaphora is critically determined by configuration (e.g., c-command) of the antecedent-anaphor relation. However, they do not appear to be in clear accord with the proposal (see Reinhart this volume for discussion) that bound and free anaphora develop independently in first language acquisition.

In fact, several aspects of the results reviewed above suggest that children consult grammatical factors for both free and bound anaphora similarly. Syntactic configuration is consulted in determining constraints both on free, e.g., pronoun, anaphora (see Lust and Clifford, Lust et al., this volume) and on various anaphor types that may be related to 'bound' anaphora. (*See* Lust et al. and Sherman and Lust for related results.) In particular, the Directionality Constraint was argued above to reflect a structure-dependent constraint which has a wide range of application across anaphor types and domains that included both free and bound anaphora. For example, the backward pronouns in the study reported in Lust and Clifford in this volume are c-commanded by their following antecedent. They thus are "bound". Children applied the directionality constraint similarly on these pronouns as an other backward pronouns which were not in a c-commanded environment. This constraint would then unite the grammar of both free and bound anaphora at early stages of acquisition, under the rubric of a parametrically determined reflex of structure-dependence.[26]

3.3 *Distinction of Grammatical Construal and Coreference Judgment in Anaphora*

At the same time, the results reviewed above indicate that a distinction between a pragmatics-based *coreference judgment* in anaphora (which is symmetric and reflexive) and a grammatical *linking or construal relation* in anaphora (which relates the anaphor and antecedent terms and which is asymmetric and irreflexive) has psychological reality in first language acquisition. The constraints which hold on each are distinct.

This is argued in Lust, Loveland and Kornet (1980) and corroborated by findings reported in this volume (see Hust and Brame 1976 for this early linguistic distinction). In Lust, Loveland and Kornet (1980) it was shown that two different tests of grammatical competence differentially tapped one of these components or the other more directly, thus confirming their psychological distinction. The imitation task evidences grammatical construal more directly. It exposes the asymmetric linking of antecedent and anaphor in the child's production of a linear string (although evidence shows that the imitation task also taps the coreference judgment indirectly). The act out test of comprehension more directly reveals coreference judgment assigned to the model sentence in the child's act-out behaviors; (although these behaviors arguably must also reflect anaphoric construal at some level more indirectly).

This different task sensitivity to distinct components of anaphora was replicated in article 6 reported in this volume. Here children again showed the forward directionality constraint for pronouns in imitation, where the comprehension task data showed that the children were aware that coreference judgments were significantly blocked on these forward pronouns. By showing that different tasks can differentially access factors related to distinct components of anaphora, these results suggest that these components of anaphora are psychologically distinct.

These results (3.1–3.3) suggest that a grammar-pragmatics distinction may be best represented as differentiating components of anaphora, not types of anaphora, in first language acquisition.

4. SUMMARY OF RESULTS OF FIRST LANGUAGE ACQUISITION STUDIES

Several conclusions are supported by results of the studies collected in this volume and reviewed here.

1. Although children do consult linearity in determining syntactic domains in early acquisition of anaphora, certain studies suggest that this linearity is not independent of the structure of the sentence in which anaphora appears. (See in particular, Lust and Clifford in this volume, and section IV.1.4.3 above). It is not autonomous. Although children acquiring English do evidence a forward directionality constraint on anaphora, this constraint is not based on an autonomous principle of

precedence. Current research is further testing this claim (e.g., Carden, this volume, Lust, Chien and Gray, in preparation).

2. The results of these studies of first language acquisition of anaphora in English leave open the possibility that the directionality principles children do use in early hypothesis formation are a reflex of parametric properties of the structure of the grammar of the language being acquired, and thus follow as a consequence of independent grammatical and structure-dependent principles. The parameter of 'branching direction' has been proposed to formalize these claims.

3. Although children do differentiate overt NP such as lexical pronouns from empty categories (e.g., IV.2.1.3 above and Lust et al. and Sherman and Lust in this volume), they do generalize over both overt and empty NP in applying general grammatical principles of structure-dependence (e.g., Lust et al. and Sherman and Lust, this volume, and Tavakolian, 1977). There is no general developmental primacy of phonetically overt over phonetically null anaphors.

4. Although children do differentiate lexical pronouns and reflexive pronouns, they do generalize over both in applying general grammatical principles of structure dependence over both (e.g., IV.2.2.2 above).

5. The empirical data from the study of first language acquisition do not support the claim that children are first forming hypotheses regarding anaphor differentiation in terms of specific features of individual nominal categories, based on their phonetic form, and independent of the syntactic domain in which they occur (e.g., Roeper, and Sherman and Lust).

There is initial suggestion in the acquisition data that the properties of various types of anaphors are differentiated in terms of the syntactic domain in which the anaphors occur, in a way which is independent of the phonetic form of the anaphor. Empty categories (null anaphors) for example are assigned properties differentially depending on the domain in which they occur where domain is differentiated by presence or absence of tense as well as by configuration (e.g., coordinate or subordinate structures). (Compare Lust et al. and Sherman and Lust results for example.) (IV.2.1.3 above.)

In general, the reflexive pronoun may be interpreted as a pronoun in certain domains, just as the pronoun may be interpreted as a reflexive in others (IV.2.2.2.1 above).

6. In particular, the evidence does not support the claim that children's initial hypotheses interpret all nominal categories as "BT

anaphor." For example, they do not generally hypothesize that "pronouns are reflexives," and thus apply grammatical principles to pronouns which are particular to reflexives. It has been suggested that this hypothesis is not well motivated theoretically (III.2. above); the initial empirical data also do not support it (e.g., Lust and Clifford, Lust et al., and Sherman and Lust, *see* IV.2.2.2 above).

7. If anything, the initial data tentatively support the conclusion that the default case may be that in some domains (where structure does not disambiguate), children's earliest hypotheses characterize a null NP as a pronoun (e.g., Roeper, and Lust et al.), and a reflexive as a pronoun (Padilla Rivera, 1985). (See IV.2.1.3 above.) (See Wexler and Chien, to appear).

8. There is initial evidence from earlier literature in the field that young children may allow a pragmatic component to override the application of grammatical structure-dependent principles (IV.3). There is indication, however, that the pragmatic principles are independent of the structural principles (cf., IV.3.3 above). They interact with them; they do not supplant them (IV.3). The forward directionality constraint was argued not to reflect an autonomous, solely pragmatically-determined, principle of surface precedence (IV.1.). There is also evidence that anaphoric construal and a judgment of coreference may be distinguished in anaphora for the child (IV.3.3). One may be grammatically determined; one pragmatically determined. At this time however, there is no evidence in support of a qualitative distinction between free and bound anaphora types in terms of the pragmatic-grammatical distinction (e.g., Lust et al. above) although the research on this set of issues has just begun (IV.3.2).

9. Although evidence for the Binding Principles in early first language acquisition is still under investigation, the results reviewed above reveal the basis for these principles in acquisition: *viz.*, structure-dependence, sensitivity to configuration such as involved in command, non-autonomous use of precedence, general theory construction (i.e., theory of anaphora), where principles range over anaphor types, equal competence for null and phonetically realized anaphor types, and differentiation of anaphor type with regard to configurational domain.

10. The development of 'control' structures (involving the null anaphor categorized as PRO) is integrally related to the general structure-dependent theory of anaphora which the child is constructing. It is not initially dependent on development of the lexicon in a manner

which is independent of sentence grammar (particularly configurational aspects of sentence-grammar). (*See* Sherman and Lust, this volume, and Cohen Sherman, 1983.)

V. *CONCLUSIONS*

1. GENERAL CONCLUSIONS AND NECESSITY FOR FURTHER RESEARCH

In general, the results of the experimental research now completed on first language acquisition of anaphora suggest that children consult configurational structure in determining relations between antecedent and anaphor. They do so to determine distribution and interpretation of anaphors. In doing so, they generalize over anaphor types, treating different anaphor types as subject to the same general grammatical principles in some domains in spite of phonetic differences. They use configurational structure to both license and block possible antecedent-anaphor relations. In addition, children consult domain in determining specific properties of anaphor types (e.g., pronouns or BT-anaphors like reflexives). Further research must investigate more specifically what properties of configuration are critical to generalization and which to differentiation of anaphor types.

The research results reviewed here also suggest that first language acquisition is constrained not only by *structure-dependence* of the child's initial hypotheses, but also by both *parameters* and *principles* involved in grammar construction. Further research, both theoretical and empirical, must pursue the more precise identification of these three sets of components and of their interrelation.

The evidence reviewed here has been argued to suggest that it is not the case that precedence relations are integrated into the child's grammar before hierarchical or configurational relations are. Rather, pronoun anaphora is structure-dependent from earliest stages of acquisition, whether forward pronouns or backward pronouns are involved; and general principles apply across both pronoun and non-pronoun anaphora from earliest stages. Carden's article (this volume) argues that certain of these data and other new data on pronouns can be interpreted to oppose this conclusion. Further study must evaluate both these new empirical studies and the revisions in linguistic theory which Carden proposes in conjunction with them.

The results also provide evidence on the manner in which a cognitive, i.e. pragmatic, and a grammatical component each provide independent principles to determine acquisition of anaphora. Further research must assess more specifically the interactions of these independent sets of factors in acquisition.

2. IMPLICATIONS FOR LINGUISTIC THEORY

The results reviewed above accord with general linguistic theory in that they are consistent with the basic premises of UG, viz., structure-dependence, not merely an autonomous principle of surface prece-dence, constrains children's early hypotheses in language acquisition.

The results also accord with certain specific proposals in theory of anaphora, e.g., the proposal that linearity may be eliminated from statement of grammatical principles and be derived as reflex of the structure in which it occurs (e.g., Reinhart 1976, 1983a, b, this volume, Higginbotham, 1980.) This proposal has been integrated in current versions of BT, e.g., Chomsky 1981a. With regard to anaphor type differentiation, the results support a theory which generalizes over phonetic shape of anaphor type and consults domain in which anaphor type occurs to compute specific anaphor type properties, e.g., whether bound or free, whether BT anaphor or pronoun.

Further work on current issues in linguistic theory are critical to direction of further experimentation in acquisition of anaphora. Current work on the specification of the structural domains which differentiate anaphor types (e.g., Freidin, this volume) is critical to further refinement of the description of the structural sensitivities which children are now documented as displaying, and to design of further experimental tests of the nature of these sensitivities. Current linguistic work on the interaction of pragmatics and grammar, specifically with regard to the characterization of anaphora in terms of coreference and construal and the place of principle C in the grammar, must critically direct further work on acquisition in this area (e.g., Reinhart, this volume; Lasnik, 1976, 1981; Higginbotham, 1983).

Current work on the precise formulation of parameters relevant to configuration and directionality in natural language will critically inter-sect with acquisition results reported here (e.g., Cinque, 1977, Travis, 1983, 1984; Koopman, 1983; Koster, 1984; Kayne, 1984).

3. TOWARD A THEORY OF ACQUISITION OF ANAPHORA

With regard to acquisition of anaphora, the theory supported by the data reviewed here is distinct from one which proposes that the child begins with a-grammatical principles for one type of anaphora, viz., pronoun anaphora, and must '*acquire restrictions*' for pronouns which are grammatical through qualitative restructuring of their knowledge of language. Rather, the data reviewed here suggested that children *release restrictions* on anaphora. The initial restrictions result from grammatically determined constraints. The constraints are determined by "structure-dependence" and they are released under the guidance of structure-dependence. The principles children bring to bear are not specific to pronouns, but generalize over anaphor type. Children appear to bring several anaphor types under a general theory of anaphora, at the same time that they distinguish these types.

The general theory of anaphora which children develop involves grammar construction. Thus, general principles and parameters of grammar, not only specific properties of the stimulus sentence, determine the acquisition data.

4. TOWARD A GENERAL THEORY OF FIRST LANGUAGE ACQUISITION

In general, the results of the studies reviewed here allow several predictions for first language acquisition, which may contribute to a comprehensive theory of acquisition. They predict that the child's general theory of language (i.e. its grammar) will not be in all ways identical at early and late stages of acquisition. They predict that children's early theory of language will be more constrained than an adult's in the sense that the child's early hypotheses lead to the belief that the language has fewer options than the adult grammar for this language actually allows. It predicts that evidence for such constraints may be strongest at earliest levels. This is because it is these levels which evidence the constraints most purely, i.e., when they are least contaminated by experience of the allowed options of the language. With experience, the child learns the structural options (variations, permutations and exceptions) that the specific language allows. For example, s/he will learn that unmarked embedding orders (e.g., postposed adverbial subordinate clauses or adverbial PP phrases as in the "3-D study") can be grammatically permuted to preposed position in English. Learning of these variations leads to realization of possible structure-dependent variation in the linearity relations of antecedent and anaphor.

This theory is consistent with the critical fact of language acquisition, *viz.*, that it occurs over time, i.e., specific language knowledge is not instantaneous. It begins to formalize what the principled nature of the differences in language knowledge may be with change from an initial state S_0 to a final state S_n involving 'adult' (attained) knowledge of language.

Findings reviewed here begin to answer critical questions of acquisition theory, viz., why do certain data 'trigger' a change in hypotheses about what is possible in a language at one time in development, and not before (cf. Manzini and Wexler, to appear). If knowledge changes because of 'new' data/information, why was this data not available to the child at an earlier time? This problem exists since there is no evidence that input data is ordered for the child in ways relevant to complex grammatical factors studied here or to the developmental patterns observed here (see Gleitman et al., 1984, Wexler and Culicover, 1980, section 2.7). The findings reviewed here support the conclusion that specific early 'constraint' on language acquisition is determined by underlying competence for natural language. This competence serves to determine what constitutes critical data for the child at early stages. The constraint reflects underlying sensitivities to certain aspects of the wide array of data to the exclusion of others. It determines that certain features of language are most salient initially. It forces dependence on unmarked structural properties of the language being acquired in accord with universal parameters of grammar organization. The constraint determines that data pick-up be organized in accord with these. In acquisition, the details of specific grammatical structures which are relevant to the parameter at issue must be worked out to a certain degree before various incoming data can be integrated in the developing grammar in a structure-dependent way. This takes time.

This theory has the consequence that the child's acquisition is characterized by a necessity for positive evidence mainly, e.g. positive evidence of the various structural permutations that the specific language allows, in order that it extend its range of grammatical options to the full set allowed in adult grammar. The existence of the constraint determines that negative evidence is not essential to the acquisition process. The child does not have to *learn* by correction to be structure-dependent.

At the same time, the results support a developmentally efficacious theory in that they support developmental continuity between early states and the final state. Although constraint is lifted with development, the basic structure-dependence of the constraint is continuous with the adult language. For example, in the adult grammar for anaphora, linearity and/or precedence relations cannot be applied without sensitivity to configuration. English is a right-branching language, and well-formed grammar of anaphora in English requires structure-dependence which consults this fact. A constraint of UG appears to insistently focus the initial state on these properties necessary to the adult grammar. This type of finding serves to explain how the adult state is correctly achieved. It does not require major qualitative shifts in the nature of language knowledge as would be necessary for example in a theory which requires the child to shift its grammar qualitatively, away from non-linguistic principles which are not efficacious for the adult language, or away from semantic principles which are not intrinsic to the grammatical/syntactic phenomenon at issue.

NOTES

[1] I thank James Gair, Noam Chomsky, Guy Carden, Howard Lasnik and John Bowers for critical discussion of the issues raised in this introduction. I thank Vicki Griffin and Shawn Lovelace for excellent manuscript preparation; Wendy Snyder, Michiko Edwards, and Ling Wu for research assistance; and David Hannah for bibliographic assistance. This article was prepared with the partial support of NSF grants BNS — 8318983, 8206328, and 7825115, and Cornell University, College of Human Ecology small grant awards.

[2] All of the studies generally assume that the theory of UG involves subcomponents which include: the lexicon, syntax (a categorical component and a transformational component), a PF (phonetic form) and a LF (logical form) component (Chomsky, 1981a, 5).

[3] Although early in the history of generative grammar it was believed that pronouns were 'derived' by transformational rules from full noun phrases (i.e., by a pronominalization transformation), linguistic study subsequently showed that this was not true. See Wasow 1979, pp. 13—38 for a review of the literature leading to these results.

[4] The principles which determine the interpretation and distribution of anaphors are believed to involve a semantic interpretative component of grammar, operating at either S-structure or LF or both. 'S-structure' is a level of syntactic representation which reflects both gaps and configurational bracketing of surface structure (cf., Chomsky, 1975, 1981a).

[5] This argument is due to Jim Gair.

[6] Note that this proposal is more complex than is usually recognized. What is essential

to a 'specifically linguistic' principle has never been articulated. More crucially there is not a precise statement of cognitive faculties which are distinctly 'non-linguistic.' Sinclair (1978, 1967) on the other hand has suggested that there are deep unifying principles which general cognition and linguistic representation share. In this volume, the acquisition studies deal with specific factors like 'syntactic domain' of anaphora which *have* been defined by linguistic theory and with factors like 'linear precedence' which *can* be defined obviously by general cognition. However, they do not deal with deeper issues wherein the structural principles may be also viewed as deriving from general cognition in some way which could be defined through future study.

[7] Age does not correlate precisely with language development. Since few measures of language development exist, except for the MLU (mean length of utterance, cf. Brown, 1973) and this measure is not predictive at upper levels of language development, studies of language development are forced to group Ss more generally by *age*. This means that behavioral data must be evaluated in terms of statistical significance of factorial variance within groups since variance may be assumed to be caused by several independent variables.

[8] This is not a necessary view. For a different perspective, see Borer and Wexler's 'maturational theory' wherein properties of UG are proposed to 'unfold' gradually over time (to appear).

[9] A host of studies of memory development (e.g., Piaget and Inhelder, 1973) have suggested that what develops in memory cannot be separated from general principles of cognitive development having to do with concept formation and operational thinking. Recent work has argued that 'age differences in memory are due to differences in the amount of semantic knowledge a child possesses for encoding and cueing and not to capacity differences" (Ceci and Howe, 1978, studying 7–13 year olds). More recent work with younger children which attempts to separate a measure of memory development and measure of language development experimentally (in a study of children 18 months to 5 years) reports that above the MLU of 4, "memory scores did not predict measures of spontaneous language complexity nor sentence imitation scores independent of age" (Blake et al., 1984, 1).

[10] Langacker's proposal is relevant to either a 'pronominalization' transformation or a semantic interpretive rule for pronouns, as he notes (1969, 161).

[11] See Kayne 1981 for study of 'why should there exist a c-command requirement' (143) and for relation of this notion to the general notion of dominance and to the specific notion of "paths."

[12] Earlier Ross 1967 had also shown forward pronouns to be blocked in certain cases, e.g., "*Realizing that $Oscar_i$ was unpopular didn't bother him_i." (See also Culicover, 1976 for related work.)

[13] Chomsky argued that a '+an +pron' lexical category did not exist for logical reasons. See Bouchard 1982 for debate on whether it exists with empty categories.

[14] Certain proposed components of UG do appear to involve relations of precedence. For example, if word order (e.g., SVO, SOV, etc.) is a parameter of UG (see Chomsky, 1982, for example) then it does. Current work on the typological validity of a 'word order' parameter however has questioned the theoretical status of this parameter. See Travis, 1983 and 1984 for example. Travis suggests for example that 'word order' may be a reflex of several distinct grammatical parameters, e.g., head direction, theta direction, or case direction. It is possible also that the typological generality that 'non-initial

subject orders (as in VOS order for example) are rare' is a function not of specifically grammatical principles but of general cognitive assimilation of subject to topic. UG may intersect in modular fashion with such factors. Similarly, although it has been proposed that WH-movement is always leftward i.e., to a preceding position in a sentence, there is some evidence from left-branching SOV languages that rightward movement, which obeys subjacency constraints, does occur (e.g., work on Sinhalese by Gair, 1983). This would suggest that direction of movement was also sensitive to, perhaps dependent on, parametric structure such as branching direction. Resolution of these speculations must await further linguistic work on the parameters and principles of UG (Chomsky, pc.).

[15] Note too that these results in II.3.4 do not deny the possible apparent fact that preference for forward pronouns may vary in strength from language to language and may in fact be stronger in Japanese and/or Chinese than in English. These results suggest, however, that the explanation of these data cannot be simply in terms of a binary valued +/- 'precedence only' principle of grammar.

[16] For example both Lasnik and Higginbotham (pc and class lectures) have suggested that a range of data, e.g., i and ii, is not accounted for by the present formulation of Reinhart's pragmatic principle. In cases like i and ii for example, there is no bound variable alternative which *should* have been used.

(i)   *We like me
(ii)   *John and Mary saw him/himself

In addition, speakers must be able to 'intend coreference' without using a bound variable form in sentences like iii since a reflexive pronoun is not possible here.

(iii)   Whenever people come to *him, John* turns them away

If speakers accept this lexical pronoun form in iii but not in 67 or 68, this would suggest that the speaker's intended coreference must be independent of the pronoun/reflexive anaphor type choice. But application of the communicative strategy requires that the speaker link coreference judgment and anaphor type choice. If they link these only when grammatically possible, this would suggest that application of the pragmatic strategy must consult the independent grammatical facts (whether a pronoun or reflexive is possible). Thus, the grammatical constraints on pronouns and anaphors would be independent of the pragmatics/grammar distinction.

[17] In each study specifications of 'significant' errors are standardized. For example, agreement 'errors' are generally not considered significant in studies of anaphora.

[18] Standardized scoring criteria in this study determined that 'correctness' in the act out task also required that basic syntactic and semantic aspects of the two clause structure of the stimulus sentence (other than coreference) be correctly represented.

[19] In this act out task, scoring criteria differed from the Lust, Loveland, and Kornet study above by assessing only the referential aspects of the response to the complement clause.

[20] The nature of pretraining differs across act-out tasks. Thus Solan 1983 for example trained children on "The horse kicked him," which required the child to associate an external referent with a pronoun. This may have trained the child to associate the pronoun deictically more than other studies which simply pretrained the child that s/he had the option to use same or different subjects in interpreting complex sentences. In

addition, some of Tavakolian's sentences required the child to use all three dolls that were made available to the child, as in "The sheep tells the duck for him to hit the pig" for example. This also may have had the effect of encouraging the child to use all dolls placed before it more than other tasks did that always used sentences only referring to a selection from the reference set. Finally, more subtle aspects of task administration and scoring may also be involved in this difference across studies. (See Notes 18 and 19 for example.) In the Tavakolian and Solan studies, noncoreference is usually a near exact complement of coreference judgments without an independent category of errors in which coreference cannot be scored. This is not the case for the Lust et al. studies.

[21] In a way this problem provides a precise example of a general problem in first language acquisition. How can children process 'primary linguistic data' before they have the grammatical knowledge which must *result* from the mapping of PLD to grammatical competence. (See Fodor, Bever and Garrett, 1974 for explicit formulation of this problem.)

[22] The sentences tested in IV.1.1 and 1.2 involved subordinate clauses. In these structures where the subordinate clause is preposed, this clause is represented as Chomsky-adjoined to the main clause. Thus, the main clause subject neither c-commands nor S-commands the preceding antecedent or anaphor. Thus "When $Mary_i$ slept, she_i snored" is possible.

[23] Goodluck 1981 argues that the temporal 'after' clause may be attached to the VP by children, not to S.

[24] Most of the examples (for test of children's sensitivity to command) involve forward anaphors. This is because test of sensitivity to command on backward anaphors (e.g., comparisons of allowed coreference on sentences which optionally allow backward anaphora, e.g. 113, with sentences like 111 which obligatorily disallow anaphora) are difficult because of the general directionality constraint against backward anaphora in acquisition. Thus the means for amount of coreference on any type of backward anaphora on any task are extremely low, making significant statistical comparison difficult.

[25] Another study (Matthei 1981) also suggests that children may be treating anaphors like pronouns. In this case Matthei tested the 'each other' reciprocal anaphor, in a comprehension (act-out) task, on sentences i—iv.

i.   The horses said that the cows jumped over each other
ii.   The horses said the cows jumped over each other
iii.   The cows want the lambs to kiss each other
iv.   The pigs noticed the boys patting each other

Matthei's subjects were 17 Ss, 4,2—6,6 years old. The design allowed him to test what reference children would choose for the anaphor 'each other', in particular to test whether they would choose a non-local antecedent, e.g. matrix clause subject. Most of the responses Matthei found did involve the main clause subject. This held regardless of complement type according to Matthei. Main clause subject responses would be predicted if the children were treating 'each other' like a pronoun, e.g. 'them', rather than as an anaphor.

The results in this experiment do not clearly support this conclusion, however. This is because although some children simply chose the matrix subject as antecedent of the anaphor, most responses (64.4%) involved children choosing *both* the subject and the second NP as antecedent of the 'each other' term. Thus, in (i) for example they would have the cows and the horses jump over each other. Use of the second NP as subject of the complement is not consistent with interpretation of the 'each other' as a pronoun, since principle B rules out pronoun interpretation here, as in v.

v.   *The horses said that *the cows* jumped over *them*

The results more closely suggest that the 'each other' is not analyzed as an anaphor or a pronoun yet by the young child. Rather the development of the reciprocal semantics of the term, common to an 'each . . . the other' reading seems to determine children's responses (where the quantifier 'each' may have no distributive reading). The claim that children may not assign a bound anaphor reading which can be represented by 'each other' is supported by Potts et al. (1979) in which children rarely at the three or four year age (25% and 37% respectively) use a reciprocal in a sentence completion task which allows it, e.g.: "Sometimes when dogs see other dogs, they bark. These dogs are barking at . . ."

[26] Goodluck 1981, 157 had hypothesized that the directionality constraint may apply only to 'optional' forms of anaphora, on the basis of her earlier experimental data. Her earlier results on this issue did not replicate in the study reported in Lust et al. in this volume or in a subsequent study completed by Goodluck, to appear.

REFERENCES

Amidon, A. and P. Carey: 1972, 'Why five-year olds cannot understand *before* and *after*', *Journal of Verbal Learning and Verbal Behavior* **11**, 417−23.

Berwick, R.: 1982, *Locality Principles and the Acquisition of Syntactic Knowledge*, unpublished doctoral dissertation, MIT.

Berwick, R. and A. Weinberg: 1984, *The Grammatical Basis of Linguistic Performance*, MIT Press, Cambridge, Mass.

Berwick, R. and Wexler, K.: to appear, 'Parsing efficiency, binding, c-command and learnability', in B. Lust (ed.), *Studies in the Acquisition of Anaphora, Vol. 2, Applying the Constraints*, D. Reidel, Dordrecht.

Bickerton, D.: 1975, 'Some assertions about presuppositions about pronominalization', in R. E. Grossman, L. J. San, and T. Vance (eds.), *Papers from the Parasession on Functionalism*, Chicago Linguistic Society, Chicago, pp. 24−35.

Blake, J., G. Quastaso, W. Austin, and E. Vingilis: 1984, unpublished manuscript, 'Memory capacity and language complexity', York University, Toronto.

Bolinger, D.: 1979, 'Pronouns in discourse', in T. Givon (ed.), *Discourse and Syntax, Syntax and Semantics* **12**, Academic Press, New York.

Borer, H. and K. Wexler: to appear, 'The maturation of syntax', in T. Roeper and E. Williams (eds.), *Parameter Setting*, D. Reidel, Dordrecht.

Bouchard, D.: 1982, 'On the content of empty categories', unpublished doctoral dissertation, MIT.

Bowers, J.: 1982, 'Parasitic gaps', in W. Harbert (ed.), *Cornell University Working Papers in Linguistics* **4**, 1−10.

Bresnan, J.: 1978, 'A realistic transformational grammar', in M. Halle, J. Bresnan, and G. Miller (eds.), *Linguistic Theory and Psychological Reality*, MIT Press, Cambridge, Mass.

Bresnan, J.: 1982a, 'Control and complementation', *Linguistic Inquiry* **13**, 343–434.

Bresnan, J.: 1982b, 'Control and complementation', *The Mental Representation of Grammatical Relations*, MIT Press, Cambridge, Mass., 282–390.

Brody, M.: 1984, 'On contextual definitions and the role of chains', *Linguistic Inquiry* **15**, 355–380.

Brown, R.: 1973, *A First Language*, Harvard University Press, Cambridge, Mass.

Carden, G.: 1982, 'Backwards anaphora in discourse context', *Journal of Linguistics* **18**, 361–287.

Ceci, S. and M. Howe: 1978, 'Semantic knowledge as a determinent of developmental differences in recall', in *Journal of Experimental Child Psychology* **26**, 230–45.

Chapman, R.: 1978, 'Comprehension strategies in children', in J. Kavanaugh and W. Strange (eds.), *Speech and Language in the Laboratory, School and Clinic*, MIT Press, Cambridge, Mass.

Chipman, H. and J. Gerard: to appear, 'Proximity strategy in the acquisition of subject control sentences', in B. Lust (ed.), *Studies in the Acquisition of Anaphora: Applying the Constraints, II*, D. Reidel, Dordrecht.

Chomsky, C.: 1969, *The Acquisition of Syntax in Children from 5 to 10*, MIT Press, Cambridge, Mass.

Chomsky, N.: 1975, *Reflections on Language*, Pantheon, N.Y.

Chomsky, N.: 1980, *Rules and Representations*, Columbia University Press, New York.

Chomsky, N.: 1981a, *Lectures on Government and Binding*, Foris, Dordrecht.

Chomsky, N.: 1981b, 'A note on non-control PRO', *Journal of Linguistic Research* **1**, 1–11.

Chomsky, N.: 1982, *Some Concepts and Consequences of the Theory of Government and Binding*, MIT Press, Cambridge, Mass.

Cinque, G.: 1977, 'Toward a unified treatment of island constraints', in W. Dressler and W. Meid (eds.), *Proceedings of the Twelfth International Congress of Linguistics*, Innsbrucker Beitrage zur sprachwissenschaft, 344–348.

Clifford, T. H.: 1984, *Acquisition of Pronouns in the First Language Acquisition of English: A Study of Natural Speech*, unpublished M.A. thesis, Cornell University, Ithaca, N.Y.

Cohen Sherman, J.: 1983, 'The acquisition of control in complement sentences: The role of structural and lexical factors', unpublished doctoral dissertation, Cornell University, Ithaca, N.Y.

Culicover, P.: 1976, 'A constraint on coreferentiality', *Foundations of Language* **14**, 109–118.

Dale, P.: 1976, *Language Development* (2nd Ed.), Holt, Reinhart, and Winston, N.Y.

Deutsch, W. and J. Koster: 1982, 'Children's interpretation of sentence internal anaphora', *Papers and Reports on Child Language Development* **21**, 39–45.

Ferreiro, E.: 1971, *Les Relations Temporelles dans le langage de l'enfant*, Droz, Paris.

Fisher, K.: 1985, *The Syntax and Semantics of Anaphora in Khmer*, unpublished Master's thesis, Cornell University, Ithaca, N.Y.

Fodor, J., T. Bever, and M. Garrett: 1974, *The Psychology of Language*, McGraw Hill, New York.

INTRODUCTION 99

Gair, J.: 1983, 'Non-configurationality, movement, and Sinhala focus', paper presented at the Linguistic Association of Great Britain, Newcastle.

Gary, J. O., and S. Gamal-Eldin: 1982, *Cairene Egyptian Colloquial Arabic*, Lingua Descriptive Studies, North-Holland Publishing Co., Amsterdam.

Gleitman, L., E. Newport, and H. Gleitman: 1984, 'The current status of the Motherese Hypothesis', in *Journal of Child Language* 11, 43—79.

Goodall, T. G.: 1984, *Parallel Structures in Syntax*, unpublished doctoral dissertation, University of California, San Diego.

Goodluck, H.: 1981, 'Children's grammar of complement subject interpretation', in S. Tavakolian (ed.), *Language Acquisition and Linguistic Theory*, MIT, Cambridge, Mass., pp. 139—166.

Goodluck, H.: to appear, 'Children's interpretation of pronouns and null NPs: An alternative view', in Lust, B. (ed.), *Studies in the Acquisition of Anaphora*: (Volume 2), *Applying the Constraints*, D. Reidel, Dordrecht.

Gundell, J. K.: 1980, 'Zero NP-Anaphora in Russian: A case of topic-prominence', in J. Kleiman and A. Ojeda (eds.), *Papers from the Parasession on Pronouns and Anaphors, April 18—19*, Chicago Linguistic Society, Chicago, 139—146.

Hammerton, M.: 1970, 'Disputed interpretation of a pronoun', *Nature* **227**, 202—000.

Harbert, W.: 1983, 'On the definition of binding domains', in D. Flickinger (ed.), *Proceedings of the West Coast Conference on Formal Linguistics II*, Stanford University, Stanford, California.

Higginbotham, J.: 1980, 'Anaphora and GB: Some preliminary remarks', in J. Jensen (ed.), *Proceedings of the Tenth Annual Meeting of the North Eastern Linguistic Society* **9**, 223—236, Ottawa, Canada.

Higginbotham, J.: 1983, 'Logical form, binding and nominals', *Linguistic Inquiry* **14**, 395—420.

Huang, C.-T. J.: 1982, *Logical Relations in Chinese and the Theory of Grammar*, unpublished doctoral dissertation, MIT.

Huang, C.-T. J.: 1984, 'On the distribution and reference of empty pronouns', *Linguistic Inquiry* **15**, 531—574.

Hust, J. and M. Brame: 1976, 'Jackendoff on interpretative semantics', *Linguistic Analysis* **2**, 243—277.

Ingram, D., and C. Shaw: 1981, 'The comprehension of pronominal reference in children', unpublished paper, The University of British Columbia.

Jacobson, P.: 1982, 'Evidence for gaps', in P. Jacobson and G. K. Pullum (eds.), *The Nature of Syntactic Representation*, D. Reidel, Dordrecht, 187—228.

Jakubowicz, C.: 1984, 'On markedness and binding principles', *Proceedings of the North Eastern Linguistic Society* **14**, 154—182.

Kayne, R.: 1981, 'Unambiguous paths', in J. Koster and R. May (eds.), *Levels of Syntactic Representation*, Foris, Dordrecht.

Kayne, R.: 1984, *Connectedness and Binary Branching*, Foris, Dordrecht.

Koopman, H.: 1983, 'The syntax of verbs: From verb movement rules in the Kru languages to universal grammar', unpublished doctoral dissertation, McGill University, Canada.

Koster, J.: 1978, *Locality Principles in Syntax*, Foris, Dordrecht.

Koster, J.: 1981, 'Configurational grammar', in R. May and J. Koster (eds.), *Levels of Syntactic Representation*, Foris, Dordrecht.

Koster, J.: 1984, 'Global harmony', *Tilburg Papers in Language and Literature* **61**, Tilburg University, the Netherlands.

Kuno, S.: 1972a, 'Functional sentence perspective: A case study from Japanese and English', *Linguistic Inquiry* **3**, 269—320.

Kuno, S.: 1972b, 'Pronominalization, reflexivization, and direct discourse', *Linguistic Inquiry* **3**, 161—195.

Kuno, S.: 1973, *The Structure of the Japanese Language*, MIT Press, Cambridge, Mass.

Kuno, S.: 1975, 'Three perspectives in the functional approach to syntax', *Papers from the Parasession on Functionalism*, Chicago Linguistic Society, 276—335.

Kuno, S.: to appear, 'Anaphora in Japanese.'

Langacker, R. W. : 1969, 'On pronominalization and the chain of command', in D. Reibel and S. Schane (eds.), *Modern Studies in English*, Prentice-Hall, Englewood Cliffs, N.J., pp. 160—187.

Lasnik, H.: 1976, 'Remarks on coreference', *Linguistic Analysis* **2**, 1—22.

Lasnik, H.: 1981, 'On two recent treatments of disjoint reference', *Journal of Linguistic Research* **1**, 48—58.

Lasnik, H. and Saito, M.: 1984, 'On the nature of proper government', *Linguistic Inquiry* **15**, 235—290.

Lasnik, H. and S. Crain: to appear, 'On the acquisition of pronominal reference', *Lingua*.

Lust, B.: 1974, 'Conjunction reduction in language of young children: Studied with particular concern for the directionality of the deletion component', unpublished Ph.D. dissertation, City University of New York Graduate Center.

Lust, B.: 1977, 'Conjunction reduction in child language', *Journal of Child Language* **4**, 257—287.

Lust, B.: 1981, 'Constraint on anaphora in child language: A prediction for a universal', in S. Tavakolian (ed.), *Language Acquisition and Linguistic Theory*, MIT Press, Cambridge, Mass., 74—96.

Lust, B.: 1983, 'On the notion "principal branching direction", a parameter of universal grammar', in Y. Otsu, H. Van Riemsdijk, K. Inoue, A. Kamio, and N. Kawasaki (eds.), *Studies in Generative Grammar and Language Acquisition*, International Christian University, Tokyo, 137—151.

Lust, B. and Y-C. Chien: 1984, 'The structure of coordination in first language acquisition of Mandarin Chinese: Evidence for a universal', *Cognition* **17**, 49—83.

Lust, B., Y-C. Chien, and L. Mangione: 1984a, 'First language acquisition of Mandarin Chinese: Constraints on free and bound null anaphora', in S. Hattori and K. Inoue (eds.), *Proceedings of the Thirteenth International Congress of Linguists*, Gakushuin, Tokyo, 1127—1130.

Lust, B., L. Mangione, and Y.-C. Chien: 1984b, 'Determination of empty categories in first language acquisition of Mandarin Chinese', Cornell University, Working Papers in Linguistics, 6, 151—165.

Lust, B. and L. Mangione: 1983, 'The principal branching direction parameter constraint in first language acquisition of anaphora', in P. Sells and C. Jones (eds.), *Proceedings of the 13th Annual Meeting of the North Eastern Linguistic Society*, University of Massachusetts, Amherst, 145—160.

Lust, B., Y-C Chien, and S. Flynn: to appear, 'What children know: Comparison of methods for the study of first language acquisition', in B. Lust (ed.), *Studies in the Acquisition of Anaphora: Vol. 2, Applying the Constraints*, Cornell University, Ithaca, N.Y.

Lust, Gair, & Mangione: in preparation, 'A note on precedence and UG', unpublished manuscript, Cornell University.

Lust, B., Y-C Chien, and D. Gray: in preparation, 'What Children Know About What They Say', Cornell University, Ithaca, N.Y.

Lust, B. and T. Clifford: 1982, 'The 3D study: Effects of depth, distance and directionality on children's acquistion of anaphora', in J. Pustejovksy and P. Sells (eds.), *Proceedings of the Twelfth Annual Meeting of the North Eastern Linguistic Society*, MIT, Cambridge, Mass., pp. 174—186 (also this volume).

Lust, B., K. Loveland, and R. Kornet: 1980, 'The development of anaphora in first language: Syntactic and pragmatic constraints', *Linguistic Analysis* 6, 359—391.

Lust, B. and C. Mervis: 1980, 'Development of coordination in the natural speech of young children', *Journal of Child Language* 7, 279—304.

Matthei, E.: 1981, 'Children's interpretations of sentences containing reciprocals', in S. Tavakolian (ed.), *Language Acquisition and Linguistic Theory*, MIT Press, Cambridge, Mass.

Manzini, R. and K. Wexler: to appear, 'Parameters and learnability in binding theory', in T. Roeper & E. Williams, *Parameter Setting*, D. Reidel, Dordrecht.

May, R.: 1981, 'On the parallelism of movement and bound anaphora', *Linguistic Inquiry* 12, 477—483.

McCray, A.: 1980, 'The semantics of backward anaphora', in J. Jensen (ed.), *Proceedings of the Tenth Annual Meeting of the North Eastern Linguistic Society*, University of Ottawa, Ottawa, 329—344.

Mohanan, K. P.: 1981, 'On pronouns and their antecedents', unpublished paper, MIT.

Mohanan, K. P.: 1982a, 'Pronouns in Malayalam', *Studies in the Linguistic Sciences* 11, 67—75.

Mohanan, K. P.: 1982b, 'Grammatical relations and anaphora in Malayalam', in A. Marantz and T. Stowell (eds.), *MIT Working Papers in Linguistics* 4, 163—190.

Mohanan, K. P.: 1983, 'Functional and anaphoric control', *Linguistic Inquiry* 14, 641—674.

Montalbetti, M.: 1984, 'After binding: On the interpretation of Pronouns', unpublished doctoral thesis, MIT, Cambridge, Mass.

Nakai, S.: 1976, 'A study of anaphoric relations in Japanese', unpublished manuscript, University of Massachusetts, Amherst.

Osherson, D. and T. Wasow: 1976, 'Task-specificity and species-specificity in the study of language: A methodological note', in *Cognition* 4, 203—214.

Oshima, S.: in preparation, 'Anaphora: A GB approach', unpublished manuscript.

Oshima, S.: 1979, 'Conditions on rules: Anaphora in Japanese', in G. Bedell, E. Kobayashi, and M. Muraki (eds.), *Explorations in Linguistics: Essays in Honor of K. Inoue*, Kenkejusha.

Oshima, S.: 1980, 'Anaphora in old English', Research reports of the Kochi University, 29, 11—43.

Otsu, Y.: 1981, *Universal Grammar and Syntactic Development in Children: Toward a Theory of Syntactic Development*, unpublished doctoral dissertation, MIT.

Padilla Rivera, J.: 1985, *On the Definition of Binding Domains in the First Language Acquisition of Anaphora in Spanish. The Modular Role of Binding Principles and Lexical Factors*, unpublished doctoral dissertation, Cornell University, Ithaca, New York.

Piaget, J. and B. Inhelder: 1973, *Memory and Intelligence*, Basic Books, Inc., N.Y.

Pinker, S.: 1984, *Language Learnability and Language Development*, Harvard University Press, Cambridge, Mass.

Potts, M., P. Carlson, R. Cocking, and C. Copple: 1979, *Structure and Development in Child Language*, Cornell University, Ithaca, N.Y.

Read, C. and V. Chou Hare: 1977, 'Children's interpretation of reflexive pronouns in English', in F. R. Eckman and A. J. Hastings (eds.), *Studies in First and Second Language Acquisition*, 98.

Reinhart, T.: 1976, *The Syntactic Domain of Anaphora*, unpublished doctoral dissertation, MIT, Cambridge, Massachusetts.

Reinhart, T.: 1981, 'Definite NP anaphora and c-command domains', *Linguistic Inquiry* 12, 605—636.

Reinhart, T.: 1983a, *Anaphora and Semantic Interpretation*, Croom Helm, London.

Reinhart, T.: 1983b, 'Coreference and bound anaphora: A restatement of the anaphora questions', *Linguistics and Philosophy* 6, 47—88.

Rizzi, L.: 1983, *Issues in Italian Syntax*, Foris, Dordrecht.

Roeper, T. and E. Williams: to appear, *Parameter Setting*, D. Reidel, Dordrecht.

Roeper, T., M. Rooth, L. Mallis, and Akiyama: in preparation, 'The problem of empty categories and bound variables in language acquisition', unpublished manuscript, University of Massachusetts, Amherst.

Ross, J.: 1967, 'On the cyclic nature of English pronominalization', *To Honor Roman Jacobson*, Mouton, The Hague, 1669—1682. Reprinted in 1969 in D. Reibel and S. Schane (eds.), *Modern Studies in English*, Prentice-Hall, Englewood Cliffs, N.J., 187—200.

Saito, M.: 1984, 'On the definition of c-command and government', in C. Jones and P. Sells (eds.), *Proceedings of North Eastern Linguistics Society* 14, 402—417.

Shatz, M.: 1978, 'Children's comprehension of their mother's questions — directives', in *Journal of Child Language* 5, 39—46.

Sinclair, H.: 1978, 'The transition from sensory-motor behavior to symbolic activity', in L. Bloom (ed.), *Readings in Language Development*, John Wiley and Sons, N.Y.

Sinclair de Zwart, H.: 1967, *Acquisition du langage et developpement de la pensee*, Dunod, Paris.

Solan, L.: 1977, 'On the interpretation of missing complement NP's', *Occasional Papers in Linguistics* 3, University of Massachusetts, Amherst.

Solan, L.: 1981, 'The acquisition of structural restrictions on anaphora', in S. Tavakolian (ed.), *Language Acquisition and Linguistic Theory*, MIT Press, Cambridge, Mass., pp. 59—73.

Solan, L.: 1983, *Pronominal Reference: Child language and the Theory of Grammar*, D. Reidel, Dordrecht.

Tai, J. H.-Y: 1973: 'Chinese as a SOV language', *Papers from the 9th Regional Meeting*, Chicago Linguistic Society, 1, 397—413.

Tavakolian, S.: 1977, *Structural Principles in the Acquisition of Complex Sentences*, unpublished doctoral dissertation, University of Massachusetts, Amherst.

Tavakolian, S.: 1978, 'Children's comprehension of pronominal subjects and missing subjects in complicated sentences', in H. Goodluck and L. Solan (eds.), *Papers in the Structure and Development of Child Language*, Occasional Papers in Linguistics, 4, University of Massachusetts, Amherst, pp. 145—152.

Taylor-Browne, K.: 1983, 'Acquiring restrictions on forwards anaphora: A pilot study', *Calgary Working Papers in Linguistics* 9, 75—99.

Travis, L.: 1983, 'Word order change and parameters', in I. Haik and d. Massam (eds.), *MIT Working Papers in Linguistics*, 5, 277—289.

Travis, L.: 1984, *Parameters and Effects of Word Order Variation*, unpublished doctoral dissertation, MIT, Cambridge, Mass.

Van Riemsdijk, H. and E. Williams: to appear, *Introduction to the Theory of Grammar*, MIT Press, Cambridge, Mass.

Veluppillai, A.: 1981, 'Cleft sentences in Tamil', *The Sri Lanka Journal of the Humanities* 7, 82—106.

Warburton, I. and N. S. Prabhu: 1972, 'Anaphoric pronouns: Syntax vs. semantics', in *Journal of Linguistics* 8, 289—292.

Wasow, T.: 1979, *Anaphora in Generative Grammar*, E. Story-Scientia, Ghent.

Wexler, K. and Y-C Chien: to appear, 'The development of lexical anaphors and pronouns', in *Papers and Reports on Child Language Development*, Stanford University.

Wexler, K. and Culicover, P.: 1980, *Formal Principles of Language Acquisition*, MIT Press, Cambridge, Mass.

Whitman, J.: 1982, 'Configurationality parameters', in J. Pustejovsky and P. Sells (eds.), *Proceedings of the 12th Annual Meeting of the North Eastern Linguistic Society*, University of Massachusetts, Amherst, 222.

Williams, E.: 1981, 'Language acquisition, markedness and phrase structure', in Tavakolian, S. (ed.), *Language Acquisition and Linguistic Theory*, MIT Press, Cambridge, Mass.

Williams, E.: 1980, 'Predication', *Linguistic Inquiry* 11, 203—238.

Williams, E.: 1978, 'Across-the-board rule application', *Linguistic Inquiry* 9, 31—43.

Williams, E.: 1977, 'Discourse and logical form', *Linguistic Inquiry* 8, 101—139.

PART A

THEORETICAL BASE

THOMAS WASOW

REFLECTIONS ON ANAPHORA

1. THE ROLE OF ANAPHORA STUDIES IN GENERATIVE GRAMMAR

Generative grammarians have been studying anaphora[1] for two decades, since the publication of Lees and Klima's seminal paper, 'Rules for English Pronominalization'. During this period, the generative literature on anaphora has grown to massive proportions. While many of the avenues explored in that literature have proved to be dead ends, and many issues remain unresolved, I believe that important insights have been attained. My purpose in this paper is to survey what I consider to be the major achievements of the work on anaphora of the past twenty years. I do not pretend to be presenting any novel discoveries; my aim, rather, is to distill what is most significant out of a large and often confusing literature.

Like the other contributions to this volume — indeed, like almost all work in generative grammar — this paper assumes a psychological perspective on linguistic research. I assume, that is, that the primary reason for investigating the structure of natural languages is to learn about the organization and functioning of the human mind. In particular, I share Chomsky's oft repeated opinion that the most striking feature of language is the contrast between the structural complexity of natural languages and the ease with which children learn to speak them. It is this "inductive leap" between linguistic experience and knowledge that Chomsky has characterized as "the fundamental problem of linguistic theory" (Chomsky (1972; 67)). It is evident that the present volume addresses this fundamental problem especially directly. In my review of the anaphora literature, I shall attempt to address as directly as possible the relevance of that literature to psychological issues, particularly to the acquisition problem.

An appropriate place to begin my survey is with an attempt to characterize what anaphora is. I will not be so bold as to offer a definition: a particularly successful empirical investigation may end with a definition, but research in progress typically involves imprecise "seat

107

B. Lust (ed.), Studies in the Acquisition of Anaphora, Vol. I, 107—122.
© 1986 *by D. Reidel Publishing Company.*

of the pants" characterizations of the phenomena in question. Loosely, then, the study of anaphora deals with pronouns, other "pro-forms" (e.g., *do so*), and ellipsis. These constructions share a number of properties, the most obvious being that they derive their interpretations in a context from their association with other elements in the context. Others will be discussed below.

What is it about anaphora that has led linguists to write so much on it? I can think of several plausible answers. First, and most obviously, anaphoric elements are a pervasive fact of life in natural languages, so any theory that purports to characterize speakers' linguistic abilities must address itself to the phenomenon of anaphora. Second, the rules governing the interpretation of anaphoric elements appear to be a part of a speaker's knowledge of language which is not explicitly taught. While adults may provide children with instruction regarding the case marking or gender of pronouns, parents do not seem to tell children how pronouns are associated with antecedents and interpreted. Further, the rules governing these aspects of anaphora show little if any variation across languages. Thus, they are excellent candidates for part of the language learner's innate endowment (as was pointed out by Witten (1970)). C. Chomsky's (1969) pioneering study of the acquisition of pronominal reference lends additional plausibility to this idea, indicating that mastery of pronominal anaphora occurs at a fairly uniform age, and is largely independent of the child's level of general syntactic develop-ment. In short, the study of anaphora may address the "fundamental problem" of language acquisition in an especially direct way. Third, the study of anaphora holds particular interest for linguists because it seems to involve the interaction of all of the standard components of a theory of language: pragmatics, semantics, syntax, and phonology. When anaphoric elements derive their interpretation from the non-linguistic context, their analysis belongs to the domain of pragmatics; when pronouns are interpreted as "bound variables",[2] they affect the seman-tics; and in determining linguistic antecedents for anaphoric elements, both tree configurations and stress level are relevant, so syntax and phonology are involved.

One especially intriguing aspect of the study of anaphora is its relationship to other phenomena investigated by generative gram-marians. This is an issue that is central to the anaphora literature of the past decade. In my dissertation (Wasow (1972), published in revised form as Wasow (1979)), I argued that rules of anaphora should be treated as an entirely separate module of linguistic theory, governed by different principles from those at work in other grammatical components. There seemed to me to be a strong *prima facie* case for this. At least the following three properties appear to distinguish anaphora rules from other well-studied types of rules. First, they are discourse rules. That is, the elements involved in anaphoric relations may be in separate sentences, possibly involving separate speakers; indeed, they need not even be linguistic elements at all. This is in marked contrast to other standard rules of grammar such as the transformations of *Wh*-movement or Comparative deletion, which operate strictly sentence internally. Second, anaphora rules are bidirectional, in the sense that anaphoric elements may either precede or follow their antecedents, as illustrated in (1)

(1) a. Those who want to *do so* can *get a drink.*
    b. Those who want to *get a drink* can *do so.*

If anaphora rules were to be formulated using standard transformational notation (as they were in the work of the mid-sixties), these rules would have to have two structural changes to accomodate examples like (1). No other rules studied by generative grammarians have this property. Third, anaphora rules are apparent exceptions to virtually all of the constraints on grammatical rules which have been proposed. For example, Pronominalization, if formulated as a transformation, can violate Ross's (1967) Complex NP Constraint (2a), Sentential Subject Constraint (2b), and Coordinate Structure Constraint (2c),[3] Chomsky's (1973) Specified Subject Condition (2d), Subjacency Condition (2e), and Tensed Sentence Condition (2f), and Wexler and Culicover's (1980) Binary Principle (2g) and Freezing Principle (2h).

(2) a. *Help* is available for students who need *it.*
    b. That the media ignored *them* upset *the demonstrators.*
    c. *My children's* favorite toys are the playhouse and *their* dolls.
    d. *The protesters* were unhappy about the newspaper's story about *them.*
    e. *The reporters* wrote stories about the judge's attack on *them.*
    f. We told *the victims* that we would compensate *them.*
    g. *Students* claim that we believe that *they* should do nothing but study.
    h. *The candidate* leaked to the media a very damaging story about *his* opponent.

Similar examples can be constructed using elliptical constructions, as (3) illustrates.

(3)   Students who have finished the assignment should help students who have not.

In spite of the initial plausibility of treating anaphora rules as qualitatively different from other rule types, there has been considerable resistance to such a bifurcation. Indeed, a major thrust of the last decade of research in generative grammar has been the attempt to formulate principles of sufficient generality to encompass all categories of grammatical phenomena. Chomsky (1973) led the way in this regard, by proposing that the same constraints which govern transformations also apply to an interpretive rule (previously discussed by Helke (1971)) assigning disjoint reference to certain pairs of noun phrases. The existence of a rule of coreference (or, in this case, non-coreference) which behaved like a transformation and unlike an anaphora rule cast considerable doubt on the desirability of making a categorical distinction betwen the two rule types. Lasnik (1976) took a major step towards eliminating the distinction by suggesting that all definite pronominal anaphora could be accounted for by means of the disjoint reference rule, properly formulated. In effect, Lasnik argued that assignment of reference was free, except for certain cases in which two expressions are grammatically constrained to refer to distinct entities. What had been discussed in the literature as definite pronominal anaphora was simply the residue of cases in which coreference was *not* blocked. Thus, on his theory, there is no pronominal anaphora rule, so one apparent counterexample to the generality of Chomsky's conditions was removed.

Unfortunately, Lasnik's proposal did not suffice to eliminate all anaphora rules (or to assimilate them to other independently necessary rule types). Its critical shortcoming is its identification of anaphora with coreference. As had been pointed out by Postal (1967) and others, identity of reference appears to be neither necessary nor sufficient for the existence of an anaphoric relation. Non-nominal anaphora (e.g., "VP Deletion" or *do so* provides the obvious candidates for non-coreferential anaphora; "sloppy identity" (Ross (1969)) is another. Conversely, asserted coreference normally does not permit anaphora.

(4) a.   Pat will read the paper after Chris does.
    b.   The man who gave *his paycheck* to his wife was wiser than
         the man who gave *it* to his mistress.
    c.   The Falkland Islands are the Malvinas Islands.[4]

For these and other reasons, recent attempts to develop a unified theory
of conditions on rules have not attempted to reduce anaphora to
coreference, but have made use of various kinds of coindexing, which
plays a role both in the syntax and in the interpretation (see especially
Chomsky (1980, 1981)).

An important innovation preparing the way for this coindexing
approach was the development of trace theory (see Lightfoot (1980) for
a summary). The central claim of trace theory is that a constituent which
is transformationally displaced leaves behind a phonetically null copy,
which is anaphorically bound to the moved constituent. As Fiengo
(1974) observed, this treatment makes it possible to analyze various
conditions on movement rules as constraints on the anaphoric binding
between the moved element and its trace. Consequently, much recent
research has been devoted to trying to formulate principles of anaphoric
binding which are sufficiently abstract and general to cover such
apparently diverse phenomena as the distribution of reflexive and
reciprocal pronouns, the distribution of displaced *Wh*-elements with
respect to their "gaps", the scope of quantifiers, and the interpretation of
"missing" infinitival subjects. Thus, anaphora (albeit, of a restricted sort
— cf. footnote 1) has assumed a truly central role in much current
syntactic theorizing.[5]

Given the importance attributed to anaphora in so much recent
linguistic research, together with the centrality of the learnability
problem in motivating most generative research, the significance of the
present volume becomes apparent. If the foremost goal of linguistic
theory is to discover what the child brings to the task of language
acquisition, and if much of the structure of language is determined by
the conditions on anaphor-antecedent pairings, then determining what
children know about anaphoric relations should be an especially
enlightening avenue of investigation.

2. MAJOR ACCOMPLISHMENTS IN THE STUDY OF ANAPHORA

There are several obvious questions that might be asked about anaphoric elements. Unfortunately, the literature is not always clear about which questions are being addressed. I would like to distinguish at least three:

(i)   What is the syntactic distribution of anaphoric elements?
(ii)   What governs the choice of antecedents for anaphoric elements?
(iii)   What interpretation should be given to a particular anaphoric element in a particular context?

Much confusion in the anaphora literature has been the result of treating proposed answers to question (ii) as though they were answers to questions (i) or (iii). In fact, (ii) has been the focus of most generative work on anaphora, although some progress has also been made towards answering (iii). Surprisingly little has been said in answer to (i), so I shall ignore (i) in what follows. Instead, I shall summarize what I consider to be the three most important contributions to our understanding of anaphora which have resulted from attempting to answer (ii) and (iii).

2.1. *The Structural Conditions on Anaphora*

No issue has occupied so much of the anaphora literature as the proper formulation of the structural conditions governing anaphor-antecedent pairing (see, among many others, Lakoff (1968), Langacker (1970), Postal (1970), Ross (1970), Lasnik (1976), Reinhart (1976), Wasow (1979)). One proposal, which enjoyed widespread acceptance for perhaps a decade was Langacker's formulation, which I will call the "Precede-Command Condition" (or "PCC" for short). Roughly, this condition limits intrasentential anaphora to cases in which the anaphoric element does not both precede and command its antecedent. An element A *commands* another element B if every S-node dominating A dominates B; that is, one element commands another if it is in a "higher" clause. This condition correctly blocks the indicated anaphoric relations in (5), while permitting those in (6).

(5) a.   *It* is available to students who need *help.*
    b.   *Doing so* upset most people who *saw that movie.*

(6) a. Students who need *it* can get *help.*
    b. Most people who *did so* regret *seeing that movie.*

Various counterexamples to the PCC were pointed out quite early (Lakoff (1968)), leading to a number of proposed modifications. The first of these to gain widespread acceptance was Reinhart's suggestion that the left-right asymmetry of the PCC was an artifact of the generally right-branching character of English constituent structure. In place of the PCC, Reinhart proposed what I will call the "C-Command Condition" (CCC): intrasentential anaphora is limited to cases in which the anaphoric element does not c-command its antecedent. An element A *c-commands* another element B if every branching node dominating A dominates B, i.e., if A is in a "higher" constituent.[6] The CCC makes the same predictions as the PCC in most cases, but where they differ, the CCC seems to fare somewhat better. For example, the CCC permits the indicated anaphoric relations in (7) while ruling out those in (8), whereas the PCC makes the opposite predictions.

(7) a. *Their* mother loves *the children.*
    b. In *his* apartment, *John* smokes pot.
    c. The chairman hit *him* on the head before *John* could say a word.
(8) a. Near *the children, they* saw a snake.
    b. In *John's* apartment, *he* smokes pot.

These differences between the PCC and the CCC are a natural focus for the attention of child language specialists. C. Chomsky's (1969) classic investigation of children's mastery of the syntactic conditions governing anaphora assumed the correctness of the PCC. More recent acquisition research provides support for the CCC over the PCC (e.g., Solan (1981)). Among many other interesting and relevant results is the discovery that left-right asymmetries in children's use of anaphora correlate with the direction of branching in the language being learned (see Lust and Clifford (1982)).

Successful though the CCC is, in general, it is not entirely without problems. McCray (1980) presents many examples in which the CCC is violated, including those in (9).

(9) a. *He* didn't give her a diamond ring because, although he's madly in love with her, *Walter's* just not ready to tie the knot.
    b. The teacher warned *him* that in order to succeed, *Walter* was going to have to work an awful lot harder from now on.

McCray argues — correctly I think — that such examples do not show that the CCC (or something similar) is *wrong*, but only that it can be overriden by pragmatic factors. McCray makes some interesting though somewhat vague suggestions about the nature of the relevant pragmatic factors, but in the absence of a fully worked out account of examples like (9), the CCC can be regarded as no more than a very promising hypothesis about the answer to question (ii) above.

Research on question (ii) has provided one very fruitful spin-off. Both the notions of "command" and "c-command", originally formulated in the effort to answer (ii), have played major roles in the syntactic theorizing of the past fifteen years. For example, trace theory made it possible to deduce the so-called "insertion prohibition" of Chomsky (1965; 146) from the CCC: if every moved constituent leaves behind an anaphorically bound trace, then it follows from the CCC that there can be no "lowering" transformations. Further, the c-command relation has been invoked in the formulation of numerous other syntactic conditions and rules, for example, in the definition of "government" (see Chomsky (1981; 163—166).

2.2. *The 'Deep/Surface' Anaphora Distinction*

The second major result to come out of the generative literature on anaphora is Hankamer and Sag's (1976) discovery of a fundamental division between two distinct types of anaphoric relations, which they label "deep" and "surface" anaphora. The central difference between them is that only the former permit non-linguistic antecedents (or, as Hankamer and Sag put it, "pragmatic control").[7] A minimal pair to illustrate this contrast is *do it* and *do so*, the former of which is a deep anaphor, the latter, a surface anaphor. Thus, while both (10a) and (10b) are possible, in the context indicated (11a) is fine, but (11b) sounds extremely odd.[8]

(10) a. Everyone tried to *stand on their head*, but only Pat succeeded in doing *it*.
b. Everyone tried to *stand on their head*, but only Pat succeeded in doing *so*.
(11)   [Pat watches Chris and Lee unsuccessfully trying to stand on their heads, and says:]
a. I can do it.
b. ??I can do so.

Correlating with the requirement for a linguistic antecedent is a requirement of some sort of structural non-distinctness.[9] For example, a surface anaphor in the active voice may not take a passive antecedent, whereas deep anaphors operate under no such constraint. Hence (12c) sounds far worse than either (12a) or (12b)

(12) a. The FBI *taped our conversations*, but I don't know why they *did so.*
    b. Our conversations were taped by the FBI, but I don't know why they did it.
    c. Our conversations were taped by the FBI, but I don't know why they did so.

Similar contrasts have been exhibited with other examples of deep anaphora (including definite pronominal anaphora, "One(s) Pronominalization", "Null Complement Anaphora") and surface anaphora ("Verb Phrase Deletion", "Sluicing", "Stripping").

In discovering a fundamental and systematic division in the domain of anaphora, Hankamer and Sag not only brought to light an intriguing new array of data, they also introduced an important desideratum for any theory of anaphoric relations. For example, Lasnik's proposal, sketched above, that grammars assign only *non*-coreference to ordinary pronouns does not appear to be extendable to cases of surface anaphora. Leaving aside reservations about Lasnik's idea voiced earlier, I see no plausible way of accounting for contrasts like (12) if the choice of antecedents is treated as essentially extragrammatical. But if Lasnik's treatment cannot be extended to surface anaphora, then an account is needed of the fact that this type of anaphora is not subject to the usual island constraints.

Hankamer and Sag's distinction should also be of considerable interest to psycholinguists, for the natural place to seek *an explanation* of the existence of the distinction is in theories of anaphoric processing. Sag and Hankamer (1980) have put forward a hypothesis about the psychological basis of the deep/surface anaphora distinction. A concise statement of their theory is the following:

[A]s a new piece of discourse is produced, what is comprehended first is a propositional representation. . . . [A]t any given point in a discourse, what is present in the mind of a comprehender is a pair: a model of the discourse to date, and a propositional representation of (part of) the immediately preceding discourse. As the discourse proceeds, the content of the propositional representation, which is held in short-term memory, is integrated into the model. At some point then the propositional representation is discarded, making room for new propositional representations in a presumably quite limited short-term register. (pp. 10—11)

Deep anaphors, then, are those which derive their interpretations from the "model of the discourse", whereas surface anaphors depend on the short-term "propositional representations".[10] I believe that this conjecture merits serious experimental investigation. Further, it seems to me that the acquisition of the deep/surface anaphora distinction is a potentially very fruitful avenue of research for developmental psycholinguists.

2.3. *Sloppy Identity*

The third major accomplishment of generative research on anaphora that I would like to mention is the discovery and solution of the problem of what Ross (1969) dubbed "sloppy identity". The problem arises from thinking of anaphoric elements as *substitutes* for other expressions (their antecedents, in cases where these are elements of the language). This way of thinking leads one to expect that anaphoric elements are entirely eliminable through the device of replacing them with the expressions they are substitutes for. However, it was noted by Ross, Lakoff, and others in the late '60's that such an expectation would be erroneous. There are a number of constructions in which replacing an anaphoric element with its antecedent leads to a crucial alteration of the meaning, or even to ungrammaticality. Some examples are provided in (13).

(13) a. I haven't finished my preparations, but you have.
     b. Hortense can stand on her head, but Sheldon can't do it.
     c. Pat and Chris are lawyers, and Lee is, too.

It is clear that the most natural interpretations of (13a & b) are not the same as (14a & b), and that (14c) differs from (13c) in grammaticality.

(14) a. I haven't finished my preparations, but you have finished my preparations.
     b. Hortense can stand on her head, but Sheldon can't stand on her head.
     c. *Pat and Chris are lawyers, and Lee is lawyers, too.

Notice, incidentally, that this phenomenon appears with both deep and surface anaphoric elements.

Such examples indicate that a simple substitution of linguistic antecedents is inadequate as an 'explication of the meaning of anaphoric elements. Having falsified this simple and obvious hypothesis, linguists puzzled for several years over what to replace it with. Lasnik (1976; 20) suggests informally that such cases of apparent "deletion under nonidentity", may be explainable by analyzing the nonidentical parts as bound variables in "logical representation"; this would permit the anaphoric element and its antecedent to be analyzed as "identical (rather than sloppily identical) open sentences". This same idea is worked out in considerable detail by Sag (1976) and Williams (1977a), making rich use of Church's lambda calculus to provide the requisite logical representations.

I will not go into the technical details of Sag's or Williams's analyses here. The major insight can, I think, be explained without going into the formalism. In essence, it is that the antecedents of anaphoric elements are semantic units. Thus, for example, there is a property of 'having finished one's preparations', which may be thught of, if one wishes, as a function (call it f) from world-time pairs to sets of individuals i.e., just the set of individuals who have finished their preparations in the world in question at the time in question. (13a) asserts that I am not in the set which results from applying f to the real world at the present time, but that you are. (14a) asserts something quite different. Sag (1976) shows that an analysis along these lines has far-reaching consequences, deriving and verifying numerous interesting predictions from this approach.

The research on sloppy identity is of particular interest (among other reasons) because it establishes a precise criterion for identifying semantic units, providing an unusually direct window into the mechanisms for the composition of meanings.[11] This should, in my opinion, make it especially interesting to psycholinguists as well.

3. DIRECTIONS FOR FUTURE RESEARCH

The results discussed in the previous section are illustrative of the sort of insight that has emerged from twenty years of generative research on anaphora. As is usually the case when progress is made, at least as many questions have been raised as have been answered. In this concluding section, I would like to briefly summarize a few of these.

Probably the most gaping hole in our present understanding of anaphora is the absence of any explicit theory of the pragmatic factors involved. There is, of course, a good deal of relevant literature, but there are no *theories* of the pragmatic aspects of anaphora which can compare in rigor or coverage with the available accounts of the syntactic and semantic factors. This is a problem not limited to the study of anaphora: it is quite generally the case that the development of pragmatic theory has lagged behind that of syntactic and semantic theory. However, this lacuna is particularly noticeable in the domain of anaphora. Given the way in which pragmatic factors interact with and even override the syntactic and semantic factors in anaphora, it is very difficult to draw any firm conclusions at all about anaphora in the absence of a better understanding of the pragmatic factors. In particular, it is extremely difficult to design psycholinguistic experiments to test hypotheses abut the mental representation or acquisition of the syntax and semantics of anaphora, because it is so hard to control adequately for the pragmatic factors, which play such a central role in actual language use.

Moreover, learning more about the psychological mechanisms involved in anaphora is, in my opinion, an essential next step in our understanding of this topic. We now have fairly sophisticated theories of some of the formal properties of anaphoric relations. In order to turn these into genuine *explanations*, we will need to learn about the role of those formal properties in actual language use.

For example, I believe that one result of the research discussed in sections 1 & 2 has been to establish that the relation of anaphora is not fully reducible to that of identity of reference. If this is true, one is naturally led to ask why human languages should be so constituted as to make a distinction between anaphora and coreference. I think that the place to look for an answer to this question is in the psychology of language. In particular, it seems plausible that a formal relation of anaphora (especially bound anaphora, which is often syntactically flagged) might ease the burden on the language user by reducing the amount of pragmatic inferencing required to interpret utterances.

Similarly, I believe that such discoveries as the c-command condition and Hankamer and Sag's deep/surface anaphor distinction are in need of *explanation*, and that the most likely source of such explanation is in terms of learnability and processability. Sag and Hankamer's conjecture about the processing basis of their distinction is a first step in this direction, but it needs to be subjected to careful laboratory testing. Likewise, Berwick and Wexler (1982 and to appear) conjecture that the c-command restriction may serve to vastly simplify both language acquisition and processing, but their proposal, like Sag and Hankamer's, remains speculation, in the absence of experimental data.

This is why studies like the one presented in this volume are timely. Our understanding of anaphora has come a long way in the past twenty years, but further progress will depend on investigating the manner in which our knowledge of language is employed in actual languge use.

NOTES

[1] I use the term "anaphora" here in the way it was used in such works as Jackendoff (1972) and Wasow (1979). Some of the recent "Government-Binding" literature (e.g., Aoun (1981)) uses the same term in a more restricted way, limiting it to what I would call "bound" or "obligatory" anaphora, e.g., reflexive or reciprocal pronouns. See below for a few more remarks on what anaphora is.

[2] A paradigm example of such a case would be (i).

(i)   Every contestant believes that she will win.

A natural interpretation for this example is rendered as something like (ii), where the pronoun corresponds to the last occurrence of the bound variable, x.

(ii) $(\forall x)$ (x is a candidate $\rightarrow$ x believes x will win)

[3] Ross's formulation of his constraints limits them to certain classes of rules (his "chopping rules"), so anaphora rules are not literally exceptions. The point here is that anaphora rules behave differently from other classes of rules in that they are insensitive to syntactic "islands".

[4] Lasnik dismisses examples like (4c) as irrelevant, but his reasons suggest that he uses the term "reference" in a somewhat nonstandard (and unclear) way. Actually, I find examples like (4c) potentially more problematical than (4a & b). If expressions are taken to refer to functions of the appropriate types (as is standardly assumed in model theoretic semantics), then it may well be possible to treat the anaphoric elements in (4a & b) as coreferential with their antecedents (see Sag (1976, 1981) and section 2.3 below). (4c) does not apear to be similarly accomodated.

[5] To my knowledge, little is said about ordinary non-bound anaphora in the literature under discussion. I presume that something like Lasnik's position could be maintained, replacing his rule of non-coreference with a rule assigning distinct indices.

[6] As Reinhart recognizes, "c-command" is the same as Klima's (1964) notion of "in construction with". Reinhart's name for it seems to have caught on better than Klima's did, presumably because it reflects the asymmetry of the relation more clearly. It is interesting that Langacker (1970) explored the possibility of using "in construction with" in place of "command", concluding that this was not a tenable idea, in part on the basis of acceptability judgements which Reinhart questions. The idea of using "in construction with" in place of "command" was also put forward by Culicover (1976), who independently came upon essentially the same idea as Reinhart, though he is rarely cited for it.

[7] Hankamer and Sag actually list a number of properties which they claim cluster to distinguish the two types of anaphora. Most of the criticism of their distinction has focused on this purported clustering, arguing that one or more of the proposed properties does not, in fact, correlate with some of the others (see, e.g., Schachter (1977) and Williams (1977b), and see Hankamer (1978) and Sag (1979) for responses to these criticisms). In my opinion, some of this criticism is well-taken: Hankamer and Sag did overstate their case. I am convinced, nevertheless, that their distinction is a real and extremely important one.

[8] Because of their ability to take pragmatic control, deep anaphors are often subject to ambiguities absent from surface anaphors. A nice example of this is provided by example (i), reported in a recent CBS radio newscast as having been seen on a sign in a dry cleaning establishment.

(i)   Should you feel that we have failed you in any way, we will be only too glad to do it again.

Notice that the unintended interpretation of (i) would be the only available interpretation if *do it* were replaced by *do so*.

[9] Hankamer and Sag argue that surface anaphors are introduced by transformations that replace a full constituent under identity with something else in the sentence. In later work, Sag (1976) argues that it is not identity of surface syntactic form that is relevant, but identity of "logical form". Sag (1981) replaces this condition with one of semantic identity. I do not wish to get into the details of the choice among these alternatives here. The point is simply that the possibility of pairing a surface anaphor with an antecedent is constrained by structural properties of the potential antecedent in ways inapplicable to deep anaphors, even when the latter take linguistic antecedents.

[10] For a criticism of this proposal and an alternative, see Murphy (1982; Chapter 3).

[11] Notice, incidentally, what is implied by the conjunction of this conclusion and the position of Sag and Hankamer (1980) that the deep/surface anaphora distinction is attributable to a two-stage comprehension process. As noted above, sloppy identity occurs with surface anaphors, as well as deep anaphors. This suggests that both Sag and Hankamer's "propositional representation" and their "model of the discourse" are representations of meanings, in some sense. Hence, this might provide evidence on the controversial question of whether an "intermediate" level of meaning representation like Chomsky's "LF" or Bresnan and Kaplan's "functional structures" is motivated.

REFERENCES

Aoun, Y.: 1981, *The Formal Nature of Anaphoric Relations*, unpublished doctoral dissertation, MIT, Cambridge, Mass.

Berwick, R. & K. Wexler: 1982, 'Parsing efficiency, binding and c-command', in D. Flickinger, M., Macken and N. Wiegand (eds.), *Proceedings of the First West Coast Conference on Formal Linguistics*, Stanford University, Stanford, California, pp. 29–34. (Also in Lust, B. (ed.), 1985.)

Berwick, R. and K. Wexler: to appear, 'Parsing efficiency, binding, c-command and learnability', in B. Lust (ed.), *Studies in the Acquisition of Anaphora, Volume 2, Applying the Constraints*, D. Reidel, Dordrecht.

Chomsky, C.: 1969, *The Acquisition of Syntax in Children from 5 to 10*, MIT Press, Cambridge, Mass.

Chomsky, N.: 1965, *Aspects of the Theory of Syntax*, MIT Press, Cambridge, Mass.

Chomsky, N.: 1972, 'Some empirical issues in the theory of transformational grammar', in S. Peters (ed.), *The Goals of Linguistic Theory*, Prentice-Hall, Englewood Cliffs, N.J., pp. 63–130.

Chomsky, N.: 1973, 'Conditions on transformations', in S. Anderson and P. Kiparsky (eds.), *A Festschrift for Morris Halle*, Holt, Rinehart and Winston, New York, pp. 232–286.

Chomsky, N.: 1980a, 'On binding', *Linguistic Inquiry* **11**, 1–46.

Chomsky, N.: 1981b, *Lectures on Government and Binding*, Foris, Dordrecht.

Culicover, P.: 1976, 'A constraint on coreferentiality', *Foundations of Language* **14**, 109–118.

Fiengo, R.: 1974, *Semantic Conditions on Surface Structure*, unpublished doctoral dissertation, MIT.

Hankamer, J.: 1978, 'On the nontransformational derivation of some null VP anaphors', *Linguistic Inquiry* **9**, 66–74.

Hankamer, J. and I. Sag: 1976, 'Deep and surface anaphora', *Linguistic Inquiry* **7**, 391–426.

Helke, M.: 1971, *The Grammar of English Reflexivization*, unpublished doctoral dissertation, MIT.

Jackendoff, R.: 1972, *Semantic Interpretation in Generative Grammar*, MIT Press, Cambridge, Mass.

Klima, E.: 1964, 'Negation in English', in J. Fodor and J. Katz (eds.), *The Structure of Language*, Prentice-Hall, Englewood Cliffs, N.J., pp. 246–323.

Lakoff, G.: 1968, 'Pronouns and reference', unpublished paper.

Langacker, R. W.: 1970, 'On pronominalization and the chain of command', in D. Reibel and S. Schane (eds.), *Modern Studies in English*, Prentice-Hall, Englewood Cliffs, N.J., pp. 160–187.

Lasnik, H.: 1976, 'Remarks on coreference', *Linguistic Analysis* **2**, 1–22.

Lees, R. and E. Klima: 1963, 'Rules for English pronominalization', *Language* **39**, 17–28.

Lightfoot, D.: 1980, 'Trace theory and explanation', in E. Moravcsik and J. Wirth (eds.), *Syntax and Semantics 13: Current Approaches to Syntax*, Academic Press, New York, pp. 137–166.

Lust, B. and T. Clifford: 1982, 'The 3D study: Effects of depth, distance and directionality on children's acquisition of anaphora', in J. Pustejovsky and P. Sells (eds.), *Proceedings of the Twelfth Annual Meeting of the North Eastern Linguistic Society*, MIT, Cambridge, Mass., pp. 174–186, (also this volume).

McCray, A.: 1980, 'The semantics of backward anaphora', in J. Jensen (ed.), *Proceedings of the Tenth Annual Meeting of the North Eastern Linguistic Society*, University of Ottawa, Ottawa, pp. 329–344.

Murphy, G.: 1982, 'Understanding anaphora', unpublished doctoral dissertation, Stanford University.

Postal, P.: 1970, 'On coreferential complement subject deletion', *Linguistic Inquiry* **1**, 439–500.

Postal, P.: 1967, 'Linguistic anarchy notes', unpublished manuscript.

Reinhart, T.: 1976, *The Syntactic Domain of Anaphora*, unpublished doctoral dissertation, MIT.

Ross, J.: 1967, *Constraints on Variables in Syntax*, unpublished doctoral dissertation, MIT.

Ross, J.: 1969, 'Guess who?', in R. Binnick et al. (eds.), *Papers from the Fifth Regional Meeting*, Chicago Linguistic Society, Chicago.

Ross, J.: 1970, 'On the cyclic nature of English pronominalization', in D. Reidel and S. Schane (eds.), *Modern Studies in English*, Prentice-Hall, Englewood Cliffs, N.J., pp. 187–200.

Sag, I.: 1976, *Deletion and Logical Form*, unpublished doctoral dissertation, MIT, Cambridge, Mass. (Reproduced by Indiana University Linguistics Club).

Sag, I.: 1979, 'The nonunity of anaphora', *Linguistic Inquiry* **10**, 152–164.

Sag, I.: 1981, 'Partial variable assignment functions, verb phrase ellipsis, and the dispensibility of logical form', unpublished paper, Stanford University.

Sag, I. and J. Hankamer: 1980, 'Toward a theory of anaphoric processing', in J. Barwise and I. Sag (eds.), *Stanford Working Papers in Semantics Volume 1*, Stanford Cognitive Science Group.

Schachter, P.: 1977, 'Does she or doesn't she?', *Linguistic Inquiry* **8**, 763–772.

Solan, L.: 1981, 'The acquisition of structural restrictions on anaphora', in S. Tavakolian (ed.), *Language Acquisition and Linguistic Theory*, MIT Press, Cambridge, Mass., pp. 59–73.

Wasow, T.: 1972, *Anaphoric Relations in English*, unpublished doctoral dissertation, MIT.

Wasow, T.: 1979, *Anaphora in Generative Grammar*, E. Story-Scientia, Ghent.

Wexler, K. and Culicover, P.: 1980, *Formal Principles of Language Acquisition*, MIT Press, Cambridge, Mass.

Williams, E.: 1977a, 'Discourse and logical form', *Linguistic Inquiry* **8**, 101–139.

Williams, E.: 1977b, 'On deep and surface anaphora', *Linguistic Inquiry* **8**, 692–696.

Witten, E.: 1970, 'Pronominalization: A handbook for secret agents', unpublished paper, Brandeis University.

TANYA REINHART

CENTER AND PERIPHERY IN THE GRAMMAR
OF ANAPHORA

In recent years serious attempts have been made to subject the anaphora, or 'binding', conditions proposed in theoretical studies to an empirical investigation using either adult anaphora or language acquisition data. Many of these studies concentrated mainly on problems of definite NP coreference. This reflects a prevailing assumption in theoretical studies of anaphora that the core issues in the case of pronominal anaphora (i.e. anaphora involving pronouns) are those of intended-coreference with definite NP's. While an alternative interpretation of pronouns as bound variables is known to exist, it is assumed to be a restricted LF phenomenon.

Although I contributed my share to this contention, I believe, now, that it leads to serious theoretical problems, which are discussed in Reinhart (1983b). Here I will argue that the core issue of the binding theory (or the syntax of anaphora) is that of bound-variable anaphora. This type of anaphora is not dependent upon the semantic properties of the antecedent, and, contrary to the common assumption, it is found also with definite antecedents. From the perspective of the grammar, it is the problem of unbound coreference which is the exceptional case, requiring specific constraints (which may not even belong to the grammar at all, as argued in the appendix).

As we shall see in Section 5, the problems with definite NP coreference are reflected in the empirical studies of this issue. I will argue that if the question is the psychological reality of the binding conditions of the grammar, bound anaphora, rather than coreference, should be studied.

1. THE INTERPRETATION OF PRONOUNS: TWO TYPES OF ANAPHORA

Analyses of anaphora assume at least implicitly two types of anaphoric relations. The first is the relation labelled traditionally 'coreference', which is illustrated in (1).

(1)   Christopher$_i$ likes his $_i$ bear.
(2)   He likes Christopher's bear.

123

B. Lust (ed.), Studies in the Acquisition of Anaphora, Vol. I, 123–150.
© 1986 by D. Reidel Publishing Company.

The interpretation given in recent analyses to the (optional) coindexing of the pronoun and the antecedent in (1) is that of 'intended coreference', i.e. the speaker intends the choice of reference or value for the pronoun to be identical to that of 'Christopher'. (Chomsky 1981, p. 314; Lasnik 1981) ('Reference' as used here need not be an object in the world, but a fixed value in some specified domain.) Sentence (2), in which the syntactic conditions do not allow the coindexing of the pronoun, can not be used with intended reference in mind. In a theory assuming contraindexing for the non-coreference in (2) (e.g. Chomsky 1980; Lasnik 1976, 1981), the contraindexing will be interpreted as indicating that the speaker purports not to believe that these two NP's are coreferential (Higginbotham 1980a). In other words, this type of anaphora interpretation defines a relation between linguistic structures and their potential uses for the purpose of expressing referential intentions, rather than defining referential or semantic relations between expressions in the sentence.[1] It would be appropriate to label it the pragmatic interpretation of anaphora, or pragmatic coreference.

A rather different type of anaphora is illustrated in (3) and (4).

(3) a. Each of the boys$_i$ brought his$_i$ bear.
   b. For all x (x is a boy), x brought x's bear.
(4)   Which boy$_i$ e_i brought his$_i$ bear?

The coindexed pronouns in (3) and (4) are interpreted as variables bound by the operator corresponding to the antecedent, as in (3b) or the operator binding the antecedent as in (4). Unlike the coindexed pronoun in (1), the coindexed pronouns in (3)–(4) do not have a fixed value; their value would depend upon the choice of value for the operator, i.e. the choice of a boy.

I will refer to the interpretation of pronouns (or other elements) as bound variables as *bound (variable) anaphora*. This use is different from the current use of the term *bound anaphora* in the GB framework, which is a syntactic rather than semantic term. However, I will argue in Section 4 that the two are consistent.

Current GB studies assume that these two types of interpretation are determined by the type of antecedent entering the coindexing relation. In (3) and (4) the antecedent is a quantified NP (or its trace). Since such NP's have no reference, it is senseless to talk about their intended reference or coreference and they can only enter bound variable relations. Referential antecedents (e.g. definite NP's and proper names), on the other hand, enter intended coreference relations, with one widely recognized exception: when the pronoun is reflexive or reciprocal it is interpreted as a bound variable regardless of the status of its antecedent. (See, e.g. Chomsky 1982, p. 83). The reason commonly given for this is that, unlike other pronouns, reflexives and reciprocals cannot refer independently or deictically. (Another acknowledged, though often ignored, case of bound variable anaphora with a definite antecedent will be mentioned directly.)

The assumption that bound variable anaphora depends (except for reflexives) on the properties of the antecedent has led, in the current framework, to the assumption that its syntactic distribution is captured at LF, independently of the binding conditions. I will first examine this LF mechanism, in the next section, and then argue, in Section 3, that the assumption that bound anaphora is determined by the type of antecedent is wrong and that no special conditions are needed for it.

2. THE CONDITIONS ON BOUND VARIABLE ANAPHORA

The structural condition on bound variable anaphora is believed (following Reinhart 1976) to require that the antecedent c-commands the pronoun, as in (5) below. This is a stronger condition than that restricting pragmatic coreference, which requires only that the pronoun does not c-command the antecedent. The difference between the two conditions can be observed through a comparison of (6) and (7).

(5) a. *No boy$_i$* brought his$_i$ teddy bear to the party.
   b. Who$_i$ t_i brought his$_i$ teddy bear to the party?
   c. *Each of the southern planets$_i$* was deserted by its$_i$ residents.
   d. In front of him$_i$ *each participant$_i$* held a candle.

(6) a. *His$_i$ bear accompanied *no boy$_i$* to the party.
   b. *Who$_i$ did his$_i$ teddy bear accompany t_i to the party?
   c. *People from *each of the southern planets$_i$* deserted it$_i$.
   d. *The rebellion against *every tyrant$_i$* destroyed him$_i$.
   e. *According to everyone$_i$ he$_i$ is an unappreciated genius.
   f. *According to him$_i$ everyone$_i$ is an unappreciated genius.

(7) a. His$_i$ bear accompanied *Christopher$_i$* everywhere.
   b. People from *the southern planet$_i$* deserted it$_i$.
   c. The rebellion against *Java the Hut$_i$* destroyed him$_i$.
   d. According to *Winnie$_i$* he$_i$ is the smartest bear in the world.

The binding conditions (Chomsky 1981) permit the coindexing of the antecedent with the pronoun in both (6) and (7), since in all these cases the pronoun does not c-command the antecedent. (Note that in (6e, f) and (7d) the PP is sentential, hence it is not c-commanded by the subject pronoun. See Reinhart, 1981a, for the arguments.) Nevertheless, while pragmatic intended-coreference is indeed permitted in (7), bound variable anaphora is not permitted in the equivalent cases of (6). Such cases are often referred to as the *weak crossover phenomena*, following the terminology of Wasow (1972) (which derives from Postal).

The difference in the distribution of pragmatic and bound variable anaphora is captured in the GB theory by assuming a special LF mechanism for the latter. While all sentences are subject to the binding conditions, when the antecedent is quantified the special LF conditions filter out inappropriate binding permitted by the general binding conditions. Current proposals concerning the exact formulation of these conditions are Higginbotham's (1980b) mechanism for controlling the coindexing of empty nodes in LF and the bijection principle of Koopman and Sportiche (1981) and Chomsky (1982).[2] Both analyses yield the result that in bound variable anaphora the antecedent's position in surface structure (i.e. its trace at LF) must c-command the pronoun (see fn. 2 for details). There are several unsolved problems with this syntactic condition. However, since I am concerned here with the overall organization of the anaphora picture and not with the structural details, I will not discuss them here. (For a survey of the problems, see Reinhart 1983a, 1983b.)

3. BOUND VARIABLE ANAPHORA WITH DEFINITE ANTECEDENTS

The common contention in the anaphora theory, then, has been that bound variable anaphora is a rather marginal issue, restricted to quantified antecedents, while the 'mainstream' of the anaphora problems consists of definite NP anaphora, which is believed to be interpreted as intended-coreference only and which is captured by the binding conditions. Although this was also my position in Reinhart (1976), I would argue now that this contention is mistaken.

3.1 The Facts

The relevant facts indicating that bound variable interpretation of anaphora is not restricted to quantified antecedents have been around, in fact, for quite a while, and they are usually labelled *sloppy identity phenomena* following Ross (1969). (For some discussion, see also Wasow, this volume.) To see what is at issue here let us consider the interpretation of (8).

(8) Charlie Brown$_i$ talks to his$_i$ dog and my neighbor Max does too/and the same is true of my neighbor Max.

(9) a. *Pragmatic coreference interpretation*:
       Max talks to Charlie's dog.
   b. *Bound variable interpretation*:
       Max talks to Max's dog.

The interpretation of conjunctions like (8) requires the copying of the missing predicate from the first conjunct into the second. The coindexing in the first conjunct indicates that we are considering, at the moment, only the case where the pronoun is intended to corefer with *Charlie Brown*. Under this assumption we still arrive at the two interpretations in (9) for the second conjunct. The question is, then, what is the source of the ambiguity in the second conjunct, given the fact that the first conjunct seems unambiguous. The answer (given, e.g., by Keenan 1971, Sag 1976, Williams 1977 and Partee 1978) is that the first conjunct is, in fact, ambiguous. One interpretation, which we have been assuming all along for definite NP antecedents, is that of intended, or pragmatic, coreference. Under this interpretation a reference (Charlie Brown) is fixed for the pronoun in the first conjunct. Talking to Charlie's dog is, then, the property which is copied into the second conjunct, yielding the interpretation (9a). The second interpretation, however, requires treating the pronoun as a bound variable. We need to assume that the first conjunct contains some open formula, *x talks to x's dog*, which is satisfied by Charlie Brown in the first conjunct and by Max in the second. This interpretation is commonly obtained by deriving a predicate $\lambda x(x$ *talks to x's dog*) (Sag 1976, Williams 1977). The predicate being copied, then, is that of talking to one's own dog rather than of talking to Charlie's dog. This interpretation (9b) is the one labelled 'sloppy identity'. A more successful name for it might be, simply, *bound-variable interpretation*, which indicates that the 'identity' at issue is not of reference (or value) but, rather, of variables.

What we have seen, then, is that definite NP's may enter bound anaphora relations and that this interpretation of pronouns is, therefore, independent of the semantic status of the antecedent. The ambiguity of the first conjunct in (8) is not noticeable if the sentence occurs alone, since the two interpretations happen to be equivalent, under normal conditions. Possibly, this would explain why the bound anaphora interpretation of definite NP anaphora has been overlooked by the 'mainstream' of anaphora studies or perhaps dismissed as strictly a discourse phenomenon. It would be interesting, therefore, to observe that it is possible to find cases where the two interpretations are distinguishable independently of discourse deletion.[3]

When the quantifier *only* is involved, as in (10) and (12), the two interpretations differ in their truth conditions.

(10)   Only Winnie$_i$ thinks he$_i$ is smart.
(11) a. Nobody but Winnie thinks Winnnie is smart.
     b. Nobody but Winnie thinks himself smart.
(12)   Only Sophie$_i$ voted for her$_i$ father.

Under the pragmatic interpretation, (10) entails (11a), i.e. thinking that Winnie is smart is the property attributed to Winnie alone. Under the bound variable interpretation, it is thinking oneself to be smart ($\lambda x(x$ thinks x is smart)) which is attributed to Winnie only, i.e. (11b) is entailed. It is clearly possible for one interpretation to be false while the other is true. Similarly in (12), it is possible that while many people voted for the person who happens to be Sophie's father, Sophie is the only one among them who, by doing so, voted for her own father. In this case the pragmatic interpretation of the anaphora is false, while the bound variable interpretation is true.

In other cases the two interpretations yield different (pragmatic) presuppositions for the sentence (13):

(13)   Even Linda is fed up with her husband.
(14) a. Most people are fed up with Linda's husband.
     b. Most women are fed up with their husbands. (For most women x, x is fed up with x's husband.)

Sentence (13) presupposes either (14a) or (14b), and it is possible for the sentence to be true if any one of these is true while the other is false.

The presupposition in (14a) is derived from the pragmatic interpretation of the anaphora in (13), and (14b) is derived from its bound variable interpretation.

In most cases, however, the disambiguation of the two interpretations is possible only in context. Although the distinctions involved here are subtle, it seems that the two contexts given for (15) in (16) each force a different interpretation of the anaphora in (15). (The example is based on an observation made by Evans, 1980. See fn. 3.)

(15) Charlie is convinced he is a genius.

(16) a. I know what Charlie and Linda have in common: Charlie is convinced he is a genius and Linda is convinced she is a genius too.

b. I know what Charlie and Linda have in common: Charlie is convinced he is a genius and Linda is convinced he is a genius too.

In (16a) the property argued to be common to Charlie and Linda is that of considering oneself a genius, which is based on the bound variable interpretation of anaphora. In (16b) the common property is that of considering Charlie a genius, i.e. the pragmatic interpretation of anaphora.

Such examples show that the ambiguity of definite NP anaphora is independent of discourse deletion. Although this ambiguity may not be noted in isolation, once the appropriate context is supplied it becomes clear. However, the discourse deletion context is the clearest case where the ambiguity always surfaces. Therefore, it is convenient to use such contexts as tests for whether a given anaphora case has the bound variable interpretation or not.

3.2 The Structural Conditions

While definite NP anaphora is ambiguous, in principle, between the bound variable and the pragmatic interpretations, it is not the case that whenever intended coreference is possible bound variable interpretation is also possible. Our next step will be to observe that the latter is possible precisely under the same structural conditions assumed for bound variable anaphora with quantified antecedents, examined in Section 2.

The studies of sloppy identity concentrated only on one type of discourse context — that of VP 'deletion' as in (8). This results in allowing bound variable interpretation only in cases where the antecedent is the subject (see Sag 1976, Williams 1977). To see the full range of this interpretation we need to look at other types of discourse 'deletion', as in (17) and (18). These constructions may be labelled 'bare-argument deletion' since the second conjunct contains only the argument. Such constructions usually allow several construals of the deleted part, and the one intended here is indicated in brackets.

(17) a. We asked Linda$_i$ to read her$_i$ paper and Lucie too (i.e. and we asked Lucie . . . too).
   b. Christopher brought Winnie$_i$ a nice jar of honey on his$_i$ birthday and Rabbit too (i.e. and he brought Rabbit . . . too).
   c. You could probably find Charlie$_i$ in his$_i$ room right now, but not Snoopy (i.e. but you could not find Snoopy . . .).
   d. In his$_i$ spaceship Solo$_i$ found a suspicious object and Skywalker (did) too.

In all the sentences of (17) the bound variable interpretation ('sloppy identity') is possible, e.g. the second conjunct in (17a) can mean that we asked Lucie to read Lucie's paper and in (17b) that Christopher brought Rabbit honey on Rabbit's birthday. It will be recalled that this interpretation requires an open formula or predicate in the first conjunct (e.g. Christopher's buying x honey on x's birthday), which is later satisfied by the argument in the second conjunct. In all cases, the antecedent in the first conjunct c-commands the pronoun, just as it does in the VP-deletion cases like (8) where the antecedent is the subject. So the conditions for bound variable anaphora are met.

Now let us consider some cases where the bound variable interpretation is not possible.

(18) a. Her$_i$ dog talks to Lucie$_i$, when he is in a good mood, and to Linda too.
   b. The rebellion against Java the Hut$_i$ bothered him$_i$ and the rebellion against the other tyrant (did) too.
   c. People from the southern planet$_i$ deserted it$_i$, and people from the western planet (did) too.
   d. According to Charlie$_i$, he$_i$ is the smartest creature on earth, and according to Snoopy too.

In all these cases anaphora is permitted in the first conjunct. However, placing them in the discourse-deletion context shows clearly that the anaphora relation here is only of the pragmatic type. No bound-anaphora is involved, since the second conjunct cannot have the bound (sloppy identity) interpretation. The second conjunct does not have the meaning that Linda's dog talks to Linda in (18a). Likewise, (18b) does not entail that the other tyrant was bothered by the rebellion against him and (18d) does not mean that according to Snoopy, Snoopy is smart. These are precisely the structures of the 'weak crossover' we have been discussing in (6) and (7), where the antecedent does not c-command the pronoun. We saw there that although pragmatic coreference is permitted with definite NP, when the antecedent is quantified bound anaphora is not possible.

Returning to the cases like (10)—(13) which show the ambiguity independently of context, we may observe that here, too, this ambiguity will not show up when the antecedent does not c-command the pronoun.

(19) a. Only a few relatives of Max$_i$ voted for him$_i$.
 b. Only the most devoted groupies of Charlie$_i$ think he$_i$ is a genius.
 c. Even the jokes about Nora$_i$ do not discourage her$_i$.
(20) Only his$_i$ father voted for Max$_i$./His$_i$ father voted only for Max$_i$.

The anaphora in these sentences is only pragmatic. In (19a) the only question at issue is who voted for Max. It does not have the interpretation which attributes the voting of some relatives of x for x to Max only. Similarly, (19b) cannot entail that for no person x, except for Charlie, the groupies of x think that x is a genius, and (19c) does not presuppose that for most people jokes about them do not discourage them. In (20), too, there is clearly no anaphora ambiguity (the interpretation that Max is the only person whose father voted for him is unavailable), though this may also be related to independent issues of the scope of *only*.

I will leave it to the reader to verify that bound anaphora with definite NP's is possible under the same syntactic conditions permitting quantified NP anaphora, namely when the antecedent c-commands the pronoun. A larger body of examples and relevant structures, as well as a survey of some crucial residual problems, are given in Reinhart (1983b).

We may conclude that, with respect to bound anaphora, there is no difference between quantified and definite antecedents — both can bind a pronoun (in the sense of binding a variable) and in precisely the same syntactic environments. The difference between them is only that definite NP's allow pragmatic coreference in addition. This, however, follows from the fact that pragmatic coreference involves a direct assignment of reference to a pronoun. If there is a definite NP around, its reference can be assigned to a given pronoun even if it is not bound by that NP. Since quantified NP's do not have a reference they cannot 'lend' a reference to an unbound pronoun. What this means, then, is that, contrary to the common assumption, the general or 'basic' anaphora interpretation shared by all types of NP's is the bound variable interpretation, and the grammar must specify, first, the conditions for this type of interpretation. The exceptional case which is affected by semantic properties of the antecedent, is the case of pragmatic coreference and not, as previously believed, bound variable anaphora.

4. BOUND ANAPHORA AND THE BINDING CONDITIONS

It would be interesting to note now that the conceptual shift in the picture of anaphora proposed in the previous section does not require any changes in the binding conditions assumed in GB, but only a change in their interpretation. The binding system of Chomsky (1981) is given in (21)–(22).

(21)   *Definition of binding*:
        α is bound by β if and only if α and β are coindexed and β c-commands α (the binding will be A or $\bar{\text{A}}$ type, depending on the position of β)

(22)   *Binding conditions*:
        (A) An anaphor is bound in its governing category
        (B) A pronominal is free in its governing category
        (C) An R-expression is free

A crucial property of this system is that it distinguishes two types of coindexing: 'bound' and 'unbound'. A 'free' node is not necessarily uncoindexed; it may be coindexed with an NP not c-commanding it. Consequently, the system distinguishes, syntactically, between the same classes we observed before:

(23)   *The pronoun is 'bound'.*
    a. Christopher$_i$ likes his$_i$ bear.
    b. Winnie$_i$ is convinced he$_i$ is a genius.
    c. We asked Linda$_i$ to read her$_i$ paper.
    d. We gave Winnie$_i$ some honey on his$_i$ birthday.
    e. Near him$_i$ Winnie$_i$ always keeps honey.
(24)   *The pronoun is coindexed but not bound.*
    a. His$_i$ bear is devoted to Christopher$_i$.
    b. The devoted groupies of Charlie$_i$ think he$_i$ is a genius.
    c. Lucie used to say behind Snoopie$_i$'s back that he$_i$ was unbearable.
    d. The rebellion against Java the Hut$_i$ destroyed him$_i$.
    e. According to Winnie$_i$ he$_i$ is a genius.
(25)   *The antecedent (R-expression) is bound: non-coreference.*
    a. *He$_i$ is devoted to Christopher's$_i$ bear.
    b. *Lucie tells him$_i$ that Charlie$_i$ is a genius.
    c. *We asked her$_i$ to read Linda's$_i$ paper.
    d. *Near Winnie$_i$ he$_i$ always keeps some honey.

In (25) the R-expressions (the antecedents) are coindexed with c-commanding pronouns; hence they are bound and the derivations are filtered out as ungrammatical by condition C of (22). Condition C together with the definition of binding in (21), captures, thus, the restriction on definite NP anaphora proposed in Reinhart (1976). The coindexing in both (23) and (24), on the other hand, is permitted by the binding conditions since in none of these cases is the antecedent coindexed with a c-commanding node; i.e. it is free, though coindexed. The crucial difference between (23) and (24), however, is the status of the pronoun: in (23) the pronoun is coindexed with a c-commanding node and hence it is bound. In (24) the node the pronoun is coindexed with does not c-command it. Hence, the pronoun is not bound (i.e. it is 'free') although it is coindexed. The two classes obtained are precisely those we distinguished in the previous section. It will be recalled that the sentences in (23) allow the bound variable interpretation, while (24) allows only pragmatic coreference. (See the discussion of (17) and (18) above.)

Since in the questions of the interpretation of anaphora, the GB framework still follows the traditional assumptions described in Section

1, this syntactic distinction which is obtained between (23) and (24) is superfluous. It follows from the independently needed definition of binding (21) and it is not reflected in the semantic interpretation of the two classes of anaphora. As we saw in Section 2, if the antecedent is definite, all coindexed pronouns are interpreted, for the present, in the same way, i.e. as cases of intended coreference. If the antecedent is quantified, its interpretation (as a bound variable) is governed, at LF, by a different mechanism.

However, the question at issue here concerns only the interpretation of the coindexing system and it is not inherent to the system itself. At the present, the interpretation of the coindexing is determined by the type of the coindexed elements: empty R-expressions (*Wh*-traces) are interpreted as variables bound by the operator which Ā-binds them (syntactically); lexical anaphors (reflexives and reciprocals) are also interpreted as bound variables, regardless of their antecedent. Pronouns are interpreted referentially along the lines of intended coreference with the antecedent they are coindexed with, etc. (see, e.g. Chomsky 1982, section 5). Thus, each type of coindexed element requires its own interpretive mechanism. However, once we discovered that pronouns can be interpreted as bound variables if and only if they are bound (syntactically), the interpretive component of the binding system can be generalized and simplified: the syntactic binding has a unique semantic interpretation as bound-variable anaphora.

Given the way the binding system is organized, the only elements that may end up bound are those lacking lexical content (empty nodes, pronouns, and lexical anaphors), all of which can, in principle, be interpreted as bound variables. (Although NP traces are not at present interpreted this way, there is no principled reason against such interpretation.) The various 'bindable' elements differ in their syntactic distribution, i.e. in the conditions under which they can be bound, and the binding system as stated guarantees their correct syntactic binding (in interaction with other components of the GB theory). Anaphors (including NP traces), for example, must be A-bound in their governing category; pronouns may be optionally A-bound, but only outside their governing category; non-anaphor empty nodes (*Wh*-traces) must be locally Ā-bound and A-free; PRO must be ungoverned. The syntactic distinctions between the lexically empty elements which are assumed by the binding theory are, therefore, needed to guarantee their correct distribution. However, there is no need to expect that these syntactic distinctions should correspond to different interpretations.

The syntactic properties of lexically empty elements determine only when they can, or must, be bound. Once they are syntactically bound, they are uniquely interpreted as variables bound either by the operator corresponding to their antecedent at LF or by the operator binding their antecedent.[4]

Recall that the binding conditions, as stated, allow unbound coindexing also, either with pronouns, as in (24), or with two R-expressions (e.g. *Those who know Charlie$_i$ adore Charlie$_i$*). Since the conditions for bound variable interpretation are not met, this type of coindexing receives the pragmatic (referential) interpretation only: the coindexed elements are intended to have the same reference.[5]

A further advantage of the interpretive system proposed here is that it also solves, automatically, the problem of quantified NP anaphora (the weak crossover problem) we observed in Section 2. Quantified NP anaphora is possible precisely when the binding system allows bound anaphora. Although the binding conditions also allow coindexing a pronoun with a non c-commanding quantified NP, such coindexings can be interpreted, as we just saw, only as intended coreference. Since such interpretation is inapplicable in the case of quantified antecedents, the coindexing in this case will be uninterpretable (in the same way that the accidental coindexing in, e.g., *Those who know every senator$_i$ like every president$_i$*, is uninterpretable though permitted by the system). No special LF mechanism such as the 'bijection principle' is needed, therefore, for these cases.

This analysis, however is not precisely equivalent to the results of the bijection principle. They differ in cases of *Wh* movement; illustrated in (25′)

(25′) a. Which paper$_1$ did you file e$_1$ without reading e$_1$?
  b. *[Whose$_1$ mother]$_2$ did the rumor about her$_2$ worry e$_2$ (though she$_2$ denied it)?

Here the *Wh* antecedent binds both anaphoric elements at SS, so the analysis proposed allows their translation as bound variables, while the bijection principle filters both out as ungrammatical, since one operator locally binds, at LF more than one argument. With respect to (25′a), the surface structure analysis seems to be correct, since parasitic gaps are increasingly viewed as grammatical, contrary to the predictions of the bijection principle. However, it fails to prevent anaphora in (25′b). Although space prevents elaborating on this, I believe that (25′b) is filtered out by other principles of the binding theory, and it hinges on the typology of anaphoric elements in the language — namely on which elements can serve as comp-bound anaphors. Pronouns, in English, cannot be COMP-bound (though they can be Ā bound). In languages with genuine resumptive pronouns in wh-questions, sentences like (25′b) were found to be acceptable (see examples in Engdahl, 1983).

We may conclude that the binding theory, under the interpretation proposed here, captures a substantial generalization about anaphora. The basic, or central, sentence-level type of anaphora is bound variable anaphora. All types of NP's may serve as antecedents here and all types of lexically empty elements (including pronouns) as anaphors. This interpretation is possible only when the anaphoric element is syntactically bound, i.e. c-commanded by the antecedent. We may now call this type *bound anaphora*, with no fear of confusion, since the anaphoric element is bound both in the syntactic sense of Chomsky defined in (21) and in the semantic sense of being interpreted as a bound variable.

We may note further that the generalization captured by the bound anaphora condition has a potential correlation in processing accounts. In Reinhart (1976 and 1983a, chapter 10) I argue that c-command domains correspond largely to the assumption of constituents, rather than clauses as the processing units to which closure applies. While in the case of intended coreference, showing this correlation (as attempted in Reinhart, 1976) is not completely straightforward, the bound anaphora conditions are precisely what we would expect if the constituent is the processing unit; since it results in placing the material which needs to be retained for binding an anaphor in a surface position which is still available when this anaphor is reached. On these issues, see also Berwick and Wexler, to appear.

As we saw, along with bound anaphora, the theory as stated also captures the other type of anaphora: pragmatic or intended coreference, which is an interpretation given to coindexing regardless of whether the expression is bound or not. This, however, is the exceptional case in the binding system. Of all anaphoric elements, pronominals are the only ones (in English) that can be used referentially (as, e.g. in *Lucie likes him*). Consequently, they can enter intended coreference relations with other referential expressions (i.e. expressions with a fixed value in some domain), just as two referential expressions may be used coreferentially. This special property of referential expressions has been incorporated into the binding theory because, as is well known, pragmatic coreference is not free: it is usually impossible when the pronoun (or a referential expression) c-commands another referential expression, as in (25). Historically, it was this problem of specifying when coreference was impossible which motivated the studies of anaphora (or, originally, of 'pronominalization') and, eventually, led to the introduction of c-command restrictions. It seemed reasonable, therefore, to include in the binding theory condition C of (22), which has the sole function of filtering out inappropriate pragmatic coreference. (All other problems originally believed to require this condition were found to be reducible to independent principles of the theory; see, e.g. Chomsky, 1982.)

In Reinhart (1983a, 1983b) I argue that, in fact, conditions like C, and, more generally, the problem of intended coreference, do not belong to the grammar at all. Rather, they follow pragmatically from the conditions on bound anaphora, with largely equivalent results. The arguments and the proposed analysis are summarized in the appendix.

If this is so, it would turn out that much of the anaphora studies have been concentrating on the 'shadows' of things rather than on the things themselves, i.e. on the pragmatic options available for speakers because of the existence of the bound anaphora mechanism in the grammar, rather than on bound anaphora.

However, whether intended coreference stays in the grammar or not is not crucial for my subsequent discussion. Either way, we saw that this is the exceptional case and the 'core' issue of sentence-level anaphora is bound anaphora.

5. EMPIRICAL ISSUES

The empirical study of anaphora has largely followed the theoretical studies in concentrating on definite NP anaphora or pragmatic coreference. I believe this direction has not proven too fruitful. Whether this problem is part of the grammar or not, it is well known that this type of coreference is dramatically affected by all types of discourse considerations (only one of which is linear order) and it would always be difficult to distinguish pragmatic and syntactic factors in interpreting the results of empirical studies here.

Let us see this first with an example of a study of adult anaphora.

Carden and Dietrich (1981) subjected sentences like (26) to an empirical investigation.

(26) a. *He* will have to report to the new Vice President, whether *McIntosh* likes it or not.
   b. We will have to put *him* under the new Vice President, whether *McIntosh* likes it or not.
   c. Whether *he* likes it or not, they would have to put *McIntosh* under the new Vice President.

The precede and command restrictions allows the italicized NP's to corefer only in (26c), while the c-command restriction (condition C of the previous section) allows coreference in both (26b, c) but not (26a). (The pragmatic strategy for intended coreference proposed in the appendix will, also, not rule out coreference in (26b).) The study was based both on counts of backward anaphora in actual texts and on laboratory experiments. The results show unequivocally, in my mind, that the coreference in both (26a) and (26b) has the same marginal status we are used to associate with ungrammatical sentences, while (26c) is both frequent in texts and scores high on coreference judgements in the experiments. It would seem, then, that the precede and command restriction is winning.

It would, however, be appropriate (as Carden and Dietrich acknowledge) to check whether there are no independent discourse conditions that could explain this result. Here, of course, we are entering a delicate area, since the discourse analyses proposed for backward anaphora are usually vague and speculative, rather than empirical. One proposal which was clearly proved wrong is Kuno's (1972) requirement that the antecedent in backward anaphora would be a topic of the previous discourse. The only existing empirical study of backward anaphora — that of Carden (1982) — clearly shows that the previous context is not what determines the distribution of backward anaphora in discourse. However, various other conditions for the use and function of backward anaphora in discourse have been proposed and it would be interesting to note that sentences like (26a, b) lie in their intersection, i.e. the competing conditions all happen to rule them out as inappropriate, pragmatically, regardless of their context.

The various proposed conditions can be divided into two types. (This division is proposed in Biller-Lappin, 1983.) The one (proposed in different wordings by Bickerton 1975, McCray 1980, and Mittwoch

1983) specifies the environment of the pronoun, requiring that it be in the pragmatically subordinate or 'non-dominant' part of the sentence. The other which I believe is implicit in Bolinger (1979), focuses on the function of the antecedent, stating that backward anaphora is possible only if the antecedent is in sentence-topic position. This approach, which I find more promising, is clearly distinct from Kuno's (1972) condition, if we assume the analysis of sentence topics proposed in Reinhart (1981b): topics are defined on expressions and not on denotations; the crucial defining property is that of pragmatic aboutness, rather than 'old information', i.e. topics are not defined by their links to the previous context but by their effect on the ongoing discourse, or the context set. Topics need not, therefore, represent old information and they are identified in each given context by an interaction of pragmatic, semantic, and syntactic considerations — including the syntactic position of the expression in surface structure. (I propose, there, a relatively explicit selection function for this procedure.)[6]

In view of the delicacy of basing an argument on discourse constraints, I would like to point out some clear cases indicating that such constraints exist.

(27) a. When he entered the room Max greeted Bill.
     b. When *she* entered the room Max greeted *Kora*.
(28) a. When he entered the room Bill was greeted by Max.
     b. When *she* entered the room *Kora* was greeted by Max.
     c. #When *she* entered the room Max was greeted by *Kora*.

In a simple, active sentence both subject and object may function as sentence topics, depending on the discourse. However, as is well known, in passive sentences the topic position is fixed and only the subject can serve as topic. Therefore such sentences can be used to test the topic-antecedent hypothesis, even without a context. We see that in (27a) *he* could refer to either Max or Bill; there is also no problem with the coreference in (27b). In (28), by contrast, the pronoun can corefer only with the subject: (28a) is not ambiguous (under coreference) and coreference in (28c) is inappropriate. The intuitions here seem substantial and possibly, if subjected to empirical experiments, the 'inappropriate' coreference in (28) (e.g. interpreting *he* as Max) will not score higher than coreference in (26a, b), though all syntactic restrictions on anaphora equally allow it.

Returning to (26a, b), both discourse conditions predict that it would

be extremely difficult to find a context in which coreference should be
appropriate here. In normal contexts the matrix clause will be conceived
of as pragmatically dominant (in the sense of Erteschik-Shir, and
Lappin 1979), so the pronoun is not pragmatically subordinate.
Although this preference can be overridden by other factors (see
examples in Mittwoch 1983 and McCray 1980), these elaborate factors
are not present in the experimental sentences. Similarly, the position of
McIntosh in these sentences is unlikely to be a topic position. (Except
for some special cases, the matrix positions have much higher preference for serving as topic than subordinate positions.) So the topic-
antecedent requirement is also not met here. On the other hand, both
conditions will select (26c) as a perfect environment for backward
anaphora: the pronoun is in the pragmatically subordinate clause and
the antecedent is in a matrix position suitable for topics.

If this is so, then, the empirical study of (26) cannot teach us anything
about the grammar. While obviously it does not support the c-command
restriction, it also does not count as a counterexample. A conclusion
that can be drawn safely from this experiment is that attempting to
evaluate the binding theory empirically, by looking at pragmatic coreference, will always be fraught with difficulties as there are too many
discourse factors that need to be considered.

First Language Acquisition Studies

We may turn now to studies of language acquisition. Although partial
support has been found for the c-command restriction on pragmatic
coreference (in, e.g. Solan 1983, Lust and Clifford 1982 and this
volume), it seems to me that, overall, the findings concerning this type of
anaphora are not too conclusive.

The crucial problem here is the directionality factor found in all
studies of the acquisition of pragmatic coreference. Of course, there is
nothing puzzling about this factor if it is atributed to pragmatic or
processing reasons; namely that forward anaphora is the easiest form of
anaphora to process while backward anaphora requires holding the
pronoun in memory and going back to it. In this case, my previous
remarks still hold, i.e. the syntax of pragmatic coreference is extremely
difficult to investigate empirically; but there is no conceptual problem
with the existence of such factors.

However, several studies point out that this directionality effect is not universal, e.g. Lust, 1983, Lust, Chien and Mangione (1984a, b), Lust and Clifford (1982 and this volume) argue that it is not found in left branching languages. This means, then, that directionality effects cannot be attributed strictly to pragmatics. These studies conclude that directionality effects in the language are determined by the 'principal branching direction' (PBD) principle, and that the child forms his first hypotheses about anaphora according to the branching direction of his language. The problem, however, is that the PBD principle itself is not related at all to the binding conditions, if pragmatic coreference is at issue. Despite the fact that English is right branching, the structures where backward anaphora is permitted by the grammar, i.e. where a preceding NP (pronoun) does not c-command a following NP, are standard and very common. (For example, every possessive subject allows, in principle, for a backward anaphora sentence.) So this picture of the grammar could not yield the directionality effect of English. If the PBD principle is correct, this means that the child makes no use at all, at the relevant stage, of the binding principles, but rather operates by an altogether independent parameter.

We should note now that the grammar yields completely different results with respect to bound anaphora. If, as we saw, bound anaphora is permitted only when the antecedent c-commands the anaphor, radical differences are predicted between right and left branching languages, since a c-commanding NP will precede the others in the first and follow them in the second. In English, for example, bound anaphora is only possible 'forwards' with the exception of only one type of structure — that involving preposed constituents (where the subject still c-commands elements to its left.) In other words, the branching direction of the language is largely irrelevant if we are considering the linear order of nodes that do not c-command each other, but it is crucially relevant if we are considering the linear order of a c-commanding node with the nodes it c-commands. If we are concentrating on bound anaphora only, no special parameter is needed — the difference in directionality effects follows directly from the binding principles.

It is significant to note here that, in fact, Lust, Chien and Mangione's (1984a, b) study of Chinese did not find that backward anaphora is uniformally easier for Chinese children than forward anaphora, but only that this is so in the case of bound anaphora. They studied two types of constructions, one with pragmatic coreference and one with bound anaphora (Wh-traces), both containing empty anaphors. (In Chinese, an empty element can function also as a pragmatic pronoun.) While the bound anaphora showed clear backward preference, no such preference was found in the case of pragmatic coreference.

It would seem, then, that there are two factors involved here, as should be expected: the one is the grammar (the binding theory) and the other is pragmatics. It is possible that the child already has, at the relevant stage, some knowledge of the major issues of the binding theory, i.e. the rules for bound anaphora, so when bound anaphora is involved there are fewer mistakes and less 'directionality' effects: the Chinese child correctly interprets it 'backwards' and the English child 'forwards'. However, when pragmatic coreference is at issue, the pragmatic factor of linear order plays a crucial role, regardless of the branching direction of the language; it might take longer for the child to learn the pragmatic subtleties of the use of backward anaphora.

I believe, therefore, that the question at issue should be that of the acquisition of bound anaphora, rather than of pragmatic coreference. Several studies of bound anaphora acquisition with empty anaphors already exist (e.g. Goodluck, 1978; Lust, et al., 1981 and this volume; Roeper, 1983 and this volume). I hope that the discussion in Section 3 may add another area to such inquiries, namely that of the study of bound anaphora with pronouns. Quantified antecedents would not be too convenient to test bound anaphora with, in view of the difficulties involved here even in adult grammar. However, the 'sloppy identity' phenomena might possibly exist quite early, or at least, this could be checked. In English, such study will have the further advantage of neutralizing the pragmatic directionality effect, since it may be confined to c-command distinctions in sentences involving forward anaphora only, as in most of the examples discussed in Section 3.

APPENDIX: A PRAGMATIC ANALYSIS OF INTENDED COREFERENCE

This appendix summarizes the arguments given in Reinhart (1983a, 1983b) for why the problem of intended coreference (or condition C of the binding theory) need not belong to the grammar.

As a starting point we may note that non-coreference arises precisely in the same syntactic environments that bound anaphora is possible in: when a given NP c-commands the other, then, if the c-commanded NP is an anaphoric element, it can be bound by the first, and if it is not,

condition C prevents its coindexing, i.e. prevents a coreference interpretation. On the other hand, if neither NP c-commands the other,
bound anaphora is impossible regardless of whether any of these NP's is
a pronoun. In such environments, pragmatic coreference is possible with
no restrictions. This complementary distribution of bound anaphora and
non-coreference follows, by definition, from the binding conditions, but
for an illustration, the examples in (30)–(34) below can be consulted.

There is no reason, however, why this complementary distribution
should be captured by the grammar, since it follows from Gricean
requirements on rational use of the language for communication. The
relevant maxim here is 'manner': be as explicit as the conditions permit.
In a rational discourse we would expect that if a speaker has the means
to express a certain idea clearly and directly he would not choose,
arbitrarily, a less clear way to express it. When syntactically permitted,
bound anaphora is the most explicit way available in the language to
express coreference, as it involves direct dependency of the pronoun
upon its antecedent for interpretation. So, if this option is avoided we
may conclude that the speaker did not intend coreference. An approximation of the pragmatic strategy governing decisions about intended
coreference is stated in (29).

> (29) a. *Speaker's strategy*: When a syntactic structure you are using
>   allows bound-anaphora interpretation, then use it if you
>   intend your expressions to corefer, unless you have some
>   reasons to avoid bound-anaphora.
>   b. *Hearer's strategy*: If the speaker avoids the bound anaphora
>   options provided by the structure he is using, then, unless he
>   has reasons to avoid bound-anaphora, he didn't intend his
>   expressions to corefer.'

The way this strategy works is illustrated in (30)–(34). Coindexing is
used here for bound anaphora; italics indicate intended coreference, and
the symbol '#' indicates pragmatic inappropriateness.

> (30) a. Winnie$_i$ ate his$_i$ honey.
>   b. # *He* ate *Winnie*'s honey.
>   c. # *Winnie* ate *Winnie*'s honey.
> (31) a. The doctor told Tigger$_i$ that he$_i$ was sick.
>   b. # The doctor told *him* that *Tigger* was sick.

(32) a. Tigger$_i$ pities himself$_i$.
    b.# *Tigger* pities *Tigger*.
(33) a. A party without *Winnie* is inconceivable for *him*.
    b. A party without *him* is inconceivable for *Winnie*.
    c. A party without *Winnie* is inconceivable for *Winnie*.
(34) a. Those who know *Snoopy* adore *him*.
    b. Those who know *him* adore *Snoopy*.

In the structures of (30)–(32), the (a) sentences allow bound anaphora, since one NP c-commands the other and the second is a pronoun or anaphor. In the (b) sentences the same structures are used but the bound anaphora option is avoided by choosing a different placement of the NP's. In this case the hearer will infer that the reason for avoiding this option is that the speaker did not intend coreference. In the structures of (33)–(34), on the other hand, the grammar does not allow for bound anaphora, regardless of the possible placements of pronouns and antecedents, since neither of the relevant NP's c-commands the other. In this case, then, the hearer can infer nothing about the referential intentions of the speaker from the structure and placement of the NP's, and whether the NP's are intended as coreferential or not can be determined on the basis of discourse information alone. Pragmatic coreference, then, is an available option, regardless of placement of full NP's and pronouns.

The pragmatic strategy (29), then, can do the work of principle C, so this principle need not be incorporated in the grammar. This would mean that the only interpretable coindexing in the grammar would be in the cases of bound anaphora, as described in Section 4. If we continue to assume a free indexing system, as assumed by the binding theory, the NP's of the (b) sentences in (30)–(32) may still end up accidentally coindexed, as well as the NP's in (33)–(34). However, this coindexing will have no interpretation: as we saw in Section 4 the interpretation of syntactic binding translates a bound anaphoric element (an empty node, a pronoun, or an anaphor) into a variable bound by the c-commanding NP. If a full NP ends up syntactically bound it cannot be interpreted, since it cannot be translated as a bound variable. Similarly, the unbound coindexing which can be obtained accidentally in (33)–(34) will have no interpretation, since the translation procedure applies only to bound elements. Thus, we eliminate from the grammar the pragmatic inter-pretation of coindexing: intended coreference is not controlled by coindexing but, rather, two free NP's can be pragmatically coreferential, subject to the strategy (29).

Note that this means also that intended coreference in (35) is not, in fact, blocked by the grammar.

(35)   Winnie adores him.

Condition B of the binding theory, (22), prohibits only the coindexing of *him* and *Winnie* which, if permitted, would result in bound anaphora incorrectly. However, as we just saw, free NP's allow pragmatic coreference, subject to (23). So here, too, it would not be the grammar that blocks coreference, but the strategy (29): since bound anaphora interpretation is available for this structure if a reflexive pronoun is used, avoiding it indicates a non-coreference intention. I believe this is a correct result. (For more discussion, see Reinhart, 1983b.)

So far, we saw that a pragmatic analysis of coreference along the lines of (29) is equivalent to the syntactic analysis in yielding the same results. Next, we should look at some advantages of the first over the second.

A crucial difference between the syntactic and the pragmatic analysis of intended coreference is that the latter predicts that the cases violating principle C should be possible if there are good pragmatic reasons to avoid bound anaphora while still intending coreference. As we saw in Section 3, such cases may not be easy to find, since the two interpretations are normally equivalent. However, in (13)—(16) we observed environments where the two interpretations can easily be distinguished. Precisely in these environments, serious counterexamples for the syntactic analysis have been pointed out by Evans (1980).

(36) a.   I know what Ann and Bill have in common. She thinks that Bill is terrific and *he* thinks that *Bill* is terrific. (Adopted from Evans, 1980 (49))
    b.   Everyone has finally realized that Oscar is incompetent. Even *he* has finally realized that *Oscar* is incompetent. (Evans, 1980 (52))
    c.   Only Winnie thinks Winnie is smart.
    d.   Only Churchill remembers Churchill giving the speech about blood, sweat, toil, and tears. (Fodor, 1975 p. 134)

Although the structures used in these examples allow bound anaphora, it is not the interpretation which is intended; e.g. in (36a) it is the property of finding Bill terrific which is taken to be shared by Ann and

Bill, while it is possible that x's finding x terrific is true of Bill but not of Ann. When *only* is involved, the pragmatic and the bound interpretations differ in truth conditions; therefore no special context is needed to justify the avoiding of bound anaphora in (36c) and (36d).[7] The strategy (29) has, then, a principled way to acount for uses like (36): pragmatic coreference is permitted since the speaker has a reason to avoid bound anaphora.

Further support for a pragmatic approach (in general) comes from largely discussed problems of handling coreference by a coindexing mechanism. (Lasnik 1976, Chomsky 1981, section 5.1)

(37)   Charlie told Lucy that they were invited to a party.

The plural pronoun in (37) cannot be coindexed with any of the singular antecedents; still, intended coreference is possible. Recall that in the present theory, intended coreference intrasententially can be obtained only via coindexing, and a lack of coindexing indicates that the NP's are not intended as coreferential. In a pragmatic approach, there is no coindexing, to begin with, and the interpretation of (37) involves establishing a set of referents (Charlie and Lucy) and choosing the same set for the pronouns.

Another problem that can be resolved if non-coreference is pragmatically determined is that, in general, violations of condition C which involve two full NP's are much easier to process than violations involving a pronoun and a full NP. (Lasnik's (1976) observation about the similarity between the two cases, which was incorporated into the non-coreference rules has been often challenged (see Evans, 1980; Bach and Partee, 1980). The strategy (29) also does not explicitly distinguish these two cases. However, since what is involved here is the ease of identifying coreference when the bound-anaphora option needs to be avoided, it is generally the case that the reference of a full NP is more easily recoverable than the reference of a pronoun. So, independently of (29), it should be easier to identify intended coreference of two identical full NP's than of a pair of a pronoun and a full NP which do not allow bound-anaphora interpretation.

Finally, if non-coreference is determined pragmatically, we may expect that many discourse considerations not captured by (29) may also interfere. In fact, several studies point out less systematic empirical counterexamples to condition C (e.g. McCray, 1980; Gueron, 1979).

Such counterexamples will still violate (29), but since this is a pragmatic strategy, there is more room to attempt an explanation for them.

A possible objection that might be raised against the pragmatic approach is that the intuitions in the core cases of non-coreference, such as (31) or (35), are as substantial as intuitions about ungrammaticality in the standard cases, so they should be considered ungrammatical. However, such arguments should be taken with due caution. However clear our intuitions are here, what we cannot have intuitions about is whether our judgement of such sentences is due to our grammar or to our pragmatic strategies. On such issues, only the theory can decide. To take a familiar example, our intuitions tell us that the sentences in (38) are problematic.

(38) a. The dog that the man that the woman invited liked disappeared.
  b. *Here is the dog that the man who owns t disappeared.

They may be judged as ill-formed or unprocessable. However, our intuitions could not tell us that in (38a) the difficulty is due to processing problems, while in (38b) it is because the sentence violates a condition on movement, i.e. that (38a) is grammatical while (38b) is not. We are used to viewing (30b) and (35) as ungrammatical; possibly, if twenty years ago the questions of anaphora had been stated differently, our feelings concerning their theoretical status would have been quite different.

NOTES

[1] This type of interpretation is needed to deal with certain problems in the syntactic analysis of coreference (and primarily of non-coreference), which were pointed out by Evans (1980). Some of the difficulties were already acknowledged in Lasnik (1976).

[2] Higginbotham's (1980b) conditions restrict the coindexing of pronouns with empty nodes: at LF, after QR has applied, the antecedent position of a quantified NP is filled with an empty trace, just like the trace left by *wh*-movement. In fact, Higginbotham states the structural condition on this coindexing in terms of linear order, rather than c-command. However, in a later paper (1980a) he arrives at a formulation similar to that based on c-command. Chomsky (1982) derives the same results from the so-called *bijection principle* which requires that at LF each operator binds one and only one argument. *Binding* is used here in its syntactic definition, i.e. coindexing with a c-commanded NP. In (5b), e.g. (Who$_i$ t_i brought his$_i$ teddy bear to the party?), it can be argued that the operator corresponding to *who* binds, syntactically, t_i, while the

coindexed his_j is bound by t_i, and not directly by *who*. In (6b), on the other hand (*Who$_i$ did his$_j$ teddy bear accompany t_i to the party?), the trace t_i does not syntactically bind the coindexed pronoun given the definition of syntactic binding above. Hence, the coindexing here would mean that both t_i and his_j are bound by *who*, in violation of the bijection principle, and the derivation will be filtered out.

[3] The examples used here are based on the same contexts argued in Evans (1980) to allow violation of the noncoreference requirement. This is not an accident, and these cases are discussed again in the appendix.

[4] A formal statement of the interpretive rule for the translation of bound pronouns is proposed in Reinhart (1983a), (1983b) using λ abstraction, although alternative formulations are, of course possible. Given the current picture of LF, if the antecedent is quantified (or a *Wh*-constituent) no special mechanism is needed for the translation of the pronoun, since the antecedent is, anyway, translated as an operator. In all other cases, however, an operator must be created for the purpose of binding the pronouns.

[5] Recall that in environments where a pronoun can be syntactically bound, pragmatic coreference is still possible, i.e. the sentence is ambiguous. Since, in the current system, pragmatic coreference interpretation requires that the pronoun be coindexed, we will still need a special convention for the interpretation of syntactically bound pronouns, stating that they can be interpreted either as bound-variables or as coreferential, pragmatically. This problem will be eliminated if, as I argue in the appendix, pragmatic coreference is not governed by coindexing at all.

[6] If this is the correct approach, I believe that the function of backward anaphora in actual discourse might be, contrary to common assumptions, that of introducing a new topic into the discourse. Again, this need not be new information elements, but an element that did not serve as topic in the immediately preceding discourse, even if it was mentioned. Of course, in the absence of an empirical text-study, this speculation is just as good or bad as any other. Some observations which support this hypothesis are found in Biller-Lappin's (1983) informal examination of literary texts.

[7] Higginbotham (1980b and in a work in preparation) argues that the coreference in (36c) could be explained also on syntactic grounds: the NP in the *only* phrase does not c-command the other.

REFERENCES

Bach, E. and B. Partee: 1980, 'Anaphora and semantic structure', in J. Kreiman and A. Ojeda (eds.), *Papers from the Parasession on Pronouns and Anaphora*, Chicago Linguistic Society, Chicago, pp. 1—29.

Berwick, R. and K. Wexler: to appear, 'Parsing efficiency, binding, c-command and learnability', in B. Lust (ed.), *Studies in the Acquisition of Anaphora, Volume 2, Applying the Constraints*, D. Reidel, Dordrecht, Holland.

Bickerton, D.: 1975, 'Some assertions abut presuppositions about pronominalization', in R. E. Grossman, L. J. San, and T. Vance (eds.), *Papers from the Parasession on Functionalism*, Chicago Linguistic Society, Chicago, pp. 24—35.

Biller-Lappin, Y.: 1983, 'Backward anaphora in discourse', unpublished master's thesis, Tel Aviv University.

Bolinger, D.: 1979, 'Pronouns in discourse', in T. Givon (ed.), *Discourse and Syntax, Syntax and Semantics* **12**, Academic Press, New York.

Carden, G.; 1982, 'Backwards anaphora in discourse context', *Journal of Linguistics* **18**, 361–387.

Carden, G. and T. Dietrich: 1981, 'Introspection, observation and experiment: An example where experiment pays off', in P. D. Asquith and R. N. Giere (eds.), *Proceedings of the 1980 Biennial Meeting of the Philosophy of Science Association* **2**, East Lansing, Mich., pp. 583–597.

Chomsky, N.: 1980a, 'On binding', *Linguistic Inquiry* **11**, 1–46.

Chomsky, N.: 1981b, *Lectures on Government and Binding*, Foris, Dordrecht.

Chomsky, N.: 1982b, *Some Concepts and Consequences of the Theory of Government and Binding*, MIT Press, Cambridge, Mass.

Engdahl, E.: 1983, 'Parasite gaps, subject extraction, and the ECP', *Working Papers in Scandanavian syntax* **6**, University of Trondheim, Norway.

Erteschik-Shir, N. and S. Lappin: 1979, 'Dominance and the functional explanation of island phenomena', *Theoretical Linguistics* **6**, 43–87.

Evans, G.P: 1980, 'Pronouns', *Linguistic Inquiry* **11**, 337–362.

Fodor, J. A.: 1975, *The Language of Thought*, Harvard University Press, Cambridge, Mass.

Goodluck, H.: 1978, *Linguistic Principles in Children's Grammar of Complement Subject Interpretation*, unpublished doctoral dissertation, University of Massachusetts.

Gueron, J.: 1979, 'Rélations de coréférence dans le phrase et dans le discours', *Langage Française* **44**, 42–79.

Higginbotham, J.: 1980a, 'Anaphora and GB: Some preliminary remarks', in J. Jensen (ed.), *Proceedings of the Tenth Annual Meeting of the North Eastern Linguistic Society* **9**, 223–236, Ottawa, Canada.

Higginbotham, J.: 1980b, 'Pronouns and bound variables', *Linguistic Inquiry* **11**, 679–708.

Keenan, E.: 1971, 'Names, quantifiers and a solution to the sloppy identity problem', *Papers in Linguistics* **4**, 211–232.

Koopman, H. and D. Sportiche: 1982, 'Variables and the bijection principle', *The Linguistic Review* **2**, 139–160.

Kuno, S.: 1972a, 'Functional sentence perspective: A case study from Japanese and English', *Linguistic Inquiry* **3**, (3), 269–320.

Lasnik, H.: 1976, 'Remarks on coreference', *Linguistic Analysis* **2**, 1–22.

Lasnik, H.: 1981, 'On two recent treatments of disjoint reference', *Journal of Linguistic Research* **1**, 48–58.

Lust, B.: 1983, 'On the notion "principal branching direction", a parameter of universal grammar', in Y. Otsu, H. Van Riemsdijk, K. Inoue, A. Kamio, and N. Kawsaki (eds.), *Studies in Generative Grammar and Language Acquisition*, International Christian University, Tokyo, pp. 137–151 (originally presented at Workshop on Linguistic Theory and First Language Acquisition, Thirteenth International Congress of Linguists, Tokyo).

Lust, B., Y-C. Chien, and L. Mangione: 1984a, 'First language acquisition of Mandarin Chinese: Constraints on free and bound null anaphora', in S. Hattori and K. Inoue (eds.), *Proceedings of the Thirteenth International Congress of Linguists*, Gakushuin, Tokyo, pp. 1127—1130.

Lust, B., L. Mangione, and Y.-C. Chien: 1984b, 'Determination of empty categories in first language acquisition of Mandarin Chinese', *Working papers in Linguistics* **6**, Cornell University, Ithaca, N.Y.

Lust, B. and T. Clifford: 1982, 'The 3D study: Effects of depth, distance and directionality on children's acquisition of anaphora', in J. Pustejovsky and P. Sells (eds.), *Proceedings of the Twelfth Annual Meeting of the North Eastern Linguistic Society*, MIT, Cambridge, Mass., pp. 174—186 (also this volume).

Lust, B., L. Solan, S. Flynn, C. Cross and E. Schuetz: 1981, 'A comparison of null and pronominal anaphora in first language acquisition', in V. Burke and J. Pustejovsky (eds.), *Proceedings of the Eleventh Annual Meeting of the North Eastern Linguistic Society*, University of Massachusetts, Amherst, pp. 205—218 (also this volume).

McCray, A.: 1980, 'The semantics of backward anaphora', in J. Jensen (ed.), *Proceedings of the Tenth Annual Meeting of the North Eastern Linguistic Society*, University of Ottawa, Ottawa, pp. 329—344.

Mittwoch, A.: 1983, 'Backward anaphora and discourse structure', *Journal of Pragmatics* **7**, 129—39.

Partee, B. H.: 1978, 'Bound variables and other anaphors', in D. Waltz (ed.), *Proceedings of TINLAP* **2**, University of Illinois, Urbana.

Reinhart, T.: 1976, *The Syntactic Domain of Anaphora*, unpublished doctoral dissertation, MIT, Cambridge, Massachusetts.

Reinhart, T.: 1981a, 'Definite NP anaphora and c-command domains', *Linguistic Inquiry* **12**, 605—636.

Reinhart, T.: 1981b, 'Pragmatics and linguistics: An analysis of sentence topics', *Philosophica* **27**, 59—94.

Reinhart, T.: 1983a, *Anaphora and Semantic Interpretation*, Croom Helm, London.

Reinhart, T.: 1983b, 'Coreference and bound anaphora: A restatement of the anaphora questions', *Linguistics and Philosophy* **6**, 47—88.

Roeper, T.: 1983, 'How children acquire bound variables', in Y. Otsu, H. van Riemsdijk, et al. (eds.), *Studies in Generative Grammar and Language Acquisition*, International Christian University, Tokyo, pp. 129—135 (also this volume).

Ross, J.: 1969, 'Guess who?', in R. Binnick et al. (eds.), *Papers from the Fifth Regional Meeting*, Chicago Linguistic Society, Chicago.

Sag, I.: 1976, *Deletion and Logical Form*, unpublished doctoral dissertation, MIT, Cambridge, Mass.

Solan, L.: 1981, 'The acquisition of structural restrictions on anaphora', in S. Tavakolian (ed.), *Language Acquisition and Linguistic Theory*, MIT Press, Cambridge, Mass., pp. 59—73.

Solan, L.: 1983, *Pronominal Reference: Child Language and the Theory of Grammar*, D. Reidel, Dordrecht.

Wasow, T.: 1972, *Anaphoric Relations in English*, unpublished doctoral dissertation, MIT.

Williams, E.: 1977a, 'Discourse and logical form', *Linguistic Inquiry* **8**, 101—139.

ROBERT FREIDIN

FUNDAMENTAL ISSUES IN THE THEORY
OF BINDING*

Within the current framework of the Extended Standard Theory of
generative grammar, the Government-Binding theory (henceforth GB)
of Chomsky 1981, two lexical NPs are interpreted as having the same
intended reference if they bear the same index. Under an optimally
simple formulation, coindexing is achieved by a rule "index NP". Thus
there is no special rule of coindexing or any special prohibition against
coindexing by the basic indexing rule (see Freidin and Lasnik 1981 for
discussion). This rule generates representations of sentences where
lexical NPs are interpreted as coreferential as in (1—3).

(1)   How many people that John$_i$ knows does John$_i$ really like?
(2)   Mary$_i$ knows that she$_i$ is clever.
(3)   They$_i$ often annoy each other$_i$.

It is possible to generate different grammatical sentences by eliminating
the coindexing in (1) and (2), but the elimination of coindexing in (3)
yields an illformed representation. The expression *each other* in (3) is a
lexical bound anaphor which has no intrinsic reference of its own and
must get its reference from some NP antecedent in the sentence in
which it occurs. The pronoun *she* in (2) also has no intrinsic reference;
but unlike the bound anaphor, a pronoun can get its reference outside
the context of the sentence in which it occurs. The proper name *John* in
(1) presumably has an intrinsic reference — in which case coindexing in
(1) does not fix the reference of the second occurrence of *John*, but
rather establishes that both names designate the same individual. In
what follows, bound anaphors and pronouns will be referred to as
anaphoric elements and the NP with which each is coindexed in a
sentence will be designated its *antecedent*.
    The rule of indexing as formulated generates representations of
anaphoric relations which do not occur — e.g. (4—6).

(4)   *Mary$_i$ knows that Mary$_i$ is clever.
(5)   *John$_i$ likes him$_i$.
(6)   *They$_i$ think that each other$_i$ are crazy.

B. Lust (ed.), *Studies in the Acquisition of Anaphora, Vol. I*, 151—188.
© 1986 *by D. Reidel Publishing Company.*

The examples in (1–6) show that coindexed NPs have a restricted distribution independent of their linear order (since this order is identical for each anaphoric element/antecedent pair). Moreover, the distribution of coindexed NPs differs according to NP-type. Coindexed names do not occur in the same contexts as coindexed pronouns (compare (4) and (2)), and coindexed pronouns do not occur in the same contexts as bound anaphors (compare (5) and (3)).

Within GB the limited distribution of coindexed NPs is accounted for by three general principles – one for each NP-type mentioned above. These principles, commonly referred to as Principles A, B, and C, are given schematically in (7).

(7)   A: an anaphor must be bound in domain D.
         B: a pronominal must be free in domain D'.
         C: a name must be free.[1]

These principles constitute a theory of binding. They are interpreted as conditions on syntactic representations at some particular level or levels in a derivation, rather than as conditions on the application of the indexing rule (i.e. on the indexing derivation itself). Under this interpretation the principles in (7) define wellformedness of binding representations.[2]

An explication of the binding theory as instantiated in Principles A–C must address the following fundamental issues concerning the formulation and application of these principles.

(8)   i.   What is the proper definition of 'bound' for Principle A?
      ii.   Is the relation 'free' for Principles B and C defined as 'not bound'?
      iii. How is domain D characterized for Principle A?
      iv.   Is domain D' of Principle B identical to the domain D of Principle A; and if not, how is it different?
      v.   To what extent does the binding theory account for the distribution and typology of empty categories?
      vi.   At what level(s) of representation do the various binding principles hold?

The following discussion is meant to be illustrative rather than definitive. It is an attempt to elucidate current work on the binding theory from the perspective of the fundamental issues raised.

The remainder of this paper is organized as follows. Questions (i) and

(ii) which deal with the structural relation between anaphoric elements and their antecedents are discussed in section 1 in terms of a single hierarchical relation, *c-command.* Section 2 covers the analysis of domain D of Principle A. The proper characterization of domain D' of Principle B as differentiated from domain D of Principle A is the focus of section 3. Section 4 deals with the application of binding theory to empty categories and the related issue of the typology of empty categories. Section 5 contains a preliminary discussion of question (vi). The determination of what levels of representation the various binding principles apply to turns out to be a complicated matter. The final section provides a brief summary of the major points in the preceding sections.

1. ON THE HIERARCHICAL RELATION BETWEEN ANAPHORIC ELEMENTS AND THEIR ANTECEDENTS

In GB the relation 'bound' is defined in terms of the structural relation 'c-command'. An NP is bound if it is coindexed with a c-commanding NP, where c-command is defined as in (9).

(9)   A node α c-commands a node β if neither node dominates the other and the first branching node which dominates α also dominates β (cf. Reinhart 1976, 1981).[3]

This relation holds between the coindexed NPs in (2—6), but crucially not in (1). By definition, the two instances of the name *John* are not bound; hence they are free even though they are coindexed. This definition of 'free' as 'not bound' also holds with respect to Principle C in the following structures, where c-command domains of the coindexed names are indicated by brackets.

(10) a. [John's$_i$ mother] thinks that [John$_i$ is unhappy]
     b. [Mary's$_i$ brother] admires [Mary's$_i$ boyfriend]
     c. Bill returned [Sam's$_i$ bicycle] to [Sam's$_i$ house]

For Principle C, the definition of 'free' as 'not bound' appears to be sufficient.

For Principle A, the definition of 'bound' based on c-command holds for the basic cases. However there are certain constructions in which an anaphor occurs in a position which is not c-commanded by its antecedent.

(11) a. pictures of himself$_i$ [embarrass John$_i$]
  b. John$_i$ is embarrassed by pictures of himself$_i$

In contrast to (11b), the anaphor in (11a) is not c-commanded by its antecedent.

There are several reasons for not modifying the definition of 'bound' (or alternatively 'c-command') to accommodate (11a) under Principle A. The definition of 'bound' as it stands correctly predicts that if the anaphor in (11a) is replaced by a name, then coindexing is allowed since neither coindexed NP c-commands the other.

(12)   [pictures of John$_i$] [embarrass John$_i$]

If the definition of 'bound' is changed for anaphors, then either (12) should be illformed on a par with (4) — which is false, or we must abandon the common thread between Principles A–C, the structural relation of c-command. Secondly, if object NP can bind NPs in embedded subjects, then there is no way to rule out binding of subjects as in (13) without ad hoc complications of the structural definitions involved.

(13)   *Each other$_i$ annoyed the men$_i$

While it could be argued that (13) is ruled out by Principle C since *the men* is not free, an analysis where an object NP may bind a subject NP would predict incorrectly that (14) is also illformed by Principle C.[4]

(14)   The men$_i$ annoyed each other$_i$

Next, while the so-called 'picture NP reflexive' cases (e.g. (11)) are acceptable, an anaphor in the subject position of an NP whose antecedent is the object of the matrix verb seems significantly less acceptable.

(15)   *Each other's$_i$ pictures annoyed the women$_i$

Therefore it is reasonable to consider cases like (11a) as outside the range of core phenomena.

Additional evidence for this conclusion comes from the fact that 'picture NP reflexives', unlike other reflexives, can have split antecedents as in (16a) — in contrast to (16b).

(16) a. i. John talked to Mary about pictures of themselves.
      ii. John gave Mary pictures of themselves.
    b. *John talked to Mary about themselves.

Note further that this property is limited to reflexives and therefore should not be considered as a general property of lexical bound anaphors, as illustrated in (17).

(17) a. *John talked to Mary about pictures of each other.
    b. *John gave Mary pictures of each other.

(See Bouchard 1982 and Lebeaux to appear for further discussion).

Another construction in which an anaphor does not occur in a c-command relation with its antecedent is given in (18).

(18)   John talked to Mary$_i$ about herself$_i$

If the anaphor is replaced with a coindexed copy of the name *Mary*, the result is illformed (excluding emphatic stress on the second instance of the name).

(19)   *John talked to Mary$_i$ about Mary$_i$

According to the simplest version of the binding theory, the object of *to* should c-command the object of *about*. This is also necessary if Principle B is to account for the illformedness of (20).

(20)   *John talked to Mary$_i$ about her$_i$

In short, the binding theory makes the correct predictions for all NP-types in this construction if the object of *to* c-commands the object of *about*.

This c-command analysis could be realized in at least two ways. If the verb *talked* and the preposition *to* are reanalyzed as a V, as in (21), then c-command will hold between the relevant NPs in the appropriate manner.[5]

(21) $[_{VP}[_V[_V talked]$ to$]$ NP $[_{PP}$ about NP$]]$

Alternatively, *to* might be analyzed as a case-marker adjoined to NP (cf. *of* in nominals like *the destruction of the city*) rather than a prepositional head which projects its own phrasal category distinct from NP and thereby blocks c-command between the two NPs. Clearly some special analysis of (18—20) is required in order to maintain the generalization captured by the binding theory as it applies to these constructions.[6]

For the remainder of the discussion the c-command formulation of 'bound' will be assumed as the core notion.

2. DOMAIN D OF PRINCIPLE A

As illustrated in (6), the condition that an anaphor must be c-commanded by its antecedent is not sufficient to determine the distribution
of anaphors. Therefore the basic c-command requirement must be sup-
plemented with a domain statement which specifies the subdomain(s) of
a sentence in which an anaphor cannot be free (even when it is bound in
the sentence). We say that this subdomain is *opaque* to binding with
respect to an antecedent outside the subdomain. Ungrammaticality due
to binding across an opaque domain will be referred to as an *opacity
effect.*

The following paradigms give the basic cases to be accounted for.

(22) simple sentences
  a. anaphor in subject position:
    i. *Each other$_i$ left.
  b. anaphor in object position:
    i.   We$_i$ admire each other$_i$
    ii. *John$_i$ admires each other$_i$

(23) complex sentences
  a. anaphor in subject position:
    i. *We$_i$ expect [(that) each other$_i$ will win]
    ii. We$_i$ expect [each other$_i$ to win]
  b. anaphor in object position:
    i. *We$_i$ expect [(that) Mary will admire each other$_i$]
    ii. *We$_i$ expect [Mary to admire each other$_i$]

The paradigm shows that an anaphor must be bound in the minimal
finite S containing it. This accounts for the illformed examples in (22)
as well as in (23.a.i) and (23.b.i), but does not account for (23.b.ii)
where the anaphor is bound in the minimal finite S containing it (= the
matrix S). Therefore it is necessary to specify a second opaque domain
for anaphors — namely the domain a subject. This is independently
motivated for binding into NP, as will be discussed below.

The specification of two domains for Principle A (i.e. the domains
of subject and finite S) creates an apparent problem with respect to
overlap. Both domains pick out (22.b.ii) and (23.b.i). This overlap is
problematic if, as in previous work (cf. Chomsky 1973, 1976), the two
domains are taken as defining two distinct conditions on the distribution
of anaphors (e.g. the Tensed S Condition (TSC) and the Specified
Subject Condition (SSC)) *and* violations of more than one condition are

assumed to increase ungrammaticality. This second assumption is not borne out for the anaphora paradigms above since (22.b.ii) and (23.b.i) are not significantly more ungrammatical than other illformed examples in the paradigm. Nonetheless, the overlapping specifications have been considered a defect in the formulation of conditions on the distribution of anaphors (see Chomsky 1977, 1980, and 1981).

Two solutions for this problem have been proposed. Chomsky 1980 sought to characterize two non-overlapping conditions, the SSC plus the Nominative Island Condition (NIC), where the domain of tense is dropped in favor of a prohibition against anaphors bearing nominative case. The NIC proposal has the empirical advantage of accounting for the grammaticality of (24), in contrast to the TSC and its variants (e.g. the Propositional Island Condition (PIC) of Chomsky 1977).

(24) We$_i$ expected [that [$\left\{ \begin{array}{l} \text{each other's}_i \text{ pictures} \\ \text{pictures of each other}_i \end{array} \right\}$] would appear

in the newspaper]]

In (24) the anaphors are free in the domain of tense (in the embedded S) but are not in the nominative case. Another advantage of the NIC is that it accounts for opacity effects in infinitival complements in Portuguese (see Rouveret 1980) and Turkish (see George and Kornfilt 1981) where infinitival subjects may be marked for agreement with the complement verb. Such subjects are marked in the nominative case. As predicted by the NIC, anaphor subjects are prohibited in these constructions.[7]

Nonetheless, there are several problems with the NIC proposal. While examples like (24) are acceptable in English, they tend to be illformed in other languages. In Dutch, for example, comparable examples with reflexives are ungrammatical (see Lasnik and Freidin 1981 for further discussion). Secondly, the NIC does not account for opacity effects in Turkish gerunds where the subject is marked genitive when the subject agrees with the verbal form, and genitive anaphor subjects are prohibited as illustrated in (25).[8]

(25) *yazar-lar$_i$ [birbir-lerin$_i$-in   viski-yi
      author-PL   each other-their-GEN   whisky-ACC

      iç-tik-lerin]-i   san-iyor-lar
      drink-GER-3PL-ACC   believe-PRES-3PL

      'The authors believe that each other drank the whisky'.

This example suggests that it is not simply a prohibition against anaphors with certain morphological properties which accounts for opacity in these examples, but rather that opacity is determined in terms of syntactic domains. The NIC does not define a syntactic domain, and therefore is not an island condition in the usual sense. For example, although the bracketed NP in (24) is marked nominative, it is not an opaque domain for binding. Icelandic presents yet another empirical problem for the NIC analysis. In Icelandic, finite indicative clauses are opaque to binding, whereas infinitival clauses are not − even when binding occurs across a subject as in (26).[9]

$$
\begin{array}{lllll}
(26) & \text{hann}_i & \text{telur} & [\text{mig}_j & \text{hafa} & \text{se} & \text{sig}_i] \\
& \text{he} & \text{believes} & \text{me} & \text{to have} & \text{seen} & \text{himself}
\end{array}
$$

Icelandic does not appear to observe the SSC. If it does not, then the opacity effects for non-subjects in finite clauses cannot be due to the SSC (see Harbert 1982b for further discussion). For Icelandic the notion 'opaque domain' for binding must be defined in terms of some characterization of 'finite clause'.

If we reject the NIC, then the opacity effects for subjects of infinitivals in Portuguese and Turkish should also fall under our characterization of 'finite clause'. (Note that this characterization does not use the term 'finite' in its time reference sense.) Since the agreement element (henceforth AGR) occurs in all the relevant examples under discussion, 'finite clause' can be characterized as the domain of AGR − assuming that AGR is a grammatical formative in INFL (= inflection) which is an immediate constituent of S and hence c-commands both VP and the syntactic subject in S. This analysis accounts for (25), which is not covered by the NIC.

Because for English the SSC is needed independently of a finite clause condition on binding (see (23.b.ii), the problem of overlapping domains arises again since the domains of subject and AGR overlap for non-subject NPs. A second solution to this problem is to give a single specification for domain D of Principle A so that the domains of subject and AGR follow from this specification. Initially this was accomplished in the GB framework by attempting to integrate the binding theory with notions of case as follows. Considering the core cases (22−23), we note that an anaphor must be bound in the minimal S-domain in which it receives case.[10] Under this unitary characterization (23.a.i) and (23.b) are illformed because the anaphors in them are assigned case in the embedded S-domain and are free in that domain. In contrast, the anaphor in (23.a.ii) is assigned case by the matrix verb and is bound in the matrix S, which is the minimal S-domain in which the anaphor receives case.

In GB theory this analysis is formalized in terms of the notion of government, since case is assigned to NPs under government by a case-assigning element (e.g. V or P). Thus domain D of Principle A is designated as the *governing category* of the anaphor, where governing category is defined as the minimal S or NP containing the anaphor and a governor of the anaphor. In S, the governors will be V, A, P, and AGR in INFL − in effect, the heads of maximal phrasal projections in $\overline{S}$ (see Freidin 1983) with the additional stipulation that INFL qualifies only with it contains AGR.[11]

While this characterization accounts for the S-paradigm as given in (22−23), it does not generalize to the paradigm for binding in NP given in (27−28).

(27) simple sentences
    a. subject position:
        i. They$_i$ read [$_{NP}$each other's$_i$ books]
    b. object position:
        i. They$_i$ read [$_{NP}$books about each other$_i$]
        ii. *They$_i$ read [$_{NP}$John's books about each other$_i$]
        iii. John read [$_{NP}$their$_i$ books about each other$_i$]

(28) complex sentences
    a. subject position:
        i. They$_i$ expect [$_{\overline{S}}$that [$_S$[$_{NP}$each other's$_i$ books] will be favorably reviewed]]
        ii. They$_i$ expect [$_S$[$_{NP}$each other's$_i$ books] to be favorably reviewed]
        iii. *They$_i$ expect [$_{\overline{S}}$that [$_S$John will favorably review [$_{NP}$each other's$_i$ books]]]
        iv. *They$_i$ expect [$_S$John to favorably review [$_{NP}$each other's$_i$ books]]
    b. object position:
        i. They$_i$ expect [$_{\overline{S}}$that [$_S$[$_{NP}$books about each other$_i$] will be well received]]
        ii. They$_i$ expect [$_S$[$_{NP}$books about each other$_i$] to be well received]

iii. *They$_i$ expect [$_{\overline{s}}$that [$_s$[$_{NP}$John's books about each other$_i$] will be well received]]

iv. *They$_i$ expect [$_s$[$_{NP}$John's books about each other$_i$] to be well received]

v. *They$_i$ expect [$_{\overline{s}}$that [$_s$John will read[$_{NP}$books about each other$_i$]]]

vi. *They$_i$ expect [$_s$John to read [$_{NP}$books about each other$_i$]]

The paradigm illustrates that the subject position in NP is always transparent to binding by a c-commanding NP ((27.a) and (28.a.i—ii)) unless a c-commanding subject intervenes ((27.b.ii) and (28.a.iii—iv)). Thus the paradigm for NP diverges from that of S in two ways: 1) the subject of NP is always transparent, in contrast to the subject of S, which is transparent only when AGR is absent; and 2) the object position in NP is transparent when there is no subject ([NP, NP]), whereas the object position is almost always opaque to binding from outside S (but cf. (40) below). The theory in which domain D of Principle A is specified as the governing category of the anaphor (as defined above) can only account for opacity effects on binding across subjects of NP. The transparency of NP with respect to binding cannot be accounted for by a mechanism similar to $\overline{S}$-deletion (as in the S-paradigm — see footnote 11) since there is no exceptional case marking into NP to motivate such a proposal.

For NP, the relevant factor which determines its transparency for binding is the presence or absence of a syntactic subject. The SSC is the only relevant opacity condition for NP. Even a c-commanding AGR does not induce opacity in NP, as illustrated in (28.a.i) and (28.b.i). With respect to binding then, there is a basic asymmetry between S and NP. Therefore the governing category analysis of the S-paradigm, which collapses the SSC and the relevant variant of the TSC under a single specification of opaque domain, does not generalize to NP.[12]

Given that the SSC must be included in the domain statement for Principle A, we once again confront the problem of potential overlap with the other part of the domain statement which accounts for opacity of subjects in the S-paradigm. As discussed above, Turkish and Portuguese suggest that AGR rather than tense is the relevant factor for opacity. Since AGR is always linked to a syntactic subject, there is some motivation for considering the agreement element as a kind of (shadow) subject. Using this observation, we can unite AGR with syntactic subjects (i.e. [NP, S] and [NP, NP]) under the designation 'SUBJECT' (read "capital subject") — see Chomsky 1981:209ff. Under this analysis the domain statement for Principle A reduces to 'domain of SUBJECT'.[13]

This formulation of Principle A accounts for both the S- and NP-paradigms, with the exceptions of (28.a.i) and (28.b.i). In these latter cases the anaphor is free in the domain of a SUBJÉCT (= AGR of the sentential complement). This analysis is corrected by modifying the definition of opaque domain so that an AGR element does not function as a SUBJECT for anaphors contained in an NP which is coindexed with it. Note that in the cases where AGR functions as a SUBJECT with respect to an anaphor (i.e. the NIC cases), the anaphor is coindexed with the AGR element. Coindexing of the anaphor in (28.a.i) with AGR in the embedded S gives the representation (29).

(29) They expect [$_\bar{S}$that [$_S$[$_{NP_i}$each other's$_i$ books] AGR$_i$ will be favorably reviewed]]

This yields an indexed representation of the sentential complement subject where the referential index of the NP is also carried by a subpart of the NP itself. The interpretation of the coindexing in (29) would be that *each other* is coreferential with the NP *each other's books* — which is of course incorrect. As proposed in Chomsky 1981, this indexing can be excluded by a general prohibition against NPs of the form (30), where *i* is a referential index.

(30) *[$_{NP_i}$ ... NP$_i$ ...]

(30) is empirically motivated by the impossibility of coindexing a pronoun contained in a NP with the NP itself, as in (31).[14]

(31) *[$_{NP_i}$ the owner of his$_i$ boat] goes sailing on weekends.

If indexing applies freely as assumed, then some constraint is needed to rule out (31), since it does not fall under Principle B. (See Chomsky 1981:212f. for further discussion).

Following Chomsky 1981, (30) can be incorporated into the formulation of the domain statement for Principle A by modifying the specification 'SUBJECT'. Since AGR in (28.a.i) and (28.b.i) should not count as a SUBJECT for anaphor binding, it can be considered 'inaccessible' to the anaphors by virtue of (30). Thus the domain statement of Principle A is further modified to (32).

(32)   Principle A: an anaphor must be bound in the domain of an
               accessible SUBJECT.

Accessibility is defined in terms of (30) and "in the domain of" requires
that the SUBJECT c-command the anaphor.[15]
    The grammaticality of (28.a.i) and (28.b.i) constitutes evidence for
this formulation of Principle A with respect to AGR. A similar argument holds for the lexical subjects of infinitival equatives.[16]

(33)   Mary believes those to be pictures of herself.

(33) has the indexed representation (34).

(34)   Mary$_i$ believes [$_S$ those$_j$ to be [$_{NP_j}$ pictures of herself$_i$]]

The infinitival subject must be coindexed with the complement of
equative *be* and hence is not an accessible SUBJECT for the anaphor,
given (30).
    There is a certain naturalness in formulating the domain statement of
Principle A in terms of accessible SUBJECT. Since anaphors must get
their reference from an antecedent in the sentence in which they occur,
it is appropriate to formulate the domain in which they must be bound
in terms of a potential antecedent (i.e. syntactic subject or the agreement
element which entails the existence of a subject). The notion 'subject' is
crucial here because the simpler structural notion of c-commanding NP
is not sufficient. Thus in (35) *John* c-commands *each other* but does not
block proper binding of the anaphor by the subject *we*.[17]

(35)   We$_i$ told John lies about each other$_i$

Why "subject" rather than "c-commanding NP" is relevant for binding
remains to be explained. As noted by Wayne Harbert, this question is
related to the question of why in many languages (e.g. Romance and
Germanic (excepting English and Icelandic), and Japanese) the only
possible antecedents for anaphors are subjects.
    As formulated in (32), Principle A still does not cover all the core
cases. Consider (36) for example.

(36)   *[$_{NP_i}$ pictures of himself] AGR$_i$ are always on display.

AGR cannot be considered an accessible SUBJECT for the anaphor
himself because coindexing of the anaphor with AGR would yield a
violation of (30). Thus the anaphor does not occur in the domain of an

accessible subject; and therefore (36) is not excluded by Principle A as formulated above. In Chomsky 1981 this problem is resolved by stipulating that an anaphor must be bound in root S. This stipulation is in addition to the domain statement in (32), and in essence constitutes a default condition with respect to (32).

The default condition is unnecessary if we assume that, by definition, an anaphor must be bound to an antecedent (see Freidin 1978:fn.7). Under this assumption, Principle A is a condition on *proper binding*, where it is given that the anaphor is in fact antecedent-bound. We then reformulate (32) as (37):

(37)   Principle A: an anaphor cannot be free in the domain of an accessible SUBJECT.

(37) defines the notion 'opaque domain' for anaphor binding. Where an anaphor occurs unbound in a sentence (e.g. (22.a.i), (22.b.ii), and (36)), the sentence is illformed because it does not satisfy the basic requirement for anaphors — that they be bound to some antecedent. The requirement is needed independently of (36) to exclude (22.a.i). In the latter example, the anaphor is bound to an accessible SUBJECT — i.e. AGR. The example is illformed nonetheless because AGR is not a possible antecedent since it has no intrinsic reference. This suggests that 'bound' should be interpreted as 'antecedent-bound' rather than 'coindexed with a c-commanding element'.

So far we have been assuming that the definition of SUBJECT covers all syntactic subjects. This holds for 'referential' lexical subjects and their empty category counterparts (i.e. trace), and in addition PRO.

(38) a. NP trace:
         *John$_i$ seems to us$_j$ [$_S$ e_i to like each other$_j$]
     b. WH trace:
         *Which boy$_i$ do they$_j$ believe [$_S$ e_i to like each other$_j$]
     c. PRO:
         *We$_i$ persuaded John$_j$ [$_{\overline{S}}$ PRO$_j$ to like each other$_i$]

In (38a–b) the anaphor is free in the domain of a trace subject and in (38c) it is free in the domain of a PRO subject. In comparison with referential NP, however, nonreferential (or pleonastic) *it* does not appear to have a strong opacity inducing effect, as discussed in Freidin and Harbert 1983. For example, (39b) is relatively wellformed in comparison to (39a), which is ungrammatical.

(39) a. *They$_i$ expect [$_S$ John$_j$ to seem to each other$_i$ [$_S$ e_j to be crazy]]
   b. They$_i$ expect [$_S$ it to seem to each other$_i$ [$_S$ that John is crazy]]

As illustrated in (40), wellformedness in these constructions is not significantly affected by the addition of AGR to the complement of *expect*.

(40) a. *They$_i$ expected [$_S$ that John$_j$ AGR would seem to each other$_i$ [$_S$ e_j to be crazy]]
   b. They$_i$ expected [$_S$ that it AGR would seem to each other$_i$ [$_S$ that John is crazy]]

(40b) is on a par with (39b) — i.e., it is relatively wellformed in comparison with the ungrammatical (40a).

Given this statement of the facts,[18] a distinction between 'referential' and 'nonreferential' subjects is necessary for the formulation of Principle A. Such a distinction can be given in terms of thematic relations (or θ-roles). Referential subjects bear θ-roles and thus constitute θ-subjects, in contrast to non-θ-subjects like nonreferential *it*. Only θ-subjects qualify as accessible subjects. This account can be extended to the NIC effect if the θ-status of the syntactic subject is somehow transferred to AGR.[19] Thus where AGR is linked to a θ-subject, the INFL projection (= S, etc.) constitutes the domain of a θ-SUBJECT. Where S contains a syntactic θ-subject and no AGR, the domain of the θ-SUBJECT is the c-command domain of the syntactic subject. This analysis has a certain naturalness in that non-θ-subjects are not possible antecedents for anaphors since they are inherently nonreferential. (For further details see Freidin and Harbert 1983).

To summarize, lexical anaphors are subject to two conditions:

(41) a. an anaphor must be bound to an antecedent
   b. a bound anaphor may not be free in the domain of an accessible θ-SUBJECT.

(41a) is part of the definition of 'anaphor'; whereas (41b) constitutes a condition on proper binding which we call Principle A of the binding theory.

3. DOMAIN D' OF PRINCIPLE B

As formulated in (7) above, Principle B requires that a pronoun be antecedent-free in a domain D'. The interpretation of 'free' here is not, strictly speaking, the converse of the interpretation of 'bound' as required for anaphors. Binding for anaphors entails coreference; whereas freedom for pronouns entails the stronger requirement of *disjoint reference* — see Lasnik 1976 and Higginbotham 1980a:fn.1).[20] In the following discussion the examples cited do not distinguish between disjoint reference and noncoreference.

The S-paradigm for bound pronouns shows a systematic correspondence with the analogous paradigm for anaphors.

(42)   simple sentences
  a. *John$_i$ admires him$_i$
(43)   complex sentences
  a. pronoun in subject position:
    i. John$_i$ expects [$_\bar{S}$ that he$_i$ will win]
    ii. *John$_i$ expects [$_S$ him$_i$ to win]
  b. pronoun in object position:
    i. John$_i$ expects [$_\bar{S}$ that Mary will admire him$_i$]
    ii. John$_i$ expects [$_S$ Mary to admire him$_i$]

The correspondence between (42—43) and the analogous paradigm for anaphors (22—23) is that bound pronouns cannot occur in positions where anaphors are properly bound, and conversely, anaphors cannot be properly bound in positions where bound pronouns may occur. This correspondence motivated earlier analyses (e.g. Chomsky 1981) in which the domain statements of Principles A and B were taken to be identical.

Although this analysis holds as a first approximation, it fails for the larger class of cases. Thus with the NP-paradigm for bound pronouns (44—45) the generalization fails almost in its entirety.

(44)   simple sentences
  a. pronoun in subject position:
    i. John$_i$ read [$_{NP}$ his$_i$ book]
  b. pronoun in object position:[21]
    i. John$_i$ doesn't read [$_{NP}$ books about him$_i$]
    ii. John$_i$ doesn't read [$_{NP}$ Mary's books about him$_i$]
    iii. *Mary doesn't read [$_{NP}$ John's books about him$_i$]

(45)   complex sentences
    a. pronoun in subject position:
      i.   John$_i$ expects [$_{\bar S}$ that [$_S$ [$_{NP}$ his$_i$ book] will be favorably reviewed]]
      ii. John$_i$ expects [$_S$ [$_{NP}$ his$_i$ book] to be favorably reviewed]
    b. pronoun in object position:
      i.   John$_i$ expects [$_{\bar S}$ that [$_S$ [$_{NP}$ books about him$_i$] AGR will be well received]]
      ii. John$_i$ expects [$_S$ [$_{NP}$ books about him$_i$] to be well received]
      iii. John$_i$ expects [$_S$ [$_{NP}$ Mary's book about him$_i$] to be well received]
      iv. John$_i$ expects [$_{\bar S}$ that [$_S$ [$_{NP}$ Mary's book about him$_i$] AGR will be well received]]
      v.   John$_i$ expects [$_{\bar S}$ that [$_S$ Mary AGR will read [$_{NP}$ books about him$_i$]]]
      vi. John$_i$ expects [$_S$ Mary to read [$_{NP}$ books about him$_i$]]

With the exception of (44.b.iii) where a pronoun in NP must be free with respect to the subject of that NP (cf. the corresponding case for anaphors (27.b.iii)), NP does not have the same opacity effects for pronouns as it does for anaphors. NP is an opaque domain with respect to disjoint reference whether or not the NP contains a syntactic subject.[22] This suggests that the notion 'accessible SUBJECT' is therefore not the correct notion for formulating the domain statement of Principle B. Since a pronoun − in contrast to anaphors − does not require that an antecedent be present in S, the notion 'accessible subject' is unmotivated with respect to disjoint reference (see Huang 1983 for further discussion).

Nonetheless, formulating Principle B in terms of accessible SUBJECT does account for the S-paradigm. An alternative formulation must therefore account for the opacity of finite S and the c-command domain of infinitival subject as well as the opacity of NP. The opacity effects for NP with respect to disjoint reference follow without further stipulation if domain D' for Principle B is formulated in terms of 'governing category', defined in the literature as follows.

(46) α is a *governing category* for β where α is the minimal maximal phrasal projection (i.e. of a lexical head) containing β.

Reference to a governor is superfluous since reference to a maximal phrasal projection entails the existence of a lexical head which governs the phrasal constituents of its projection. Unfortunately there are two defects with this simple definition: 1) it fails to account for the S-paradigm; and 2) it incorrectly predicts that AP, PP, and VP will also be opaque with respect to disjoint reference, as indicated in (42) for VP and (47) for AP.[23]

(47)   *John$_i$ is [$_{AP}$ proud of him$_i$]

Huang 1983 proposes that the domain statement of Principle B be formulated in terms of government and the presence of a SUBJECT. Thus Principle B states that "a pronoun must be free in its governing category," where governing category is redefined as in (48) (cf. Huang 1983: (14)).

(48) α is a *governing category* for β iff α is the minimal category containing β, a governor of β, and a SUBJECT.

Huang assumes that the lexical head of NP is a SUBJECT of NP (analogous to AGR which is considered the nominal head of the INFL projection (see Chomsky 1981)). Therefore NP is always a governing category for pronouns since the head N is both governor and SUBJECT with respect to pronominal NP constituents of the NP.

This proposal also encounters problems with the S-paradigm. In (49) VP is the minimal category (= maximal phrasal projection of a lexical head) containing a governor of the pronoun *her* (= V) and a SUBJECT (= *her*).

(49)   *Mary$_i$ [$_{VP}$ believes [$_S$ her$_i$ to be clever]]

Since, as Huang notes, the accessibility of SUBJECT to the pronoun is not conceptually relevant to pronoun binding, VP will fit the definition of governing category for the pronoun. To define the matrix S as the governing category for (49), we could require that the SUBJECT be distinct from the pronoun. This comes dangerously close to reintroducing the notion of accessibility into the definition of governing category for pronouns. For (50) however we must do just that if (48) is to be maintained in some form.

(50)   *Mary$_i$ [$_{VP}$ seems [$_{PP}$ to her$_i$] [$_S$ e_i to be unhappy]]

VP is again the minimal maximal projection containing the pronoun *her*, a governor of the pronoun (= the preposition *to*), and a SUBJECT (=

e_i). Requiring that the SUBJECT c-command the pronoun reinstates the notion of accessibility.

The problem with formulating domain D' for Principle B is to characterize what is common to NP and S — excluding VP and AP — and in addition allow for the transparency of subjects of infinitivals without resorting to the notion of accessible SUBJECT. Only in this way can we avoid having to stipulate NP and S as binding categories for pronouns.

One common feature of S and NP — in addition to allowing syntactic subjects — is that both are domains in which θ-roles are assigned by predicates (i.e. verbs, predicate adjectives, and certain nominals), as illustrated by the sentence/nominal pair in (51).

(51) a.   The mayor criticized the city council.
     b.   The mayor's criticism of the city council

Since V and A may assign a θ-role to an NP outside of their maximal projections (VP and AP) — e.g. to a subject of S, they do not count as "θ-domains".

(52)   A θ-*domain* of α, a predicate (= V, A, or N), is the minimal domain in which α assigns it θ-roles to arguments.[24]

A θ-domain constitutes a *complete functional construct*. Note that this is a type (as opposed to a token) distinction since S functions as a θ-domain even when the sentential subject is a non-θ-position, as in (50).

In order to account for the transparency of infinitival subjects in the S-paradigm for pronouns, it is necessary to incorporate the notions of government and θ-domain in the formulation of the domain statement for Principle B.

(53)   Principle B: a pronoun must be free in the θ-domain of its governor.

In (49), the binding domain for the pronoun *her* will be the θ-domain of *believes* — i.e. the matrix S. In (50), the preposition *to* which governs the pronoun *her* does not assign the pronoun a θ-role independently of the matrix verb *seems*. Therefore the θ-domain of the preposition will be identical to that of the verb — i.e. the matrix S. In the case of AGR, however, it is unnatural to talk about its θ-domain since AGR does not assign a θ-role to the subject it is coindexed with. This problem can be avoided if we mentioned instead the θ-domain of the predicate which is constructed with AGR. Thus the domain statement of Principle B might be more appropriately formulated as "the minimal θ-domain containing a governor of the pronoun."

It is worth noting in conclusion that the notions "θ-domain" and "domain of subject" are conceptually connected in that a subject marks the periphery of a θ-domain.

4. BINDING THEORY AND EMPTY CATEGORIES

In GB it is assumed that the binding theory applies to empty categories as well as to lexical NP-types, and therefore provides a typology of empty categories similar to that of lexical NPs (see Chomsky 1981, 1982). A critical examination of this assumption follows.

To a large extent this view is based on the observation of earlier analyses (e.g. Chomsky 1976) that the opacity effects for lexical anaphors in the S-paradigm extend to NP-trace and PRO.[25] It was assumed that NP-trace and bound PRO could be considered as empty category analogues to lexical anaphors and that their distribution would then follow from the same principles that determined the distribution of lexical anaphors (i.e. the SSC and TSC of the earliest accounts and their descendents).

This analysis is not supported by the opacity effects in the NP-paradigm since neither NP-trace nor PRO may occur as arguments of nominals.

(54) a. *John$_i$ read [$_{NP}$ PRO$_i$ books]
　　 b. *John$_i$ was received [$_{NP}$ e_i book]

(54a) cannot be interpreted as 'John read his own books' and (54b) is not a wellformed variant of *John's book was reviewed*. (54b) is independently excluded by the Case Filter (Chomsky 1980, 1981) since the NP containing the lexical item *book* is not marked for case by the passive predicate *reviewed*. To exclude PRO from a variety of positions (e.g. in (54a)), Chomsky (1981) analyzes PRO as a pronominal anaphor and therefore subject to both Principle A and Principle B. In this analysis the binding domains for both principles are stated in terms of governing category, where specification of a governor is crucial. Thus PRO as a pronominal anaphor must be both bound *and* free in its governing category *if it has one*. The conclusion then is that PRO can only occur in ungoverned positions — i.e. subject of gerunds and infinitivals where $\bar{S}$-deletion does not apply (cf. Aoun and Sportiche 1983).

Given that the binding domains for Principles A and B are distinct with respect to the NP-paradigm as discussed above, it no longer follows as a theorem of the binding theory that PRO must be ungoverned. Specifically, the nonoccurrence of PRO in NP is not explained by the binding theory.[26] Furthermore, given the formulations of Principles A and B above, the binding theory now accounts for the relevant cases of PRO binding, given in (55), as follows.

(55) a. *John$_i$ saw PRO$_i$
     b. *John$_i$ expects [$_{\bar{S}}$ that PRO$_i$ AGR$_i$ will win]
     c. *John$_i$ expects [$_S$ Mary to like PRO$_i$]
     d. John$_i$ expects [$_{\bar{S}}$ PRO$_i$ to like Mary]

(55a) is excluded because PRO-binding violates Principle B (although it satisfies Principle A). (55b) is illformed because PRO is free in the domain of an accessible SUBJECT (= AGR$_i$) and therefore violates Principle A, though it satisfies Principle B. (55c) is illformed for the same reason, where the accessible SUBJECT here is the syntactic subject *Mary*. This analysis of PRO as a pronominal anaphor excludes the illformed cases, but is only partially relevant for the wellformed (55d). With respect to Principle A, the matrix S is the binding domain for PRO. Thus PRO satisfies Principle A in (55d). Since $\bar{S}$ is a barrier to government, PRO is ungoverned in (55d) and therefore neither satisfies nor violates Principle B. If PRO were governed (i.e. if $\bar{S}$-deletion had occurred), then PRO-binding in (55d) would violate Principle B. If a lexical pronoun *him$_i$* were substituted for PRO$_i$ in (55d), then to avoid the Case Filter the lexical pronoun must be marked for case, hence governed and thus in violation of Principle B. For (55d) then it is irrelevant that PRO is analyzed as a pronominal, in contrast to (55a) where it is crucial.

This leaves the problem of the nonoccurrence of PRO in NP. If we take it as an axiom of the theory that PRO cannot occur in a governed position, then the full distribution of PRO (including non-control PRO, which doesn't behave like an anaphor in any event) is accounted for. Of course this eliminates the motivation for analyzing control PRO as a pronominal anaphor. Its distribution would be accounted for by the above-mentioned PRO-axiom and the lexical property of particular verbs which allow (or require) control structure complements (e.g.

persuade (obligatory control) vs. *expect* (optional control) — see Jackendoff 1972).[27]

The distribution of NP-trace patterns exactly like that of lexical anaphors in the S-paradigm — compare (22—23) with (56—57).

(56)   simple sentences
        John$_i$ was awarded [$_{NP_i}e$] \$1,000.

(57)   complex sentences
        a. trace in subject position:
            i. *John$_i$ was expected [$_{\bar{S}}$that [$_S$ [$_{NP_i}e$] AGR$_i$ will win]]
           ii. John$_i$ was expected [$_S$ [$_{NP_i}e$] to win]
        b. trace in object position:
            i. *John$_i$ was expected [$_{\bar{S}}$that [$_S$Mary would admire [$_{NP_i}e$]]]
           ii. *John$_i$ was expected [$_S$Mary to admire [$_{NP_i}e$]]

As with lexical anaphors, the subject of an infinitival complement is transparent to binding from the matrix clause.

In the NP-paradigm, however, NP-trace is generally disallowed, as illustrated by a comparison of illformed examples like (58) and (59) with the corresponding wellformed examples (60) and (61).

(58)   *John$_i$ was discovered [$_{NP}$pictures (of) e_i]
(59)   *John$_i$ discovered [$_{NP}$pictures (of) e_i]
(60)   [$_{NP_j}$pictures of John] were discovered [$_{NP_j}e$]
(61)   John$_i$ discovered [$_{NP}$pictures of himself$_i$]

The ungrammaticality of (58) is predicted within case theory since the NP *pictures of e*, being governed by the passive participle, will not be assigned case — in violation of the Case Filter, which requires that a lexical NP be case-marked. The ungrammaticality of (59) follows from the theory of predicate/argument structure, which prohibits a single NP from being assigned more than one argument function in a sentence.[28] In (59), *John* is assigned the argument function of subject of *discovered* and in addition the argument function of object of the nominal *pictures* via trace-binding, in violation of the condition on the uniqueness of argument assignment. Because case theory and the theory of predicate/argument structure independently predict the nonoccurrence of NP-trace in NPs, the NP-paradigm for NP-trace provides no motivation one way or the other for considering NP-trace as an anaphor.

Another instance where NP-trace does not pattern like a lexical anaphor involves binding across non-θ-subjects. While it appears that an anaphor may be free in the domain of an accessible non-θ-subject (see (39b) and (40b) above), a NP-trace may not (as noted in Freidin and Harbert 1983).

(62)   *He$_i$ was expected [$_{\bar{S}}$ for [$_S$ it to be insulted [$_{NP_i}$ e]]]
          cf. It was expected for him$_i$ to be insulted [$_{NP_i}$ e]

(62) cannot be explained as a violation of the Case Filter or conditions on predicate/argument structure. It could be excluded under Principle A if NP-trace is analyzed as an anaphor with the proviso that nonlexical anaphors are not sensitive to the distinction between θ-subjects and non-θ-subjects.

NP-trace is unlike a lexical anaphor in yet another way. It does not bear a θ-role independently of its binder. While a lexical anaphor receives its reference from its binder, the NP-trace transmits a θ-role to its binder. Reference is not at issue. Suppose that for NP-trace the domain of accessible SUBJECT does not involve the θ/non-θ distinction as indicated in (62). Then the binding domain for anaphors with respect to the S-paradigm could be reformulated in terms of θ-domain since both formulations are equivalent with respect to the S-paradigm. (Recall that the NP-paradigm is not relevant for the formulation of binding domains with respect to NP-trace). Thus a θ-role can only be transmitted within a θ-domain, just as reference can only be transmitted within a θ-domain (defined in terms of accessible θ-SUBJECT). NP-trace, like a lexical anaphor, may not be free in its binding domain.

The distinction between NP-trace and WH-trace is based on the different properties of these traces in wellformed structures. NP-trace is always caseless, whereas a corresponding WH-trace (i.e. in an NP-position) is always case-marked (see Lasnik and Freidin 1981). There is also a distinction between the binders of the two types of trace. NP-trace is always bound by an NP in a grammatical function (GF) position (e.g. subject), while WH-trace is always bound by a phase in COMP, a non-grammatical-function ($\overline{\text{GF}}$) position. In the GB framework, a GF position is designated as an A-position; and a $\overline{\text{GF}}$ position, as an $\overline{\text{A}}$-position (where "A" stands for "argument"). NP-trace is properly bound when it is A-bound in its binding domain. WH-trace is properly bound when it is $\overline{\text{A}}$-bound subject to certain locality requirements (e.g. Subjacency, see Chomsky 1977, 1981). Given that PRO is ungoverned, then it too, like NP-trace, is a caseless empty category.

The case-marked/caseless distinction is therefore sufficient to differentiate empty categories that function like anaphors from WH-trace. This functional interpretation of empty categories contrasts with a derivational interpretation in which an NP-trace is a trace resulting from movement between A-positions, as opposed to a WH-trace, which results from moving a WH-phrase to an $\overline{\text{A}}$-position (COMP).

Before exploring the functional analysis of empty categories, let us first determine the status of WH-trace with respect to the binding theory. The binding theory as presented above is a theory of A-binding. NP types are determined on the basis of behavior with respect to Principles A, B, and C as applied to A-binding. To determine the status of WH-trace, we consider its behavior with respect to A-binding. The simplest case is given in (63) where the WH-trace (e_i) is A-bound by the pronoun *he*.

(63)   *$[_{\overline{S}}$who$_i$ $[_S$did he$_i$ see $e_i]]$

The coindexing in (63) expresses the interpretation 'which person is such that that person saw himself?'. Because the question *who did he see?* has no such interpretation, this representation must be excluded. The question cannot be asked with intended coreference between the subject and object of *see*. To express this intended coreference, the question must be formulated as *who saw himself?*. Therefore a WH-trace does not behave like a lexical anaphor. The example does not distinguish between the two remaining possibilities for the status of WH-trace — as a name or a pronoun — since both must be A-free in S.

The two possibilities can be distinguished in the subject position of a finite sentential complement, where a pronoun may be bound but a name must be free (cf. (43.a.i) vs. (4)). The construction which distinguishes between the binding of pronouns and names shows that WH-trace behaves like a name rather than a pronoun. Consider the following paradigm.

(64)a.i. John$_i$ said $[_{\overline{S}}$he$_i$ won]
   ii.*He$_i$ said $[_{\overline{S}}$John$_i$ won]
   b.i. $[_{\overline{S}}$who$_i$ $[_S$ e_i said $[_{\overline{S}}$he$_i$ won]]]
   ii.*$[_{\overline{S}}$who$_i$ $[_S$did he$_i$ say $[_{\overline{S}}$ e_i won]]]

In (64.a.i) and (64.b.i) the pronoun is free in this binding domain, thereby satisfying Principle B. In (64.a.ii) the name *John* is bound, and therefore this representation violates Principle C. Similarly, intended coreference between the subjects of *say* and *won* in (64.b.ii) is not

possible, in contrast to (64.b.i). Assuming that the WH-trace has the
status of a name, (64.b.ii) is excluded under Principle C as well.[29]

So far, we have empty categories that behave like anaphors (NP-trace
and control PRO) and names (WH-trace) with respect to the binding
theory. Whether there are empty categories that behave like pronouns
remains to be determined. If there are, then the typology of empty
categories would seem to mirror the typology of lexical NPs (with
perhaps the exception of pleonastic elements — though see Chomsky
1982). Evidence for empty categories behaving like lexical pronouns is
open to interpretation. Putting aside the question of whether they exist
in English (see again Chomsky 1982), let us consider some evidence
from Spanish.

In Spanish, empty categories occurring in the subject of finite clauses
must be differentiated.[30] The empty categories in (65) illustrates the
standard paradigm for NP-trace with raising verbs.

(65) a. Ellos$_i$ parecen [$_S$ e_i haber   ganado]
         They   seem   to have won

     b. *Ellos$_i$ parecen [$_{\bar{S}}$ que [$_S$ e_i han   ganado]]
         They   seem   that   have won

In (66) however the empty categories cannot be analyzed as NP-traces
(or PRO since they are in governed positions).

(66) a. Dejé a Juan$_i$ [$_{\bar{S}}$ que [$_S$ $e_{i/*j}$ se fuera]]
         I let   Juan   go

     b. Juan$_i$ quiere [$_{\bar{S}}$ que [$_S$ $e_{*i/j}$ se vaya]]
         Juan   wants   *him/you to go

     c. Juan$_i$ no   cree   [$_{\bar{S}}$ que [$_S$ $e_{i/j}$ se vaya   ]]
         Juan   doesn't believe   that   he/you is/are going

In (66a) the empty category must be coindexed with an antecedent,
whereas in (66b) it cannot, and in (66c) coindexing is optional. Thus
only in (66c) does the empty category exhibit the same behavior as a
lexical pronoun. The obligatory coreference in (66a) and the obligatory
noncoreference in (66b) might be ascribed to lexical properties of the
matrix verb *dejar* and *querer*, just as verbs of obligatory control in
English impose (as a lexical property) coreference between their subject
(or object) and the subject of an infinitival complement. In any event,

the empty categories in (66) are distinct from NP-trace because they do not transmit a θ-role to their binder. As noted above, they are also different from PRO in that they occur in a governed position. Following standard practice, we will refer to such empty categories as pro (read "small pro").

Under this analysis, empty categories can be distinguished in terms of the properties of their binder and the structural position they occupy.

(67) A. Properties of binders:
    1. in A vs. $\overline{\text{A}}$ position:
       a. A position: NP-trace, PRO, pro
       b. $\overline{\text{A}}$ position: WH-trace
    2. with vs. without an independent θ-role:
       a. with independent θ-role: PRO, pro
       b. without independent θ-role: NP-trace, WH-trace
  B. Structural properties of the empty category:
    1. governed vs. ungoverned:
       a. governed: NP-trace, WH-trace, pro
       b. ungoverned: PRO
    2. case-marked vs. caseless:
       a. case-marked: WH-trace, pro
       b. caseless: NP-trace, PRO

(67) translates into the following feature matrix.

(68)·

	A-position	independent θ-role	governed	case-marked
WH-trace	−	−	+	+
NP-trace	+	−	+	−
PRO	+	+	−	−
pro	+	+	+	+

Given this feature analysis of empty categories, one question that arises is why are there only four empty category types when sixteen are possible.[31] For example, is there an empty category like WH-trace with respect to its binder but ungoverned and caseless? Presumably the answer depends on what empty category types are compatible with the theory of grammar. Thus an empty category which is case-marked must be governed since case-marking occurs only under government. This rules out the possibility of an empty category which is case-marked but ungoverned.

In the current GB framework then, some properties take precedence

over others. The problem is to determine which properties of empty
categories are basic and which can be predicted by the various principles of grammar. It is by no means obvious how this is to be established.
Any one feature in (68) could be eliminated and the remaining three
would still distinguish between the four empty category types. If two
features are eliminated, then the four empty categories could be distinguished only with the two features in (69).[32]

(69)   independent θ-role   case-marked
     WH-trace   −   +
     NP-trace   −   −
     PRO   +   −
     pro   +   +

This suggests that a functional determination of empty categories
minimally requires reference to at least one property of the binder and
one property of the empty category itself.[33]

The functional determination of empty categories has some intriguing
consequences for the analysis of representations containing empty
categories. Consider (70) for example.

(70)   *John$_i$ likes e_i

There are two possible derivations of (70), either by movement − in
which case e_i is a NP-trace, or by base generation − in which case the
empty category is either PRO or pro. Functionally, e_i is governed, case-
marked, and A-bound by an antecedent with an independent θ-role.
Therefore e_i does not function as a trace (see (68)) regardless of how it is
derived. Rather, it is functionally pro and hence a pronominal with respect to the binding theory. Therefore (70) violates Principle B since
pro is not free in its binding-category.

The alternative derivational analysis of the empty category in (70)
requires two different explanations for the ungrammaticality of the
example. Trace-binding here would be ruled out by the prohibition
against nonunique θ-role assignment, assuming that *John* would be
assigned a second θ-role via trace-binding (see p. 171). PRO-binding
would be excluded because PRO would be governed in violation of the
PRO-axiom; and pro-binding would violate Principle B as discussed
above.

It might appear that this analysis allows us to derive the condition on uniqueness of θ-role assignment via the functional determination of empty categories. The full derivation does not go through however. In (71), the empty category is functionally determined as pro, but would not violate Principle B.

(71)   *John$_i$ believed [$_S$ Mary to like e_i]

Since the empty category is both governed and case-marked, it cannot be analyzed as PRO; nor can it be analyzed as NP-trace because it is case-marked and has a binder with an independent θ-role. Functionally this empty category is pro. However, in English the distribution of pro is limited to parasitic gap constructions, as in (72) where e_i is a variable (WH-trace) which licences the parasitic gap e_i' (= pro) (see Chomsky 1982 for discussion).

(72)   Which letters$_i$ did you file e_i [without PRO reading e_i']

Note that e_i does not bind e_i' because it does not c-command e_i'. We might therefore assume that whatever accounts for the limited distribution of pro in English will also account for both (70) and (71) above, without recourse to Principle B, and independently of the functional determination of empty categories.

Nonetheless, the functional determination of empty categories is available within the GB framework for the analysis of derived structure. Whether it is empirically or conceptually better motivated than the derivational account of empty categories remains to be determined.[34] What is clear is that, under the derivational determination, the binding theory can be used to identify empty category types (e.g. NP-trace as an anaphor), whereas binding theory cannot be used in this way under the functional determination.

5. BINDING THEORY AND LEVELS OF REPRESENTATION

Under the assumption that the binding theory consists of a set of filters which determine the wellformedness of binding for some level (or levels) of representation, an empirical issue concerning which levels are relevant arises. In most discussions it has been assumed that Principles A, B, and C apply as a unit. This may not be correct as will be discussed below.

For the purposes of discussion, we will assume the following levels of representation.

(73)   D-structure
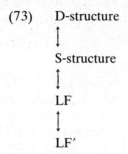
        S-structure

        LF

        LF'

The mapping from S-structure to LF establishes quantifier/variable structures via a rule of Quantifier Raising (see May 1977) and perhaps some mechanism for reconstructing phrase-markers (see Chomsky 1981) as will be discussed below. The mapping from LF to LF' (where 'LF' stands for 'logical form') yields predication-structures via coindexing (as discussed in Chomsky 1982:fn.11). Given these four levels, we may now consider what evidence might bear on the application of each of the three binding principles at each level. If a principle can apply at more than one level (as suggested in Chomsky 1981, 1982), then the number of potential binding theories is greatly increased, as is the difficulty of identifying the correct theory. Moreover, some of the evidence that bears on the issue seems to lead to paradoxes. The following discussion is offered as an illustration.

Chomsky 1981 addresses the question of levels with respect to Principle C. He notes that the rules of Quantifier Raising and scope assignment to *wh*-phrases *in situ* will map the S-structures of the sentences in (74) onto the corresponding LF structures in (75), (irrelevant details omitted).[35]

(74) a. He liked every book that John read.
     b. I don't remember who thinks that he read which book that John likes.
(75) a. (for every book *x* that John read) [he likes *x*]
     b. I don't remember (for which person *y* and which book *x* that John likes) [*y* thinks that he read *x*]

he c-commands *John* in (74), but not in (75). Since the pronoun and name are obligatorily disjoint in reference — which would be predicted if Principle C applies to (74) (i.e. at S-structure rather than LF), examples like (74) provide evidence that Principle C holds at S-structure.

There is also evidence that Principle C does not hold at S-structure. Consider the pair of sentences in (76).

(76) a. Which report that John revised did he submit?
      b. Which report that John was incompetent did he submit?

While *John* and *he* may be construed as coreferential in (76a), they must be construed as disjoint in reference in (76b). This difference in interpretation appears to be systematic, based on the distinction between the relative clause in (76a) vs. the sentential complement in (76b). Given that the sentential complement, but not the relative clause, subcategorizes the noun *report*, it may be that the subcategorization domain $\bar{N}$ is accessed in the interpretation of the variable bound by the WH-phrase. Presumably this access does not extend to relative clauses, which fall outside the subcategorization domain of the nouns they modify.

The interpretation of (76a) follows from the assumption that Principle C holds at S-structure. Unfortunately, this assumption gives the wrong result for the interpretation of (76b), where obligatory disjoint reference holds between *John* and *he* as if the pronoun c-commanded the name. At S-structure, the pronoun does not c-command the name in (76b), and therefore Principle C will not account for the only possible interpretation. One way to reinstate the appropriate c-command relationship between the name and the pronoun is to assume that some sort of reconstruction applies between S-structure and LF. That is, in LF the sentential complement of the noun (but, crucially, not the relative clause) would occur in the object position of *submit*.[36] Some support for a process of reconstruction as sketched comes from other cases of WH-movement where Principles A and B are involved.

(77) a. *How angry at John$_i$ was he$_i$?
      b. *How angry at him$_i$ was John$_i$?
      c. *How angry at him$_i$ did Mary say John$_i$ was?
      d. How angry at him$_i$ did John$_i$ say Mary was?
      e. *How angry at John$_i$ did he$_i$ say Mary was?
(78) a. How angry at each other$_i$ were they$_i$?
      b. How angry at each other$_i$ did Mary say they$_i$ were?
      c. *How angry at each other$_i$ did they$_i$ say Mary was?

(77a−b) show that disjoint reference holds between the pronoun and
the name in spite of WH-movement, which destroys the c-command
relation that held between them at D-structure. (77a) is presumably a
violation of Principle C, whereas (77b) violates Principle B. However
(77d), in contrast to (77e), shows SSC (or TSC) effects − i.e., disjoint
reference between *him* and *John* is blocked by the presence of the
intervening subject *Mary*. (78c) indicates the same effects with respect to
bound anaphora, where proper binding of *each other* by *they* is blocked
by the intervening subject *Mary*. In other words, *Mary* functions as an
accessible subject for the anaphor in spite of the fact that c-command
between *Mary* and *each other* does not hold at S-structure. These
paradigms would be accounted for under the assumption that Principles
A and B apply at some level of representation in which reconstruction
has applied to S-structure.

   It should be noted at this juncture that the notion of reconstruction is
at best problematic, as discussed in Higginbotham 1980:section 6 and
Higginbotham 1983:section 3. The major difficulty involves the analysis
for the LF-representation of sentences like (79).

   (79)   Which book about which pianist did she read?

The pronoun *she* cannot be coindexed with the variable bound by *which
pianist* in LF. This would follow under Principle C given that variables
(including WH-trace) have the status of names (see section 4 above) and
that the pronoun c-commands the relevant variable in LF. The idea is to
assimilate structures like (79) to those of (80), which contain names
instead of a variables.

   (80)   She read a book about Ingrid Haebler.

To do this, (79) would have to have an LF representation like (81).

   (81)   (for which pianist y) (for which book x) [she read [x about y]]

Yet the status of the term [x *about* y] in (81) is questionable on both
syntactic and semantic grounds.[37]

   The above discussion seems to suggest that the notion of c-command
may not be sufficient for binding theory when extended to $\overline{A}$-binding as
in the case of WH-movement and Quantifier Raising. As we have seen,
the issues surrounding this question are complex and will require
substantial clarification. The question of levels of application for the
binding theory depends in part on the prior question of the sufficiency
of c-command.

Before concluding this section, let us examine some additional evidence, which does not involve the question of the sufficiency of c-command, but instead bears on the question of whether Principles A, B, and C apply as a module at the same level(s) of representation. The evidence concerns equative constructions as discussed in section 2 with respect to the notion 'accessible SUBJECT'. A relevant example was given as (33) above, with an indexed representation (34).

(34)   Mary$_i$ believes [$_s$ those$_j$ to be [$_{NP_j}$ pictures of herself$_i$]]

In order to determine that *those* is not an accessible SUBJECT for the anaphor *herself*, *those* must be coindexed with NP$_j$. Yet given this coindexing, we might ask why (34) is not in violation of Principle C. One possible answer would be that Principle C applies at a level of representation prior to the coindexing of *those* and NP$_j$. Suppose that this coindexing results from a rule of predication which maps LF onto LF'. Then Principle A must apply at a different level of representation than Principle C. Given (34) we might assume that Principle A applies at LF', whereas Principle C applies at LF or S-structure, depending on the sufficiency of c-command for $\overline{A}$-binding. In this way there may be some motivation for distinguishing Principle C from Principles A and B. So far, however, there appears to be no motivation for separating Principles A and B in terms of the level(s) of representation to which they apply.

6. SUMMATION

The theory of binding investigated here consists of three principles which determine the distribution of bound elements – anaphors, pronouns, and names. Section 1 demonstrates that the relation between an antecedent and a bound element relevant for the operation of these principles is that of c-command. Section 2 addresses the issues involved in specifying opaque domains for anaphor binding, concluding that the notion of accessible θ-SUBJECT gives the closest fit to the facts. In section 3 it is noted that while the S-paradigms for pronoun and anaphor binding are analogous, the NP-paradigms are not. To account for these facts of pronoun binding, it is necessary to formulate the notion of opaque domain differently from that of Principle A. This is achieved by utilizing the notions of θ-domain and government, with the result that Principles A and B overlap with respect to opaque domains for the S-paradigm, but diverge in the appropriate way for the NP-paradigms. The extension of binding theory to empty categories is considered in section 4. While there is some motivation for concluding that WH-trace is subject to Principle C, it is questionable whether PRO is subject to the binding theory in any way. Furthermore, there is some evidence that NP-trace should be treated as an empty category analogue of a lexical anaphor and hence subject to Principle A. In this way, the binding theory contributes to a typology of empty categories, under which empty categories may be identified functionally or derivationally. The question of which levels of representation are relevant for the three principles of the binding theory is raised in section 5. Discussion establishes that the c-command relation of section 1 may be insufficient for cases involving $\bar{A}$-bounding. This suggests that S-structure by itself is not the appropriate level for any of the principles. Equative constructions provide evidence that Principle C should apply to a different level than Principles A and B.

This article has attempted to provide an overview of some of the fundamental issues confronting a theory of binding. At various points, alternative proposals have been considered. At the level of grammatical analysis it is often difficult to distinguish between alternatives which cover the same range of data. Yet these alternatives may not be equivalent in terms of what they suggest for processing or acquisition of language. Consider for example the issue of defining opaque domains for Principles A and B. If the definition is identical for both principles, then we might expect that a child who has acquired the S-paradigm for anaphors will also have the S-paradigm for pronouns given that Principle B is operative in his/her grammar. If, however, the definitions are different as proposed above, we might expect to find differences in the acquisition of the S-paradigms for pronouns and anaphors. For one study that argues in favor of the latter case, see Solan to appear.

NOTES

* This paper was intended as a critical review/summary of current work on binding theory circa 1983, though at some points it goes beyond this. I am indebted to Wayne Harbert for our many discussions on the binding theory. I would also like to thank Noam Chomsky, Lori Davis, Howard Lasnik, and Barbara Lust for comments on an earlier draft.
[1] The term 'name' covers common as well as proper nouns, excluding bound anaphors (i.e. reflexive pronouns and reciprocals), pronouns, nonreferential *it* and existential *there*. There is some evidence that variables — in particular, the empty category bound

by a WH-quantifier (see section 4 below) — have the status of names. See Freidin and Lasnik 1981 for an extensive discussion of this point. Chomsky 1981 uses the term 'R-expression' (for 'referential expression') rather than 'name' in the formulation of Principle C.

[2] See Freidin 1978 for discussion of conditions on rules vs. conditions on representations.

[3] For a somewhat different definition of c-command, see Chomsky 1981:chapter 3.

[4] This point is due to Wayne Harbert.

[5] See Chomsky 1981, Stowell 1981, and Manzini 1983 for discussion of the mechanism of reanalysis.

[6] It should be noted that these constructions are also problematic in another way. The *to*-phrase and the *about*-phrase may be freely ordered, as in (1).

(i) a.　　John talked to Bill about Mary.
　　b.　　John talked about Mary to Bill.

The ordering affects the distribution of anaphors so that neither PP may contain an anaphor when the *about*-phrase precedes the *to* phrase (cf. (18)).

(ii) a.　　John talked to Mary about herself.
　　b.　　*John talked about herself to Mary.
　　c.　　*John talked about Mary to herself.

If (18—20) are subject to reanalysis as discussed above, then it must be prevented from applying to constructions like (i.b). Then (ii) falls under Principle A as expected.

　　This analysis makes a prediction with respect to Principles B and C. It should be the case that (iii) and (iv) are wellformed, since the object of *about* does not c-command the object of *to*.

(iii)　　　*John talked about her$_i$ to Mary$_i$
(iv)　　　?John talked about Mary$_i$ to Mary$_i$

The prediction is false for (iii) and unclear for (iv). If 'bound' and 'free' are to be defined in terms of c-command, as the evidence bearing on Principles A and C suggests, then (iii) will have to be accounted for on other grounds. The alternative of complicating the binding theory by defining 'free' for Principle B differently than for Principle C is not well-motivated. It may be that some condition on linear order beyond what follows from c-command is necessary for pronouns. For further discussion of problems with pronouns and the c-command condition, see Reinhart 1981:section 5.

[7] See Rizzi 1981 for further arguments in favor of the NIC over the TSC/PIC.

[8] This data is from George and Kornfilt 1981 — their (37).

[9] This example is cited in Harbert 1982 and credited to Avery Andrews.

[10] The first proposal of this sort comes from Rouveret and Vergnaud 1980.

[11] The problem with this is that INFL structurally governs the subject NP of $\overline{S}$ whether or not it assigns case to the subject. The analysis could be maintained if we require that for government to hold there must be both a head and its maximal projection. Since maximal projections — especially $\overline{S}$ — are considered to be barriers to government and hence to case assignment, it could be claimed that exceptional case-marking of lexical subjects in infinitival complements lacking a *for* complementizer requires $\overline{S}$-deletion (see Chomsky 1981). Under the stricter requirement that government entails a maximal

projection as well as a head, INFL in exceptional case-marking constructions would not govern the infinitival subject — rather the matrix V would.

[12] See Fiengo and Higginbotham 1981 for further discussion of opacity in NP.

[13] As Chomsky notes (1981:210), the analysis provides a principled answer to the question of why S and NP should be the two governing categories under the earlier analysis. They are the two categories with subjects.

[14] That is, (31) cannot be construed as "the owner of his own boat . . .". Note however that (30) can be violated under certain conditions, as in

(i) $John_i$ is $[_{NP_j}$ the sole distributor of his_i records$]$

Thus the constraint prohibiting (31) cannot be the simple formal statement given in (30). What is at issue here is that a pronoun cannot get its reference from a NP that contains it. In (i), however, *his* is bound to *John* rather than the NP that contains it.

[15] In Chomsky 1981 the definition of 'accessible' redundantly specifies c-command.

[16] This example is due to Kevin Kearney. I am indebted to Lori Davis for calling it to my attention.

[17] It is assumed that both objects subcategorize the verb *tell* and therefore are constituents of $\overline{V}$, the subcategorization domain of V. Thus c-command follows.

[18] Chomsky 1981:214f. gives a different analysis on the basis of the following data.

(i)   *They think [it bothered each other that S] (= (84i))
(ii)   *He thinks [it bothered himself that S] (= (84ii))

Freidin and Harbert 1983 disagrees with the grammaticality judgment on (i) — although it could be a matter of sequences of tenses rather than a binding violation. Speakers who find (i) unacceptable nevertheless accept (iii).

(iii)   They think [it would bother each other that S]

The unacceptability of (ii) might be related to the fact that there is a grammatical alternative to the reflexive — i.e. the proximate pronoun, though how this relates to some principled account remains to be determined.

[19] Suppose this involves the actual transfer of the θ-property, rather than a sharing of it. Then we have an account for why AGR takes precedence over the syntactic subject. Though this approach might raise further problems concerning conditions on θ-role assignments. See note 28.

[20] For discussion of an indexing mechanism for expressing disjoint reference, see Chomsky 1980, 1981; Freidin and Lasnik 1981; Lasnik 1981; and Higginbotham 1983.

[21] Speaker judgments on these examples tend to vary for reasons that are unclear. For example, some speakers do not accept (i), but find that acceptability improves in the negative counterpart.

(i)   *$John_i$ reads [books about him_i]

Similar judgments hold for the pair *like* vs. *dislike*. For a somewhat different analysis of (i) and related material, see Chomsky 1982:fn. 24.

[22] Regarding the application of disjoint reference into NP, as mentioned in the previous footnote, note that examples like (45.b.i—ii) appear to be the standard case across languages (see Lasnik and Freidin 1981 for discussion of this with respect to the NIC). Speakers who tend towards a disjoint reference reading in the simple sentence cases find

the coreferent reading in complex sentences unexceptional. The disjoint reading in simple sentences may be due to lexical properties of the matrix verb — i.e. where there is a connection via θ-marking between the verb and its object NP. In complex sentence cases no such connection exists; hence there is no apparent way to contravene the opacity of the complement object NP.

[23] See Harbert 1983 for discussion of PP. Harbert notes that some PPs appear to block disjoint reference as in (i).

    (i)   John$_i$ put the book [$_{PP}$ beside him$_i$]

As (ii) illustrates, this is not generally the case.

    (ii)   *John$_i$ mailed the book [$_{PP}$ to him$_i$]

[24] Whether or not PP is a θ-domain is left open at this point. (50) above and (ii) of the previous footnote argue against this. (i) would conform to Principle B if PP is a θ-domain.

[25] Control PRO must have an antecedent in S, in contrast to non-control PRO (i.e. PRO$_{arb}$) as in (i).

    (i)   It is unclear [$_{\bar{S}}$ what$_i$ [$_S$ PRO$_{arb}$ to do e_i]]

Where PRO need not be bound by an antecedent, it does not function as an anaphor. If PRO$_{arb}$ is never bound to an antecedent at the level of representation where binding principles apply, then binding theory will not account for the distribution of PRO$_{arb}$. This will be assumed in what follows. Whatever accounts for the fact that PRO$_{arb}$ occurs only in ungoverned positions might also account for the distribution of control PRO in only ungoverned positions.

[26] Huang claims that PRO has only one bounding domain — i.e. the one provided by the most restrictive definition. In the case under discussion this would be the domain of an accessible SUBJECT, and thus the larger of the two possibilities. In this domain PRO must be both bound and free.

[27] This is necessary in any case so that PRO$_{arb}$ is excluded as a possible subject in the infinitival complement of these verbs. That is, *John wants to leave* is never interpreted as 'John wants someone to leave'.

[28] This will occur when an NP in a position which is assigned an argument function (θ-role) binds a trace in a position which is also assigned an argument function. The basic idea is that movement operations are restricted to moving constituents into non-argument positions only (i.e. positions which are not assigned an argument function). In terms of trace binding, the antecedent of a trace cannot occur in an argument position (θ-position in the terminology of Chomsky 1981). See Freidin 1978, Borer 1979, and Chomsky 1981 for further discussion. See also footnote 33.

[29] See Freidin and Lasnik 1981 for a detailed discussion of these cases, and Chomsky 1982 for a different analysis involving a functional definition of empty categories in terms of the local binder of the empty category. Basically, Chomsky suggests that because the empty categories in (63) and (64.b.i) are locally A-bound by antecedents in θ-positions, they function as PRO. Therefore the examples are illformed because they contain governed PRO, which is prohibited. For some important criticism of this analysis, see Brody 1984.

[30] I am indebted to Carlos Piera for the following examples.

186   R. FREIDIN

³¹ See Bouchard 1982 and Sportiche 1983 for further discussion.
³² Note that the other features make a 3-to-1 distinction in contrast to the 2-to-2 distinction of the features in (69). That is why they don't work here.
³³ It is claimed in Chomsky 1981 and 1982 that one argument for the functional determination of empty categories is that the existing types virtually partition the distribution of NPs. This would follow if there were only one (structural) type of empty category, where the distinctions among the four subtypes are made in terms of their function. This argument is unconvincing because the {PRO, pro}/trace distinction is crucial for both the theory of predicate/argument structure (see footnote 28) and the Empty Category Principle (ECP) of Chomsky 1981 which requires that an empty category be 'properly governed' [the exact definition of proper government need not concern us here]. In contrast to trace-binding, PRO-binding is immune to the prohibition against binding between argument positions since PRO and its binder always have independent θ-roles. Furthermore, PRO, unlike trace, is immune to the ECP since it is never governed. Similarly for pro. If {PRO, pro} were structurally distinct from trace — i.e. $[_{NP} [_N e]]$ for {PRO, pro} vs. $[_{NP} e]$ for trace, then there might be some principled explanation for the immunity of {PRO, pro} based on this structural difference. The alternative of appealing to the independent-θ-role-of-the-binder feature of {PRO, pro} to distinguish them from trace will not account for their immunity to the ECP in non-control constructions.
³⁴ See Chomsky 1982:sections 3 and 5 for further discussion based on somewhat different assumptions about the analysis of empty categories.
³⁵ These examples are from Chomsky 1981:197. The grammaticality of (74b) seems dubious at best.
³⁶ Exactly how this is to be implemented is far from clear, and raises several complicated issues involving the specification of quantifier/variable structures in LF. van Riemsdijk and Williams 1981 propose an intermediate level of structure between D- and S-structure, designated NP-structure, which indicates only the results of NP-movements (excluding, crucially, WH-movements). If Principle C applies at NP-structure, then the interpretation of (76b) is accounted for without recourse to reconstruction at LF. However, the interpretation of (76a) cannot be accounted for under this proposal. Note further that the correct interpretation of (74) follows from the NP-structure proposal or the reconstruction proposal, given that relative clauses are not affected by QR (contrary to Chomsky's analysis cited above).
³⁷ (81) might be derived by replacing the trace of the *wh*-phrase in (79) with the term [*x* of *y*]. The problem with this is that it presupposes an analysis of quantifier/variable structure which will lose May's explanation for linked quantification (see May 1977). That is, in NPs containing two quantified expressions, the more deeply embedded quantifier always has wide scope. This does not follow given the analysis under discussion.

REFERENCES

Aoun, Y. and D. Sportiche: 1983, 'On the formal theory of government', *The Linguistic Review* 2, 211–236.

Borer, H.: 1979, 'Empty subjects in modern Hebrew and constraints on thematic relations', in J. Jensen (ed.), *Proceedings of the Tenth Annual Meeting of the North Eastern Linguistic Society*, University of Ottawa, Ottawa, pp. 25—37.

Bouchard, D.: 1982, *On the Content of Empty Categories*, unpublished doctoral dissertation, MIT.

Brody, M.: 1984, 'On contextual definitions and the role of chains', *Linguistic Inquiry* **15**, 355—380.

Chomsky, N.: 1973, 'Conditions on transformations', in S. Anderson and P. Kiparsky (eds.), *A Festschrift for Morris Halle*, Holt, Rinehart and Winston, New York, pp. 232—286.

Chomsky, N.: 1976, 'Conditions of rules of grammar', *Linguistic Analysis* **2**, 303—351.

Chomsky, N.: 1977, 'On Wh-movement', in P. Culicover, T. Wasow, and A. Akmajian (eds.), *Formal Syntax*, Academic Press, New York.

Chomsky, N.: 1980a, 'On binding', *Linguistic Inquiry* **11**, 1—46.

Chomsky, N.: 1981a, *Lectures on Government and Binding*, Foris, Dordrecht.

Chomsky, N.: 1982, *Some Concepts and Consequences of the Theory of Government and Binding*, MIT Press, Cambridge, Mass.

Fiengo, R. and J. Higginbotham: 1981, 'Opacity in NP', *Linguistic Analysis* **7**, 395—421.

Freidin, R.: 1978, 'Cyclicity and the theory of grammar', *Linguistic Inquiry* **9**, 519—549.

Freidin, R.: 1983, 'X-bar theory and the analysis of English infinitivals', *Linguistic Inquiry* **14**, 713—722.

Freidin, R. and W. Harbert: 1983, 'On the fine structure of the binding theory: Principle A and reciprocals', in P. Sells and C. Jones (eds.), *Proceedings of the Thirteenth Annual Meeting of the North Eastern Linguistic Society*, MIT, Cambridge, Mass., pp. 63—72.

Freidin, R. and H. Lasnik: 1981, 'Disjoint reference and Wh-trace', *Linguistic Inquiry* **12**, 39—53.

George, L. and J. Kornfilt: 1981, 'Finiteness and boundedness in Turkish', in F. Heny (ed.), *Binding and Filtering*, MIT Press, Cambridge, Mass.

Harbert, W.: 1982a, 'In defense of tense', *Linguistic Analysis* **9**, 1—18.

Harbert, W.: 1982b, 'Should binding refer to subject?', in J. Pustejovsky and P. Sells (eds.), *Proceedings of the Twelfth Annual Meeting of the North Eastern Linguistic Society*, MIT, Cambridge, Mass., pp. 116—131.

Harbert, W.: 1983b, 'On the definition of binding domains', in D. Flickinger (ed.), *Proceedings of the West Coast Conference on Formal Linguistics II*, Stanford University, Stanford, California.

Higginbotham, J.: 1980a, 'Anaphora and GB: Some preliminary remarks', in J. Jensen (ed.), *Proceedings of the Tenth Annual Meeting of the North Eastern Linguistic Society* **9**, 223—236, Ottawa, Canada.

Higginbotham, J.: 1980b, 'Pronouns and bound variables', *Linguistic Inquiry* **11**, 679—708.

Higginbotham, J.: 1983, 'Logical form, binding, and nominals', *Linguistic Inquiry* **14**, 395—420.

Huang, C.-T.J.: 1983, 'A note on the binding theory', *Linguistic Inquiry* **14**, 554—561.

Jackendoff, R.: 1972, *Semantic Interpretation in Generative Grammar*, MIT Press, Cambridge, Mass.

Lasnik, H.: 1976, 'Remarks on coreference', *Linguistic Analysis* **2**, 1—22.
Lasnik, H.: 1981, 'On two recent treatments of disjoint reference', *Journal of Linguistic Research* **1**, 48—58.
Lasnik, H. and R. Freidin: 1981a, 'Core grammar, case theory, and markedness', in A. Belletti, L. Brandi, and L. Rizzi (eds.), *Theory of Markedness in Generative Grammar*, Scuola Normale Superiore, Pisa.
Lebeaux, D.: (to appear), 'Locality and anaphoric binding', *The Linguistic Review*.
Manzini, M. R.: 1983b, *Restructuring and Reanalysis*, unpublished doctoral dissertation, MIT.
May, R.: 1977, *The Grammar of Quantification*, unpublished doctoral dissertation, MIT.
Reinhart, T.: 1976, *The Syntactic Domain of Anaphora*, unpublished doctoral dissertation, MIT, Cambridge, Massachusetts.
Reinhart, T.: 1981a, 'Definite NP anaphora and c-command domains', *Linguistic Inquiry* **12**, 605—636.
Riemsdijk, H. van and E. Williams: 1981, 'NP structure', *The Linguistic Review* **1**, 171—217.
Rizzi, L.: 1981, 'Nominative marking in Italian infinitives and the nominative island constraint', in F. Heny (ed.), *Binding and Filtering*, MIT Press, Cambridge, Mass.
Rouveret, A.: 1980, 'sur la notion de proposition finie', *Language* **60**, 75—107.
Rouveret, A. and J. Vergnaud: 1980, 'Specifying reference to the subject: French causatives and conditions on representations', *Linguistic Inquiry* **11**, 97—202.
Solan, L.: to appear, 'Parameter setting and the development of pronouns and reflexives', Proceedings of University of Massachusetts Amherst Conference on Parameter Setting.
Sportiche, D.: 1983, *Structural Invariance and Symmetry in Syntax*, unpublished doctoral dissertation, MIT.
Stowell, T.: 1981, *Origins of Phrase Structure*, unpublished doctoral dissertation, MIT.

PART B

FIRST LANGUAGE ACQUISITION:
EXPERIMENTAL STUDIES

1. NULL (BOUND) ANAPHORA

THOMAS W. ROEPER

HOW CHILDREN ACQUIRE BOUND VARIABLES*

The heart of linguistic theory lies in the concept of a transformation. It creates the fundamental acquisition problem as well: how does a child learn to reconstruct deep structure from surface structure? In concrete terms, how does the child know where invisible noun phrases are, how does he know that there is an invisible NP after *hit* in *who did John hit*, which is linked to *who*?

The concept of a transformation (which moves *who* from the position after *hit*) has been re-analyzed in terms of a larger notion of *binding* relationships. We can say   in a sentence like *who$_i$ did John hit (trace)$_i$* that there is binding between *trace$_i$* and *who$_i$*, where *trace* is an invisible object left behind by the transformation. Although *trace* is invisible it has phonological effects which have been amply documented elsewhere (see Chomsky (1973) and notes).

The notion of *binding* encompasses not only who/trace relations but other noun/pronoun relations which can be found in sentences like *Everyone$_i$ thinks he$_i$ is smart.* The concept of binding has two aspects, each of which is important because each may undergo separate acquisition. In a sentence like *John thinks he is smart* we find the possibility of *coreference* between *John* and *he*. We can ask one question about such a sentence: How does a child learn that different noun phrases refer to a single referential object? In addition to coreferential NP's we have variable coreferential NP's, that is the relation found in a sentence like *who thinks he likes tomatoes.* In such a sentence there is a set of *he*'s and *who*'s who both think and like tomatoes. We can now ask the question: How do children learn that coreferential NP's can be variable?

In the experiment discussed below we examine how children acquire sentences where transformations, coreferential binding, and variables all interact. The surface facts are quite subtle. Thus they pose a large problem to an acquisition device unless the acquisition device is innate and knows beforehand where to look for crucial distinctions. If, in other words, the acquisition device has insight into parametric variation, then acquisition should be straightforward. We provide an analysis that is supportive of a parametric approach to acquisition and therefore supportive of current linguistic theory.

191

B. Lust (ed.), Studies in the Acquisition of Anaphora, Vol. I, 191–200.
© *1986 by D. Reidel Publishing Company.*

It has been shown generally that children shift from a linearly based approach to coreference to a structurally based approach (Tavakolian (1977), Solan (1981)). At first they allow coreference between an NP (John) and a pronoun (he) if *John* precedes *he* linearly (*John thinks he won*). When children develop tree structure, they shift to a hierarchical condition on coreference (Goodluck (1981), Solan (1983), Lust and Clifford (1982, and this volume), Hsu (1981)). Under a hierarchical condition, backwards coreference is possible if the pronoun is lower in the tree than the NP it refers to. For instance we can have coreference in the sentence *In his dissertation, John said everything,* where *his* precedes *John* but is lower in the tree. The technical definition of this hierarchical condition is known as "c-command."[1]

In a subtle experiment, Solan (1981) showed that backwards pronominalization occurs just in case the phrase with a referential noun is attached to the S-node. He found that 4-year-old children preferred to give coreference between *'im* and *Bill* in *John hit'im after Bill's run* (since temporals attach to S) but not to *John hit'im in Bill's yard* (since locatives attach to the VP). Where both *'im* and *Bill* are under the VP, the c-command principle rules out coreference.[2]

We have approached the question in a domain where the intuitions are clearer and the c-command constraint applies at a level where *variables* are involved. Note that coreference is possible if a pronoun follows (and is c-commanded by) a *Wh*-word. If the pronoun precedes the *Wh*-word, coreference fails. In other words, as these examples show, the *Wh*-word functions just like a name (see Lasnik and Freidin):

(1) a.   who knows he can sing   b.   John knows he can sing

   c.   he knows who can sing   d.   he knows John can sing

Coreference is possible in (1a, b), but not in (1c, d). Why then is it ruled out in (2) where the *Wh*-word precedes the *he*?

(2)   who does he know can sing

The answer is that the c-command principle applies at a deeper level. *He* precedes and c-commands the *trace* of *who* creating the same configuration we found in (1c):

$$\overset{\overset{\displaystyle x}{\frown}}{}$$

(3)   who does he know *trace* can sing

The generalization holds if the argument applies to deep rather than surface structure, or if it applies at surface structure between *he* and *trace*.

Now we are in a position to do an experiment. Do children understand that the c-command constraint applies between pronouns and traces? Does UG − or when does UG − tell them to apply coreference constraints to invisible NP's?

The sentences in question invite us to examine another, more sophisticated, dimension of acquisition. Suppose one answered the question in (3) coreferentially: "Why he thinks he himself can sing"; the answer would be correct. We seer 'o have lost the contrast between (1a) and (2). However, the constraint reappears when the notion of *variable* enters. In *Who thinks he can sing* there is one he who might be thinking about himself. In other words, in (1a) *who* and *he* function as bound *variables* calling for a *multiple* response. It is quite possible that the notions of *coreference* and of *bound variable* involve independent cognitive maturation. That is, a child may understand coreference before he or she understands bound variables. We designed our experiments to distinguish between simple coreference and variable coreference.

We have done four different pilot experiments involving first Piagetian techniques, then a group experiment with real objects, and finally two different picture identification experiments. We shall summarize one experiment and then present follow-up designs. We believe that this domain of experimentation should be developed with special care because it involves subtle interactions at the heart of language acquisition: movement rules and abstract levels.

We gave a group of nine children between five and seven-years old (the crucial age as indicated by earlier pilots) fourteen sentences in two counter-balanced orders (designed and carried out by T. Borowski):

(4)   who does he think wears a hat (crossover)
(5)   who thinks he wears a hat (non-crossover)

The children were given a series of pictures in which there was a prominent person and several other people all doing or wearing the same thing. The prominent person was a natural referent for *he* if the children did not select a bound-variable reading.

In one picture three children are wearing a hat. Both (4) and (5) call for the child to point to all three children. But the follow-up question differentiates them: "Who's thinking". For (4) it should be the prominent person at the side, while for (5) it is all three children. It is possible to construe (5) to mean that one person thinks another person is wearing a hat. Nonetheless we expected that the pictorial stimulus would elicit some bound-readings for those children who understand variables.

Table 1 shows the results: Here the proportion is coreference/total responses.

TABLE 1

Individual	*A*				*B*				
Child	J1	J2	T	A	R	A	J	C	B
who-verb	4/8	3/8	5/6	2/6	7/8	6/8	4/6	7/8	5/6
who did	3/6	4/6	4/6	3/6	1/6	2/6	0/8	3/6	0/8
multiple responses	1	1	1	0	2	3	2	3	3
Total			3						13

Group B exhibits essentially an adult grammar: high numbers of coreferential responses to *who-verb* matched by low coreference for *who-did*, coupled with a substantial number (13) of multiple responses on the who-verb cases. (Not all who-verb sentences called for multiple responses.) Group A exhibits a capacity for coreference but without a distinction between *who-verb* and *who-did* (roughly half were coreferential in each class). They gave only three multiple responses (all for one sentence involving two ice cream cones). Since a strong correlation exists between two variables (coreference and multiple answers), these small numbers are significant statistically: under complex randomization $i/128 = p < .01$.

If Group B has the adult grammar, then we can credit them with knowledge of the position of *trace*, the notion of variable, and the c-command principle. What principles do they have in the grammar immediately preceding this adult grammar? How do we account for the fact that Group A allows coreference in a sentence like *who does he think wants a cupcake?*

In recent work Chomsky (1982b) articulates the notion of *Extended Projection Principle*. The idea in essence is that the lexicon contains information, derived from the meaning of words, that requires verbs to have certain thematic relations (like *Agent*) which are linked to positions like subject. Therefore the lexical definition of a verb like *think* or *want* requires that subjects exist. It follows that the child does not have to have a syntactic notion of *movement* or *deletion* to know that the sequence *he thinks wants* is impossible as it stands. The verb *wants* must have a subject and therefore the child can automatically, on lexical assumptions, project an NP gap in such a sequence: *he thinks (NP) wants.*

What is the nature of the *empty category* that must intervene between *think* and *want?* Under current government-binding theory (and variants) there are only two possibilities: *trace* and *pronoun.* These options are (putatively) universal and exhaustive. The *pronoun* option, however, subdivides into two parametric possibilities: big PRO and little *pro.* The category PRO is found in non-case-marked positions, for instance in infinitives, and allows an arbitrary interpretation (it is good PRO to sing). In some languages, small *pro* can appear in tensed (governed) positions like the gap between *he thinks pro wants* and it can have definite as well as arbitrary reference. It is distinguished by the fact that it can receive case. (See Chomsky (1981), (1982) for discussion.)

Now let us advance an hypothesis:

(6)   *pronoun* is an unmarked empty category (NP) = a *primitive* empty category in linguistic theory.

We use the term *primitive* here to mean that a child has a piece of knowledge in the core of universal grammar which can be applied without *language-particular* pre-requisites. It does not mean that it can be applied with no pre-requisites. For instance, the primitive *pronoun* requires the presence of some tree-structure. However we suggest that it can be used to fill any NP position required by the lexicon without application of language-particular constraints. For instance, *agreement* rules may not yet be acquired when *pronoun* appears as a default empty category, although *government* is relevant to adult empty categories.

The fact that children do not observe disjoint reference on crossover sentences like (2) means that they cannot have projected *trace* into the empty NP position. We are led therefore to the hypothesis that the Group A children have projected some form of the empty *pronoun* in that position.

Now we must address the parametric issue: which pronoun is present, PRO or *pro*? It is conceivable that there is a primitive empty category *pronoun* which does not distinguish these options (see commentary by van Riemsdijk, this volume). However there is reason to believe that all children begin with a specific version of *pronoun.*

The term *parameter* is used because the division between these two kinds of pronoun reflects an important division between language families. One set of languages (Italian, Spanish, and many others) allow an empty subject that is case-marked, while in the other set (English, French) the subject must always be phonetically realized in case-marked positions. Consequently we have expletive subjects in sentences like *it seems that John can sing* which fulfill this function. The challenge to the English child is to realize that his language disallows (by parametric exclusion) small *pro* and allows only big PRO or an expletive.

Several recent studies argue that young children begin with the assumption that *pronoun* equals small *pro* no matter what language they eventually learn. Roeper (1981) shows evidence that sentences like "vitamin C is for to grow" exist in the language of a two-year old. The *for*-phrase with no object and no *trace* relation must then have a case-marked empty category, in other words, small *pro*. Hyams (1983) provides extensive evidence and argumentation in behalf of the hypothesis that children begin with small *pro*. In particular English-speaking children begin saying subjectless sentences ("Yes is toys in the room").

We return now to the experiment under discussion. Our argument leads to the suggestion that children in Group A project *pro* between *think* and *wants*. In effect a sentence like *he thinks pro wants a cupcake* is just like *he thinks he wants a cupcake.*[3] The element *pro* does not have to be a variable and therefore the children in Group A can recognize coreference without choosing multiple responses. In contrast, a *Wh*-word (which is a variable − it can refer to a set) must have a *variable-trace* as an antecedent. It follows that the use of *Wh*-trace has the cognitive pre-requisite that children can use bound variables.

We argue therefore that children in Group A have *who does he think pro wants a cupcake* with coreference between *who, he,* and *pro*. This suggests that children may have the capacity to generate a *Wh*-word in sentence-initial position without movement (as in *whether* sentences).

Our hypothesis about Group A's grammar is very limited. We argue that the notions of trace and variable are not playing a role, but rather a simple notion of coreference is used based on the presence of an invisible pronoun (pro). This conclusion may in fact be correct for the children between 5—7 years old. However, subsequent experimentation makes the matter more complex.

We shall give a brief overview of salient results in a subsequent experiment. It provides partial support for the claims just advanced. We gave 22 children from 8—10 years old a two-part set of 48 pictures to be marked. Each picture had three or four parts with a prominent person available. We included single-clause cross-over sentences (*whose shoes is he tying*) and non-crossover sentences (*who is tying his shoes*) and we varied the pronoun between *he, she,* and *they.* In addition we varied extraction from subject to object.

None of these changes changed the essential result. The children divided into three groups. The first group of six children chose the deictic option (prominent person, usually a Sesame Street character like Big Bird). The second group of six children, like those in the experiment reported here, treated the crossover and non-crossover sentences identically when two clauses were involved, allowing multiple coreference for both sentence types. The third group of eight children had essentially an adult grammar. The single-clause crossover received no coreferential readings, and the single-clause non-crossover received few.

The evidence suggests once again that small *pro* is present but it does not have the feature that no variable is present. Unlike in the first experiment, the middle group of children allowed there to be *multiple* coreference on the crossover sentences like (2). It is therefore not the notion of *bound-variables* which prevents children from projecting a trace in the empty category position. The children are treating *pro* as a bound variable too. Let us now step back and review both the evidence and how the notion of a parameter is used.

All of the evidence points toward the presence of small *pro.* However it does not point to the use of a parameter which changes grammars at a single stroke. (1) We find that children begin using *it seems . . .* sentences around the age of four, (2) we find that they abandon the *for to* sequence in the four-to-five year old range, and (3) they exhibit knowledge of c-command by the age of four, and (4) though it is possible to argue that single clause *Wh*-movement is lexical, the absence of sentences like *what kind did John buy Ford* suggests that three-year old children have a *trace* filling object position. Therefore it seems as if the conceptual ingredients and the parametric evidence for eliminating small *pro* are present. We can give no straightforward reason why eight-to-ten year old children should use a grammatical option which has supposedly been eliminated at the age of four.

Let us explore instead a different perspective on parameters: they contain a set of subparameters each of which must be instantiated by independent evidence. Until each subparameter is triggered, empty categories are filled by the *primitive* empty category *pro*. What differentiates a parameter from a subparameter? In effect a parameter establishes a set of subparameter hypotheses which can be triggered by minimal evidence.

Where are the subparameters? This question deserves careful and detailed investigation. In general, all boundaries and all movement rules which permit language particular variation may require subparametric evidence for this realization. The major difference between one-clause and two-clause crossover sentences is that the two-clause sentences require a two-step movement through COMP. It is this derivational path which seems to be non-instantaneously acquired. A detailed study of this matter goes beyond the scope of this paper but recent works by Klein (1982) and Roeper, Rooth, Mallis and Akiyama (forthcoming) discuss these issues.

In conclusion, our evidence supports the theory which leads to a limited inventory of empty categories (trace and pronoun). The fact that an NP position is present (dictated by the Extended Projection Principle) and has freedom of reference is precisely what is predicted by the projection of *pro* onto the empty position. The fact that it is *pro* and not PRO which we must posit for this position is consistent with the theory of the so-called pro-drop parameter and with a variety of naturalistic evidence gathered from children.

We are led to two kinds of elaboration of linguistic theory: (1) empty categories must be divided into primitive and non-primitive, and (2) the instantiation of a parameter requires the instantiation of a set of subparameters which in turn requires a number of data points. We have designated one empty category as *primitive* because it provides a necessary step in the acquisition process. We have now the beginning of a biological explanation for why there are a variety of empty categories: the distribution of *traces* cannot be directly projected by the child. He must first construe all empty categories as *pronouns*.

NOTES

* The series of experiments discussed in this paper has had a long evolution. T. Borowski, C. Clifton, L. Frazier, J. Randall, K. Wexler, and E. Williams were all involved in the first phase of research. M. Rooth, S. Akiyama and L. Mallis in the second. We have received helpful comments from a wide variety of audiences, including GLOW, University of Massachusetts colloquia, Cornell University colloquia, and MIT Linguistics colloquia. Research was supported by NSF BNS 80–14326.

[1] See Reinhart (1976) and Chomsky (1981) for revisions. The technical formulation is stated negatively: the first branching node dominating a pronoun may not also dominate the reference noun.

[2] See Solan (1983) and Higginbotham (1980) for discussion of the application of the principle to Logical Form instead. The basic idea is clear although there are some interesting variations in how the principle is formulated. We hope to develop acquisition work to parallel some of the newly found relevant data in this domain.

[3] We are indebted to N. Chomsky for suggesting this line of reasoning to us.

[4] Bloom et al. report that *Wh*-words are learned one-by-one with respect to particular verbs. This is also compatible with the ideas that initially children generate *Wh*-words in place and later learn to connect them with specific syntactic positions. The idea is also compatible with various "functional" approaches to invisible NP phenomena.

REFERENCES

Bloom, L., P. Lightbrown and L. Hood: 1980, 'Wh-questions: Integration of language and thought to explain the sequence of acquisition', unpublished manuscript, Columbia Teachers College, New York.

Chomsky, N.: 1973, 'Conditions on transformations', in S. Anderson and P. Kiparsky (eds.), *A Festschrift for Morris Halle*, Holt, Rinehart and Winston, New York, pp. 232–286.

Chomsky, N.: 1981, *Lectures on Government and Binding*, Foris, Dordrecht.

Chomsky, N.: 1982, *Some Concepts and Consequences of the Theory of Government and Binding*, MIT Press, Cambridge, Mass.

Goodluck, H.: 1978, *Linguistic Principles in Children's Grammar of Complement Subject Interpretation*, unpublished doctoral dissertation, University of Massachusetts.

Goodluck, H.: 1981, 'Children's grammar of complement subject interpretation', in S. Tavakolian (ed.), *Language Acquisition and Linguistic Theory*, MIT, Cambridge, Mass., pp. 139–166.

Higginbotham, J.: 1980, 'Pronouns and bound variables', *Linguistic Inquiry* **11**, 679–708.

Hsu, J.: 1981, *The Development of Structural Principles Related to Complement Subject Interpretation*, unpublished doctoral dissertation, City University of New York.

Hyams, N.: 1983, *The Acquisition of Parameterized Grammars*, unpublished doctoral dissertation, City University of New York. (to appear) Reidel.

Klein, S.: 1982, *Syntactic Theory and Developing Grammar*, unpublished manuscript, University of California at Los Angeles.

Lasnik, H. and R. Freidin: 1981b, 'Disjoint reference and Wh-trace', *Linguistic Inquiry* **12**, 39—54.

Lust, B. and T. Clifford: 1982, 'The 3D study: Effects of depth, distance and directionality on children's acquisition of anaphora', in J. Pustejovsky and P. Sells (eds.), *Proceedings of the Twelfth Annual Meeting of the North Eastern Linguistic Society*, MIT, Cambridge, Mass., pp. 174—186 (also this volume).

Otsu, Y.: 1981, *Universal Grammar and Syntactic Development in Children: Toward a Theory of Syntactic Development*, unpublished doctoral dissertation, MIT.

Phinney, M.: 1981, *Syntactic Constraints and the Acquisition of Embedded Sentential Complements*, unpublished doctoral dissertation, University of Massachusetts.

Reinhart, T.: 1976, *The Syntactic Domain of Anaphora*, unpublished doctoral dissertation, MIT.

Roeper, T.: 1981, 'Core grammar and a parametric theory of triggers', unpublished paper, University of Massachusetts.

Roeper, T., M. Rooth, L. Mallis, and S. Akiyama: in preparation, *The Problem of Empty Categories and Bound Variables in Language Acquisition*, unpublished manuscript, University of Massachusetts, Amherst.

Solan, L.: 1981, 'The acquisition of structural restrictions on anaphora', in S. Tavakolian (ed.), *Language Acquisition and Linguistic Theory*, MIT Press, Cambridge, Mass., pp. 59—73.

Solan, L.: 1983, *Pronominal Reference: Child language and the Theory of Grammar*, D. Reidel, Dordrecht.

Tavakolian, S.: 1977, *Structural Principles in the Acquisition of Complex Sentences*, unpublished doctoral dissertation, University of Massachusetts, Amherst.

Tavakolian, S.: 1981, 'The conjoined clause analysis of relative clauses', in S. Tavakolian (ed.), *Language Acquisition and Linguistic Theory*, MIT Press, Cambridge, Mass.

2. PRONOUN (FREE) ANAPHORA

BARBARA LUST AND TERRI CLIFFORD

THE 3D STUDY: EFFECTS
OF DEPTH, DISTANCE AND DIRECTIONALITY
ON CHILDREN'S ACQUISITION OF ANAPHORA

There has been much concern in recent linguistic theory for definition of restrictions on the class of grammars which might help to explain "learnability" of natural language (e.g., Baker and McCarthy, 1981). In this paper we provide empirical evidence for a 'structure-dependent' constraint on hypothesis formation in early first language acquisition of English. It concerns a central aspect of natural language, anaphora. This constraint determines that configurational structure is necessary to the computation of grammatical anaphora. This structure-dependent constraint is argued to be stronger than non-linguistic principles for anaphora, which the child may access. We argue that the empirical evidence for this structure-dependence supports a theory such as that proposed by Chomsky 1977, 1981 which claims that biologically determined cognitive capacities for natural language provide linguistically significant constraints on the form of possible representations of possible human language.

1.0 ANAPHORA

"Anaphora" will be used here in the general sense (although not the specific technical sense of Chomsky, 1981) to refer to the relation in natural language wherein a proform (i.e., an anaphor) is interpreted by reference to another term (which may be a name) in a sentence or discourse. For example, in 1, the pronoun "he" is interpreted by reference to the name "John" (under its most likely interpretation with neutral stress). Likewise, in 2, the "null anaphor" is interpreted by reference to the name "John".

(1)   *John* read the play and *he* smoked a pipe.
(2)   *John* read the play and *Ø* smoked a pipe.

Sentence 1 in this paper will be said to exemplify a relation of *pronoun anaphora*; sentence 2, a relation of *null anaphora*. We will be concerned with pronoun anaphora in this study. Although the term "anaphora" is used in current linguistic theory of Universal Grammar in a way which

B. Lust (ed.), Studies in the Acquisition of Anaphora, Vol. I, 203—243.
© 1986 *by D. Reidel Publishing Company.*

is restricted not to include pronouns (Chomsky, 1981), we use the more general sense of the term here, *viz.* as one phenomenon covered by the subsystem of UG called "binding theory", which is concerned with "relations of anaphors, pronouns, names and variables to possible antecedents" (Chomsky 1981, 6).

Although it is well known that some anaphora can be determined by extra-syntactic (pragmatic as well as discourse) factors (e.g., Hankamer & Sag, 1976; Williams, 1977a, b; Hammerton, 1970; Kuno, 1972a, b, 1975; Stenning, 1978), we will be concerned with sentential anaphora in this study, not with discourse or contextual anaphora.

In this paper we assess the role in first language acquisition of English of 3 "locality" conditions which characterize relations between a pronoun and an antecedent within a sentence: *Directionality, Depth* and *Distance.* (See Koster, 1981 for discussion of "locality" principles (in general).) We define each of these conditions below, and report results of an experimental study which varied these three conditions factorially.

On the basis of our experimental results, we argue that, contrary to what might be expected, children in their computation of anaphora do not critically consult the factor of *distance.* This factor is based on surface and non-linguistic facts about language. They do critically consult the factor of *depth.* This factor is related to the configurational structure of language. They do also consult the factor of *directionality.* This factor establishes linear order between antecedent and anaphor.

Critically, in this study, however, children are shown not to consult *directionality* in a manner which is independent of configurational structure and based on surface linearity alone. Children are shown to *block* a directionality principle when configurational structure requires this. The factor of linear order is thus shown to be overriden by the factor of configurational structure when these two are at odds.

These results are argued to critically support the structure-dependent nature of children's early hypotheses regarding anaphora in the language they are acquiring. They help to define the nature of the constraints which structure these early hypotheses.

1.1 *Directionality*

Previous research has shown that a *directionality constraint* characterizes anaphora in young children's language (e.g., Lust, 1981). In first language acquisition of English, children (2 to 7 years) showed a strong preference for forward anaphora. In forward anaphora, the anaphor *follows* the governing term to which it is related, as in 3. In backward anaphora, the anaphor *precedes* the governing term as in 4.

(3)   *Oscar* bumped the wall when *he* found the penny.
(4)   When *he* closed the box, *Cookie Monster* lay down.

In an elicited imitation task, for example, young children acquiring English found it significantly easier to imitate sentences with forward anaphora (such as 3), than those with backward anaphora (such as 4). Moreover, children reduced redundancy only in a forward direction. For example, given a sentence such as 5 to imitate, children frequently converted to a sentence like 6, but never to a sentence like 4, even though 4 is a grammatical option.

(5)   When *Cookie Monster* closed the box, *Cookie Monster* lay down.
(6)   When *Cookie Monster* closed the box, *he* lay down.

When asked to imitate backward pronoun anaphora such as in 4, children often reversed the order of the name and pronoun to give forward anaphora as in 6. Other research has independently supported these directionality findings and confirmed that this phenomenon also characterizes several forms of null anaphora and generalizes from experimental data to natural speech (e.g., Tavakolian, 1977; Solan, 1978, 1983; Lust and Mervis, 1980; Lust, Solan, Flynn, Cross & Schuetz, 1981, and this volume). Elsewhere we have studied further the nature of this effect, which we refer to as a "directionality constraint" (Lust, Loveland, Kornet, 1980.)

1.1.1 *The Nature of the Directionality Cosntraint*

The 'directionality constraint' could reflect a simple principle of surface linear order: An antecedent must *precede* an anaphor to which it is related. This principle could be computed on surface facts. It could be autonomous, that is, independent of configurational structure. In general, linearity is a general cognitive relation which is not specifically linguistic (e.g., Wasow, 1979, 61; Reinhart, 1976). Elsewhere, based on English acquisition data alone, it has been theorized that the early directionality constraint in English might be based on a sensitivity to autonomous linear order (Tavakolian, 1977, 1978; Carden, 1981, also this volume; Solan, 1983; Roeper, this volume).

As Reinhart has noticed (1976), however, in a right branching language like English, what precedes will usually also 'command' what follows, in a sentence. (Below we define the concept 'command' which characterizes a configurational relation between terms.) Thus the forward directionality constraint in child language *could* reflect sensitivity to a correlation of linear order and a structural relation like command. In support of this thesis, research has confirmed that children acquiring a left-branching language, such as Japanese or Chinese, do not show the forward directionality constraint found in children acquiring English (Lust & Wakayama, 1979, 1981; Lust & Chien, 1984; Lust, Mangione and Chien, 1984). An early paper by Roeper 1973, presented German acquisition data which also suggested that children might modulate linear order in early anaphora with regard to the structure of this language.

The psycholinguistic issue of whether children are sensitive to both linearity and configuration in anaphora is paralleled by a linguistic issue. Whether both linear order and command are equally important in the grammatical theory of anaphora has long been debated in linguistic study of anaphora and is currently still debated (Higginbotham, 1980; Lasnik, 1976; Reinhart, 1976, 1981).

1.1.2 *Command*

While Langacker (1970) had argued that a pronoun may not "precede and command" its antecedent, Reinhart (1976) argued that the critical grammatical factor may be "c-command," and that it may be unnecessary to involve the linear principle of 'precede' in grammar. Sentences like 7, she argued, do not allow anaphoric interpretation between a name and pronoun. (The asterisk means that coreference is not allowed between name and pronoun underlined.) Such sentences show that the critical constraint is that a pronoun may not *c-command* an antecedent, even if it is *preceded* by an antecedent.

(7)   *Near Dan_i, he_i saw a snake

They suggest that c-command, not linearity, determines well-formedness of anaphora.

"Command" relations crucially refer to dominance relations in the constituent structure of a language. They are generally defined over configurational (or geometric, i.e., tree-structure) representations of a sentence. In a general sense, term A has been said to "command" term B, if a defined node X which dominates the term A also dominates the term B in this configurational structure. Various definitions of command differ in their specification of X and its relation to A. (See also the introduction to this volume for further references on this concept.)

A general configurational representation over which a command relation is defined (where A commands B) is shown in 8a. 8b shows that this relation characterizes the relation between name and pronoun in 7.

(8) a.

(8) b.

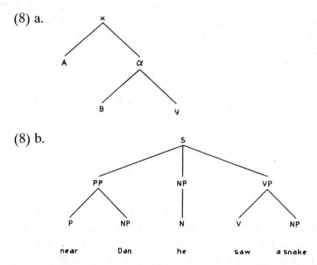

In Chomsky's current theory of Universal Grammar, command relations are believed to be critical in determining well-formed anaphora, as well as other grammatical subsystems. Chomsky has recently articulated the centrality of the notion 'command' in binding theory: "... it is a configurational property — presumably c-command — that determines the operation of the binding theory, not a requirement that anaphors (or pronominals ...) search for subjects or objects as antecedents, in some sense of this notion that has any independent sense apart from the configurational properties" (Chomsky, 1981, 154).

There are a number of unresolved issues which regard command, such as at how many levels of natural language representation command is relevant to anaphora (e.g., syntactic and/or semantic), and whether command applies differentially to different types of anaphors (e.g., pronouns as well as various types of null anaphors). There is general agreement, however, that if any type of command is involved in anaphora, syntactic command is, and that it is relevant to all anaphoric types in binding theory, although it may apply to these differently. We will concentrate in this paper thus on syntactic command, and consider its relevance to acquisition of pronoun anaphora.

Of the several different definitions of "command" (see Saito 1984, and Solan, 1983 for a helpful review) we use a notion of "command" called "c" command in the experimental design of the stimulus sentences in our study. This is generally defined as the case where the *first branching* node above the commanding term also dominates the commanded term (Reinhart, 1976, 1981), as in the figures 8 above.

1.1.3 *Previous Acquisition Research on Command*

There has been some evidence in the child language literature that children *are* sensitive to dominance relations in their language such as represented by "command." There have been two studies which more directly address the issue of whether children are sensitive to "command" relations within a language in early forms of anaphora.

Solan (1983) tested 5–7 year old children (mean age 6,7) by an act-out task on comprehension of 8 sentence types involving right-branching complementation of a main clause and backward pronominalization from the complement to the main clause. *Position* of pronoun (subject or object) in the main clause, *type* of complement (NP or S), and *place* of complement attachment (VP or S) varied factorially. Solan's results showed significant main effects of each of the varied structural factors on amount of children's backward anaphora judgments, in a comprehension test. These results suggested that the children were sensitive to the structural factors manipulated, all of which involve dominance. For example, Solan's results showed that children made significantly fewer backward anaphoric judgments with VP-attachment of complements than with S-attachment. Since VP-attachment provides a configuration where main clause object c-commands the terms of the complement, this result may reflect a greater avoidance by children of anaphora in the c-command situations.

All Solan's examples reflected backward anaphora. Thus although these data suggest that children may be sensitive to dominance relations such as command, they leave open the issue of the relation of this sensitivity to the forward directionality constraint.

In another study, Lust, Loveland, Kornet (1980) tested whether children were sensitive to dominance relations and also varied directionality of pronouns. In this study (3—8 year old) children in an act-out comprehension task frequently blocked coreference judgments between name and pronoun in sentences like 9 or 10 as well as 11; although they freely gave coreference judgments in sentences like 1.

(9)   *On top of *Ernie's* head, *he* rubbed the tissue
(10)   *Under *Cookie Monster, he* threw the donut
(11)   *He* rolled over when *Big Bird* opened the box

In sentences 9, 10, and 11, the pronoun commands the name and thus anaphora is blocked in adult grammar, as in 7. Sentences 9 and 10 have the name preceding the pronoun (forward pronominalization) while 11 has the pronoun preceding the name (backward pronominalization). These results were especially important because if children had a directionality constraint which was simply based on forward linear order (i.e., name simply must precede the pronoun) children should have attributed coreference in 9 and 10 although they may not have in 11. These results suggest then, as Solan's had, that children might be sensitive to relations of command. Further, these results suggested that the forward directionality constraint in English child language may be sensitive to the structural relation between the pronoun and antecedent. This study varied different types of command without distinguishing them, however, e.g., that in 9, or 10, and 11.

Both the Solan and the Lust, Loveland, Kornet studies then suggest that young children acquiring English are sensitive to specific relations of command (reflecting dominance) in early anaphora. However, they do not directly provide conclusive evidence that children's forward directionality constraint is not based on strictly linearity alone, independent of command. The critical question is: *do children allow configurational factors, such as reflected by command structure, to override the directionality principle they hold favoring foward anaphora?* If so, this will provide critical evidence that the forward directionality constraint in first language acquisition of English is not independent of the configurational structure of English sentences, and is thus not based on linearity alone.

1.2 *Depth*

If children are sensitive to dominance relations, then we might expect children to be sensitive to *depth* of embedding (i.e., increase in number of phrase embeddings) of the antecedent name relative to pronoun (or of the antecedent pronoun relative to the name), since 'depth' is a property of dominance. If children consult dominance relations in a sentence in applying the forward directionality principle, then we might expect the factor of *depth* to interact with their computation of forward anaphora. For example, we might expect children to distinguish 9 from 10. There is an extra phrasal node between name and pronoun in 9 relative to 10. If dominance is consulted in the anaphora in these sentences, then we might predict increased *depth* to aid, not hinder children's control of these sentences. If dominance is involved in children's *directionality* constraint, and not only linear order, it might be expected that the directionality constraint should be accentuated where there is more *depth* in the stimulus sentences.

In fact, in adult grammar, depth of embedding does appear to influence interpretation of anaphora. Compare for example the apparently greater likelihood of a coreferential judgment in a sentence like 12 compared to 7.

(12)   Near Dan's fertile garden, he built a potting shed.

The name *Dan* is embedded in an extra phrase node in 12.[2]

1.3 *Distance*

It is possible that children would block forward anaphora in a sentence like 10 simply because the name and pronoun are immediately adjoined; i.e., there is no *distance* between name and pronoun. This result on anaphora in 10 would not require postulating that children were sensitive to the dominance relations this sentence involves. Increased *depth* of embedding, for example, in 12, compared to 7, also often includes increased *distance* between name and pronoun. Evidence of sensitivity to depth of embedding then does not necessarily mean that children are sensitive to dominance, unless this factor is clearly distinguished from the factor of distance. It too could reflect children's alternative sensitivity to a non-linguistic factor, *distance*.

2.0 THE 3-D STUDY: HYPOTHESES TESTED

In this study we test the thesis that in first language acquisition of English, the language learner's forward *directionality* constraint is not independent of sensitivity to dominance. We hypothesize, that children will evidence modulation of their forward directionality constraint when the command relations within their language are reversed. For example, they will modulate their directionality constraint in sentences like 9—10 above. These sentences reverse the unmarked right branching direction of English, and thus critically manipulate the usual command relations in English sentences.

Specifically, we test whether children who are acquiring English will block the anaphora they usually impose in a *forward* direction, when command relations are reversed, e.g., like 7, 9, or 10. A structure like 8b is assumed for sentences like these.[3] What precedes in these cases does not command (as in unmarked English right-branching sentence structure) but what follows commands (in subject position).

If children do modulate their anaphora in accord with dominance relations, thus breaking the usual (forward) directionality constraint, this would confirm not only that children are sensitive to dominance relations in their language but that the 'directionality' constraint previously observed in child language does consult configurational structure. It is not autonomous. It includes a sensitivity to dominance.

We also test the effects of two other factors which characterize the relation between a name and an anaphor: i.e., *distance* between name and pronoun and degree of *depth* of embedding between them. We evaluate the roles of these factors in children's acquisition of anaphora, independent of the factor of *direction*. We hypothesized that if children are sensitive to configurational structure, the grammatical factor of syntactic dominance, i.e., *depth* of embedding, would significantly affect children's anaphora. We hypothesized that *distance* would not be an overriding factor. If *distance* were significant it would only be so in interaction with *depth*, e.g., in sentence 9. If there were only added distance, and no added depth in an antecedent-pronoun relation, the *distance* factor would not be significant in itself.

We evaluate whether the three factors of *direction*, *depth* and *distance* affect children's computation of anaphora through 2 measures: a measure of children's production (imitation) and a measure of their comprehension.

Both production and comprehension tasks were necessary to this study because a finding that children evidence a forward directionality constraint in production (imitation) would not necessitate a conclusion that they compute an anaphora or coreference judgment in these cases. The comprehension task allows us to test this directly.

In general, children would be predicted to recognize the sentences tested in this study as marked, both for imitation and comprehension. This is because the sentences reverse the unmarked right-branching structure of English and conflict with the forward directionality principle children construct for English.

2.1 *Method*

2.1.1 *Design*

Children were tested on 2 examples each of the eight sentences types exemplified in Tables I and II for both their *imitation* and *comprehension*, respectively. All the sentences in Tables I and II represent a condition of reversed dominance. They all involve preposed prepositional phrases as do 9 and 10. What occurs in the preposed prepositional phrase in these structures is c-commanded by the following term in main clause subject position as 8b shows. Forward pronominalization is blocked in the adult grammar on these sentences. Only backward pronominalization is possible on them.[4]

Sentences on Table I and II varied factorially in pronominalization *Direction* (*forward* (pronoun follows name) and *backward* (pronoun precedes)), *Depth* of embeddedness of the antecedent pronoun or name in the preposed phrase (i.e., one or two phrases deep) and *Distance* between name and pronoun (separation by one word (+Distance) or no separation (−Distance)). These 3 independently varied factors constitute the "3-D" factors of this study.

Varying in *Direction*, sentences with forward pronominalization had a name in the preposed prepositional phrase and a pronoun as subject of the main clause, e.g., 1−4 on Tables I and II. Sentences with backward pronominalization had a name as subject of the main clause, and a pronoun in the preposed prepositional phrase, e.g., sentences 5−8 on Tables I and II. Varying in *Depth* of embeddedness, sentences with one NP embedding of the term within their preposed prepositional phrase are exemplified by "On *Cookie Monster, he* . . ." (−Depth), e.g.,

TABLE I
Examples of Sentences in Imitation Task on 3-D Study

Forward	Backward

+Depth

+Distance

1. On the side of *Ernie's* face, *he* put the kleenex.

5. Under the bottom of *his* foot, *Ernie* rolled the ball.

−Distance

2. Under the leg of *Ernie*, *he* threw the lollipop.

6. Under that toe of *his*, *Oscar* dropped the ice cream.

−Depth

+Distance

3. On *Cookie Monster*, quickly, *he* poured the chocolate milk.

7. On *him*, quietly, *Big Bird* spilled the grape juice.

−Distance

4. Under *Oscar the Grouch*, *he* quietly bounced the ball.

8. On *him*, *Cookie Monster* quickly poured the orange juice.

4 and 8 on Tables I and II. Sentences with 2 NP embeddings are exemplified by "Under the foot of *Ernie*, he ..." (+Depth), e.g., 2 and 6 on Tables I and II.[5] *Distance* between name and pronoun varied in "+Depth, +Distance" sentences such as "On the side of *Ernie's* face, *he* ... ," 1 and 5 on Tables I and II, and in "+Depth, −Distance" sentences such as "Under the leg of *Ernie, he* ...", 2 and 6 on Tables I and II. *Depth* and *Distance* were varied independently. In the condition of "−Depth," sentences without distance were represented by examples like "Under *Oscar the Grouch, he* ... ," e.g., 4 and 8 on Tables I and II. Sentences '+Distance' in this "−Depth" condition involved an adverb interposed between the simple preposed prepositional phrase and the main clause, e.g., "On *Cookie Monster*, quickly, *he* poured the chocolate milk," e.g., 3 and 7 on Tables I and II. It was assumed that the adverb in the "+distance" condition did not significantly change syntactic structure, but merely added distance between name and pronoun without increasing depth. There were 2 examples of each of the 8 conditions

TABLE II
Examples of Sentences in Act-Out Task on 3-D Study

Forward	Backward

+Depth

+Distance

1. On the top of *Oscar's* head, *he* rubbed the donut.

−Distance

2. Under the foot of *Ernie*, he put the pillow.

5. Under the toe of *his* foot, *Ernie* put the donut.

6. On that foot of *his*, *Cookie Monster* dropped the donut.

−Depth

+Distance

3. Under *Big Bird*, quickly, *he* threw the choo-choo train.

−Distance

4. On *Cookie Monster,* he quickly dropped the choo-choo train.

7. On *him*, quietly, *Oscar the Grouch* rubbed the pillow.

8. Under *him*, *Big Bird* quietly pushed the choo-choo train.

shown on Tables I and II. Thus there were 16 3-D sentences for both imitation and comprehension.

In addition, four subordinate clause sentences with directionally varied pronouns, e.g., 3 and 4 above, were also tested in this study although they will not be reported in this paper except as baseline comparisons of performance. There were thus 20 sentences in all for both imitation and comprehension, 16 of the 3D type shown on Tables I and II, and 4 subordinate clause type. All sentences were 12 syllables long and were uniformly controlled in lexicon, pragmatic content, and general sentence structure.

The overall design thus allowed for a 3 factor ANOVA ($2 \times 2 \times 2$) with independent 2-valued factors of *Direction, Depth, Distance* (the 3-D factors) and repeated measures giving the basic 8 sentence types. An additional between-group factor, *Development,* varied age group in nine six-month age groups as shown on Figure 1. Results on these 3-D sentences could be compared by design to results on sentences with subordinate clauses. We focus on 3-D sentence results in this paper. Unless specified otherwise, all results refer to the 16 3-D sentences.

2.1.2 Tasks

The elicited imitation task involved a methodology which has been established in previous research to tap children's language competence (Lust, 1977; Lust, Loveland, Kornet, 1979 and Slobin and Welsh, 1973). The comprehension task involved an act-out task with children's dolls, now established in the literature as a test of comprehension (e.g., Sinclair, et al., 1976; Goodluck and Solan, 1978; Lust, Loveland & Kornet, 1980). Both tasks are studied in some detail in Lust, Chien and Flynn, to appear.

2.1.3 Procedures

Half the children received the imitation test first. Half received the comprehension test first. Both tests were divided into 2 randomized batteries of 10 sentences each. In most cases, all testing was completed in one session of approximately 1/2 hour.

For imitation and comprehension tasks, one experimenter administered the task, while another observed and transcribed the comprehension task results. All sessions were tape recorded. Imitation task data were transcribed from tapes. For 20% of the subjects, a third experimenter was present to provide independent transcription of the interpretation and imitation task results; allowing test of reliability of recording and scoring procedures.

Reference Set for the Interpretation Task. The reference sets for each of the interpretation batteries consisted of 3 Sesame Street dolls (6 dolls for the 2 batteries) which corresponded to the names mentioned in the sentences. The dolls were not displayed during the imitation task. Several small props were also available to the child for use in the interpretation task (e.g., a candy, an ice cream cone, a block, etc.).

Pretraining. A set of pre-training sentences preceded both the imitation and the interpretation tasks. *For the imitation task,* these pre-training sentences consisted of a set of (i) single clause sentences, (ii) double clause coordinated sentences with 2 different subject names, (iii) double clause coordinated sentences each with the same repeated subject names. Imitation of these sentences was elicited to determine (a) that the child understood the imitation task in general; (b) that the child could imitate a multiple clause structure; and (c) that (s)he could imitate one with *more than one* subject, as well as one with a *single* subject. This guaranteed that the child would be aware that the task neutrally allowed anaphora (and coreference) options to include *either* coreference with the named doll or noncoreference. Successful pre-training consisted of the child's correct imitation of at least one of each of the 3 structural types. If a child did not at first succeed the pretest items, at least one model or prompt was given. No child who did not eventually pass pretraining participated in the test sequence.

For the comprehension task, a similar set of 3 single and multiple clause structures was administered as pretraining. A similar criterion for successful pretraining was adopted, *viz.*, successful acting out of at least one of each of the 3 structural types. Successful interpretation involved use of either one or two dolls and relevant props in actions specified in the model sentences.

2.1.4 *Scoring*

All data were independently scored by 2 persons (or by 3 persons in the portion of the sample subjected to reliability test), according to established criteria briefly summarized below (and available in full on request). All differences were resolved by rechecking of tapes and/or discussion of scoring criteria. Four measures were scored, two for each task, as follows.

Imitation Measures: All data were scored for (i) *correctness* and for (ii) *errors on anaphora* structure.

Correctness. Incorrect were all changes in anaphora or basic clause structure. Thus (a) clause reversals; (b) omission of clause; (c) conflation to a single clause; (d) movement or repetition of prepositional phrase, and (e) movement or omission of the adverb, for example, were all incorrect. Imitation errors, such as inflection omission or tense changes, etc., were allowed in imitations scored as correct.

Anaphora errors, which were all incorrect, included all changes in the pronoun or relation between noun and pronoun: e.g., pronoun direction reversal, substitution of NP for a pronoun and vice versa, double pronominalization, deletion of NP or pronoun, noun in apposition and addition of pronoun or NP. All scored anaphora errors maintained the general syntactic two-clause structure of the sentence.

Comprehension task Measures: Generally, the same criteria were applied in the comprehension task as in the imitation task. All comprehension data were scored for (i) *correctness* and for (ii) *coreference judgments* (CRJ).

Correctness. Sentences were scored correct only if both phrase and clause were acted out. With regard to pronoun interpretation, all forward pronominalization sentences in Table II were scored correct only if a *non*-coreferential choice of a doll was made to interpret the pronoun. All backward pronominalization sentences in Table II were scored correct if the child chose either a coreferential or a noncoreferential doll to interpret the pronoun. A judgment of coreference was operationally defined as the child's use of the same doll for interpretation of the pronoun and the name, in any order. Substitution of a different doll or prop for the named one was scored incorrect in all cases. All scored judgments of coreference maintained reference to both the phrase and the main clause in the sentence and used a single doll to represent each. An additional type of error unique to the act-out task was the use of the *child's self as an agent* rather than either the named doll or another doll. This was scored as incorrect in all cases, and analyzed as a unique error.

Reliability results: Independent transcription and scoring by two observers, calculated for 20% of the data resulted in 96% agreement on imitation data scoring and 92% on act-out (correct/incorrect scores).

2.1.5 *Subjects*

94 Ss were tested, ranging from 3,5 to 7,11 (years, months). Mean age was 5,7. All subjects were monolingual, from local Ithaca daycare centers and grammar schools, and showed no overt language disorder.

2.2 *Results*

For all results, we assume a .01 level of statistical significance in analyses. Score range is 0—2 since there were two exemplars for each condition.

2.2.1 *Imitation Data*

Success. Mean numbers of items correct on children's imitation of each condition of the 16 3-D sentences are shown in Table III. Mean number of anaphora errors are shown on Table IV. Overall mean correct was low on these sentences (only .93). (This may be compared to 1.49 on a comparable set of sentences with subordinate clauses.) As predicted, then, children treat these as marked structures, although by the age of 7 (last 2 groups) children approach 75% correct as Figure 1 shows.

Developmentally, correct imitation on these sentences increased with age over the 9 age groups tested, as shown in Figure 1; *Development* (F(8,85) = 6.78, p < .001). *Development* did not interact significantly with any of the other factors, however, suggesting that the effects of the 3-D factors were relatively constant over the whole age range studied.

Analysis of Variance on amount of successful imitation of these sentences showed that the factors of *Direction* and *Depth*, were each significant in determining children's success in imitation: *Depth* (F(1,85)

TABLE III

Mean Number of Items Correct in the *Imitation* Task of 3-D Study

(*by Direction, Depth, Distance and Developmental Level*)[a]

Developmental Levels	Forward					Backward					Group Mean
	+Depth		−Depth		Mean	+Depth		−Depth		Mean	
	+ Dist	− Dist	+ Dist	− Dist		+ Dist	− Dist	+ Dist	− Dist		
I 3,5−3,11	0.58	0.58	0.25	0.17	0.40	0.17	0.33	0.08	0.17	0.19	0.29
II 4,0−4,4	0.83	0.92	0.17	0.5	0.61	0.42	0.58	0.58	0.17	0.44	0.52
III 4,5−4,11	1.30	1.30	0.80	1.00	1.10	0.70	0.70	0.50	0.40	0.58	0.84
IV 5,0−5,4	1.40	1.30	0.50	0.80	1.00	1.0	0.9	0.6	0.3	0.70	0.85
V 5,5−5,11	1.30	1.2	0.2	0.4	0.78	0.9	1.0	0.4	0.5	0.70	0.74
VI 6,0−6,4	1.6	1.6	0.9	1.6	1.43	1.0	1.4	0.8	1.0	1.05	1.24
VII 6,5−6,11	1.7	1.8	0.8	1.2	1.38	1.4	1.3	1.2	1.0	1.23	1.30
VIII 7,0−7,4	1.8	1.8	1.3	1.6	1.63	1.6	1.6	1.4	1.1	1.43	1.53
IX 7,5−7,11	1.9	1.9	1.2	1.2	1.55	1.2	0.8	1.2	0.9	1.03	1.29
Overall Groups	1.35	1.35	0.66	0.92	1.07	0.90	0.94	0.73	0.60	0.79	0.93

[a] Score range 0−2.

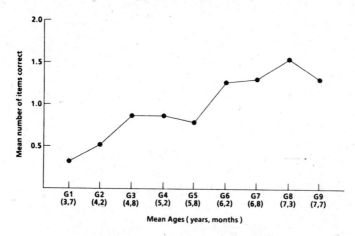

Fig. 1. Development of Correct Imitation on 3D Study.

= 87.25, p < .001); *Direction* (F(1,85) = 32.24, p < .001). Forward pronominalization was in general significantly easier (1.07) to imitate successfully than backward pronominalization (.79), signifying that children applied a general forward *Directionality* principle also on production of these sentences, even though forward anaphora is blocked on them. Sentences with increased *Depth* were in general significantly easier for children to imitate (mean number of items correct was 1.14) than those with less depth (mean .73), suggesting that children did consult the dominance relations in these sentences. *Distance* was not significant as a main effect (F(1,85) = 0.68, p = .41).

Moreover, the factors of *Depth* and *Direction* interacted significantly in a 2-way interaction (F(1,85) = 14.34, p < .001) and together these interacted with *Distance* in a 3-way interaction (F(1,85) = 7.47, p < .01) in children's imitation. As can be seen in Figures 2a & b, increased depth increases imitation success for both forward and backward pronominalization (whether or not there is distance between name and pronoun). Critically, however, the *directionality* effect (favoring forward over backward pronominalization) holds more strongly where there is increased *depth* (sentences 1,2 vs 5,6 on Table I) (F(1,85) = 50.06, p < .001) rather than less depth (F(1,85) = 3.65, p = .60) (sentences 3,4 vs 7,8), as the figures show. This would be predicted, as we stated above, if children associated the *directionality* constraint with dominance, which the *depth* factor reflects.

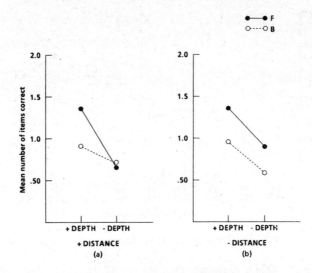

Figs. 2a & b. Amount of Correct Imitation on Various Conditions of 3D Study
(*Direction* × *Depth* × *Distance*).

Distance can be seen from Figures 2a and b to have a very restricted
effect. It is only where there is a forward direction and no depth (3 vs 4).
The factor of added *distance* without *depth* (3 on Table I) significantly
depresses the amount of correct imitation of forward pronominalization.
In this condition of (−*Depth*, +*Distance*), the *Directionality* effect is
nullified as seen in Figure 2a. That is, forward and backward pronominalization are not distinguished by children in this condition. This might
follow if children expected forward directionality of anaphora to cohere
with right branching embedding. They would thus find the increased
distance in this condition (e.g., 3 on Table I) *without* correspondent
increased embedding, to be disturbing. They thus do not apply the
forward directionality constraint here.

These results show that the Directionality effect is linked to *Depth* of
embedding. Although it also holds where there is no depth (7 and 8 on
Table I) the *Directionality* effect is smaller here, and can be nullified in
this condition by the insertion of distance (without depth) between the
name and pronoun.

In summary, children show a directionality constraint overall favoring
forward over backward pronominalization on production of these sen-

tences. Since these sentences do not allow forward anaphora, this might suggest that children's *directionality* constraint is independent of configurational structure. However, overall mean correct imitation is depressed, signalling that children did find these sentences marked. Since the markedness of these sentences results from their reversed dominance structure, and its conflict with forward directionality of anaphora, it is possible that children recognized this conflict. In support of this view, the factor which reflects dominance, *viz. depth*, is significant in children's correct imitation of these sentences; and the *directionality* effect is significantly modulated by (in fact, increased by) *depth*. *Distance* is not critical unless in interaction with *depth*, as well as *Direction*.

Anaphora Error. An analysis of anaphora errors allows more precise evaluation of the effects of the 3-D factors on children's imitation. 58% of all errors on imitation of these 16 3-D sentences (31% of items) involved anaphora errors (as defined above). (This may be compared with 47% of all errors which involved anaphora errors (12% of items) on the 4 comparable sentences with subordinate clauses.)

TABLE IV

Mean Number of Items with Anaphora Errors in Imitation Task of 3-D Study

	Forward					Backward					Group Mean
	+Depth		−Depth		Mean	+Depth		−Depth		Mean	
Developmental Levels	+ Dist	− Dist	+ Dist	− Dist		+ Dist	− Dist	+ Dist	− Dist		
I (3,5−3,11)	0.58	0.42	1.33	0.50	0.71	1.42	1.08	0.92	0.75	1.04	0.88
II (4,0−4,4)	0.67	0.83	1.25	0.67	0.86	1.17	1.08	0.67	1.00	0.98	0.92
III (4,5−4,11)	0.50	0.30	1.00	0.60	0.60	0.90	1.00	1.20	0.90	1.00	0.80
IV (5,0−5,4)	0.20	0.10	0.60	0.40	0.31	0.60	0.70	0.50	0.40	0.55	0.44
V (5,5−5,11)	0.20	0.30	1.10	0.80	0.60	0.80	0.70	1.30	0.80	0.90	0.75
VI (6,0−6,4)	0.30	0.30	1.00	0.00	0.40	0.40	0.60	0.70	0.80	0.63	0.51
VII (6,5−6,11)	0.20	0.20	0.90	0.00	0.33	0.30	0.60	0.80	0.70	0.60	0.46
VIII (7,0−7,4)	0.00	0.10	0.60	0.20	0.23	0.10	0.30	0.20	0.40	0.25	0.24
IX (7,5−8,0)	0.00	0.10	0.70	0.40	0.30	0.40	0.70	0.70	0.80	0.65	0.48
Overall Groups	0.31	0.31	0.96	0.40	0.50	0.70	0.77	0.78	0.73	0.75	0.62

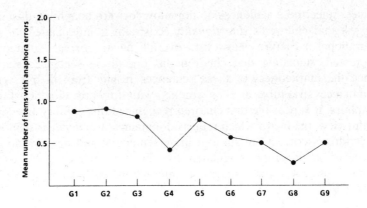

Fig. 3. Anaphora Errors Over all Groups in Imitation of 3D Sentences.

As can be seen from Table IV and Figure 3, anaphora errors on the 16 3-D sentences significantly decrease with age, decreasing most significantly between groups 2 and 4 (*Development*, F(8,85) = 3.97, p < .001). Again *Development* did not significantly interact with any of the other factors in amount of anaphora error.

Anaphora error on the 3-D sentences was also found to vary significantly with each of the 3-D factors. *Direction* significantly affected amount of anaphora error, with significantly more error on the backward cases (.75) than on the forward (.50) (F(1,85) = 17.11, p < .001). *Depth* also significantly affected amount of anaphora error (F(1,85) = 15.36, p < .001), with significantly more anaphora errors in the −Depth condition (.72) than in the +Depth (.52). Moreover, anaphora errors showed a similar set of significant interactions as the overall amount correct data did, with a similar pattern of results. Although *Distance* significantly affected amount of anaphora error, it again interacted with *Depth*.

These anaphora error results suggest that the structural pattern of results reflected in success rate of children's imitation is critically due to their handling of the anaphora in these sentences.

Prepositional Phrase (PP) Errors. Errors of movement, copying and reconstruction of the PP in these sentences occurred on both backward and forward anaphora, shown in examples 13 and 14 below. (Overall, 13% of items involved a prepositional phrase error.)[6]

(13) a. E: On him, Cookie Monster quickly poured the orange juice.
   b. Child: Cookie Monster poured the orange juice on him
       (*movement*)
   c. Child: On him Cookie Monster poured the orange juice on
       him (*copy*)
   d. Child: Cookie Monster poured the orange juice under
       Ernie's foot (*reconstruction*)
(14) a. E: Under Oscar the Grouch, he quietly bounced the ball
   b. Child: He quietly bounced the ball under Oscar the Grouch
       (*movement*)
   c. Child: Under Oscar the Grouch, he quietly bounced the ball
       under Oscar the Grouch (*copy*)
   d. Child: Quietly Oscar bounced, bounced on his head the ball
       him (*reconstruction*)

All of the 16 3-D stimulus sentences involved preposed PP. However, children made more errors on the preposed prepositional phrase
(e.g., moving, copying, reconstructing or omitting it) on sentences which
had backward anaphora (sentences 5−8 on Table I) than they did on
those with forward anaphora (1−4). Sixty-three percent of prepositional
phrase errors were on backward anaphora while 37% were on forward
anaphora sentences. Children *omitted* these preposed prepositional
phrases nearly equivalently in both forward and backward anaphora
cases (6% out of forward items; 8% out of backward items respectively).
However, they moved, copied or reconstructed the prepositional phrase
to a postposition substantially more often when the model involved
backward pronominalization (46% of all errors on backward items),
e.g., 13b, or c, or d, than in forward, 14b or c or d (27% of all errors on
forward items).

Children in fact only rarely changed PP position without also changing anaphora direction. For example they never maintained backward
anaphora and also changed PP position, as in converting 13a to 15.
They only rarely convert 14a to 16 (2% of PP conversions *on forward*
pronominalization).

(15)   He quickly poured the orange juice on Cookie Monster.
(16)   Oscar the Grouch quietly bounced the ball under him.

Overall, 49% of PP conversions also involved a clear pronominalization
direction change. Conversion (movement, copy or reconstruction) of the

prepositional phrase in backward pronominalization may and usually did involve a reversal of pronominalization direction; backward to forward as in conversion of 13a to 13b (4%) or c (55%). Many (41%) were reconstructions as in 13d. (None of the small amount of PP conversions on forward pronominalization involved pronominalization direction change to backward (as in 14a to b); only 17% of PP conversions on 14a converted to 14c. The remainder of forward pronominalization changes were of the reconstruction type, e.g., 14d.)

These results suggest that pronominalization direction and branching direction were correlated in children's production. The directionality principle in child language which favors forward pronominalization is fundamentally related to a preference for rightward branching as in postpositioned PPs (e.g., 13 b−d) as opposed to preposed PPs. These results suggest that the forward directionality constraint in pronominalization in first language is tightly linked to a sensitivity to dominance, specifically to the dominance involved in the language's branching direction.

Children's errors on imitation of these sentences which varied with the 3-D factors were thus not simply due to the marked preposed prepositional phrases. In their imitation, children's errors on the preposed prepositional phrases were tightly linked to their anaphora errors, and to the factor of *Direction*.

Summary of Imitation Data. Imitation results thus show a replication of the *directionality* effect, involving a preference for forward pronouns. However, imitation data also suggest a sensitivity to dominance and interaction of this sensitivity with pronoun *direction*. Children consider these stimulus sentences (which have conflicting dominance and *direction*) to be marked. They significantly associate the *directionality* constraint with increased *depth*, imitate the sentences more successfully with more *depth*, and adjust the preposed PP to show correct unmarked command for forward pronouns.

2.4.2 *Act-out Task*

Success Rate. Table V shows mean numbers correct on the act-out task of the 16 3-D sentences exemplified in Table II. (Overall, only .50 of these sentences were correctly interpreted, as compared to 1.0 on the similar set of 4 subordinate sentences.)

TABLE V

Mean Number of Items Correct in the *Comprehension* Task of 3-D Study
(*by Direction, Depth, Distance* and *Developmental Level*)

Developmental Levels	Forward +Depth + Dist	Forward +Depth − Dist	Forward −Depth + Dist	Forward −Depth − Dist	Forward Mean	Backward +Depth + Dist	Backward +Depth − Dist	Backward −Depth + Dist	Backward −Depth − Dist	Backward Mean	Group Mean
I 3,5−3,11	0.25	0.17	0.25	0.17	0.21	0.42	0.67	0.58	0.42	0.52	0.36
II 4,0−4,4	0.58	0.08	0.08	0.08	0.21	0.33	0.67	0.50	0.08	0.40	0.30
III 4,5−4,11	0.4	0.4	0.2	0.1	0.28	0.3	0.1	0.1	0.5	0.25	0.26
IV 5,0−5,4	0.3	0.2	0.3	0.0	0.2	0.3	0.3	0.3	0.3	0.30	0.25
V 5,5−5,11	0.3	0.1	0.2	0.0	0.15	0.5	0.5	0.3	0.5	0.45	0.30
VI 6,0−6,4	0.6	0.6	0.4	0.6	0.55	0.6	0.9	0.5	0.9	0.73	0.64
VII 6,5−6,11	0.3	0.3	0.1	0.1	0.2	0.8	0.5	0.4	0.6	0.58	0.39
VIII 7,0−7,4	0.8	0.6	0.9	0.9	0.8	1.0	1.4	1.1	1.0	1.13	0.96
IX 7,5−7,11	0.8	0.7	1.0	0.9	0.85	1.1	1.4	1.2	1.5	1.30	1.08
Total overall	0.48	0.34	0.37	0.31	0.38	0.59	0.71	0.55	0.63	0.62	0.50

Comprehension of these sentences improved significantly with *Development* ($F(8,85) = 4.96$, p < .001), as did imitation. As shown in Figure 4, major development in comprehension success was between Groups 5−9 (5,7−7,11 yrs, mos).

Direction of anaphora again significantly affected comprehension success ($F(1,85) = 26.96$, p < .001.) However, in this case, comprehension was significantly more successful on backward pronominalization sentences (e.g., 5−8 on Table II) (mean correct .62) than on forward (mean correct .38) (e.g., 1−4 on Table II). Neither *Depth* nor *Distance* was significant as main effect in act-out success.[7]

Since coreference judgments (i.e., choice of the doll named to interpret the pronoun) were wrong in the forward pronominalization cases and correct in the backward, and since backward pronominalization allowed either coreference or noncoreference, increased success on backward cases could have been due simply to increased probabilities of success due to increased response options in the backward case. Analyses of children's coreference judgments are necessary to evaluate whether this was the sole source of children's greater comprehension success on backward anaphora in these sentences. These analyses showed that it was not.

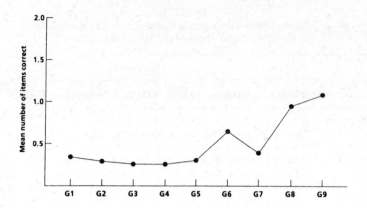

Fig. 4. Development of Correct Comprehension of 3D Sentences.

Coreference Judgments. As described above, children's behaviors on the act out task, where they were presented with a reference set of 3 dolls, were categorized in several types. (1) Children could use the same doll to interpret the name given in the sentence and the pronoun (a *coreference judgment*). (2) They could use a second doll to interpret the pronoun, but the doll named to interpret the *name* (*noncoreference judgment*). Both (1) and (2) require that the child maintain a two part (both main clause and PP) structure in their response. In addition, (3), children could *use themselves* to be the referent of either the doll named or the pronoun, and thus themselves perform the action of the clause. If children do this on sentences with forward pronouns, e.g., sentence 1 on Table I, they are distinctly *not* using the named doll (in this example, "Ernie") to interpret the pronoun, which they have the option of doing and which they most frequently do in this task. Finally (4) children could and did make a variety of *primitive errors* on the task, e.g., act out only one part of the complex sentence (e.g., omit the PP), or omit the main clause completely or in part. If a child commits significantly more of such errors in certain conditions of the experiment, this cannot be due to chance. It can be viewed as reflecting the factors which were experimentally varied to create this condition.

In this particular 3-D experiment, the coreference judgments are critical. If children simply apply a *forward directionality* constraint on these 16 3-D sentences as on others (e.g., the unmarked sentences in English with subordinate clauses, e.g., our 4 tested here like those in other previous studies) and do not consult the structure of these (3-D) sentences, then they should simply make significantly more coreference judgments on the forward pronouns than on the backward, just as they do on sentences with subordinate clauses and unmarked structure.

Table VI shows mean number of *coreference* and *noncoreference* judgments (between pronoun and name) across all conditions of the 16 3-D sentences. Analysis of children's *coreference* judgments (choosing doll named to interpret the pronoun as well as name) confirmed that children made significantly more coreference judgments in backward cases (mean .46 items) than in forward (mean .36 items), $(F(1,85) = 10.02, p = < .01)$ on the 3-D sentences. (On the 4 subordinate clause sentences tested in this study, in contrast, children made significantly more coreference judgments on forward (mean 1.31) than on backward (mean .36) pronouns.) Children thus block the forward *directionality* effect on the 3-D sentences. The fact that the means for coreference judgments are low for both forward and backward pronouns in the 3-D sentences does not invalidate the significance of this finding. The imitation data showed that the children do hold a general *Directionality* principle which says that in general 'pronouns go foward' in English. The subordinate clause data in the comprehension task confirms this also. Thus one would not expect a very large number of coreference

TABLE VI
Coreference Judgment by Direction.
Choice of Doll Named for Pronoun Interpretation (+CR), or of Alternative Doll (−CR)
in Comprehension of 3-D sentences

Developmental Levels	Forward Pronoun		Backward Pronoun	
	+CR	−CR	+CR	−CR
I	12 (13%)	8 (8%)	23 (24%)	17 (16%)
II	14 (15%)	10 (10%)	25 (26%)	13 (14%)
III	11 (14%)	9 (11%)	9 (11%)	10 (13%)
IV	10 (13%)	9 (11%)	17 (21%)	10 (13%)
V	12 (15%)	10 (13%)	12 (15%)	17 (21%)
VI	12 (15%)	23 (29%)	15 (19%)	28 (35%)
VII	19 (24%)	8 (10%)	26 (33%)	12 (15%)
VIII	20 (25%)	31 (39%)	18 (23%)	30 (38%)
IX	26 (33%)	33 (41%)	29 (36%)	33 (41%)
Total	136 (18%)	141 (19%)	174 (23%)	169 (22%)

judgments on backward pronouns. The critical aspect of this 'amount of coreference' judgment, on 3-D sentences remains: Children do not show more coreference judgments in the forward condition than in the backward on these 3-D sentences. The forward (*Directionality*) principle seen elsewhere in children's anaphora is thus significantly modulated on these 3-D sentences. If children's *Directionality* principle only consulted linear order of antecedent and pronoun, this result would not be predicted.

Amount of *noncoreference* judgments are also critical in this study. If children do not treat the forward sentences in terms of their antecedent-pronoun linearity alone, then they might be predicted to explicitly block coreference by choosing a second doll on forward 3-D sentences at least as much as they do so on backward pronouns in general. Usually (on unmarked sentences with subordinate clauses) children make more noncoreference judgments on backward than on forward sentences, although there is usually not a high degree of such extra-sentential reference in this task. Most responses are usually coreferential, especially where this is grammatically allowed. (On the 4 subordinate clauses tested in this study 27% of the backward pronoun items were given a noncoreferential reading by choice of another doll; only 5½% of forward pronouns were.)

In the 3-D sentences, overall, children made a similar number of non-coreference judgments in both forward (19% of items) and backward pronominalization cases (22%) $(F(1,85) = 3.16, p = .08)$. In addition, overall there were as many *noncoreference* judgments as *coreference* judgments in the data (21% of items showed coreference, 21% showed noncoreference). These results clearly show that children blocked coreference on these 3-D sentences, reducing it to an amount equivalent to noncoreference; and treating the forward as equivalent to backward in amount of noncoreference.

This pattern of results distinguishes these data from other in the literature, e.g., that testing children's comprehension of subordinate clauses with varied anaphora direction, where coreference judgments predominate in children's responses (e.g., Lust, Solan, Flynn, Cross and Schuetz, this volume). The increase in coreference judgments on backward over forward cases and the general depression of coreference judgments on the forward cases in these 3-D sentences suggest that children are not treating these forward pronominalization cases like others. This suggests that the children are sensitive to the dominance factor which is reversed in these sentences. They do consult this factor, not only the linear order of pronoun and name, in computing the anaphora in these sentences.[8]

Use of Self Behaviors. Further confirmation that children were not treating these cases of forward pronominalization like other forward anaphora, is shown by the high amount of the children's use of themselves as referents of the pronoun in the forward pronoun cases as opposed to backward. As Table VII shows, on a large number of items (39%), in the forward cases, children used themselves in the act out task for main clause agent. For example, for "On the belly of *Oscar, he* dropped the candy," the child did not have Oscar drop the candy, but did so him(her)self (onto Oscar). This behavior suggests a type of blocking of coreference between the name (*Oscar*) and the forward pronoun (*he*), since the antecedent name is *not* used to interpret the following pronoun in this case, as it is in others.

TABLE VII
Use of Self as Agent Subject in Comprehension Task
of 3-D Study

Developmental Levels	Forward	Backward
I	32 (33%)	15 (16%)
II	39 (41%)	23 (24%)
III	38 (48%)	23 (29%)
IV	36 (45%)	17 (21%)
V	44 (55%)	21 (26%)
VI	34 (43%)	18 (23%)
VII	38 (48%)	27 (34%)
VIII	19 (24%)	18 (23%)
IX	14 (18%)	11 (14%)
Total	294 (39%)	173 (23%)

It might be thought that this effect was due to a simple constraint on the child's interpretation such that main clause subjects should have self as agent, and therefore that this effect was unrelated to anaphora direction or dominance. However, this error occurred substantially less often on backward pronominalization cases as shown on Table VII (only 23% of items with backward pronouns showed this error).[9] This difference suggests that at least part of the source of this "self as agent" effect may be attributed to the child's attempt to block coreference in the forward cases. Moreover use of self is significantly more rare in children's interpretation of other anaphora, and does not differ by direction. (For example, on the 4 subordinate clause sentences tested in this study, such use of self occurred only on 8% of forward items, 7½% of backward.)

The Effect of 3-D Factors on CRJ. In support of the view that children consulted the dominance relations in the 3-D sentences, the factor of *depth* was also significant in determining amount of coreference judgments. There were significantly more coreference judgments in the +depth (.49) than −depth (.33) conditions (F(1,85) = 18.35, p = .001). A significant *Direction x Depth* interaction (F(1,85) = 11.96, p < .001) also showed that depth affected amount of coreference judgment more on forward pronominalization than on backward. If *Depth* reflects dominance, then children again are seen to modulate their *Directionality* principle by reference to sentence structure, not simply by linearity alone.

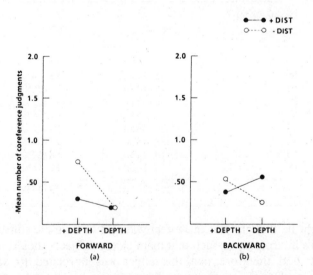

Figs. 5a & b. Amount of Coreference Judgment in Comprehension in Various Conditions of 3D Study (*Direction, Depth & Distance*).

As Figures 5a and b suggest, however, *Distance* also had a significant main effect on amount of children's coreference judgments, with overall significantly more coreference judgments made where there was no distance (.46) than with distance (.36) (F(1,85) = 7.68, p = .01). However, *Distance* significantly interacted with *Direction* (F(1,85) = 14.93, p < .001) and with *Depth* (F(1,85) = 26.05, p < .001). These interactions reflected the fact that the distance factor also only significantly affected forward pronominalization (+Distance .25; −Distance .47), not backward (+ Distance .48; −Distance .45). The *Depth* × *Distance* interaction further specified that decreased distance increased coreference judgments on forward pronominalization only where there was increased depth.

The *Depth* factor, a specific property of dominance, therefore significantly increased amount of coreference judgment. The *Distance* factor is significant in interaction with *Depth*, and children modulate amount of coreference judgment with regard to these factors. They mainly modulate forward prominalization.

Development was not significant in determining amount of coreference judgments on these sentences (even though overall amount correct did improve significantly with age) and did not interact significantly with any of the other factors. This signifies that children's patterned sensitivity to the 3-D factors we varied is relatively constant over development in effects on comprehension as it was in effects on production (imitation data).

In summary, analysis of children's coreference judgments then confirm that children do have a forward *Directionality* principle, as was seen in the imitation task. Children continue to show a low amount of coreference judgments on the backward pronouns even on these 3-D sentences. Critically, however, results of the comprehension task show that children do not apply a directionality principle autonomously of the dominance structure in these sentences. On these 3-D sentences with reversed dominance, children significantly block the forward *Directionality* principle. They show more coreference judgments overall in backward than forward cases, show as much noncoreference as coreference overall, and as much noncoreference judgments in forward as in backward cases. Moreover, these analyses show children to be sensitive to the manipulated factors in their amount of coreference judgment, in particular to the *depth* factor, which reflects dominance. The *distance* factor is restricted in its effects.

3. CONCLUSIONS

Directionality. The results of this study in general support findings from previous research that children acquiring English as a first language demonstrate a *directionality* principle favoring forward pronoun anaphora. They show this to be true even when the adult grammar of English would disallow forward pronoun anaphora, e.g., by preposing of certain embedded complements as in the sentences with preposed PP in this study.

However, at the same time, results of this study show that this *directionality* constraint is not applied independently of the syntactic dominance relations in the configuration of these sentences. Children modulate their established directionality constraint by these dominance relations in these sentences confirming that this constraint is not based on sensitivity to linear order alone. This modulation was seen both in imitation and in comprehension task results.

Depth. In both imitation and comprehension tasks, children showed that they consulted the structural property of *depth* of embedding in these sentences. Increased embedding significantly improves children's success at imitating these marked sentences; their forward directionality principle is accentuated with increased depth. In comprehension data, depth of embedding increases coreference judgment particularly with forward pronouns. Since *depth* is a property of dominance, these effects confirm that children did consult the configurational structure of these sentences and modulated their forward *directionality* by it.

Distance, a non-linguistic factor, is not an overriding factor in children's pronoun anaphora, whether in production or comprehension. It is rarely a main effect in these statistical data, signalling the lack of generality of this factor; and when it is significant, it is seen to be restricted by interaction with the factor of *Depth. Distance* alone then cannot explain children's apparent sensitivity to *Depth.*

4. DISCUSSION

Universal Grammar. In general, these results support a theory wherein childrens' early first language is constrained by general, abstract and structure-dependent principles of grammar. They are consistent with a version of Universal Grammar which includes configuration (dominance) as central to the characterization of well-formed anaphora (cf. Chomsky, 1981; Koster, 1981). Children's differential but structured responses to the 3-D sentences in our study, which involve reversed command, and their specific reaction to the *Depth* factor, which reflects dominance, support this conclusion.

Linear Order. Children alternatively could have used a *Directionality* principle based on linearity alone on these sentences. In this case, they would have reacted just to the surface fact of whether pronouns linearly *preceded* or *followed* names. They would thus have treated the 3-D sentences just like other sentences with other dominance relations which have pronouns proceeding or following names (e.g., previous studies with subordinate clauses, or the 4 subordinate clause sentences tested in this study). They did not. If surface linearity was an autonomous surface principle in children's anaphora, one might also expect *distance* between terms to have been a significant factor. As a property of the physical stimulus, *distance* might have been expected to have general regular significant effects on children's computation of the surface facts relevant to determining linear order between pronoun and antecedent. It did not.

In keeping with the basic tenets of UG, then, children's hypotheses regarding anaphora appear to be constrained to be structure-dependent. Children do not apply autonomous principles of linearity or surface distance. Their hypotheses consult the configurational structure, specifically the dominance structure of the sentences they are presented. The "locality" principles children bring to bear on early hypothesis formation towards a grammar of anaphora are crucially configurationally determined.

These results are consistent with a linguistic model for anaphora which involves configuration in the characterization of well-formed anaphora, and treats linearity as derivative (e.g., Reinhart, 1976).

Command. As noted above, current theories of UG have specified "command" as central to characterization of grammatical structure. Command reflects dominance in a particular way.[10]

The configuration of our stimulus sentences was designed to reflect the general property of dominance by varying the command relations between name and pronoun, as we described above. Thus our results, showing that children were sensitive to this manipulation and did structure their responses in accord with it, suggest that children were sensitive to command, as a reflection of configuration and dominance.

However, other aspects of our results suggest that children's sensitivity to dominance was more general than command alone. Children's sensitivity to the *Depth* factor as a relation of dominance in this study is independent of *command.* Sensitivity to command alone would not have predicted children's sensitivity to *depth* found in this study. In addition, if command were the only factor in children's sensitivity to configuration of these sentences, children would have simply reversed their directionality principle for pronominalization on these reversed dominance sentences and favored backward pronominalization. As mentioned above (see Note 2), command is binary-valued by the definition in 1.1.2 regardless of depth of embedding of related terms. For example, in the case of a forward pronoun, e.g., 1–4 on Tables I and II, the pronoun commands the preceeding name in all cases. There is no reason, given this fact alone, that children should have had an easier time imitating these when the name was more deeply embedded. or why they should have given more coreference judgments in this case, unless they were sensitive to a property of dominance that went beyond command; and unless they had linked their directionality principle to this more general property.

The Nature of the Forward Directionality Constraint

The results of this study help to disambiguate the nature of the forward directionality constraint. Since children in this study did not apply this constraint uniformly on the 3-D sentences as they do on unmarked English sentences, such as those with subordinate clauses, but significantly modulated this constraint, these data suggest that this constraint may critically involve forward linearity to correlate with rightward command, or right branching direction, as Reinhart had proposed.

The results in this study showing effects of *depth* (viz., that it aided children in overcoming the markedness of the sentences, that it accentuated their forward directionality constraint, and increased coreference judgments in a forward direction) support the view that children's early forward directionality constraint in English may be critically linked to the right branching nature of English.

Markedness of the 3-D Stimulus Sentences

The results of this study have implications for a theory of first language acquisition which invokes 'markedness' (e.g., Chomsky, 1981). The sentences (Table I and II) of this study are "marked" variants of English: not only are they infrequent, but adult anaphora judgments on these are notoriously insecure and counter-arguments to the unique role of c-command in such data exist (cf., Carden, 1981b and this volume). The highly structured and dominance-dependent results in this study suggest, however, that children bring principles derived from a theory compatible with unmarked structures to bear even on these marked structures (viz., forward anaphora corresponds to rightward branching, which is primary in this language).

Although the general depression of children's performance (both production and comprehension) on the sentences tested in this study might be thought to be explained by the marked nature of these sentences types, the highly significant and subtle sensitivities to the 3-D dimensions varied in this study cannot be so explained and suggest that children's general depression on successful production and comprehension of these sentences is structure-based. At some level children must find the reversed dominance structure of these sentences to be in conflict with the forward *directionality* principle they have established for their language.

Proposed Alternative Explanations

Several specific alternative explanations have been considered for certain specific aspects of our data. We consider a few of these below.

Task. The convergence of production data (imitation task) and comprehension data (act-out task) in this study rule out any possible alternative explanation for the data in this study which are based on task or mode of language behavior.

Depth is a Semantic Factor. One reviewer has suggested that increased depth usually correlates with increased semantic or conceptual complexity. Therefore effects we found due to *Depth* could be due to this semantic factor, not to any syntactic aspects of dominance or embedding involved in this factor. As we noted above, however, (see Note 5), not only did we control this factor to a minimum, in our design of the *Depth* factor variations, but our results are not consistent with this interpretation of the *Depth* factor. For example, there is no reason why increased semantic complexity would have led to *increased* success in the imitation of these sentences or more coreference judgments on them. Critically there is no reason why this semantic factor should have interacted with the *Directionality* factor as it did, accentuating the *forward* directionality principle.

Distance Manipulation. Additionally, it might be thought that the statistical significance of the *depth* factor in children's correct imitation might be due to our manipulation to achieve *distance* without *depth*. It might be due simply to children's mishandling of the inserted adverbs (e.g., "quickly") (since the −*depth* condition sentences which involve +*distance* (e.g., 3 and 7 on Table I) involve an inserted adverb between subject and predicate). The fact that this factor of depth had differential effects on forward and backward pronouns as shown in Figure 2a; and the fact that increased depth significantly increased successful imitation of sentences without distance where the adverb was not inserted after the subject (Figure 2b) suggested that this inserted adverb could not completely explain these results. Further argument that children were sensitive to *depth* and not merely to the inserted adverbs, is provided by the fact that anaphora errors were specifically affected by this factor of *depth*.

The Preposed PP is a Sentence Adjunct. One reviewer has suggested that preposed PP's must grammatically be sentence adjuncts, not VP adjuncts. Rather than qualifying the predicate in the main clause of these sentences, these PP's modify the subject of the main clause and the whole proposition. Thus for example, in sentence 1 on Table II, the *he* (who does the rubbing) must be located "on the top of Ernie's head." This interpretation would have the consequence that children give many noncoreference judgments since this event is physically impossible with a coreference reading. The view that these sentences require such a sentence-adjunct reading requires that a sentence like the following (where the PP is subcategorized by the V) is ungrammatical.

(17)   Near the tree, John put the ball.

Although this reviewer does assign ungrammaticality to this sentence we do not concur and have been unable to find support for this judgment elsewhere.

Moreover, even if the PP's were interpreted as this proposal suggests, this would not explain why *Directionality* had its effects (e.g., both forward and backward pronouns should disallow coreference equally on this view); or why *Depth* affected the results as they did.

The Preposed PP is Topic. One reviewer has suggested that children may analyze preposed PP's as topics. It is unnatural to topicalize a pronoun, they claim. Therefore backward pronouns would be a particular source of difficulty, and children would modulate their coreference judgments accordingly.

If this proposal were true, it might predict that children would imitate forward pronouns better than backward as they did in this study. However, it would not predict that they would assign as much or more coreference judgment to the backward pronoun as they do, in the comprehension task. Children's imitation errors, wherein they move the locative phrase to sentence final position, also does not support the view that the children were treating the PP as topic. The effect of the *Depth* factor in this study is also not explained by such a 'topicalization' principle.

Subcategorized Verbs. Several (4) of the 16 items in the act-out task involved the verb 'put,' (one of each pair of items in 4 conditions) while the others included verbs such as 'dropped' or 'threw.' In the imitation task one out of each of 3 of the 4 pairs of items included 'put'; 3/16 items. Since the verb 'put' is distinct from the other verbs used in being strictly subcategorized to take a locative complement, it would be possible that the amount of coreference judgment children made on sentences with these verbs would be significantly increased over those with other verbs if the child was operating on this lexical subcategorization factor. If so, this lexical subcategorization factor (regardless of dominance facts) might explain either our *Directionality* or our *Depth* results.

However, in general, since 'put' verbs are distributed similarly over direction variants in imitation task, they could not explain the critical directionality effects on this test. In particular, the *depth* effect on amount correct imitation was significant both on items with (.67 vs .39) and without (.68 vs .27) 'put' and there was no significant difference between these ($t(93) = 1.79$, $p = .07$). Moreover, the same *Directionality* effect (favoring forward pronominalization) held significantly both on items with (.67 vs .52) and without (.68 vs .38) 'put' and there was no significant difference between the differences between these $(t(93) = 1.68, p = .10)$.

On the act-out task, also, the *depth* factor affected amount correct sentences with and without 'put' similarly. In addition, analyses of amount of coreference judgment on forward and backward pronominalization sentences with and without 'put' (in the +Depth, +Distance condition, where there was one sentence with and one without 'put' in each direction) showed no significant differences in the effects of directionality, with more CRJ on backward than forward in each case (+, −'put'). Moreover, the 'depth' factor did not significantly differentiate +"put" and −"put" sentences in corresponding conditions $(t(93) = 2.09, p = .04)$. Thus the lexical subcategorization factor caused by the verb 'put' as distinguished from other verbs cannot be the major explanation of these results.

Use of Self as Scoring Category in the Act-Out Task

It has been suggested that it might be assumed that use of self actually *intends coreference*; the child is simply acting out the actions themselves *for* the doll named (Carden, pc; this volume). On this interpretation of data, it is argued that if we conflate 'use of self and CR' as both equal to a coreference judgment, then children would not be seen to significantly eschew CR in forward cases.

First, this interpretation of use of self would have to be empirically verified. It cannot be simply assumed, because the child in this 'self' behavior is not taking either option (+/−CR with named doll) which is available to them; and because this use of self occurs more in certain conditions than others. Second, several factors would have to be explained. Why does an increased use of self appear on these 3-D sentences, much over the normal amount in sentences with subordinate clauses? Why is there significantly more use of self on forward 3-D than on backward 3-D sentences, particularly when coreference with named doll is the usual response for forward anaphora. One might say that the 'self as agent subject' response is accentuated in the forward case because here there is a pronoun in main clause subject position (thus an unresolved agent) while in backward cases there is already a name in subject position (a resolved agent). However, the pronoun only reflects an unresolved agent, if anaphora is *not computed* for this pronoun, i.e., if coreference is blocked. Third, even if one conflates all 'use of self' with all coreference judgments (by use of same doll), a conflation which would ignore any possible intended noncoreference in self responses, children would still be seen not to be applying a forward directionality constraint to these data. (In this case they would be showing a similar amount of "coreference" judgment on backward as on forward: .57 on forward; .56 on backward, $F(1,85) = .42$, $p = .52$, a nonsignificant difference.)[11]

In the absence of viable alternative explanations, then, our results support the view then that while children acquiring English do hold a forward directionality constraint, this constraint is not independent of configurational structure. These results support a general theory of acquisition of anaphora which involves early structure-dependent constraint on the child's early hypothesis-formation, thus contributing to learnability of this central aspect of grammar.

NOTES

[1] This paper was supported by the National Science Foundation under grant #BNS−7825115, and by a seed grant from the College of Human Ecology, Cornell University at early stages. A preliminary version of this paper was presented at the North Eastern Linguistic Society Meeting, MIT, November, 1981.

We are grateful to the Cornell Nursery School and several Ithaca Schools (IACC, South Hill, SHCCC, Caroline, Fall Creek, Danby) for allowing us to conduct this study with their children.

We thank Lila Gleitman for extensive insightful comments, which led to extensive revision of an earlier version of this paper. We thank Suzanne Flynn for her insight and assistance at every step of the preparation of this study, Yu Chin Chien for her assistance throughout, especially in data analysis, and James Gair, Bob Freidin, Larry Solan, and Tatsuko Kaneda Wakayama for insightful discussion of the anaphora acquisition issues. We thank Guy Carden for continued thoughtful provocation concerning the issues and data raised in this paper.

We thank Caleb Rossiter for significant discussion of acquisition questions at early stages, and Julie Mersereau, Barbara Krawiec, Karen Gevirtz and Bill Gerzog for their help in data collection. We thank Blair Hoffmann for extensive and insightful help in data analysis, and Wendy Snyder and Lynn Okagaki for critical comments. Finally we thank Vicki Griffin for tireless help in manuscript preparation.

[2] Notice that the factor of 'c-command' is defined independently of *depth*. A term is either commanded or not by another term no matter how deeply it may be embedded. In general, however, the *Depth* factor is clearly linked to the general factor of dominance, which 'command' reflects, since it measures degree of embedding. We include it within our design both for this reason, and because it is necessary to isolate this factor from the factor of *distance* in order to evaluate the latter clearly.

[3] Figure 8b reflects a marked structure within English. Such structures have become critical in the linguistic literature which studies constraint on anaphora in (adult) grammar because they are one of few cases in English where forward anaphora is blocked in this language.

[4] The forward sentences are not generally considered anaphoric at all in adult grammar. The terms 'forward' or 'backward' pronominalization are used here thus only to refer to the fact that the pronoun either follows or precedes the name, respectively, in these sentences. Adult judgments vary on structures like 9—10, 12, and on sentences such as those on Tables I and II. The judgment that anaphora is blocked in all forward cases such as on Table I, and allowed in all backward cases, is the general assumption in the linguistic literature, however. The factors of *depth* and *distance* do not alter the c-command relations in these sentences. Thus they are assumed not to affect the anaphora judgments associated with *direction* on these sentences.

Note that these variations in adult judgments will not directly affect the interpretability of our results in our study. Coreference judgments do not affect the scoring of the imitation results at all. They do determine the scoring of correct or incorrect in the test of comprehension of these sentences as we explain below; but since our scoring is regularized on these sentences these data are clearly interpretable. Moreover, we report children's judgments of coreference on these sentences independently of whether adults (or adult grammars) consider these judgments "right" or "wrong."

[5] This manipulation was necessary because as noted above, the '+distance' condition usually necessitates added depth. *Distance* and *Depth* factors are thus often confounded; e.g. compare "Near *Ernie*, he, ..." to "Near *Ernie's* face, *he* ..." The latter adds distance but also an extra phrase node (depth) between name and pronoun. Notice that greater depth usually involves greater semantic complexity by virtue of the extra phrase node in +Depth. As can be seen from the examples given in the text and from Tables I and II, however, our +/−Depth manipulation involves minimal semantic differentiation. Thus "Under the foot of Ernie" (+Depth) and "under Ernie" (−Depth) are almost equivalent semantically.

[6] Only 3% of children's prepositional phrase errors involved exact movement of the prepositional phrase from preposed to postposed position; 46% involved exact copy where original preposed PP was left in place but *also* repeated at the end of the sentence; the remainder involved *reconstructions* where a new or changed prepositional phrase was constructed in postposition (with or without the original prepositional phrase mentioned).

[7] *Direction* and *Distance* interacted significantly ($F(1,85) = 8.26$, $p < .01$) in comprehension success, suggesting that the Directionality effect (B < F) on Comprehension success held more strongly in the case where there was no *distance*. (B = .67, F = .32 in −Distance). Where there was increased distance, the directionality effect was weakened (B = .57, F = .43 in +Distance). Coreference judgment analyses below however, suggest that these apparent effects of *distance* in comprehension are linked to the *depth* factor.

[8] We discuss only critical results here. Additional results were obtained. Analysis of CRJ showed that each of the 3D factors significantly affected amount of CRJ. It also showed that each 2 way interaction among the factors was significant. There was a *Direction X Distance* interaction ($F(1,85) = 14.93$, $p < .002$) as there had been in analysis of amount correct on comprehension. Here *distance* was found to affect amount

of forward more than backward coreference judgments and a *directionality* effect is seen to hold mainly in the +Distance condition.

Directionality X Depth was also significant with Depth affecting amount of CRJ on Forward, more than Backward (F(1,85) = 11.96, p = .0009). And *Depth X Distance* was significant (F(1,85) = 26.05, p = .000), with *depth* showing an effect mainly where —*Distance*.

These results generally suggest that children in comprehension are mainly modulating forward anaphora by sensitivity to the factors of *depth* and *distance*, but not modulating backward anaphora significantly.

[9] In this error on backward, children use the named doll as pronoun and replace the name by themselves. Another 10% of backward items used self as main clause agent (replacing name of doll) and used *a different* doll as referent of the backward pronoun. Since it was not clear in these responses how much of the sentence the child actually remembered, they were not included in these analyses. However, even if they were interpreted as a form of NCR judgment on backward cases by the child, there were only very few of these and the statistical comparison of amount of use of self as main clause agent still shows a significantly greater amount of the self as agent-subject response on forward over backward cases (F(1,22) = 30.66, p < .001).

[10] The relation between 'dominance' and command is more indirect than we have explicated in the text. Although the notion 'command' is defined in terms of dominance, note for example that in the case where A 'commands' B, as in Figure 8a, A does not itself directly dominate B, although what dominates A does dominate B. A is thus intuitively 'higher in the tree' than B. (See Kayne, 1981 on this issue.)

[11] This statistical comparison involves *all* use of self behaviors (cf. footnote 9).

REFERENCES

Baker, C. and J. L. McCarthy: 1981, *The Logical Problem of Language Acquisition*, MIT Press, Cambridge, Mass.

Carden, G.: 1981, 'Blocked forwards coreference', paper presented at the Linguistic Society of America Winter Meeting, New York.

Carden, G.: 1982, 'Backwards anaphora in discourse context', *Journal of Linguistics* **18**, 361—387.

Chomsky, N.: 1977, 'On wh-movement', in P. Culicover, T. Wasow, and A. Akmajian (eds.), *Formal Syntax*, Academic Press, New York.

Chomsky, N.: 1980, *Rules and Representations*, Columbia University Press, New York.

Chomsky, N.: 1981, *Lectures on Government and Binding*, Foris, Dordrecht.

Dresher, E. and N. Hornstein: 1979, 'Trace theory and NP movement rules', *Linguistic Inquiry* **10**, 65—82.

Evans, G.: 1980, 'Pronouns', *Linguistic Inquiry* **11**, 337—362.

Fodor, J., T. Bever, and M. Garrett: 1974, *The Psychology of Language*, McGraw-Hill, New York.

Goodluck, H. and L. Solan (eds.): 1978, *Papers in the Structure and Development of Child Language*, Occasional Papers in Linguistics, 4, University of Massachusetts, Amherst, Mass.

Gueron, J.: 1980, 'On the syntax and semantics of pp extraposition', *Linguistic Inquiry* **11**, 637—679.

Hammerton, M.: 1970, 'Disputed interpretation of a pronoun', *Nature* **227**, 202—000.

Hankamer, J. and I. Sag: 1976, 'Deep and surface anaphora', *Linguistic Inquiry* **7**, 391—426.

Higginbotham, J.: 1979, 'Anaphora and GB: Some preliminary remarks', *North Eastern Linguistic Society Proceedings, X*, Ottawa.

Higginbotham, J.: 1980, 'Pronouns and bound variables', *Linguistic Inquiry* **11**, 679—708.

Kayne, R.: 1981, 'Unambiguous paths', in J. Koster and R. May (eds.), *Levels of Syntactic Representation*, Foris, Dordrecht.

Koster, J.: 1981, 'Configurational grammar', in R. May and J. Koster (eds.), *Levels of Syntactic Representation*, Foris, Dordrecht.

Kuno, S.: 1972a, 'Functional sentence perspective: A case study from Japanese and English', *Linguistic Inquiry* **3**, 269—320.

Kuno, S.: 1972b, 'Pronominalization, reflexivization, and direct discourse', *Linguistic Inquiry* **3**, 161—195.

Kuno, S.: 1975, 'Three perspectives in the functional approach to syntax', papers from the Parasession on Functionalism, Chicago Linguistic Society, 276—335.

Langacker, R. W.: 1970, 'On pronominalization and the chain of command', in D. Reibel and S. Schane (eds.), *Modern Studies in English*, Prentice-Hall, Englewood Cliffs, N.J., pp. 160—187.

Lasnik, H.: 1976, 'Remarks on coreference', *Linguistic Analysis* **2**, 1—22.

Lust, B.: 1977, 'Conjunction reduction in child language', *Journal of Child Language* **4**, 257—287.

Lust, B.: 1981, 'Constraint on anaphora in child language: A prediction for a universal', in S. Tavakolian (ed.), *Language Acquisition and Linguistic Theory*, MIT Press, Cambridge, Mass., pp. 74—96.

Lust, B. and Y.-C. Chien: 1984, 'The structure of coordination in first language acquisition of Mandarin Chinese: Evidence for a universal', *Cognition* **17**, pp. 49—83.

Lust, B., K. Loveland, and R. Kornet: 1980, 'The development of anaphora in first language: Syntactic and pragmatic constraints', *Linguistic Analysis* **6**, 359—391.

Lust, B., L. Mangione, and Y.-C. Chien: 1984, 'Determination of empty categories in first language acquisition of Mandarin Chinese', Working papers in Linguistics, 6, Cornell University, Ithaca, N.Y.

Lust, B. and C. Mervis: 1980, 'Development of coordination in the natural speech of young children', *Journal of Child Language* **7**, 279—304.

Lust, B., L. Solan, S. Flynn, C. Cross and E. Schuetz: 1981, 'A comparison of null and pronominal anaphora in first language acquisition', in V. Burke and J. Pustejovsky (eds.), *Proceedings of the Eleventh Annual Meeting of the North Eastern Linguistic Society*, University of Masachusetts, Amherst, pp. 205—218 (also this volume).

Lust, B. and T. Wakayama: 1979, 'The structure of coordination in children's first language acquisition of Japanese', in F. Eckman and A. Hastings (eds.), *First and Second Language Acquisition*, Newbury House, Rowley, Mass., pp. 134—152.

Lust, B. and T. Wakayama: 1981, 'Word order in first language acquisition of Japanese', in P. S. Dale and D. Ingram (eds.), *Child Language — An International Perspective*, University Park Press, Baltimore, pp. 72—90.

May, R.: 1981, 'On the parallelism of movement and bound anaphora', *Linguistic Inquiry* **12**, 477–483. .

Reinhart, T.: 1976, *The Syntactic Domain of Anaphora*, unpublished doctoral dissertation, MIT, Cambridge, Massachusetts.

Reinhart, T.: 1981, 'Definite NP anaphora and c-command domains', *Linguistic Inquiry* **12**, 605–636.

Roeper, T.: 1973, 'Theoretical implications of word order, topicalization and inflections in German language acquisition', in C. Ferguson and D. Slobin (eds.), *Studies of Child Language Development*, Holt, Rinehart and Winston, New York, pp. 41–554.

Saito, M.: 1984, 'On the definition of c-command and government', in C. Jones and P. Sells (eds.), *Proceedings of North Eastern Linguistics Society* **14**, 402–417.

Sinclair, H., J. Berthoud-Papandropoulou, J. P. Bronckart, H. Chipman, E. Ferreiro, and E. Rappe DuCher: 1976, 'Recherches en psycholinguistique genetique', *Archives de Psychologie* **44**, 157–175.

Slobin, D. and C. Welsh: 1973, 'Elicited imitation as a research tool in developmental psycho-linguistics', in C. Ferguson and D. Slobin (eds.), *Studies of Child Language Development*, Holt, Rinehart and Winston, New York, pp. 485–496.

Solan, L.: 1978, *Anaphora in Child Language*, unpublished doctoral dissertation, University of Massachusetts.

Solan, L.: 1983, *Pronominal Reference: Child language and the Theory of Grammar*, D. Reidel, Dordrecht.

Stenning, K.: 1978, 'Anaphora as an approach to pragmatics', in M. Halle, J. Bresnan, and G. Miller (eds.), *Linguistic Theory and Psychological Reality*, MIT Press, Cambridge, Mass., pp. 162–200.

Tavakolian, S.: 1977, *Structural Principles in the Acquisition of Complex Sentences*, unpublished doctoral dissertation, University of Massachusetts, Amherst.

Tavakolian, S.: 1978, 'Children's comprehension of pronominal subjects and missing subjects in complicated sentences', in H. Goodluck and L. Solan (eds.), *Papers in the Structure and Development of Child Language*, Occasional Papers in Linguistics, 4, University of Massachusetts, Amherst, pp. 145–152.

Wasow, T.: 1972, *Anaphoric Relations in English*, unpublished doctoral dissertation, MIT.

Wasow, T.: 1979, *Anaphora in Generative Grammar*, E. Story-Scientia, Ghent.

Williams, E.: 1977a, 'Discourse and logical form', *Linguistic Inquiry* **8**, 101–139.

Williams, E.: 1977b, 'On deep and surface anaphora', *Linguistic Inquiry* **8**, 692–696.

3. DISTINGUISHING BOUND AND
FREE ANAPHORA

BARBARA LUST, LARRY SOLAN, SUZÁNNE FLYNN,
CATHERINE CROSS AND ELAINE SCHUETZ

A COMPARISON OF NULL AND PRONOUN ANAPHORA IN FIRST LANGUAGE ACQUISITION[1]

1.0 INTRODUCTION

In this paper we report selected results of an experimental study of the acquisition of certain forms of anaphora in first language acquisition of English. The results of this study provide evidence that children who are acquiring English distinguish a phonetically realized pronoun with free anaphora from a null nominal category with bound anaphora in environments such as those shown in 1 and 2. At the same time, however, the data from this study provide evidence that at early language levels children apply general principles to constrain both null and pronoun anaphora similarly in these environments. Specifically (a) children generalize certain grammatical restrictions which hold on free pronoun anaphora as in 1 to hold also on bound null anaphora as in 2; and (b) they fail to observe certain grammatical restrictions which should hold on bound null anaphora as in 2 and not on pronoun anaphora as in 1.

(1) a.   John saw Tom when he ran down the street.

     b. John_i saw Tom_j when $\text{he}_{i,j,k}$ ran down the street.

(2) a.   John saw Tom when Ø.running down the street.

     b. John_i saw Tom_j when PRO_i running down the street

1.1 *The Anaphoric Structure of 1 and 2*

The basic grammatical facts about 1 and 2 are well known.[2] They involve similar configuration as 3 shows.

(3)

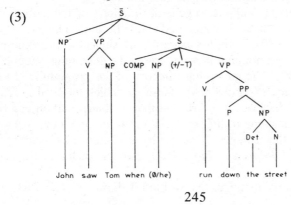

245

B. Lust (ed.), Studies in the Acquisition of Anaphora, Vol. I, 245–277.
© 1986 *by D. Reidel Publishing Company.*

Both 1 and 2 involve embedded adverbial 'when clauses' which are sometimes called "adjuncts." They both involve types of NP anaphors in subordinate clause subject position. We are using the terms 'anaphor' and 'anaphora' here in a general sense.[3] In general, 1 and 2 represent forms of anaphora where interpretation of the NP subject of the subordinate clause is determined by reference to interpretation of some other term.

In sentence #1, this NP is filled in surface structure by the lexical pronoun 'he.' The subordinate clause is tensed. The pronoun may be construed in relation to another NP in the sentence, such as e.g., subject or object of the main clause, or, its interpretation may optionally be determined by context (discourse or other pragmatic context) (as suggested by coindexing in 1b).

In sentence #2, this subject NP is phonetically null. The subordinate clause is non-tensed. A rule of control construes the interpretation of this null NP to obligatorily accord with the subject of the main clause, namely 'John.' In 2 it cannot be 'Tom' who is running down the street, in contrast with 1.[4] The null NP is designated as 'PRO' in 2b. 2b reflects subject control of PRO by coindexing. We use the notation 'PRO' here to refer to a nominal category which does not have phonetic content but is 'pronominal' in that it shares certain properties with pronouns in this domain (Chomsky, 1981a).

The anaphor types in 1 and 2 both are 'pronominals' in that they both have a feature structure (gender, number, person), which must be matched to the features of the NP to which they are related in interpretation. They differ in that the pronoun in 1 "in addition has a phonological matrix" (Chomsky, 1981a; 102, 61). The PRO in 2 "is, in effect, a pronoun lacking a phonological matrix" (102).

Both pronominals are subject to general principles of that subset of Universal Grammar which is concerned with 'Binding Theory' (BT) (Chomsky, 1981a, 1982). Both, for example, are subject to the Binding Principle 'B,' i.e., "a pronominal must be free in its governing category" (Chomsky, 1982, 20). The governing category of the pronoun in 2 for example, is the tensed subordinate clause in which it occurs. The pronoun signals the fact that it is "free" in that its interpretation can be determined by either name in the main clause, 'John' or 'Tom', or by a referent external to the sentence. It cannot have an antecedent within its own sentence, e.g., *'*John* likes *him*'. PRO also cannot have one, e.g., *'*John* likes *PRO*'.

The pronominals are distinguished within BT, however. The 'PRO' in

Sentence 2 has properties both of a pronoun and of a 'BT-anaphor', which is bound. (See footnote 3). Chomsky (1981a, 191) writes: "Notice that PRO is like overt pronouns in that it never has an antecedent within its clause ... PRO also resembles anaphors in that it has no intrinsic referential context but is either assigned reference by an antecedent or is indefinite in interpretation, lacking specific reference." Thus, in BT, PRO is regarded as 'pronominal anaphor'. While the interpretation of the pronoun in 2 may be determined by pragmatic context (one indication of its being 'free'), PRO in 1 must have a grammatical antecedent within the sentence (an indication of its being a 'bound' anaphor) and that antecedent is the subject. PRO is thus subject not only to principle B, but also to principle A of the BT, i.e., 'An anaphor is bound in its governing category'. Because PRO is subject to both principles A and B of BT, Chomsky derives the "basic property" of PRO, viz., that it is "ungoverned" (See Chomsky, 1982, 21).

It follows from these principles that in a tensed clause (as in 1), a pronoun, not a PRO, must appear in subject position because the tense of this clause is a governor. In a nontensed clause (as in 2), a PRO, not a pronoun must appear, since this position is ungoverned.

(4)   *John saw Tom when Ø ran down the street.
(5)   *John saw Tom when he running down the street.

Thus the tense of the embedded clause and the choice of null or pronoun in examples 1 and 2 are closely linked grammatically.

In summary, in 1 and 2, both the anaphor types (pronoun and null) appear in similar configurations, as suggested by 3. They are both pronominals, although they differ in phonetic content. By virtue of general principles, they differ in the tense of the domain in which they occur and they correspond to different anaphora relations (free or bound).[5]

2.0 THE STRUCTURE OF THIS STUDY

In this study we evaluated whether children distinguish the anaphora represented by a pronoun and a null anaphor (PRO) in sentences like 1 and 2. We asked whether first language acquisition of the null anaphora PRO) in these cases is subject to the same principles or constraints which hold on first language acquisition of pronoun anaphora. Specifically, we tested whether the two constraints in 6 which have previously been found to hold on pronoun anaphora in first language acquisition of

English, would hold similarly on acquisition of null anaphora (PRO) in these domains. This finding would provide evidence of the generality of the constraints which children bring to bear on early first language acquisition. It would support the claim that these constraints are not determined by phonetic form of anaphor type, and that null anaphors are recognized in children's theory of anaphora. If children generalize over pronoun and PRO in early acquisition of anaphora, this would suggest that children unify these anaphor types under a single category, e.g., 'pronominal'. Since 1 and 2 involve similar configurational domains, this result would be consistent with the view that children apply general constraints on anaphora by consulting configurational domain rather than phonetic form of anaphor type, in determining anaphora.

Finally, if children generalize constraints to PRO which are applicable in adult grammar only to pronoun, then we can more precisely determine the nature of children's early hypotheses regarding anaphora, and provide empirical evidence regarding the 'unmarked' forms of anaphora. In this case, the children would be treating pronoun as unmarked and PRO as marked.

2.1 Constraints Tests

We tested both pronoun and PRO for the following constraints which have been found to hold on pronoun acquisition in previous studies.

(6)   *Constraints on first language acquisition (of English)*
   i. *Directionality*
      The anaphor must *follow* the related term in early child language (Tavakolian, 1977, 1978; Lust, 1981; Lust, Loveland & Kornet, 1980; Solan, 1978, 1983).
   ii. *Pragmatic Context*
      Pragmatic context (e.g., discourse context) may determine the referent of an anaphor (Kuno, 1972a, 1972b, 1975; Stenning, 1978; Reinhart, 1976, 1983a, b this volume; Lasnik, 1976; Lust, Loveland and Kornet, 1980).

First, we tested whether the 'directionality constraint' (6i), would also hold on null anaphora in certain domains. Previous research has shown that children favor forward pronominalization as in 7a and resist backward pronominalization as in 7b. However, a similar effect has not been confirmed for null anaphora as in 2. In fact, some research has suggested that this directionality constraint might not hold on acquisition of null anaphora like 2 (Goodluck, 1978, 1981).

(7) a. *Forward Anaphora*
Tommy ran fast because *he* heard a lion.
Jenna drank some juice while *she* was having lunch.

(7) b. *Backward Anaphora*
Because *he* heard a lion, *Tommy* ran fast.
While *she* was having lunch, *Jenna* drank some juice.

Second, we tested whether the 'pragmatic context' constraint would hold on null anaphora. By this constraint (6ii), a term which is mentioned in a previous utterance determines the reference of an anaphor in a following utterance. In previous study of acquisition of pronoun anaphora, sentences like 8a which establish a pragmatic (discourse) context, have been shown to significantly affect children's interpretation of pronoun anaphora in a following utterance such as 8b. (See Lust, Loveland and Kornet, 1980 for example.)

(8) *Pragmatic Context — Pronoun Anaphora*
a. I'm going to tell you a little story about *Cookie Monster.*
b. When *he* closed the box, *Cookie Monster* lay down.

If children generalize the 'directionality' constraint in 6i from pronoun to null anaphora, they are generalizing a constraint which is unnecessary to null anaphora, unless children in some way conflate null (PRO) and pronoun anaphora in these domains in their application of the principles which constrain acquisition of anaphora.

If children generalize the pragmatic context constraint in 6ii to null anaphora, however, they are generalizing a constraint which is not only *not* necessary, but actually inconsistent with the adult grammar for this form of anaphora in English. Null anaphora, such as in 2, does not allow pragmatic control, but must be grammatically controlled by subject. If children apply the pragmatic context constraint to null as well as to pronoun anaphora in the domains we tested, then they are not only *generalizing* a constraint over both anaphor types, but they are failing to observe a specific grammatical restriction on null anaphora in this domain. They are generalizing a property of *pronouns* to *PRO*.

2.1 *Method*

2.1.1 *Design*

In this study we tested 101 Ss from age 3;1 to 7;11 years (mean age 5,5) on sentences types exemplified in Tables I and II. In a factorial design with repeated measures, these sentences varied according to *Anaphor type* (*pronoun* or *null* PRO) and *Directionality* of anaphor (*forward* or *backward*). The sentences involved adverbial subordinate 'when' clauses. Forward anaphora involved postposed subordinate clauses as in 7a. Backward anaphora involved subordinate clauses which were preposed to the left of the main clause as in 7b.

The 4 types of sentences resulting from multiplication of the 2 factors were tested by standardized procedures in both an *elicited imitation* task which measured children's production, and an *act-out task* which measured children's comprehension (See Tables I and II). In the elicited imitation task, the child was asked to repeat each sentence after the adult experimenter and the success or errors (structural conversions) in

TABLE I
Stimulus Sentences
IMITATION

Forward	Backward
I. *Pronoun*	III. *Pronoun*
1. *Billy* dropped the penny when *he* saw the cat.	5. When *he* colored the books, *Tommy* drank the milk.
2. *Billy* read the book when *he* ate the dinner.	6. When *he* sang a song. *Jimmy* opened the door.
II. *Null*	IV. *Null*
3. *Johnny* washed the table, when Ø drinking juice.	7. When Ø dressing the baby. *Daddy* dropped the book.
4. *Bill* ate the apple, when Ø coloring the book.	8. When Ø cutting the grass, *Jimmy* walked the dog.

Experimental Design Control Sentences

9. When *Daddy* chased the cat, *he* picked a flower.
10. When *Tommy* read the book, *he* ate the ice-cream.

TABLE II
Stimulus Sentences
COMPREHENSION (ACT OUT)

Forward	Backward
I. *Pronoun*	III. *Pronoun*
1. *Fozzie* tickled *Kermit Frog,* when *he* dropped the car.	5. When *he* dropped the tissue, *Kermit* rubbed *Scooter.*
2. *Ernie* tickled *Big Bird,* when *he* dropped the penny.	6. When *he* pushed the penny, *Ernie* pinched *Oscar.*
II. *Null*	IV. *Null*
3. *Scooter* squeezed Fozzie, when Ø dropping the tissue.	7. When Ø hitting the block, *Scooter* kicked Fozzie Bear.
4. *Big Bird* patted Oscar, when Ø pushing the car.	8. When Ø pushing the car, *Big Bird* patted Ernie.

the child's responses were analyzed. In the act-out task, children were asked to illustrate the meaning of the sentence by choosing a doll or dolls from a reference set of 3 dolls and demonstrating the administered sentence with their actions on available props. The child's success at representing a correct meaning for the sentence, as well as the child's choice of referent for interpretation of the anaphor were analyzed in their act-out behavior.

Both imitation and comprehension sentences were designed so that coreference to either subject or object, or noncoreference, was semantically and pragmatically possible to an equivalent degree. All sentences were equal in syllable length and reflected appropriate controls on lexical content across types.

Experimental design control sentences such as 9 and 10 on Table I were also tested to insure that simple preposing of subordinate clause, rather than backward anaphora, did not significantly explain directionality results. Sentences 1 and 5 on Table I differ, for example, not only in that 1 involves forward anaphora and 5 involves backward anaphora, but 1 involves a (more unmarked) postposed subordinate clause, while 5 involves a (more marked) preposed cause. The control sentences had preposed subordinate clauses but forward anaphora. If children have difficulty with backward anaphora due to *directionality of anaphora,* then control sentences like 9 (or 10) on Table I should be significantly more accessible to children than the experimental sentences like 5 (or 6) on this table since both have preposed clauses, but anaphora direction differs. If there is a significant increase in children's facility with a sentence like 1 (or 2) on Table I over one like 9 (or 10) (control) this would suggest that clause order is a significant factor for children. However, if the difference between 1 (or 2) (postposed forward) and 5 (or 6) (preposed backward) is significantly greater than the difference between 1 (or 2) (postposed forward) and 9 (or 10) (preposed forward), this would suggest that children are significantly sensitive to an anaphora directionality factor; a factor which is independent of the clause order factor, and which operates over and above it.

In the comprehension task, one half the sentences were preceded by a *Pragmatic Lead* to the object of the main clause. That is, in half the items the sentence was preceded by a sentence which named the *object* of the main clause as topic. For example: "Now I'm going to tell you a story about *Fozzie Bear*. When Ø hitting the block, **Scooter** kicked *Fozzie Bear*." The lead was misleading for null anaphora which requires obligatory coreference between the main clause subject and the null anaphor. The lead was compatible with the pronoun, since the pronoun allows free coreference with subject, object or other referent.

The structure of the sentences in the act-out task were the same for conditions both with and without PL. They resembled the sentences of the imitation task, except that the act-out sentences all involved actions that were both physically "act-outable" by the child and discrete enough to allow accurate reliability in transcription and scoring. All sentences involved two names (of dolls) in subject and object position of main clause, and a subject anaphor (pronoun or null) in the subordinate clause which involved an action on a prop.

The design allowed factorial analysis (by ANOVA) on the 3 factors, *Anaphor Type* (2) × *Directionality* (2) × *Age Group* (10), for both imitation and comprehension tasks, with an additional (fourth) factor, presence or absence of *Pragmatic Lead* (to the object) on the comprehension task. A significance level of .01 was accepted for significance. (We speak of > .01 but < .05 as "approaching significance".)

2.1.2 Procedures

Each child was administered 20 sentences for imitation, and 16 sentences for comprehension. There were two sentences for each condition. (Score range was 0—2.) The sentences were divided into two randomized batteries of 8 sentences each, to allow one or two sittings with a child depending on attention span. A different set of three dolls was used for each comprehension battery in order to avoid boredom on the part of the child. The dolls available included the familiar sets: Big Bird, Ernie, Oscar the Grouch; and Fozzie Bear, Kermit the Frog, Scooter. Sentences with and without pragmatic lead were randomly interspersed in each battery according to design. Half the children received the imitation task first; half received the comprehension task first.

Pretraining. Before beginning the task, all subjects were pretrained on sentences which involved a single clause, e.g., "Kermit threw the penny" to develop basic understanding of the task. In addition they were tested on two types of two-clause sentences which involved either same subject or different subjects across clauses, e.g., *"Oscar* turned around and *Oscar* threw the penny;" or *"Scooter* pushed the car and *Ernie* sat down." This was done in order to ensure that the child began the task with the clear assumption that *both coreference across clauses and non-coreference* were equivalently possible responses. No child was allowed to proceed to the experimental sentences until they had successfully responded to each of these practice types.

2.1.3 Scoring

Imitation. Imitation behaviors were scored correct only if the child made no significant change in syntax or semantics of the stimulus sentences. Omission of any major constituent or change in vocabulary or embedding, for example, constituted an error. Changes in inflection alone (including tense) or in determiners alone were not considered incorrect.

"Anaphora errors" in imitation were scored if they included any change in the anaphor-antecedent relation while maintaining 2-clause structure, e.g., change of anaphora direction, expansion of the anaphor to a lexical noun, or conversion from one anaphor type to another, for example changing pronouns to null or null to pronun.

Act-Out. Act-out behaviors were scored as correct only if the child demonstrated both of the two clauses in the stimulus sentence, where actions, dolls and props matched the stimulus (according to written standardized criteria).[6] Grammatical functions of subject and object relations in both clauses of the stimulus sentence were necessarily maintained in the child's actions for a correct score. Pronoun interpretation was scored correct if the child chose either subject or object or third doll as referent of the pronoun. Null interpretation was scored correct only if the child chose subject. The children's use of themselves as referent of the pronoun or null was scored incorrect.

Coreference judgments (CRJ) were specifically scored as to whether the children chose *subject, object, a third doll* or *themselves* as referent for the anaphor, for both pronoun and null. "Strict" coreference judgments are reported in this paper. A "strict" subject choice, for example, involved a coreference judgment to subject of main clause, where all other aspects of the child's behavior were correct; (e.g., child also used correct actions, second doll and prop without mistake).

2.1.4 *Reliability Tests*

All imitation data were scored independently by 2 persons according to the written criteria. A random 20% of the imitation data was transcribed by 2 persons in order to ascertain transcription reliability.

All act-out data was scored by 2 persons independently for both correct/incorrect and coreference judgment scores according to the written criteria. All cases of discrepancy were resolved by reconsulting the original data.

In addition, a random 20% of the data (two from each age group) involved independent transcriptions of act-out behaviors by two different persons, followed by independent scoring of each transcript in order to ascertain transcription reliability.

2.2 *Subjects*

There were 53 males and 48 females (grouped in ten 6-month age groups) from local nursery school and day care centers. All were English monolingual, without speech or language handicap. Mean ages for each of the ten groups are shown on the bottom of Figure 1.

3.0 RESULTS

3.1 *Imitation Results*

3.1.1 *Amount Correct*

Mean numbers of correct imitation responses are shown in Figure 1. There was a significant main effect for *Age Group* ($F(9,91) = 4.91$, p < .0001). Mean number of correct responses more than doubled from .5 in Group 1 to 1.2 in Group 2. Scores increase slowly to Group 7 and then level off, remaining relatively constant from Groups 7 to 10 with about 75% correct. Within the age we measured, then, the major period of growth in successful production of these structures appears to occur between the ages of 3;0 and 5;3 years with relatively little gain between 5;3 and 8;0.

Children did not significantly differentiate null and pronoun forms in the amount correct on their imitation. Pronoun anaphora was only very slightly easier to imitate overall ($F(1,91) = 3.57$, p = .06; $\overline{X}_{Pron} = 1.35$, $\overline{X}_{Null} = 1.22$). There was, however, a significant main effect of *Directionality*. *Forward* forms were significantly preferred over backward

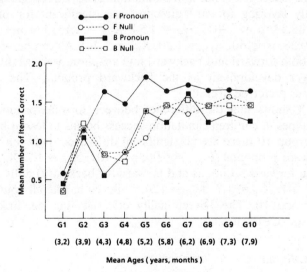

Fig. 1. Development of Correct Imitation of Sentences with Forward and Backward Pronouns or Nulls.

$(F(1,91) = 10.82$, p $= .005$; $\overline{X}_{Forward} = 1.37$, $\overline{X}_{Backward} = 1.19)$. This replicates the Directionality effect found in previous studies.

Analyses of the experimental design control sentences showed that this directionality effect is independent of the pre- and post-posing difference in subordinate clause between forward and backward sentences. Sentences with preposing (control sentences like 9 (or 10)) were significantly more difficult for children ($\overline{X} = 1.35$) than those with postposed clause order ($\overline{X} = 1.54$) even when both involve forward pronouns. However, there was a significantly greater ease of imitation of preposed sentences when they involve forward pronouns ($\overline{X} = 1.35$) than when they involve backward pronouns ($\overline{X} = 1.15$). Moreover, there was a significantly greater difference between success on the experimental sentences which vary both anaphora direction and clause order, than there was between sentences which vary in clause order but maintain forward direction. This shows that the directionality effect is general and independent of clause order in the stimulus sentences. This again replicates results of previous study (cf. Lust, 1981).

As Figure 1 suggests, there was also a significant interaction of *Directionality* and *Anaphor type* $(F(1,91) = 18.67$, p $< .001)$ in determining success of children's imitation. The Directionality effect significantly favoring forward direction was significant for pronouns $(F_{(1,91)} = 28.23$, p $< .001$; $\overline{X}_{FP} = 1.54$, $\overline{X}_{BP} = 1.15)$ but not for null $(F_{(1,91)} = 0.28$, p $= .60$; $\overline{X}_{FN} = 1.20$, $\overline{X}_{BN} = 1.24)$. As can be seen from Figure 1, both forward and backward null anaphora were as difficult to imitate over development as the backward pronoun. The forward pronoun was preferred overall.

Figure 1 shows that the difference between forward pronouns and the other types in children's imitation success begins to lessen by group 5 and at group 10 there are no significant differences between forward and backward pronouns $(F_{(1,9)} = 6.00$, p $< .01$; $\overline{X}_{FP} = 1.7$, $\overline{X}_{BP} = 1.3)$ or between forward pronouns and forward (or backward) nulls $(F_{(1,9)} = 0.47$, p $< .01$; $\overline{X}_{FP} = 1.7$, $\overline{X}_{FN} = 1.5)$. Children handle all equivalently well by group 10. The Directionality effect is thus age-linked and characteristic of early levels.

3.1.2 Anaphora Errors in Imitation

Mean number of anaphora errors in children's imitation of these sentences are shown in Figure 2.

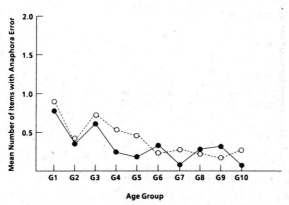

Fig. 2. Developmental Change in Amount of Anaphora Error in Imitation of Sentences with Pronouns or Nulls.

Paralleling results of the analysis of amount of correct responses, there was a significant main effect of *Age Group* ($F_{(9,91)}$ = 3.24, p < .005) on number of children's anaphora errors. Figure 2 shows that anaphora errors on both null and pronoun forms account for a large amount of children's errors in youngest groups and drops by Group 5. This shows that the anaphora involved in these sentences accounts for a significant proportion of children's success or difficulty in imitating them.

Anaphor Type ($F_{(1,91)}$ = 1.88, p = .17; $\overline{X}_{Pronoun}$ = 0.33, $\overline{X}_{Null}$ = 0.42) was not significant. There were only slightly more anaphora errors on null anaphors than on pronouns.

The effect of *Directionality* on amount of anaphora error ($F_{(1,91)}$ = 5.24, p = .02; $\overline{X}_{Forward}$ = 0.32, $\overline{X}_{Backward}$ = 0.43) approached significance. There were more anaphora errors on backward than on forward forms. Figure 3 shows this effect on pronouns and confirms that it is developmentally linked.

There was also a significant interaction between *Directionality* and *Anaphor Type* in the anaphora errors ($F_{(1,91)}$ = 45.75, p = .0001; $\overline{X}_{FP}$ = 0.12, $\overline{X}_{FN}$ = 0.51, $\overline{X}_{BP}$ =F0.54, $\overline{X}_{BN}$ = 0.33). There were significantly fewer anaphora errors on forward pronouns than on any of the other types. There were significantly more anaphora errors on backward

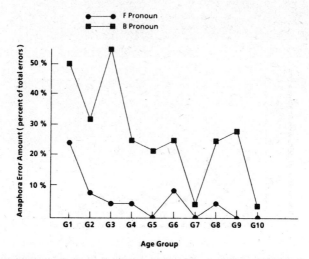

Fig. 3. Developmental Change in Directionality Effect. Amount of Anaphora Error in Imitation of Sentences with Backward Pronouns Compared with those with Forward Pronouns.

pronouns (27% of items) than on forward (6% of items) (F(1,91) = 38.91, p < .001). In the sentences with nulls, in contrast there were significantly more anaphora errors on forward nulls (26% of items) than on backward (17% of items).

First inspection of these results might suggest that although null and pronoun did not in general differ significantly in these imitation data in terms of overall success or overall amount of anaphora error, the 'directionality' constraint was not evidenced on null anaphora as it is on pronoun anaphora. Forward and backward null anaphora do not appear to differ in terms of overall amount correct in children's imitation or in terms of overall amount of anaphora error, in the way that forward and backward pronouns do. Backward nulls and backward pronouns were imitated similarly in children's imitation (e.g., Figure 1). Analysis of the nature of children's anaphora errors in imitation, however, confirms that the directionality constraint in 6i did affect both pronoun and null anaphora.

3.1.2.1 *Directionality Effects in Children's Anaphora Errors.* Four types of anaphora error occurred frequently on backward forms. All of these error types evidenced an effect of Directionality on both pronouns and nulls.

First, in children's imitation of both pronouns and nulls, backward forms were often blocked by reversing the backward direction to forward. Example 9 shows this for pronouns (23.6% of anaphora error) and 10 shows this for nulls (42.4% of anaphora error). ("E" refers to experimenter model, "S" refers to subject response in these examples.)

(9)   E: When *he* sang a song, *Jimmy* opened the door.
       S: When *Jimmy* sang a song, *he/Ø* opened the door.
(10)   E: When Ø dressing the baby, *Daddy* dropped the book.
       S: When *Daddy* was dressing the baby, he/Ø dropped the book.

In contrast, the anaphora directionality was changed in the opposite direction, i.e., forward to backward (on one forward pronominal and one forward null) in only two cases. Backward anaphora was also blocked by children's substitution of a full NP for the anaphor, i.e., creating a NP-NP structure, as in 11 and 12, or by substituting a pronoun for the antecedent, i.e., creating a Pronoun-Pronoun structure, as in 13 and 14. A fourth type of blocking in backward forms, creating a Ø-Østructure, is shown in 15 and 16. These last three conversions of backward forms accounted for an approximately equal percentage of anaphora error on both pronouns and nulls: 34.5% on backward pronouns and 36.3% on backward nulls.

NP-NP

(11)   E: When he sang a song, *Jimmy* opened the door.
       S: When *Jimmy* sing a song, *Jimmy* opened the door.
(12)   E: When Ø dressing the baby, *Daddy* dropped the book.
       S: When *Daddy* was dressing the baby, *Daddy* dropped the book.

Pron-Pron

(13)   ·E: When *he* colored the books, *Tommy* drank the milk.
       S: When *he* was coloring the books *he* drinked the milk.
(14)   E: When Ø cutting the grass, *Jimmy* walked the dog.
       S: When *he* was cutting the grass *he* walked the dog.

Ø-Ø

(15)   E: When *he* colored the books, *Tommy* drank the milk.
       S: When Ø colored the books, Ø drank the milk.
(16)   E: When Ø dressing the baby, *Daddy* dropped the book.
       S: When Ø dressing baby, Ø dropped the book.

The above errors provide evidence that children treat pronoun and null anaphora in a similar mannner in that they frequently block backward anaphora in both cases. They thus appear to apply principle 6i, the directionality constraint, to both pronoun and null in the domain of our stimulus sentences.

3.1.2.2 *Differentiation of Anaphor Types. Primacy of Pronoun.* Analyses of children's imitation error types also provided evidence that children assign a primacy to pronoun over null anaphora in the domains exemplified by our sentences.

Children regularly converted the null anaphors to pronouns (71% anaphora errors on nulls) rather than pronouns to nulls (only 31% anaphora errors on pronouns) in their imitation. This signifies that children differentiate these anaphor types, and that they generalize from the pronoun. Null to pronoun conversions as in 17 or 18 occurred significantly more often than pronoun to null conversions as in 19 or 20 ($F_{(1,91)} = 12.29, p < .001; \overline{X}_{P \to N} = 0.08, \overline{X}_{N \to P} = 0.25$).

(17)   E: *Johnny* washed the table when Ø drinking the juice.
           S: *Johnny* washed the table when *he* was drinking the juice.
(18)   E: When Ø dressing the baby, *Daddy* dropped the book.
           S: When *he* was dressing the baby, the *Dad* dropped the book.
(19)   E: *Billy* read the book when *he* ate the dinner.
           S: *Billy* read the book, when Ø ate(ing) dinner.
(20)   E: When *he* sang a song, *Jimmy* opened the door.
           S: When Ø sanging a song, *Jimmy* opened the door.

Correlation of Anaphor Type and Tense. Children's imitation changes of anaphor type showed further that they have differentiated anaphor type sufficiently to link anaphor type with the domain of tense in which it occurs. 84% of children's conversions of nulls to pronouns involved an appropriate conversion from the nontensed clause of a null anaphor to a tensed subordinate clause which is required for a pronoun. 68% of conversions of pronouns to nulls involved a conversion from tensed to nontensed clause.

3.1.2.3 *Directionality and Anaphor Type.* A main effect of *Directionality* also characterized the anaphor type conversions ($F_{(1,91)} = 16.34$, p

$< .001; \overline{X}_F = 0.25, \overline{X}_B = 0.08$). That is, anaphor type conversions on forward forms such as those in 17 occurred significantly more frequently than conversions on backward forms as in 18 or 20. The largest amount of these anaphor type conversions involved conversion of forward null to forward pronoun. There was a significant *Directionality × Anaphor Type* interaction in children's anaphor type conversions $(F_{(1,91)} = 39.68, p < .0001; \overline{X}_{FP \to FN} = 0.04), \overline{X}_{FN \to FP} = 0.46, \overline{X}_{BP \to BN} = 0.13, \overline{X}_{BN \to BP} = 0.04$).

While the forward null to forward pronoun conversion is the most frequent (accounting for 88% of all anaphor type errors and for 57% of total errors on these forms), the number of anaphor type conversions for the other three anaphor types (BP, BN, FP) is small and approximately equal. The analogous conversion on backward forms from null to pronoun accounted for only 15.2% of anaphora error on backward forms, for example. Backward null anaphora was often directionally reversed, but reversed to forward pronoun anaphora. (64% of errors on these backward nulls which converted to pronouns were converted to *forward* pronouns as in 21).

(21)　　E: When Ø dressing the baby, *Daddy* dropped the book.
　　　　　S: When, when, when *Dad* (was) dressin' baby *he* dropped a book.

Children then are clearly showing a directionality effect on nulls which is related to that on pronouns. They distinguish forward nulls mainly by converting these to pronouns.

The frequent conversion of forward nulls to forward pronouns, as in 17, explains why the Directionality factor was not significant for amount of correct responses on null forms. The frequent (incorrect) conversion of forward nulls to forward pronouns explains the depression of the number of correct responses on forward null forms and the increase in anaphora error on them.

3.1.3 *Summary of Imitation Data*

These imitation data show that at the same time that children clearly distinguish the two anaphor types that we studied, Pronoun and null (PRO), they generalize over these in application of the forward directionality constraint, 6i, treating these two anaphor types similarly in terms of this constraint. This evidences that children do generalize over both pronoun and PRO in their early acquisition of anaphora in some ways. It also shows that the directionality principle is not determined by or restricted to either one anaphor type alone.

In addition, these imitation data evidence a primacy of pronoun anaphora over null anaphora in children's frequent spontaneous conversions of null to pronoun rather than of pronoun to null anaphora.

3.2 *Comprehension Test*

3.2.1 *Experimental Design*

The 101 Ss in 10 age groups were also tested for their comprehension of the 4 basic sentence types involving the factors of *Anaphor Type* (Pronoun and Null), *Directionality* (forward or backward), and *Age* (10 age groups). Stimulus sentences for each condition are shown in Table II.

This basic design allowed us to test whether the factor of *Directionality* would generalize over both pronoun and null (PRO) anaphora in a comprehension task as it had in the imitation task. If so this would confirm the generality of the constraint and help to clarify its nature. If the directionality constraint appears in comprehension data, it is not simply a production constraint. If so, this suggests more clearly than the imitation task that the directionality principle constrains anaphora *per se*, since anaphora involves an interpretive judgment of coreference.

In the comprehension task, as specified in 2.1.1 above, sentences varied additionally as to whether they included a *Pragmatic Lead* (PL) to the *object* of the main clause. This additional factor (+/−PL) allowed us to test specifically whether Ss would allow the pragmatic context to affect null as well as pronoun anaphora, thus contravening the grammatically determined obligatory subject control of the null anaphor. If they did so, this would specifically suggest that children were generalizing from the case of free pronoun, because consultation of pragmatic context is consistent with pronoun interpretation but not with null (PRO). This generalization would be consistent with children's converting null anaphors to pronouns in the imitation task on these sentences. If the child's generalization to pronoun in the imitation task in this study is related to the child's theory of anaphora, then the frequent choice of pronoun over null in these sentences may reflect the child's generalization to free (optional) anaphora, which the pronoun represents. This would confirm that the pronoun is the unmarked case in the particular structural domains represented by our sentences.

3.2.2 Results of Comprehension Task

Results of the comprehension task reflected children's generalization of both constraints (*Directionality* (6i) and *Pragmatic Context* (6ii)) over null anaphora. They also confirmed the imitation result that children generalized from free (optional) anaphora (represented by pronoun) to bound (obligatory) anaphora (represented by the null, PRO).

3.2.2.1 *Amount Correct.* Figure 4 shows developmental curves over the 10 groups in amount correct comprehension of sentences without PL. Figure 5 shows this with PL.

Direction did not significantly determine amount of correct comprehension of pronouns overall; there was no significant difference between amount of correct comprehension on forward and backward pronouns. The "Directionality" constraint did generalize to null anaphora however, as the figures show. There were significantly more null anaphora items correct with forward anaphora ($\overline{X}$ = .525) than with backward ($\overline{X}$ =

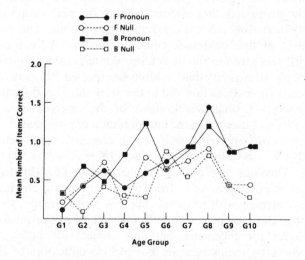

Fig. 4. Development of Successful Comprehension of Sentences with Forward or Backward Pronouns or Nulls *without* Pragmatic Lead.

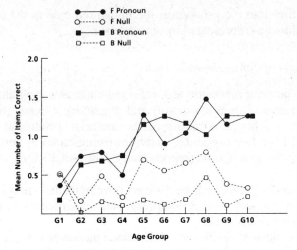

Fig. 5. Development of Successful Comprehension of Sentences with Forward or Backward Pronouns or Nulls *with* Pragmatic Lead.

.332) $(F(1,91) = 11.64, p = .001)$. This directionality effect held both without PL (FN = .58, BN = .46) and with PL (FN = .47, BN = .21).

Comparison of Figures 4 and 5 shows that the *Pragmatic Lead* significantly depressed the amount correct on null anaphora while significantly increasing amount correct on the pronoun. This confirms a generalization of the "pragmatic context" constraint to null anaphora. Since the PL was given to the object, this depression in amount correct for null anaphora suggests that children interpreted PL as determinant of reference in the null, as they did in the pronoun. This documents that children consulted pragmatic context in the interpretation of null anaphors (PRO) as they did in the interpretation of pronouns.

Sentences with pronouns were comprehended significantly more successfully ($\overline{X}$ = .87) than those with null ($\overline{X}$ = .43) $(F(1,91) = 60.43, p < .001$. This was true both with and without PL. This too would suggest that children generalize from the pronoun as unmarked. However since sentences with pronouns allowed more chances for correct response than did sentences with nulls (subject, object or third doll was scored correct for pronouns, but only subject for nulls), "amount correct" scores by themselves are not precise indicators of children's relative comprehension of pronoun and null anaphors. Analyses of children's coreference judgments are necessary to confirm this result.

3.2.2.2 *Coreference Judgments.* Coreference judgments for both pronoun and null were affected significantly by *Direction,* confirming that
children generalized the directionality effect over both of these anaphor
types. For both pronoun and null, as can be seen in Figure 6, the choice
of subject is preferred more strongly for forward anaphora than for
backward. For both pronoun and null, object choice is preferred more
for backward than for forward.

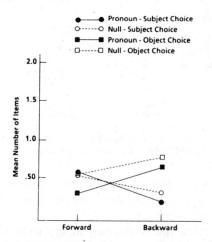

Fig. 6. Choice of Subject or Object as Antecedent in Comprehension Task
(Direction × Anaphor Type).

The *Pragmatic Lead* also affected both pronoun and null in similar
ways, as Figure 7 shows. PL (to the object) similarly increases choice of
object and decreases choice of subject for both pronoun and null
anaphora. For pronoun, PL to object increases choice of object from .34
to .61 (F(1,91) = 26.4, p < .001. For null, PL to object increases
choice of object from .49 to .84 (F(1,91) = 57.6, p < .001. For
pronoun, PL to object decreases choice of subject from .44 to .37
(F(1,91) = 2.11, p = .15, ns). For null, PL to object decreases choice of
subject from .53 to .35 (F(1,91) = 15.18, p < .001.

For both types, pronoun and null, the PL has its strongest effect in
depressing choice of subject and increasing choice of object on the
backward forms, rather than on the forward. This accords with results
found previously (LLK, 1980) on pronoun anaphora where backward
anaphora appears more sensitive to pragmatic context than does for-

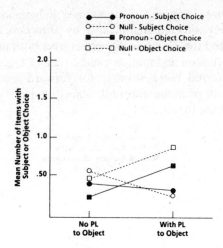

Fig. 7. Choice of Subject or Object in Comprehension Test, with and without Pragmatic
Lead to Object for Nulls and Pronouns.

ward in child language. It further supports the claim that the Directionality Constraint and the Pragmatic Context Constraint both apply
similarly to the null and pronoun.

The choice of a doll not mentioned in the stimulus sentence is a
possible correct response for act-out of sentences with pronouns, but
not for nulls. There is little choice of an extra-sentential (third doll)
referent in either pronoun or null. Only 2% of pronoun and 2½% of null
items involved the child's choice of an extra-sentential referent in the
form of a 3rd unmentioned doll (F(1,91) = .67, p = .41, ns). For both
nulls and pronouns the condition of highest appearance of 3rd doll
choice is the backward form (mean number of items is .07 for pronouns,
.05 for nulls).[7] Thus again children are seen not to differentiate pronoun
and null in terms of their reference to pragmatic context.

4.0 SUMMARY AND DISCUSSION

The data from this study provide evidence that children generalize over
structures like 1 with a pronoun and structures like 2 with a PRO. They
apply constraints 6i and ii similarly to both. The data confirm that both
the *directionality* constraint, and the *pragmatic context* constraint, are
general and not linked to specific phonetic forms, e.g., pronouns.

In addition, the evidence confirms that children treat the pronoun as the unmarked case in these structures. They assimilate the null (PRO) to pronoun. They thus deny the obligatory subject control required of PRO. In terms of Binding Theory, they ignore the 'BT-anaphor' properties of PRO.

Evidence for these conclusions was found both in children's production and in their comprehension of these structures.

(i) Children in their imitation of these structures frequently converted the null to a pronoun; rarely the reverse.

(ii) Children in their comprehension allowed pragmatic lead to influence their interpretation of PRO away from subject control just as they allowed it to influence their interpretation of the pronoun. PL affected both pronoun and PRO to a similar degree and in a similar manner.

(iii) Children generalize a directionality effect similarly over both pronoun and null. They show this in their imitation where forward pronouns are significantly easier to imitate than backward pronouns, forward nulls are preferentially converted to forward pronouns, and both backward nulls and backward pronouns are similarly avoided. They show this in their comprehension where choice of subject or object as antecedent is seen to be determined similarly by directionality of antecedent and anaphor for both pronoun and PRO. For example, for both pronoun and PRO there are more choices of subject as antecedent in the forward case (where the antecedent precedes the pronoun or PRO), than in the backward (where it follows).

(iv) In the comprehension task, children also show that they generalize both a directionality effect and a pragmatic context effect over both pronoun and PRO, in that for both pronoun and PRO, the pragmatic lead affects the choice of antecedent significantly more frequently in the backward direction, i.e., when the pronoun or PRO precedes the antecedent in the main clause.

Critically, children generalized over pronouns and PRO at the same time that they documented that they *did* differentiate the null category from the lexical pronoun. If they did not differentiate them, they would not have systematically converted the null to the pronoun in their imitation. Moreover, they differentiated these thoroughly enough to correlate them with the correct properties of tense in the domain in which they appear a large majority of the time, as their imitation data show. The data confirm then that at the same time that children distinguish the pronoun and null (PRO), they treat them unitarily at the level at which they apply the general constraints in 6 (Directionality and Pragmatic Context).

4.1 *Free Anaphora as Unmarked*

These data suggest that pronoun, not PRO, is the unmarked case in these sentences. Free anaphora is represented by the pronoun. Converging evidence supports this claim: (i) the children's spontaneous conversions of nulls to pronouns in imitation *and* (ii) the similar effects of pragmatic context on nulls as on pronouns in comprehension.

4.1.1 *Conversion of Null to Pronoun in Imitation*

The conversion from null to pronoun in children's imitation could simply reflect the child's general preference for a phonetically filled nominal category. This would be predicted by some current theories of child language (e.g., Slobin, 1973). There is some evidence for this type of phenomenon in other studies where children have been found to elaborate gaps by filling in redundant NP in imitating coordinate structures with gaps (e.g., Lust, 1976, 1977, Lust, Flynn, Chien, and Clifford, 1980; Slobin and Welsh, 1973). The full set of data suggests, however, that the phenomenon of null to pronoun conversion observed in this study is not based on a simple preference for a phonetically realized nominal category in the child. Children only rarely convert to NP. Rather, they specifically convert to pronoun, in the sentences in this study. In addition, overall in this study children did *not* find it significantly more difficult to imitate sentences with null anaphors than those with pronouns.

The conversion from null to pronoun might alternatively be thought to be a direct result of (or reflection of) the directionality constraint favoring forward anaphora. Note that children did not significantly prefer pronouns to nulls in backward forms, but only in forward ones. Children could merely choose to instantiate this directionality constraint by use of a pronoun which follows its antecedent in our sentences. The constraint itself might be thought to be in fact a production constraint defined over phonetically realized elements (*viz.*, pronouns) which must be linearly ordered in real time in keeping with on-line processing. If so, the conversion of null to pronoun is not a general preference in the child with regard to the free anaphora reflected by the pronoun but a reflex of the forward directionality effect. This explanation is disconfirmed, however, by the fact that although the anaphor type choice is clearly linked to directionality in these imitation results, the directionality effect is independent of anaphor type. It has been found in other studies on structures involving only null anaphors and no frequent conversion to pronouns (e.g., coordinate structures, Lust, 1976, 1977; Tavakolian, 1977). Results of the comprehension test in this study also evidenced the directionality constraint in children's interpretation of null anaphors. Children significantly comprehended forward null better than backward null, and attributed more subject coreference judgments to them. Thus, the children's choice of the pronoun in imitation in this study cannot be explained solely by the child's "needing" a pronoun to instantiate either a null category or the directionality factor in production. It may be viewed as representing a choice of the type of anaphora represented by the pronoun, viz., free anaphora.

4.1.2 *Effects of PC on Comprehension*

Pragmatic Context constraint is associated with pronoun, not with PRO, in adult grammar. It applies specifically to free anaphora. Children generalize this property of free anaphora to PRO in structures we studied. They frequently not only replace the null anaphor by a pronoun but they override obligatory subejct control of the bound null anaphor in these contexts under the influence of PC. This behavior provides evidence that the children's choice of pronoun in imitation of these structures reflects a related choice of free anaphora in their comprehension.

It should be observed that effects of pragmatic context in this study are indirect. The PC causes children to shift choice of antecedent from one NP to another (Subject to Object) *within* the sentence. Our experimental design did not test whether a pragmatic lead to a name which was *not* mentioned in the sentence would cause children to use this sentence-external referent as antecedent for null and pronoun. For example, this design did not present children, with a sequence like "This is a story about Ernie. John kissed Tom when Ø turning around." (Since this sequence is pragmatically unlikely, and the manipulation of 3 dolls at once is problematic for young children, an experimental design would have to be developed in order to adapt this situation for use.) It could be argued, therefore, that because the PC manipulation in this study only causes children to shift choice of antecedent *within* the sentence, that both null and pronoun therefore still have 'grammatical antecedents' and therefore both are 'BT-anaphoric' in keeping with the essential features of PRO.

The PC manipulation of this study, however, did test whether children would consult PC in the form of a previous utterance in their choice of antecedent. The results confirmed that children *do* consult this previous utterance similarly for *both* pronouns and PRO. This PC caused shifting of choice of antecedent in both cases. Consultation of PC in the form of a previous utterance for determination of anaphor antecedent is consistent with interpretation of a pronoun, but inconsistent with interpretation of PRO, whatever the possible antecedents (whether sentence-internal or sentence-external). Shifting of possible antecedents is also generally inconsistent with PRO, although consistent with pronouns, whether these antecedents are in or out of the sentence in which the PRO appears. We saw also that where choice of an external referent (3rd doll) did occur spontaneously in this study, it occurred similarly for null and pronoun. Moreover, if the effect of PL which was observed in the comprehension task is not a reflex of the assignment of free anaphora to these structures, then it is contradicted by the imitation task results in which these same children actually inserted a pronoun in their imitation of these structures, and an ad-hoc explanation must be sought for these imitation results.

4.2 *General Significance of Results*

(1) In general, these results provide evidence that at a certain level, children conflate distinct terms (pronoun and PRO) under general principles. In this sense then they are seen to be constructing a 'theory of anaphora' in first language acquisition. This theory consists of hypotheses regarding 'how the system works.' They formulate the principles of this system with regard to *direction* between antecedent and anaphor, and with regard to possible determination by *pragmatic context*. The precise form of the anaphor type, whether a phonetically filled lexical pronoun or a null category is not what determines the child's general theory.

(2) These results evidence that in their theory of anaphora, children represent a level of language structure other than the immediate

acoustic surface; in particular, they represent a *gapped* structure. (In current theory, this level is termed "S-structure" cf. Chomsky, 1980b.) The fact that children develop production and comprehension of null anaphora in close relation to pronoun anaphora and the fact that they spontaneously convert null to pronoun anaphora evidences their representation of the gap *per se* at some level.

(3) These results in general accord with a recent theory of NP's (Chomsky, 1981a) which suggests that pronoun and PRO are grammatically categorized uniformly as "Pronominals." Both share a set of feature specifications (person, gender, number). They differ essentially only in that PRO lacks the phonetic matrix which characterizes the pronoun. Children's spontaneous conversions of nulls to pronouns in their imitation may be viewed as a phonetic realization of this underlying set of features of the PRO.

4.3 More Specific Significance of Results. What is the Basis of Children's Generalization from Pronoun to PRO?

4.3.1 Binding Theory (BT)

In BT terms, it is the 'BT-anaphoric' properties which characterize PRO but not pronoun. The results of this study suggest then that children must learn to additionally assign these properties to PRO, thus differentiating PRO from pronoun. These properties would assure that PRO must have a grammatical antecedent, viz., subject, and should be insensitive to pragmatic context.

Children's generalization from pronoun to PRO in this study would be predicted by a linguistic theory which treated 'PRO' as a marked, derivative construct. Since PRO is not directly described by any of the 3 basic binding principles in BT (e.g., Chomsky, 1981, 1982), but by an intersection of 2 of these principles this aspect of current BT theory could be viewed as consistent with our results. The results would also be consistent with a theory of binding which proposed that PRO does not have 'BT-anaphoric' properties in all cases of control but may be underlyingly a pronoun (cf., Bouchard, 1982; Harbert, pc).[8]

Children's generalization from pronoun to PRO would also be consistent with acquisition theory based on BT (e.g., Van Riemsdijk, this volume; see also Roeper, this volume) which predicts that the bound variable or 'BT-anaphoric' properties of PRO must be distinguished from pronominals during the course of language acquisition.

4.3.2 *The Configurational Domain of the Sentences in This Study*

Children's treatment of PRO in this study is not identical to that in other studies. The pronoun and PRO in this study occurred in adverbial subordinate clause domains sketched in 3 above. In other studies, where PRO has occurred in different structures (e.g., VP complements, Sherman 1983 and this volume) children have not imposed either the pronoun in imitation or free anaphora in comprehension. In nulls which occur in these structures, children have not been found to substitute a pronoun significantly in imitation, or to allow PC to influence their interpretations of this null. Other researchers studying other sentences structures have also not found our results (e.g., Deutsch and Koster, 1982, Jakubowicz, 1984).

If children do not generalize properties of optional (free) pronoun anaphora over all forms of null anaphora, or over all forms of PRO, one must ask under just what conditions they do generalize this way. In particular, what about the stimulus sentences in our study provoked the generalization to free pronoun anaphora? Since the sentences in this study had the same configuration for both free and bound anaphora, it may be that children used this configurational similarity as the basis on which to generalize over these. This configuration, an embedded adverbial subordinate clause, with a 'when' connective in COMP position, was associated with free anaphora.

4.3.2.1 *The Unmarked Form of Null Anaphora in Adverbial Subordinate Clauses.* Although some languages do resemble English in permitting only subject control of null subjects in sentence structures like 2, e.g., Russian (Babby, 1978), Malayalam for some clause types (although not others) (Mohanan, 1983), many languages use null anaphora where English uses pronouns in these contexts. Such null anaphora is often optionally or pragmatically controlled, as is pronoun anaphora in these contexts in English. The language-specific aspect of null subject interpretation in English structures like 2 can be seen by comparison to similar structures in other languages, e.g., Japanese, or Sinhalese shown in 22, where the null subject is freely controlled by discourse context, as the underlining in the gloss suggests.

(22)   yudde ivərə unaamə   rajjuruwo maaligaawəTə
        war   over   became-when king   palace-DAT

        aawa. Ø enəkoTə   maaligaawə lassənəTə sarəsannay
        came. Ø come-when palace   beautifully decorate

        kiyəla bisoo wæDəkaarəyanTə kiwwa
        COMP   queen workers-DAT   said

        (The war having ended, *the king* returned to the palace.
        When Ø coming, the queen told the workers to decorate the
        palace beautifully.)

In fact, null anaphora even in English is often optionally or even
pragmatically controlled, in similar contexts where the adjunct phrase
does not include a connective, e.g., "Ø Going down the street, John saw
Tom." Here the Ø may freely refer to either John or Tom. Bresnan
(1982a, b) and Mohanan (1983) have pointed out also that PRO can
have discourse reference in English. Their examples include 23:

(23)   *Mary* sighed and looked around the room. It was unclear
        what *PRO* to do with herself now that Molly was gone.

Thus both the phonetic form of the anaphor used in these domains, and
the possible obligatory subject control of the null anaphor may be
language specific, and obligatory subject control in structures like 2 may
be exceptional even within English.[9]

4.4 *Children's Hypotheses*

Children's hypotheses regarding two types of anaphora which were demonstrated in this study thus reflect general principles which are
independent of phonetic form of anaphor and which constrain the form
of the data in the child's experience (production or comprehension).
These constraints on children's hypotheses reflect a general and abstract
Directionality principle. They also may reflect what may be the
unmarked form of anaphora in subordinate clause domains such as 1
and 2 in natural language.[10]

     Current theoretical work on the nature of PRO across languages is
necessary to the formulation of the parameter suggested here in terms of
the Binding Theory (e.g., Chomsky 1981b, Huang 1984, Gair 1983,
Mohanan, 1983). Our results accentuate the significance of these
studies.

NOTES

[1] This study was supported in part by the National Science Foundation under grants #BNS-7825115 and #BNS-8318983.

We thank James Gair, and D. T. Langendoen for critical discussion. We thank Yu-Chin Chien, Terri Clifford and Shirley Hsu for invaluable assistance in data collection and analysis. We thank Helen Goodluck for useful exchange of relevant results, and discussion.

[2] Although the basic facts surrounding structures like 1 and 2 are fairly clear, the precise representation of the anaphoric relations they reflect is not. (This is true particularly in the case of the PRO in 2.) The configurational structure assigned to structures like 1 and 2 and the role of this configuration in determining the anaphora relations they involve are still not totally resolved linguistically. (See Chomsky 1981b, Williams 1980, Manzini 1983, Smits 1983 and Mohanan 1983, for some discussion.) In particular the level of adjunction of the subordinate clause, both when postposed as in 3, and when preposed, may be ambiguous. Prior resolution of these more precise issues is not necessary to our experimental design or to our argument in this study, however. Our empirical results may in fact contribute to their resolution.

[3] See the introduction to this volume for definition of the general sense in which the term "anaphora" is used here. Chomsky's recent "Binding Theory " (BT) restricts the term 'anaphor' to NP's which are "lexically identified" as anaphors, and which require grammatical antecedents, or have "no intrinsic reference" (1981a, 218), e.g., "each other" or reflexive pronouns. Pronouns then are not 'anaphors' in this specific use of the term in this theory. Although we use the term 'anaphor' in its two senses, context makes its interpretation clear. In addition we will refer to the more specific use of anaphor in Chomsky's theory as 'BT-anaphor.'

[4] Exceptions to this claim of obligatory control by main clause subject have been noted by Langendoen (pc) and Gair (pc) who observe, for example, "When Ø walking down the street, it started to rain." Another example is "After Ø explaining it, they got the idea that *I* ordered the department heads not to talk," heard on a Radio Newscast by the Mayor of Binghamton, 1/12/82. As Langendoen adds, however, the clear unacceptability of examples like "When Ø shaving himself, Mary saw Tom" suggests the strength of the principle of main clause subject control in these contexts. See Mohanan 1983, 650, for further arguments on this issue.

[5] In general, null anaphors in English, reflect bound anaphora, not free, while pronouns reflect free anaphora, not bound. However, the principles which determine whether a term is bound or free are deeper than the phonetic content of the term itself. They concern the configuration in which the pronoun or null appear. Thus 'pronouns' can be interpreted as bound (see Reinhart this volume) and null nominal categories can be interpreted as free, in English as well as in other languages, depending upon the structural domain in which they appear. (Consider for example, the sentence, "Ø winning the war is on everyone's mind." The null here is free in reference and does not have an antecedent within the sentence in which it appears (cf. Solan, 1977, Williams, 1980).

[6] Written scoring criteria for both imitation and act-out behavior are available on request.

[7] The most natural response in the act-out task as administered here appears to be not to generate spontaneous reference to an additional doll not named in the stimulus

sentence, especially if one or more of the named dolls are possible referents grammatically. Higher amounts of sentence-external reference to other dolls available in the reference set have been found in studies where stimuli grammatically did not allow sentence internal antecedents (e.g., Solan, 1983, Lust and Clifford, this volume). In addition, in studies like this one, where the reference set consists of 3 dolls, 2 of which are mentioned in the stimulus sentence, chance alone would predict that one of the named dolls be used as antecedent. The critical point for the argument made here, however, is that even among this small amount of external reference that does occur in this study, there is no significant difference between the amount for pronouns and that for nulls ($F(1,91) = .67$, $p = .41$).

[8] Chomsky's (1982) theory of 'small pro' is another possible formulation of this concept.

[9] The frequent misreading of the 'dangling participle' in English (e.g., John saw the fire Ø running down the street) may be another indication of the weakness of obligatory subject control in such contexts.

[10] Current work in first language acquisition of languages other than English is pursuing this issue further (cf. Lust, Card Stansifer, Belazi and Clark, 1981 and in preparation for Arabic). In Arabic, for example, null anaphors may in general represent free anaphora. If children generalize to free anaphora not on the basis of phonetic form but on the basis of anaphora type, this predicts that Arabic children should generalize from pronoun to null. This would be opposite to the English pronoun in phonetic content, but similar to English in the pronoun's anaphora properties. See also Lust, Chien and Mangione 1984 and to appear for related study of Chinese.

REFERENCES

Babby, L: 1978, 'Participles in Russian: Attribution, predication and voice', *International Review of Slavic Linguistics* **3**, 5–25.

Bouchard, D.: 1982, 'On the content of empty categories', unpublished doctoral dissertation, MIT.

Bresnan, J.: 1982a, 'Control and complementation', *Linguistic Inquiry* **13**, 343–434.

Bresnan, J.: 1982b, 'Control and complementation', *The Mental Representation of Grammatical Relations*, MIT Press, Cambridge, Mass., pp. 282–390.

Chomsky, N.: 1980b, *Rules and Representations*, Columbia University Press, New York.

Chomsky, N.: 1981a, *Lectures on Government and Binding*, Foris, Dordrecht.

Chomsky, N.: 1981b, 'A note on non-control PRO', *Journal of Linguistic Research* **1**, 1–11.

Chomsky, N.: 1982, *Some Concepts and Consequences of the Theory of Government and Binding*, MIT Press, Cambridge, Mass.

Deutsch, W. and J. Koster: 1982, 'Children's interpretation of sentence internal anaphora', *Papers and Reports on Child Language Development* **21**, 39–45.

Gair, J.: 1983, 'Non-configurationality, movement, and Sinhala focus', paper presented at the Linguistic Association of Great Britain, Newcastle.

Goodluck, H.: 1978, *Linguistic Principles in Children's Grammar of Complement Subject Interpretation*, unpublished doctoral dissertation, University of Massachusetts.

Goodluck, H.: 1981, 'Children's grammar of complement subject interpretation', in S. Tavakolian (ed.), *Language Acquisition and Linguistic Theory*, MIT, Cambridge, Mass., pp. 139–166.

Huang, J.: 1984, 'On the distribution and reference of empty pronouns', *Linguistic Inquiry* **15**, 531–574.

Jakubowicz, C.: 1984, 'On markedness and binding principles', *Proceedings of the North Eastern Linguistic Society* **14**, 154–182.

Kuno, S.: 1972a, 'Functional sentence perspective: A case study from Japanese and English', *Linguistic Inquiry* **3**, 269–320.

Kuno, S.: 1972b, 'Pronominalization, reflexivization, and direct discourse', *Linguistic Inquiry* **3**, 161–195.

Kuno, S.: 1975, 'Three perspectives in the functional approach to syntax', papers from the Parasession on Functionalism, Chicago Linguistic Society, 276–335.

Lasnik, H.: 1976, 'Remarks on coreference', *Linguistic Analysis* **2**, 1–22.

Lust, B.: 1976, 'Conjunction reduction in child language'. Unpublished doctoral dissertation, City University of New York.

Lust, B.: 1977, 'Conjunction reduction in child language', *Journal of Child Language* **4**, 257–287.

Lust, B.: 1981, 'Constraint on anaphora in child language: A prediction for a universal', in S. Tavakolian (ed.), *Language Acquisition and Linguistic Theory*, MIT Press, Cambridge, Mass., pp. 74–96.

Lust, B., E. Carol-Stansifer, N. Belazi and C. Clark: 1981, and in preparation, 'First language acquisition of anaphora in Arabic: The roles of configuration and linearity. Unpublished manuscript, Cornell.

Lust, B., Y.-C. Chien, and L. Mangione: 1984a, 'First language acquisition of Mandarin Chinese: Constraints on free and bound null anaphora', in S. Hattori and K. Inoue (eds.), *Proceedings of the Thirteenth International Congress of Linguists*, Gakushuin, Tokyo, pp. 1127–1130.

Lust, B., S. Flynn, Y.-C. Chien and T. Clifford: 1980, 'Coordination: The role of syntactic, pragmatic and processing factors in its first language acquisition', *Papers and Reports on Child Language Development* **19**, 79–87.

Lust, B., K. Loveland, and R. Kornet: 1980, 'The development of anaphora in first language: Syntactic and pragmatic constraints', *Linguistic Analysis* **6**, 359–391.

Lust, B., L. Mangione, and Y.-C. Chien: 1984b, 'Determination of empty categories in first language acquisition of Mandarin Chinese', Working papers in Linguistics, 6, Cornell University, Ithaca, N.Y.

Manzini, M. R.: 1983, 'On control and control theory', *Linguistic Inquiry* **14**, 427–446.

Mohanan, K. P.: 1983, 'Functional and anaphoric control', *Linguistic Inquiry* **14**, 641–674.

Reinhart, T.: 1976, *The Syntactic Domain of Anaphora*, unpublished doctoral dissertation, MIT, Cambridge, Massachusetts.

Reinhart, T.: 1983a, *Anaphora and Semantic Interpretation*, Croom Helm, London.

Reinhart, T.: 1983b, 'Coreference and bound anaphora: A restatement of the anaphora questions', *Linguistics and Philosophy* **6**, 47–88.

Sherman, J. Cohen: 1983a, *The Acquisition of Control in Complement Sentences: The Role of Structural and Lexical Factors*, unpublished doctoral dissertation, Cornell University.

Slobin, D.: 1973, 'Cognitive prerequisites for the development of grammar', in C. Ferguson and D. Slobin (eds.), *Studies of Child Language Development*, Holt, Rinehart and Winston, New York, pp. 175–208.

Slobin, D. and C. Welsh: 1973, 'Elicited imitation as a research tool in developmental psycho-linguistics', in C. Ferguson and D. Slobin (eds.), *Studies of Child Language Development*, Holt, Rinehart and Winston, New York, pp. 485–496.

Smits, R.: 1983, 'On some free adjuncts in English and the role of elements in comp', unpublished paper, University of Amsterdam.

Solan, L.: 1977, 'On the interpretation of missing complement NP's', *Occasional Papers in Linguistics*, 3, University of Massachusetts, Amherst.

Solan, L.: 1978, *Anaphora in Child Language*, unpublished doctoral dissertation, University of Massachusetts.

Solan, L.: 1983, *Pronominal Reference: Child Language and the Theory of Grammar*, D. Reidel, Dordrecht.

Stenning, K.: 1978, 'Anaphora as an approach to pragmatics', in M. Halle, J. Bresnan, and G. Miller (eds.), *Linguistic Theory and Psychological Reality*, MIT Press, Cambridge, Mass., pp. 162–200.

Tavakolian, S.: 1977, *Structural Principles in the Acquisition of Complex Sentences*, unpublished doctoral dissertation, University of Massachusetts, Amherst.

Tavakolian, S.: 1978a, 'Children's comprehension of pronominal subjects and missing subjects in complicated sentences', in H. Goodluck and L. Solan (eds.), *Papers in the Structure and Development of Child Language*, Occasional Papers in Linguistics, 4, University of Massachusetts, Amherst, pp. 145–152.

Williams, E.: 1980, 'Predication', *Linguistic Inquiry* 11, 203–238.

4. CONTROL

SYNTACTIC AND LEXICAL CONSTRAINTS ON THE ACQUISITION OF CONTROL IN COMPLEMENT SENTENCES[1]

1. INTRODUCTION

There is currently much concern in linguistic theory for the role of the lexicon in the organization of syntax (e.g., Chomsky, 1981, Bresnan, 1982). Current linguistic theory proposes considerable restructuring of the grammar such that the lexical component is greatly expanded. This change in current grammatical theory raises interesting questions for a theory of first language acquisition. In the acquisition of complex syntax, to what degree can and do children depend on lexical knowledge and to what degree do they depend on structure-dependent knowledge, where structure-dependence is specifically determined by the syntactic component of sentence-grammar?

1.1 *Lexicon and Anaphora*

As elsewhere in this volume, the term "anaphora" is used to refer to the natural language situation in which a proform (e.g., pronoun or null anaphor) is interpreted by reference to another term in the sentence or general discourse context. The lexicon is critically involved in the grammar of anaphora in several ways. The lexicon functions critically in the identification of and location of anaphors (particularly null anaphors or "empty categories") (cf. Chomsky, 1982; Janet Fodor, 1979). For example, the hearer knows that utterances with the verb 'tell' must include a referent to 'something told' and to 'someone' told 'to'. In addition, the lexicon functions critically in that subset of anaphoric phenomena which are covered by "control theory" (Chomsky, 1982, Manzini, 1983; Bresnan, 1982).

1.2 *Control and Anaphora*

In this paper we are particularly concerned with that specific type of anaphora, which is described by a "control" relation in Verb Phrase (VP) complements, such as (1a) and (1b) below.

279

B. Lust (ed.), Studies in the Acquisition of Anaphora, Vol. I, 279–308
© *1986 by D. Reidel Publishing Company.*

(1) a.   [[*John* promises Bill] [*PRO* to leave]]

   b.   [[John tells *Bill*] [*PRO* to leave]]

These sentences embed a clause (e.g., 'PRO to leave') which (at least in surface structure) lacks an overt subject, and is untensed (infinitival) as a complement to a matrix clause (e.g., 'John promises Bill').[2] Although the complement clause lacks an overt subject, the hearer interprets these sentences as if there were a subject associated with the verb of the complement, in order to determine the predicate-argument structure of the embedded clause (e.g., in order to determine who leaves).

1.3 *Control Reflects Syntactic Structure*

The null anaphor in these embedded VPs (represented as 'PRO') reflects general syntactic properties of these complement structures. Notice that a pronoun is not possible in these structures (i.e., in a non-tensed domain) as exemplified in (2a) and (b) below.

(2) a.   *John promises Bill he to leave.
   b.   *John tells Bill he to leave.

The constraint involved in (2a) and (2b) can be seen if these sentences are contrasted with 2c–f below, which have tensed sentence complements. Here pronouns are required, and null anaphors forbidden.

   c.   John promises Bill that he will leave.
   d.   *John promises Bill that Ø will leave.
   e.   John tells Bill that he will leave.
   f.   *John tells Bill that Ø will leave.

It has been argued that the requirement for phonetically empty subjects in the non-tensed VP domain, as in 1a and b, reflects critical syntactic properties related to the anaphor type categorized as 'PRO' (e.g., Chomsky, 1981, 1982), which are associated with the VP complement structure.

1.4 *Control Reflects the Lexicon*

The null anaphor is interpreted in relation to another term in the sentence, as shown by the underlining in (1a) and (1b) in a manner dependent on the main clause verb. In (1a), it is known to be *John*, the matrix subject, who leaves, because the matrix verb is 'promise'. In (1b), where the matrix verb is 'tell', it is *Bill*, the matrix object who leaves.[3] Control structures thus integrate the lexicon and syntax in complex sentence formation.

1.5 *Linguistic Background to the Study of Control*

Analyses of control have been proposed by Bresnan (1982), Chomsky (1981), and Manzini (1983). These accounts share basic features although they differ in that Bresnan's account, based on the Lexical Functional Theory of Grammar (Bresnan, 1978, 1982), represents the grammar of control in the lexicon alone. Chomsky's account of control (e.g., Government and Binding, 1981) takes into account both lexical facts and structural considerations, such as the sentential domain (the role of INFL (inflection) and the governed or ungoverned position of empty categories) which is argued to be critical for defining type of anaphor and properties of anaphoric interpretation[4] (cf. also Williams, 1980).

1.6. *Acquisition Issues*

The linguistic issues which Chomsky and Bresnan have formulated regarding the representation of lexical and structural factors in control relations raise interesting and critical questions for a theory of control in first language acquisition. By studying the acquisition of complex sentence anaphora in sentences such as (1a) and (1b), and related structures, we address the issue of the degree to which lexical principles may guide the acquisition of the anaphora involved in this structure, and the degree to which children may bring general structural (syntactic) principles which constrain anaphora to bear on these structures also.

1.7 *Previous Acquisition Research*

There has been considerable study of children's comprehension of the verbs 'promise' and 'tell' in sentences such as (1a) and (1b) above (e.g.,

C. Chomsky, 1969; Maratsos, 1974; Tavakolian, 1978, Hsu, 1981). A review of empirical data available from these studies reveals that there are major unresolved issues with regard to the role of the lexicon and of the structure of these sentences in acquisition. (These studies are reviewed in detail in Sherman, 1983).

The major result from previous studies is that in interpreting complement sentences such as (1a) and (1b), children age 3—10 frequently assign object control to the verb 'promise' as well as to the verb 'tell' (Chomsky, 1969; Maratsos, 1974; Tavakolian, 1978; Hsu, 1981). That is, children frequently interpret *both* sentences such as (1a) and (1b) as though *Bill* (the main-clause indirect object) would leave, even though in sentences with 'promise' such as (1a) it is *John* (the main-clause subject) which is correct. A number of different explanations have been offered for this result, perhaps the most 'classic' of which is the Minimum Distance Principle (MDP), first proposed as relevant in these structures by C. Chomsky (1969). According to this principle, children generally choose the object as controller of the missing complement subject because it is the noun phrase nearest to it. In C. Chomsky's definition of the MDP, it is unclear whether distance (i.e., 'nearness' of terms) is defined in terms of surface distance or in terms of dominance relations (cf., Rosenbaum, 1970).[5] However, as it is usually referred to in the first language acquisition literature, the MDP is a surface-distance strategy. In this sense, the MDP is a processing strategy, according to which the sentence is analyzed as a linear string.

A processing strategy such as the MDP suggests that in interpreting VP complements, children access neither lexical or structural principles involved in control, but rather, consult only the relation of surface distance between anaphor and antecedent. However, because of certain limitations in the design and methodology of previous studies, this conclusion cannot be assumed.

First, all previous studies on the acquisition of control tested only VP complementation. Thus, several alternatives to the MDP are possible. For example, it is not possible to determine whether children's object control responses were due to: (a) an inability to access the subject control properties of 'promise' (as claimed), and a generalization of a principle of lexical control (as object), or (b) a general principle of object control in VP. Children may associate object control in VP with the null anaphor ('PRO') on the basis of a general syntactic principle which critically consults the (untensed) VP complement structure and/

or the null anaphor (e.g., 'PRO') in sentences such as (1). As Chomsky has pointed out (1980, pp. 32–36), in English, object control is unmarked in VP complement structures, in the sense that a wide range of verbs, in fact most verbs, require object control in this structure. This is suggested in (3a–f) below. This generalization might possibly be explained by the structurally related fact that the matrix object is the nearest c-commanding element to the null complement anaphor (e.g., Rosenbaum, 1970). 'Promise' is thus a marked exception to this syntactic generalization.[6]

(3) a.   John persuaded *Bill PRO* to go

b.   John forced *Bill PRO* to go

c.   John reminded *Bill PRO* to go

d.   John wanted *Bill PRO* to go

e.   John convinced *Bill PRO* to go

f.   John ordered *Bill PRO* to go

Previous studies also did not fully assess the degree to which children have knowledge of lexical control properties. They showed that children assign more object than subject control to both the verbs 'promise' and 'tell'. However, from the data presented, it is not possible to determine whether children gave more subject control responses in sentences with 'promise' than in sentences with 'tell' and more object control in sentences with 'tell' than in sentences with 'promise'. If they did, this would suggest that children do, in fact, differentiate lexical control properties of verbs (i.e., of 'tell' and 'promise') even though they may have a general principle of object control in VP complements.

Thus, previous studies did not fully assess children's knowledge of the lexicon, or their knowledge of complementation structure, or their knowledge of the relation between these two (See C. Smith, 1981 on the importance of this issue). To assess these possibilities, it is necessary to test the verbs 'promise' and 'tell' in other complement structures as well as in VP's.

2. THIS STUDY

In a set of experimental studies of the development of young children's competence for anaphora in English control structures, Sherman (1983a) varied not only control properties of the matrix verb, but also structural factors of complement embedding in experimental design. By varying both structural factors (i.e., syntactic domain of the complement and type of anaphor) and lexical factors (i.e., verb control), she attempted to determine the degree to which children are sensitive to each of these factors and to study how they integrate these factors in building a theory of control for the language they are acquiring.

. Although the results of Sherman's study do not critically distinguish linguistic models of control (e.g., Chomsky, 1981; Bresnan, 1982), they provide evidence that general syntactic principles, which involve general principles of anaphora, as well as lexical principles are consulted in this aspect of early child language. The results of Sherman's study also bear on the critical set of questions about the *types* of theories children have about language, which are raised by previous studies on the acquisition of control. In studying knowledge of lexical and structural factors which define control relations in acquisition, this study provides evidence on whether children's knoweldge of control at early stages is based solely on processing strategies such as a surface MDP, or whether it involves linguistic sensitivities which are related to the grammar of the language the child is acquiring.

2.1 *Rationale of This Study*

Sherman (1983a) first attempted to replicate the previous finding that children assign object control in VP complements with 'promise' as well as 'tell'. Her study hypothesized, however, that replication of this result may not merit the conclusion that children's interpretation of the missing complement subject is based on an interpretive non-structure-dependent strategy such as the MDP. Instead, she hypothesized that this finding may be explained by the fact that children hold a general principle of anaphoric control in VP complements which requires that they assign the matrix object as antecedent of the complement anaphor in these structures. The prediction for a general principle of object control in VP follows from the fact that object control in VP complements is the unmarked case in English (as shown in (3) above).

The comprehension task consisted of an act-out task in which children were asked to act-out sentences presented by the experimenter. This task has been established in the literature as a measure of the child's sentence comprehension and provides direct evidence of the child's interpretation of null or pronoun anaphora (e.g., Sinclair, et al., 1976; Goodluck and Solan, 1978; Lust, et al., 1980; Goodluck, 1981).

2.3 *Design*

Sherman, 1983, reports results of two experimental studies: (1) The Lexical Control (L-C) Study of imitation and comprehension, and; (2) The Pragmatic Lead (P-L) Study of comprehension. These studies were conducted with two different groups of children. We summarize selected aspects of design and results relevant to the hypotheses above.

In a factorial design, children were tested in the two studies on complement sentences which varied in *Control Property of the matrix verb* as either *subject control* ('promise') or *object control* (both the verbs 'tell' and 'remind' were tested). In addition, sentences varied in *Complement Type* to include both VP and sentential complementation, as exemplified in Tables 1 (Imitation) and 2 (Act-out).[10] In the tables, sentences 1, 3 and 4, for example, represented VP complements; 2, 5 and 6 represented $\overline{S}$ complements. A set of 16 of these complement sentences, ranging evenly over the 4 sentence types, 4 items of each condition (VP: subject, object control; $\overline{S}$: subject, object control) were presented within each task.

As shown in the tables, children were also tested on coordinate sentences in both imitation and act-out tasks. Coordinate sentences varied in anaphor type (null, pronoun). Sentences 7 and 8 in the tables represent the null coordinate sentences; 9 and 10 represent the pronoun coordinate sentences. In each task, children were presented with four coordinate sentences (two with a null anaphor and two with a pronoun anaphor).

Complement sentences were equated for other lexical content, tense of matrix and embedded clause and for length (9 words). The matrix clause of both VP and $\overline{S}$ complements was presented in present tense (e.g., 'John promises Bill'). Embedded sentences in sentential complements were presented in future tense because it was thought to be the most neutral in its relation to the interpretation of the pronoun anaphor. Coordinate sentences were similar to the complement sentences in length and lexical content.

TABLE I
Example Sentences — Imitation Task

Complement Sentences

Verb Type

Complement Type	S Complement	VP Complement
Subject Control (promise)	2. Jimmy promises Tom that he will drink the milk.	1. Tom promises Billy to eat the ice cream cone.
Object Control (remind, tell)	5. Bill reminds Jimmy that he will cook the dinner. 6. Jimmy tells Tom that he will ride the bicycle.	3. The lady reminds the man to eat the apple. 4. The sister tells the brother to draw a picture.

Coordinate Sentences

Anaphor Type

Null Anaphor	*Pronoun Anaphor*
7. The Mommy hugs the Daddy and pats the dog. 8. The Daddy kisses the Mom and eats the cookie.	9. Daddy hugs the boy and he closes the door. 10. Mom tickles the girl and she drinks the water.

TABLE II
Example Sentences — Act-Out Task

Complement Sentences

Verb Type

Subject Control
(promise)

1. The turtle promises the skunk to push the car.
2. Oscar promises Big Bird that he will drop the block.

Object Control
(remind, tell)

3. The monkey reminds the turtle to kick the ball.
4. The turtle tells the monkey to drop the penny.
5. Big Bird reminds Ernie that he will rub the penny.
6. Ernie tells Big Bird that he will pat the tissue.

Complement Type
S̄ Complement   VP Complement
S Complement

Coordinate Sentences

Anaphor Type

Null Anaphor

7. The turtle tickles the skunk and bumps the car.
8. The monkey pats the skunk and kicks the car.

Pronoun Anaphor

9. Ernie squeezes Oscar and he pushes the ball.
10. Big Bird kisses Oscar and he rubs the tissue.

In the L-C Study, 20 sentences (16 complement and 4 coordinate) were presented to each child in the imitation task and 20 in the act-out task. In the P-L study, children were tested on 20 sentences.[11] Within each sentence type in the P-L Study, half of the sentences were preceded by a lead which mentioned the matrix subject and half by a lead which mentioned the matrix object. To determine effect of *Pragmatic Lead* on children's interpretation of the complement anaphor, we analyzed whether the specific term mentioned in the lead (subject, object) influenced choice of antecedent. That is, did children choose the matrix subject as antecedent more often when the pragmatic lead mentioned matrix subject than when it mentioned matrix object; and did they choose matrix object as antecedent more often when pragmatic lead mentioned matrix object than matrix subject?

2.4 *Reference Set for the Interpretation Task*

The reference sets for the interpretation task consisted of either 3 Sesame Street dolls or 3 stuffed animals depending on stimulus sentences.

2.5 *Subjects*

72 *S*s divided equally into 3 age groups: 3,0—3,11 (Group I); 5,0—5,11 (Group II); 7,0—7,11 (Group III) were tested in the L-C Study. Mean age was 5 years, 5 months. 33 of the *S*s were female and 39 male. In the P-L Study, 36 *S*s divided into the same 3 age groups were tested. Mean age overall was 5 years, 6 months. 19 of the *S*s were female and 17 male. *S*s were individually interviewed in several day care, nursery and elementary schools in Ithaca, N.Y. All subjects were monolingual and had no apparent language disorder.

2.6 *Analyses*

The design allowed for parallel analyses and comparison of results on the imitation and act-out tasks in the L-C Study. The two tasks were analyzed independently by a 3-factor ANOVA ($3 \times 2 \times 2$): *Age* (I—III) $\times$ *Complement Type* (VP, $\overline{S}$) $\times$ *Verb Control Property* (Subject, Object) with repeated measures on the last two factors. In the P-L Study, the comprehension task was analyzed independently by a 4-Factor

ANOVA (3 × 2 × 2 × 2), which added *Pragmatic Lead* (Subject, Object) as a factor with repeated measures on the last three factors. Coordinate sentences in each study were analyzed separately by a 2-Factor ANOVA (3 × 2): Age (I—III) × Anaphor Type (Null, Pronoun), and compared to complement sentences by calculating percent correct for each sentence type (complement, coordinate).

For all analyses, a $p < .01$ level was used as a conservative criterion for statistical significance. Mean score range was 0—4 for complement sentences; 0—2 for coordinate sentences.[12]

2.7 *Procedures*

The complete task (imitation and act-out) took approximately 40 minutes to administer. The tasks were administered by one experimenter, while another experimenter observed and transcribed the child's responses in the act-out task. All test sessions were tape-recorded and the imitation task responses were transcribed from the tape. See Sherman, 1983, for details.

2.8 *Pretraining*

Pretraining sentences were presented to children preceding both imitation and act-out tasks in order to ensure that the child understood the nature of the tasks, to ensure that s/he could handle multiple-clause sentences, and to ensure that the child understood that coreference and non-coreference responses were equally possible in the task.

2.9 *Scoring*

All data were independently scored by 2 persons. All scoring followed an established written set of criteria which are generally described below. Two measures were scored for each task.

Imitation responses were scored for (i) correctness, and (ii) specific errors. To be considered correct, the child's response had first of all to include both clauses of the sentences, and no changes in complementation type, matrix verb, anaphor, matrix subject or object or tense of embedded clause.

Responses to the *act-out task* were scored for (i) correctness and (ii) interpretation of the complement anaphor. In general, children's responses were considered incorrect if they used an incorrect doll or prop and/or if they acted out an incorrect action. For VP complements, children had to interpret the null anaphor in accordance with the control properties of the matrix verb for the response to be scored correct. For both VP and $\overline{S}$ complements, use of *self* as agent was scored as incorrect. Only children's interpretation of the embedded clause was scored. Act-out responses were also particularly scored for choice of antecedent of the complement (i.e., whether the child selected the matrix subject, object, third doll or self as actor).[13]

2.10 *Reliability Results*

Independent transcriptions and scoring by two observers, calculated for 15% of the data resulted in 96% agreement on correct-incorrect scores and 97% agreement on error analyses on imitation data scoring. Reliability scoring on the act-out data resulted in 95% agreement on incorrect scores, and 98% agreement on scoring of the interpretation of the complement anaphor.

3. RESULTS

Overall mean correct for act-out was 2.95 or 74% correct; for imitation, overall mean correct was 2.26 or 56% correct.

Hypothesis 1: Replication of object control in VP complements
  Act-out

Children in all age groups were significantly more successful comprehending VP complements with object (2.97) than with subject control verbs (1.57) (F(2,69) = 35.98; p < .001).

Results of the L-C study of children's comprehension replicate the previous finding that children more frequently assign object control (1.04) than subject control to 'promise' (.85) in VP complements, although this difference was not significant. It is not until the oldest age group tested that children gave more subject control (1.08) than object control (.75) responses to the sentences with 'promise'.

Hypothesis 2: Evidence for lexical control
  Act-out

As Figure 1 shows, in spite of the fact that children assigned more object than subject control overall in VP complements, at the same time,

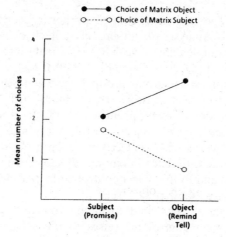

Fig. 1. Act-Out: Choice of Matrix Subject or Object to interpret null subject in VP Complements.

children (over combined age groups) gave significantly more subject control responses to the null subject when the matrix verb was the subject control verb 'promise' (1.57) than when it was an object control verb (.72) ($F(2,69) = 27.65$; p < .001). In contrast, they gave significantly more object control responses to object control verbs (3.01) than to 'promise' (2.28) ($F(2,69) = 19.70$; p < .001). This lexical effect was also seen in sentential complements. Here, children (over combined age groups) chose the matrix subject as antecedent for the pronoun anaphor significantly more often when the matrix verb was 'promise' (2.37) than when the matrix verb was 'remind' or 'tell' (1.80) ($F(2,69) = 11.18$; p < .005); and chose the matrix object as the antecedent significantly more often when the matrix verb was an object control verb (1.83) than when it was the subject control verb 'promise' (1.26) ($F(2,69) = 11.60$; p < .005). Moreover, children chose the subject (1.33) significantly more often than the object (.46) in interpreting $\overline{S}$ complements with the main verb 'promise' ($F(2,69) = 25.04$; p < .001), but they did not do so for $\overline{S}$ complements with object control verbs.

These results suggest that children (over combined age groups) differentiated verbs by their specific lexical control properties. This lexical effect was independent of complement type, since it replicated over both VP and $\overline{S}$.

Results of the act-out task in the L-C Study also showed that children's knowledge of lexical control properties *develops* over the age range studied. Analysis of amount of subject and object control responses in VP complements revealed a significant interaction of *Age* and *Verb Control* ($F(2,69) = 7.05$; $p < .005$). Figure 2 shows that children in the youngest age group, group 1, gave about as many subject control responses to object control verbs ('remind', 'tell') (1.04) as they did to the subject control verb ('promise') (1.08). In group 2, children did assign significantly more subject control to 'promise' (1.54) than to the object control verbs (.54) ($F(1,23) = 8.62$); $p < .01$); and in the oldest age group, the difference in amount of subject control responses to 'promise' (2.08) and to the object control verbs (.58) was most highly significant ($F(1,23) = 34.50$; $p < .001$).

Figure 2 also shows that children in the youngest age group gave about as many object control responses to the subject control verb (2.67) as to object control verbs (2.37). Children in group 2 assigned more object control to object control verbs (3.33) than to the subject control verb (2.42) although this difference was not quite significant ($F(1,23) = 6.84$; $p < .02$). In group 3, children assigned significantly more object control to object control verbs (3.33) than to 'promise' (1.75) ($F(1,23) = 38.62$; $p < .001$).

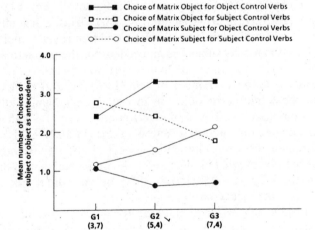

Fig. 2. Choice of Matrix Subject or Object to interpret null subject in VP Complements: *Verb Control Type × Age.*

In $\overline{S}$ complements it is also not until the oldest age group that children gave significantly more subject choices to the subject control verb (2.79) than to the object control verbs (1.96) (F(1,23) = 8.85; p < .01), and significantly more object choices to object control verbs (1.71) than to 'promise' (1.00) (F(1,23) = 7.92; p < .01).

These results show in confirmation of Hypothesis 2 that children over the age range studied develop a sensitivity to the lexical control properties of verbs.

Hypothesis 3: Evidence of sensitivity to complement structure
   3a. *Evidence of distinction in control by complement type*
   Act-out

While children overall age groups gave more object (1.27) than subject (.60) control responses in VP complements, they gave more subject (1.12) than object (.67) control responses in $\overline{S}$ complements.

Children's choice of matrix object or subject as antecedent of the complement anaphor varied significantly with *Complement Type* in a manner independent of verb type. Children gave significantly more object control responses in VP (2.64) than in $\overline{S}$ complements (1.55) (F(2,69) = 60.40; p < .001) over both verb control types and gave more subject control responses in $\overline{S}$ (2.09) than in VP complements (1.14) (F(2,69) = 47.78; p < .01) over both verb control types.

Thus, in confirmation of Hypothesis 3a, children from the youngest age distinguished control with regard to complement type. These results confirm that generalized object control for children was specific to the VP domain.

Imitation. Analysis of the amount of correct imitation revealed a significant interaction between *Verb Control Type* and *Complement Type* (F(2,69) = 28.92; p < .001). Figure 3 shows that while children found VP complements with object control verbs (3.04) easier to imitate than those with subject control verbs (2.41), they found $\overline{S}$ complements with subject control verbs (2.01) easier to imitate than those with object control verbs (1.57). This result suggests that children not only distinguish control properties of the matrix verb, but associate verb control with complement type.

Further evidence for this association is provided by children's imitation errors. The most frequent errors in the imitation task included

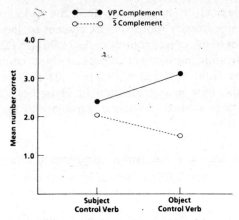

Fig. 3. Amount of Correct Imitation: Interaction of *Verb Control Type* and *Complement Type.*

change in complement type and change in verb control type, accounting for 22% and 17% of all errors, respectively. As exemplified in 7 below, children often changed a VP to a S̄ complement, as in 7a or a S̄ to a VP complement as in 7b, in their imitations.

(7) a. Stimulus: Tommy promises Bill to make a snowman.
        Response: Tommy promises Bill that he will make a snowman.
    b. Stimulus: Bill reminds Jimmy that he will cook the dinner.
        Response: Bill reminds Jimmy to cook the dinner.

Similarly, children changed a subject control verb to an object control verb as in 8a, or an object control verb to a subject control verb, as in 8b.

(8) a. Stimulus: Tommy promises Bill to make a snowman.
        Response: Tommy tells Bill to make a snowman.
    b. Stimulus: Bill reminds Jimmy that he will cook the dinner.
        Response: Bill promises Jimmy that he will cook the dinner.

Children's complement changes (as in 7), however, showed a significant interaction of *Verb Control* and *Complement Type* ($F(2,69) = 11.69$; $p < .002$). Children changed VP to sentential complements more often when the matrix verb was subject control (.21) (as in 7a) than when it was object control (.01) and changed sentential to VP complements more often when the matrix verb was object control (.32) (as in 7b) than when it was subject control (.11). That is, children changed complement type so that a subject control verb would occur with a $\overline{S}$ complement, and so that an object control verb would occur with a VP complement.

In addition, children changed subject to object control verbs significantly more often within VP complements (.12) (as in 8a) than within $\overline{S}$ (.03) and changed object to subject control verbs significantly more often within $\overline{S}$ complements (.19) (as in 8b) than within VP (.04) (F(2,69) = 17.60; p < .001). Thus, as in complement changes, children changed verb control type so that a VP complement occurred with an object control verb, and a $\overline{S}$ complement occurred with a subject control verb.

In confirmation of Hypothesis 3a, both act-out and imitation results confirm that children distinguished VP and $\overline{S}$ complements in terms of control and that object control is specifically linked to the VP domain.

3b: *Evidence of differentiation of anaphor type*
Act-out

Results of the P-L study revealed that children differentiated the

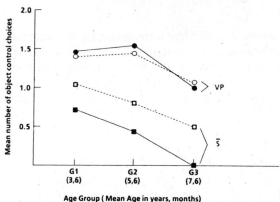

Age Group (Mean Age in years, months)

Fig. 4. Development of Object Control Responses in VP and $\overline{S}$ Complements: Effects of Pragmatic Lead.

anaphor type (null and pronoun) associated with VP and $\overline{S}$ complements. Figure 4 shows that in VP complements, amount of object control responses was about as high in sentences preceded by a pragmatic
lead to object (1.35) as in that to subject (1.29). In contrast, in sentential
complements, choice of object as antecedent was more frequent when
the lead mentioned the matrix object (.77) than when it mentioned the
matrix subject (.38). Similarly, in VP complements, choice of subject
was about as frequent when preceded by a subject (.55) as by an object
(.50) lead. In contrast, in sentential complements, children gave more
subject choices in sentences preceded by a subject (1.51) than by an object (1.15) lead. The interaction of *Pragmatic Lead* and *Complement
Type* in this study approached significance for choice of object (F(2,33)
= 6.27; p < .02), as it did for choice of subject (F(2,33) = 4.57; p <
.04).

For both subject and object choices, *Age* did not significantly interact
with any other factors. This suggested a differentiation of the properties
of null (obligatory) and pronoun (free) anaphora in the syntactic
domains of VP and $\overline{S}$ from the earliest age group studied.

These findings support the hypothesis that children distinguish the
null anaphor in VP complements as obligatory in reference and the
pronoun as free in $\overline{S}$ complements.

*Hypothesis 4: Evidence of general principles associated with anaphor
type*

   Act-out

Figure 5 shows that children's treatment of the obligatory nature of
null anaphora is general and extends beyond the domain of VP complements. As in VP complements, choice of antecedent in coordinate
sentences with a null anaphor (e.g., (5) above) was not significantly affected by *Pragmatic Lead*. Children in all age groups gave about the
same number of subject choices whether the lead mentioned the subject
(.81) or the object (.72) (F(2,33) = .66; p = .42); and they gave a similar
low number of object choices whether the lead mentioned the subject
(.06) or the object (.14) (F(2,33) = 1.25; p = .27).

However, in contrast, as in sentential complements with pronouns,
(e.g., (4b) above), the factor of *Pragmatic Le d* did approach significance in determining the antecedent in coordinate sentences with
pronuns (e.g., (6) above). *Pragmatic Lead* affected both choice of sub-

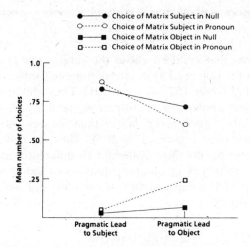

Fig. 5. Choice of Matrix Subject or Object in interpreting Coordinate Sentences with Null and Pronoun subjects under different conditions of Pragmatic Lead.

ject: $(F(2,33) = 4.69; p < .04)$ and choice of object : $(F(2,33) = 4.83; p < .04)$, although not significantly. In these sentences with pronouns, children chose the subject more often when the pragmatic lead mentioned the subject (.86) than when it mentioned the object (.67), and chose the object more often when the lead mentioned the object (.25) than when it mentioned the subject (.08).

These results signify that children associate general properties with null anaphors (obligatory) and contrast these with properties associated with pronoun anaphors (free).

Imitation. Children's imitation of coordinate sentences further showed that children do treat null anaphora similarly in a general manner. Children found both VP complements with null subjects (68% correct) and coordinate sentences with null subjects (74% correct) easier to imitate than $\overline{S}$ complements with pronoun subjects (45% correct) and coordinates with pronoun subjects (34% correct).

The above imitation and act-out results confirm Hypothesis 4. They show that children generalize principles of anaphor interpretation (i.e., treating nulls as obligatory and pronouns as free) across different syntactic domains.

Hypothesis 5: Evidence of relation of syntactic domain to anaphor type
    Act-out

Figure 5 shows that children chose the subject (1.61) significantly more often than the object (.19) in interpreting null subjects in coordinate sentences (F(2,69) = 151.64; p < .001). Thus, children gave more *subject* than object choices in coordinate sentences with nulls at the same time that they gave more *object* than subject choices in VP complements (compare Figures 1 and 5). Thus, in confirmation of Hypothesis 5, these results show that children differentiated their interpretation of null anaphors in different domains at the same time that they generalize over the null anaphor in both VP and null coordinate sentences as obligatory.

4. DISCUSSION

The results of this study replicate the previous finding in the child language literature that children overgeneralize control by the main clause object in sentences like (1) above. They replicate the finding that the subject control properties of the verb 'promise' are late in acquisition. This object control effect was shown in the developmental analysis in this study to develop between the ages of 3 and 5 and to recede by age 8.

In contrast to previous research, however, results from this study also show that this object control effect reflects the child's application of grammatical principles which are fundamental to the child's developing theory of control, and which integrate with the child's general theory of anaphora. In particular, the object control effect was seen to reflect a principle of sensitivity to complement type. The distinction between $\bar{S}$ and VP complements was seen to guide children's hypotheses regarding antecedent choice from the earliest ages studied. Children in general assign more subject control in $\bar{S}$ complements, more object control in VP complements.

The sensitivity to complement type (by which amount of control is differentiated by VP or $\bar{S}$ complement type) was shown to be a syntactic sensitivity in that it was specifically associated with the general syntax of anaphora. As we saw above ((4a) and (4b)), differentiation of complement types is syntactically linked to differentiation of anaphor types in these complements (pronoun or null (PRO)). Children in this study were shown to differentiate null control (in VP) as obligatory, and pronoun interpretation (in $\overline{S}$) as optional. Children thus not only distinguished complement types in general but distinguished them in terms of principles of anaphora which they involve. This differentiation of anaphor types moreover, is shown to be linked to the general grammatical system being developed by the child. Children's treatment of the null anaphora in VP complements as obligatory is seen to be general, since it generalizes over the nulls, in particular, coordinated VP, with null subjects, such as in (5) above. Further, object control, which is associated with this null anaphor was seen to be specifically associated with the structure of the embedded VP complement. In coordinated VP, with null subjects, such as in (5), children chose predominantly subject, not object, as antecedent in distinction from the embedded VP in (1a) or (b).

Knowledge of lexical control facts was seen to develop over the age range tested (3—8). Lexical control was seen to be an independent factor in the child's language acquisition. It was independent of the syntactic effects relegated to complement type. The lexical effects were observed whether the complement type was VP or $\overline{S}$. Similarly, the distinction between amount of control assigned due to complement type (VP, predominantly object; $\overline{S}$, predominantly subject) was seen to matter independent of verb control type involved.

These results suggest that children must learn to integrate their developing knowledge of the lexicon and its idiosyncratic control properties (e.g., 'promise' as subject control), with general syntactic principles for assigning control, which are determined by complement type. Where these conflict, as in the case of 'promise' in VP complements, syntactic principles appear to override the lexicon for a period during development. The thesis that this conflict is due to the child's syntactic principle of object control in VP, and not to a problem of assigning subject control to 'promise' in general, is supported by the finding that children in all age groups chose the matrix subject significantly more often than the matrix object in interpreting the pronoun in $\overline{S}$ complements with 'promise', but not in interpreting $\overline{S}$ complements with object control verbs.

4.1 *Possible Counterarguments*

4.1.1 *Lexical Principle: Object Control*

One could argue that children simply have a generalized theory of lexical control which says "control by object". Such an explanation however, would not account for generalization over properties of the anaphors (null and pronouns) and differentiation of anaphor interpretation with differentiation of structural domain in which anaphor occurs, which was found in this study. The general independence of the lexical control effects from complement type shows that this lexical factor could not account for this set of different sensitivities. Moreover, by the second age we measured (see Figure 2) children suggest they 'seem to know' something of the control differences across the lexical items (*promise* vs *remind* and *tell*), but they don't apply this knowledge sufficiently to override general object control in VP.

4.1.2 *A Differentiated MDP*

In explaining the generalized object control effect which we observed in this study, one might also consider the alternative that children don't use a Minimum Distance Principle on pronouns, such as in $\overline{S}$ complements, not because of a sensitivity to the difference in complement type (sentence vs VP) but because the MDP simply is not associated with pronouns, only with nulls. If so, however, there would be no explanation for why children's interpretation of nulls in coordinated VP structures resembles their interpretation of pronouns in $\overline{S}$ complements, associating the subject and not the object as antecedent of the null anaphor. This shows that children distinguish the interpretation of pronominal and null anaphor types by structure, and not only by their phonetic realization. Moreover, children clearly showed that they know the pronoun is free, and the null is not. So, a distinction in the application of the MDP would correlate with a general syntactic distinction children had made between these types. Moreover, if a simple processing principle like the MDP were at work, other factors like Pragmatic Lead would be expected to shift children's responses more easily than it did. (For further arguments against the MDP as an alternative account see Sherman, 1983b and to appear in volume 2.)

4.2 *Conclusion*

This study shows that a child language effect widely observed in the child language literature, frequently attributed to a 'processing principle' in fact reflects a behavior which is consistent with general principles for the grammar of anaphora, in particular, with the grammar of control.

The data from this study support a general model of first language acquisition which considers lexical and syntactic principles as independent, at least in part, and as complementary. The findings of this study provide evidence that the development of language, particularly of a grammar of control, lies in the progressive integration of lexical and syntactic principles.

NOTES

[1] This research was supported in part by a Dissertation Award to the first author from the College of Human Ecology, Cornell University, and by a National Science Foundation Grant BNS 7825115 to the second author. Preparation of this manuscript was supported by the MIT Center for Cognitive Science under a grant from The Alfred P. Sloan Foundation's particular program in Cognitive Science. We thank Joyce Nelsen for help in data collection, transcription and scoring, Yu Chin Chien for assistance in data analysis, and the subjects and schools in Ithaca, NY for their participation. We thank Steven Pinker for helpful comments on this manuscript.

[2] See Koster and May, 1982 and Bresnan, 1982 for discussion of the underlying representation of these structures. The design and interpretation of our results in this paper do not require full resolution of the issues addressed in these references. Although our data do bear on these issues, we will address them in a separate paper (Sherman and Lust, in preparation).

In the examples in (1a) and (1b) we represent the missing complement subject in the embedded clause as the anaphor type 'PRO', as specified by Chomsky, 1981, 1982. The null subject is specified as 'PRO' (+anaphor, +pronominal) since it is ungoverned (i.e., not governed by tense in the embedded clause and not governed by the matrix verb which governs its matrix clause (indirect) object). 'PRO' has been defined as sharing properties of both pronouns and anaphors which are bound by antecedents.

[3] Certain recent linguistic treatments argue that these differentiated control properties are not represented in the lexicon but can be accomplished by a pragmatic theory, e.g., Manzini, 1983. For the purposes of this paper, however, we will assume 'control properties of the verb' (as in Chomsky, 1981, p. 75).

[4] See Chomsky, 1981 for definition of government.

In Chomsky's theory of generative grammar and related work (e.g., Chomsky, 1981; Koster and May, 1982, Manzini, 1983), the underlying structure of VP complements is sentential. The null subject is specified as 'PRO'. The interpretation of the null subject

('PRO') is specified by a rule of control theory that coindexes a lexically unfilled complement subject NP node with an antecedent NP, specifically involving 'control properties' of the matrix verb.

Bresnan (1982) argues that control relations are properly stated in the "functional argument structure" of the verb (which specifies the semantically interpretable information expressed by a sentence) and not in the phrase structure configurations. In Bresnan's theory the semantic interpretation of sentences is provided by directly mapping the functional argument structure of the verb onto the surface structure of the sentence. In VP complements such as (1a) and (1b) above, null subjects (represented as 'PRO') in these sentences are not stipulated in phrase structure configurations, but rather, are considered to reflect a functional argument structure which is introduced and defined in the lexicon of the verb. The interpretation of the null complement subject is provided by a control equation – a functional schema associated with the lexicon which equates the functional structure of the controller (i.e., the expressed element, such as the matrix subject or object) and the controlled element (i.e., the unexpressed element or missing complement subject). For example, the lexical control information specified for the verbs 'tell' and 'promise' includes both subcategorization information, which indicates the syntactic context that the verb may appear in, and the verb's functional argument structure which is mapped onto the syntactic context. The subcategorization information specifies that these verbs (e.g., 'tell' and 'promise') may appear in a VP complement (represented as _ VP) shown in ia and iia below, respectively. The functional argument structures in ib and iib specify which argument completes the lexically unfilled subject. Thus, as shown in ib, in VP complements with 'tell' the grammatical object, NP2, completes the lexically unfilled subject. In VP complements with 'promise' the grammatical subject, NP1 completes the missing argument as shown in iib. (cf. Bresnan, 1978)

(i) a.　　tell: V NP [_ VP]
　　b.　　NP2 [(NP2)VP]
(ii) a.　　promise: V NP [_ VP]
　　b.　　NP2 [(NP1)VP]

[5] The Minimum Distance Principle was first formulated by Rosenbaum (1967). In this formulation (since adopted by N. Chomsky, 1980) Rosenbaum defined distance in terms of underlying phrase structure (i.e., dominance relations) by making reference to the number of branches on the tree which separate the NP node in the matrix sentence from the initial NP of the complement. Although C. Chomsky herself refers to Rosenbaum's original formulation of the MDP (cf. C. Chomsky, 1969, p. 11), it is unclear whether she defines distance in terms of surface distance relations, or dominance relations in her restatement of the principle.

[6] The role of the structural notion of 'c-command' (see Introduction to this volume and chapters by Wasow, Reinhart and Freidin for definition and discussion) has been proposed in certain versions of control theory (e.g., Manzini, 1983). Some studies (e.g., Goodluck 1981; Hsu, 1981) have investigated the acquisition of control relations from the point of view of properties of language such as c-command. Results of these studies suggest that children, are, in fact, constrained by the structural fact that a controller must c-command its anaphor. However, in the structures of interest in this study (i.e., (1a) and (1b)) the interpretation of the complement anaphor cannot be determined by a

structural principle such as c-command alone. First, in these structures, *both* the matrix subject and object c-command the null anaphor. Second, *both* (1a) and (1b) involve c-command equally. Third, the distinction between VP and $\overline{S}$ complement domains shown in (1) and (2) above is not determined by c-command alone. The different determination of the specific antecedent thus depends on the lexical control properties of the matrix verb as well as on the VP complement domain.

[7] Note that if children are sensitive to lexical (verb) control facts, then it is possible that children will access this lexical information in complement structures other than VP complements as well, e.g., $\overline{S}$ complements as in (2c) and (2e) above, although it is not grammatically required.

[8] In the coordinate structures like (5) for example, the subject but not the object of the first clause c-commands the null anaphor of the second clause. Thus, as indicated by the underlining in (5) choice of subject is obligatory in these sentences.

[9] In previous studies on the acquisition of control (e.g., Chomsky, 1969; Maratsos, 1974; Tavakolian, 1978), children were presented with an act-out task only.

[10] Sentences were equalized for subject and object control by including four sentences with the subject control verb 'promise' and two sentences each with the object control verbs 'remind' and 'tell' in both complement types.

[11] In the Pragmatic Lead Study, only the verbs 'promise' and 'tell' were tested.

[12] Mean score range for complement sentences was 0–4 when scored by verb control *type* (subject control, object control) within each complement type. When scored by verb (promise, remind, tell) score range was 0–2, with only the first two 'promise' sentences presented in each complement type included in the analysis.

[13] Analyses of children's responses in the act-out task focused on subject and object choices which accounted for 93% of all responses (44% and 56% respectively) in the Lexical Control Study. Both subject and object choices were considered coreference responses. Since non-coreference responses, either choosing the third doll not mentioned in the sentence, or self (the child himself as actor of the embedded clause)) accounted for only 7% of responses, these were not further analyzed.

REFERENCES

Bresnan, J.: 1978, 'A realistic transformational grammar', in M. Halle, J. Bresnan, and G. Miller (eds.), *Linguistic Theory and Psychological Reality*, MIT Press, Cambridge, Mass.

Bresnan, J.: 1982, 'Control and complementation', *Linguistic Inquiry* **13**, 343–434 (also in J. Bresnan (ed.), *The Mental Representation of Grammatical Relations*, MIT Press, Cambridge, Mass., pp. 282–390.

Chomsky, C.: 1969, *The Acquisition of Syntax in Children from 5 to 10*, MIT Press, Cambridge, Mass.

Chomsky, N.: 1980, 'On binding', *Linguistic Inquiry* **11**, 1–46.

Chomsky, N.: 1981, *Lectures on Government and Binding*, Foris, Dordrecht.

Chomsky, N.: 1982, *Some Concepts and Consequences of the Theory of Government and Binding*, MIT Press, Cambridge, Mass.

Fodor, J. D.: 1979, 'Superstrategy', in W. Cooper and E. Walker (eds.), *Sentence Processing*, Lawrence Erlbaum, N.J., pp. 249–279.

Gallimore, R. and R. Tharp: 1981, 'The interpretation of elicited sentence imitation in a standardized context', *Language Learning* **31**, 369–392.

Goodluck, H.: 1981, 'Children's grammar of complement subject interpretation', in S. Tavakolian (ed.), *Language Acquisition and Linguistic Theory*, MIT, Cambridge, Mass., pp. 139–166.

Goodluck, H. and L. Solan (eds.): 1978, *Papers in the Structure and Development of Child Language*, Occasional Papers in Linguistics, 4, University of Massachusetts, Amherst, Mass.

Hsu, J.: 1981, *The Development of Structural Principles Related to Complement Subject Interpretation*, unpublished doctoral dissertation, City University of New York.

Koster, J. and R. May: 1982, 'On the constituency of infinitives', *Language* **58**, 116–143.

Lust, B.: 1977, 'Conjunction reduction in child language', *Journal of Child Language* **4**, 257–287.

Lust, B., K. Loveland, and R. Kornet: 1980, 'The development of anaphora in first language: Syntactic and pragmatic constraints', *Linguistic Analysis* **6**, 359–391.

Manzini, M. R.: 1983, 'On control and control theory', *Linguistic Inquiry* **14**, 427–446.

Maratsos, M.: 1974, 'How preschool children understand missing complement subjects', *Child Development* **45**, 700–706.

Menyuk, P.: 1969, *Sentences Children Use*, MIT Press, Cambridge, Mass.

Rosenbaum, P. S.: 1967, *The Grammar of English Predicate Complement Constructions*, MIT Press, Cambridge, Mass.

Rosenbaum, P. S.: 1970, 'A principle governing deletion in English sentential complementation', in R. A. Jacobs and P. S. Rosenbaum (eds.), *Readings in English Transformational Grammar*, Ginn, Waltham, Mass., pp. 20–29.

Sherman, J. Cohen: 1983a, *The Acquisition of Control in Complement Sentences: The Role of Structural and Lexical Factors*, unpublished doctoral dissertation, Cornell University.

Sherman, J. Cohen: 1983b, 'The minimum distance principle reconsidered: A new explanation for previous findings', paper presented at the Eighth Annual Boston University Conference on Language Development.

Sherman, J. Cohen and B. Lust: (in preparation), 'The underlying structure of VP and S complements: Evidence from first language acquisition'.

Sinclair, H., J. Berthoud-Papandropoulou, J. P. Bronckart, H. Chipman, E. Ferreiro, and E. Rappe DuCher: 1976, 'Recherches en psycholinguistique genetique', *Archives de Psychologie* **44**, 157–175.

Slobin, D. and C. Welsh: 1973, 'Elicited imitation as a research tool in developmental psycholinguistics', in C. Ferguson and D. Slobin (eds.), *Studies of Child Language Development*, Holt, Rinehart and Winston, New York, pp. 485–496.

Smith, C.: 1981, 'Comments' (on 'Deductive model and the acquisition of productive morphology'), in C. L. Baker and J. McCarthy (eds.), *The Logical Problem of Language Acquisition*, MIT Press, Cambridge, Mass., pp. 151–164.

Tavakolian, S.: 1978, 'The conjoined clause analysis of relative clauses and other structures', in H. Goodluck and L. Solan (eds.), *Papers in the Structure and Development of Child Language*, Occasional Papers in Linguistics, 4, University of Massachusetts, Amherst, pp. 39–83.

Williams, E.: 1980, 'Predication', *Linguistic Inquiry* **11**, 203–238.

PART C

COMMENTARY

HENK VAN RIEMSDIJK

CROSSOVER BETWEEN ACQUISITION RESEARCH AND GOVERNMENT AND BINDING THEORY: COMMENTS ON THE PAPER BY TOM ROEPER[1]

As an outsider who tries to keep up with the most salient work in the domain of theoretically oriented acquisition research, I am struck by two general facts. First, compared to, say, fifteen years ago there has been a spectacular improvement in the quality and theoretical relevance of these studies over the past few years. Second, this type of acquisition research appears to remain extremely marginal within the field of developmental psycholinguistics. As for the improvement, there is, I believe, at least one factor which has been instrumental in bringing it about. This is that over the past fifteen years, a number of highly general structural principles have emerged which are more or less agreed upon and which constitute a fertile source for hypotheses that may be testable in acquisition research. As for the persisting marginal status of this type of research, I have no explanations, only regret.

Apart from their inherent interest, the abstract principles I mentioned satisfy another very important condition: by virtue of their abstract and general character, they are in many ways almost invariant. By this I mean that although there is a great deal of discussion about the exact formulation that should be adopted, about the parametrized elements in the definitions, etc., the core idea of the principle remains constant over many years. And at the present level of integration of acquisition research with the purely theoretical work, that is entirely adequate: the core notions are precise and yet flexible enough to constitute useful tools for hypothesis construction, and at the same time there is no risk that they will be rejected, abandoned and replaced within a few months or years, thereby frustrating the time-consuming acquisition research.

As an example, consider the notion of "c-command." This is one of the most central notions of present-day grammatical theory. It is the crucial notion in the theories of binding, case, government, the empty category principle, etc. Thereby it offers a wide range of empirical areas in which experimental work can be set up. The core notion of c-command can be formulated as follows:

B. Lust (ed.), Studies in the Acquisition of Anaphora, Vol. I, 311–318.
© 1986 by D. Reidel Publishing Company.

(1)   α c-commands β iff the minimal node of type φ that
        dominates α dominates β and α does not dominate β.

Again, there is much debate over several details, in particular as to the
correct characterization of φ (the most prominent possibilities being (a)
φ = a branching node, or (b) φ = a maximal projection node), but the
core definition (1), given some value for φ, is quite suitable for testing in
a multitude of ways.

Before going into greater detail, there is one more general observation which imposes itself. Acquisition research which is inspired by the
strategy outlined above cannot fail to produce results which permit a
much more specific interesting interaction with current linguistic theorizing, thereby making possible a much higher level of integration
between developmental psycholinguistics and linguistic theory. Current
syntactic theory has attained a high degree of deductive depth, sophis-
tication, and empirical coverage. As a consequence it constitutes a
powerful heuristic with which to derive predictions and lines of further
research. Some examples of this sort will be given below.

Turning now to Roeper's paper (this volume), we have a case where
acquisition data are of immediate relevance to a number of issues
currently debated. Roeper's data indicate that the strong crossover
effect is not immediately present when the child acquires rules like *Wh*-
movement, but emerges at some point between five and seven years of
age.[2] I will focus here on the interpretation which is given of this
observation: the concept of a trace acting like a variable emerges at
some point after the acquisition of *Wh*-movement and of empty categories as such. In particular it is suggested that the trace of *Wh* starts out
as something like a null pronominal such as PRO, or 'pro'.

I would like to comment first on the general line of reasoning behind
this interpretation, second on some serious problems with the proposal
and on some ways to avoid them, and third on a number of interesting
predictions which may be derived from the theory in view of data such
as Roeper's.

CLASSIFICATION OF NOUN PHRASE TYPES

One of the central areas of research in current syntactic theorizing
concerns the classification of noun phrase types. Several subtheories of
core grammar partition the set of noun phrase types into subsets such as

lexical vs non-lexical, anaphoric vs non-anaphoric, pronominal vs non-pronominal, etc. Particularly exciting is the fact that the set of non-lexical categories or empty categories is partitioned by the same distinctions. In other words, there is not a uniform type of gap, but empty categories can be either anaphors (such as NP-traces), variables (such as *Wh*-traces), PRO (such as controlled subjects). (Cf. Chomsky (1981) for a detailed discussion.) The binding theory, theta theory, case theory and a number of other components of core grammar determine the properties of these types of empty elements. More recently, Chomsky (1982) has proposed that the differences between the different types of empty elements are all purely contextual, in other words that they have no inherent features that distinguish them. This view is referred to as the functional interpretation of empty categories.

ROEPER'S INTERPRETATION OF CHILD LANGUAGE DATA

The reasoning which underlies Roeper's interpretation of his data reported in this volume (Chapter 5), then, may be taken to be something like the following. Initially the child has just the easily accessible concept of empty categories, but the further differentiation of this class into subtypes with distinct properties arises at later stages. A scenario along these lines might be something like the following:

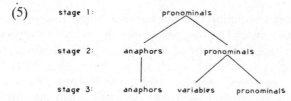

If this is a reasonable approximation, then the experiments Roeper has conducted yield evidence for the transition from stage 2 to stage 3.

Many speculations to fill in the picture become possible. We might hypothesize, for example that the transition from stage 1 to stage 2 coincides with the emergence of the concepts of government and governing category, which are crucial in distinguishing anaphors and pronominals. This would take us far beyond the scope of the present discussion, however. Note on the other hand that even at this fairly general level we already make some predictions. Roeper's examples are all bisentential, i.e., of the type (6):

(6) a.   Who$_i$ [e_i] thinks [$_s$he$_i$ can sing]
    b.(*)Who$_i$ does he$_i$ think $_s$[[e]$_i$ can sing]

In such examples the empty category (ec) is separated from the pronoun
by a clause boundary. Assuming that the ec is a pronominal element at
the early stage makes sense, because it equates (6) with (7):

(7)   He$_i$ thinks he$_i$ can sing

Note that anaphors are excluded here:

(8) a.   *he$_i$ thinks himself$_i$ can sing
    b.   *Himself$_i$ thinks he$_i$ can sing

If we compare this with the situation in a simplex clause, judgments are
reversed:

(9) a.   *He$_i$ likes him$_i$
    b.   He$_i$ likes himself$_i$

Our simple analysis in terms of (5) assumes that the children in
Roeper's group A are at stage 2. This predicts that these children should
get a noncoreference reading for (10a) but not for (10b).

(10) a. *Who$_i$ did he$_i$ see [e]$_i$
     b. Who$_i$ [e]$_i$ saw himself$_i$

So far we have been assuming that the relevant empty category has
pronominal properties instead of name-like ones. In an earlier version
of his paper, Roeper suggests that the ec starts out as PRO. However, in
the government-binding framework which we are here using, PRO is
assumed to be a pronominal anaphor. Given the binding theory of
Chomsky (1981) this assumption yields the desirable result that PRO
can only occur in ungoverned positions — essentially the subject position of infinitival clauses. In light of this, claiming that the trace of *Wh* is
PRO at some early stage would imply that at that stage *Wh*-movement is
only possible from the subject position of infinitivals. That is clearly
absurd. It would mean that the children couldn't handle cases like (11):

(11)   Who$_i$ did you see [e]$_i$

Furthermore, examples like (6) would also be excluded for the same
reason. Even more seriously, assuming that PRO can, for some reason
yet to be determined, occur in cases like (11) would make it very hard

to explain why the children cannot (presumably) say sentences like (12).

(12)   *John$_i$ saw $[e]_i$

Hence there are very good reasons for assuming that the *Wh*-trace for children at stage 2 in (5) is a pronominal element rather than a pronominal anaphor. In other words, such an ec has all the relevant properties of a real pronoun, except that it lacks a lexical realization. Such an ec has occasionally been assumed for adult grammars, especially to account for so-called "pro-drop" phenomena (cf. Chomsky (1981)).[3] This type of purely pronominal ec is often referred to as ("little") *pro*.

Let us turn now to some predictions which, unencumbered as I am by methodological know-how, seem to me easily testable. First, note that one area in which the difference between *Wh*-trace (variable) and PRO comes out very clearly is the phenomena of *wanna*-contraction in English. Essentially, *want* and *to* may contract to yield *wanna*. When PRO intervenes between *want* and *to*, contraction may apply; but when *Wh*-trace intervenes contraction is blocked:

(13) a.   Who$_i$ do you$_j$ want PRO$_j$ to see $[e]_i$
     b.   Who do you wanna see
(14) a.   Who$_i$ do you$_j$ want $[e]_i$ to see Bill
     b. *Who do you wanna see Bill

Consequently, if children have *wanna*-contraction at the relevant age, and if the trace of *Wh*-movement is PRO at that age, then these children should not have any contrast betwen (13) and (14). Of course, the prediction might come out somewhat differently if we take the ec to be pro instead of PRO, but I will not pursue this complication here.

In more general terms, the hypothesis makes some very suggestive predictions for languages that are quite different from English. Let us state the hypothesis in its most general form as follows:

(15)   At some early stage in language acquisition there is no formal distinction between pronominal elements and bound variables. Such a distinction arises between age 5 and 7.

So far, we have only dealt with (15) as it applies to empty categories. However, it is natural and fully in line with current thinking to assume that (15) carries over to lexically realized elements as well. Accordingly, we have the following situation:

(16)

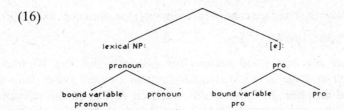

The main bifurcation between lexical NP and ec is intended as an indication that this distinction is presumably acquired before the second parameter is set. This seems entirely plausible given that the data necessary to acquire the distinction is of the most trivial and most easily accessible type.

Assuming now that the second parameter is the same one for lexical NP and ec, again the null assumption it would appear, we predict that this parameter is set at a stage comparable to that which Roeper has discovered, i.e. at age 5 to 7. This prediction will be testable if we find a language in which variables bound by a moved Wh-phrase show up as lexical pronouns in the adult grammar. Furthermore such a language must have an overt distinction between normal (free) pronouns and bound pronouns (variables) at the adult stage.

A language which could be used for this purpose is Vata, a West African language belonging to the Kru family. In Vata, a variable in the subject position must be lexically expressed, i.e. an ec is excluded in this position. Furthermore free and bound pronouns are systematically distinguished by the tone they bear: normal (free) third person pronouns bear a mid-high tone (´) while bound third person pronouns bear a low tone (`). For example:

(14) a. àlɔ́$_i$ ɔ̀$_i$ mlì là
       who he left ?   (= who left?)

   b. *àlɔ́$_i$ ɔ́$_i$mlì là

   c. ɔ́ mlì
      he left

(15) a. yī$_i$ ǹ gūgū nā ì$_i$ ɓlì là   (= what do you think
       what you think that it fell ?   happened?)

   b. *yī$_i$ ǹ gūgū nā í$_i$ ɓlì là

   c. ǹ   gūgū nā í ɓlì
      you think that it fell

(See for the data, the analysis, and discussion Koopman (1980) and Koopman & Sportiche (1982)). Extrapolating from the English case, then, our theory predicts that children acquiring Vata will not be sensitive to the tonal distinction and presumably have the mid-high tone for all third person pronouns at the earlier stage. (I am assuming here that the tones are learned at a stage prior to the stage crucial to the intended experiment — an assumption which, as far as I know, is consistent with what is known about the acquisition of tonal systems). The relevant data from Vata, which ought to be much easier to obtain than the English counterparts, could yield very strong confirmation of Roeper's hypothesis and my interpretation of it. Needless to say, disconfirmation of the hypothesis would require a thorough rethinking of this interpretation or even of the relevant aspects of the government-binding theory.

Let me finally mention another example of a language in which the extension of Roeper's hypothesis could be tested. Turkish is such a language. Turkish is an object pro-drop language, i.e. it is possible in Turkish to have an ec instead of a lexical third person pronoun in the object position (it is possible to say things like 'I discovered' alongside 'I discovered it' with the same meaning). On the other hand, variables must always be presented by an ec in the adult grammar. See Kornfilt (1977) for data and discussion. Along the same lines of argument, we would expect to find that the early stage of children acquiring Turkish exhibits free variation between the ec and the lexical pronoun in relative clauses; here the adult grammar tolerates only ec. This prediction holds under the proviso, of course, that children do have free object pro-drop at this stage.

There are many more tacks that could be taken and pursued, but I hope that the examples that I have given illustrate sufficiently that a high level of interaction has now become possible between linguistic theorizing and language acquisition research. What is particularly important to note, I believe, is that this integration is not a one way traffic but that it is mutually beneficial.

NOTES

[1] This paper was originally presented (with additional material) at the International Congress of Linguists, Tokyo, 1982.

[2] The "strong cross-over effect" refers to the phenomenon exemplified in the ungrammaticality of a sentence like "Who did *he* say (Mary kissed *t*)" with coreference between *he* and *t*. In this case, the trace left by Wh-movement to COMP (involved in question formation) is interpreted as a variable in logical form. This variable reflects a constraint like names do in that neither the trace nor the name can be coreferential with a c-commanding pronoun. Thus *"*he* said Mary kissed *Tom*" is impossible with coreference as is the Wh-sentence involving the trace. (See Roeper's chapter in this volume.) The strong cross-over phenomena are studied in Wasow 1979, 1972, developing ideas of Postal 1971. See also Chomsky 1981, e.g., p. 158; and Freidin and Lasnik 1981 (Editor).

[3] The "pro-drop" phenomenon generally refers to a parameter whereby the grammar of some languages unlike English, allows omission of subject in tensed clauses, e.g., Spanish or Italian (Chomsky, 1981) (Editor).

REFERENCES

Chomsky, N.: 1981, *Lectures on Government and Binding*, Foris, Dordrecht.

Chomsky, N.: 1982, *Some Concepts and Consequences of the Theory of Government and Binding*, MIT Press, Cambridge, Mass.

Freidin, R. and H. Lasnik: 1981, 'Disjoint reference and Wh-trace', *Linguistic Inquiry* **12**, 39—53.

Koopman, H.: 1980, 'Subject-object asymmetries in Vata', *Publications de l'ILA*, Université de Abidjan.

Koopman, H. and D. Sportiche: 1982, 'Variables and the bijection principle', *The Linguistic Review* **2**, 139—160.

Kornfilt, J.: 1977, 'Against the universal relevance of the shadow pronoun hypothesis', *Linguistic Inquiry* **8**, 412—418.

Postal, P.: 1971, *Cross-Over Phenomena*, Holt, Reinhart and Winston, New York.

Wasow, T.: 1972, *Anaphoric Relations in English*, unpublished doctoral dissertation, MIT.

Wasow, T.: 1979, *Anaphora in Generative Grammar*, E. Story-Scientia, Ghent.

BLOCKED FORWARDS COREFERENCE: THEORETICAL IMPI JCATIONS OF THE ACQUISITION DATA*

1. INTRODUCTION

A central issue in linguistic theory is the relationship between syntax and semantics. Recent work in the Government-Binding framework (e.g. Chomsky 1981, 1982) proposes a particularly simple model of the relationship, in which an abstract syntactic level of S-Structure, fairly close to a classical surface structure, serves as the sole input to Logical Form. At first glance, the familiar examples of blocked forwards coreference (5a) seem to be a problem for this proposal, since most early analyses of blocked forwards (the "Abstract Model") require coreference to be controlled at at least two levels. Reinhart (1976, 1981) apparently solved this problem, proposing an elegant analysis in which both forwards and backwards coreference were handled at a single level compatible with S-Structure. This "Surface Model" of Reinhart's has been widely accepted, and is generally assumed in current Government-Binding analyses.

Despite the appeal of the Surface Model, there is a substantial range of data that is better handled by the Abstract Model (Carden 1981, Carden and Dietrich 1981, McCawley 1984); some of these cases are sketched in section 2.4. Reinhart herself (1983b, this volume) has proposed substantial modifications in the Surface Model, building some key features of the Abstract Model into the pragmatics. It is therefore of considerable interest to look for additional sources of evidence bearing on the choice between the Surface Model and the Abstract Model.

My purpose in this paper is to survey the available evidence on the acquisition of the relevant constraints on coreference, and to discuss its significance for the Surface/Abstract debate. I will argue that the Abstract and Surface models, in their simplest forms, make sharply differing predictions about the sequence in which certain constraints should be learned. The acquisition studies that test these predictions give partially conflicting results, but I will argue that the weight of evidence supports the Abstract Model. There are, of course, various

319

B. Lust (ed.), Studies in the Acquisition of Anaphora, Vol. I, 319–357.

moves that could be made within the Surface Model; and I consider some of these in section 4.2. I conclude that the weight of the available acquisition evidence marches along with the weight of the adult evidence to support the Abstract Model against the Surface Model. This conclusion implies a need for some revision in the Government-Binding view of the relation between syntax and semantics.

2. THE THEORETICAL ISSUE

2.1 *Forwards and Backwards Coreference: The Basic Paradigm*

A. Only forwards coreference is possible:

(1) a.	*Mary* claims that *she* is a genius.	(Mary = she)
b.	**She** claims that *Mary* is a genius.	(She ≠ Mary)
(2) a.	*John* went to school after *he* finished breakfast.	(John = he)
b.	**He** want to school after *John* finished breakfast.	(He ≠ John)

B. Both forwards and backwards coreference are possible:

(3) a.	The man who loves *Mary* claims that *she* is a genius.	
		(Mary = she)
b.	The man who loves *her* claims that *Mary* is a genius.	
		(her = Mary)
(4) a.	After *John* finished breakfast, *he* went to school.	(John = he)
b.	After *he* finished breakfast, *John* went to school.	(he = John)

C. Only backwards coreference is possible:

(5) a.	Near *John,* **he** saw a snake.	(John ≠ he)
b.	Near *him, John* saw a snake.	(him = John)

Most of the time, the antecedent comes before the pronoun, as in (1a, 2a, 3a, 4a); I will call this "forwards coreference," since the coreference link runs forwards from the antecedent to the pronoun. If you try to reverse the direction, as in (1b, 2b), the coreference link is broken. In a limited range of structures, however, the pronoun can precede its antecedent, as in (3b, 4b, 5b); I will call this "backwards coreference." In a still more limited range of structures, the pronoun has to come first; (5a) has no reading with *John* coreferent with *he.* I will call this "blocked- forwards coreference."

From a descriptive point of view, a child learning this paradigm must master two contrasts: (a) He must learn when backwards coreference is possible and where it is blocked; I will call this the "blocked-backwards contrast" (1b, 2b vs 3b, 4b, 5b). (b) He must learn where forwards coreference is possible and where it is blocked, the "blocked-forwards contrast" (1a, 2a, 3a, 4a vs 5a).

There is an extensive literature discussing the analysis of this paradigm for adults; the Reinhart and Wasow papers in this volume give useful summaries with bibliographies. There are two main approaches:[1] (a) What I will call the Abstract Model, which uses a precede/S- or K-Command condition for the blocked-backwards contrast (Ross 1967, Langacker 1969, Lasnik 1976), and uses an extended Reflexive rule applied to an abstract structure for the blocked-forwards contrast (Kuno 1975, Carden 1981). (b) What I will call the Surface Model, which uses a single C-Command condition for both the blocked-backwards and blocked-forwards contrasts (Reinhart 1976, 1981, 1983a, b); Chomsky's Binding Theory (1981, 1982) uses a variant of this Surface Model.

Language-acquisition data is relevant to this debate, because, at least at first glance, the two models make differing predictions about the order of acquisition. In the Abstract Model, partially independent machinery accounts for the two contrasts, a relatively simple surface condition for the backwards contrast, and a more complex combination of rules and ordering for the forward contrast. Other things being equal, the Abstract Model thus predicts that the contrasts can be learned independently, and that the simpler backwards constraint is likely to be learned earlier. The Surface Model, in contrast, claims that a single constraint accounts for both contrasts. Other things being equal, it thus predicts that the two contrasts should be learned simultaneously.

2.2 *The Abstract Model*

The basic insight of Ross (1967) and Langacker (1969) was that backwards coreference was possible only when the pronoun was in a subordinate position. Langacker formalized this as what has been called the Precede/Command condition:[2]

(6)   The Precede/Command Condition: A pronoun must not both precede and command its antecedent.

(7)   Definition: Node X "commands" node Y iff the first "bounding node" B above X dominates Y.

The Precede/Command Condition in itself, of course, is not a complete model for coreference. At a minimum, we would need to provide formal mechanisms for coreference and for generating pronouns, we must specify the level at which (6) applies, and we must give a definition of "bounding node". The data that we will be considering provides no evidence to choose among alternative formal mechanisms, but the relevant level and the appropriate definition of bounding node will be crucial. I will propose initially that (6) holds at surface structure. Langacker, after considering other alternatives, proposed that S be the only bounding node; we can call this "S-Command." Jackendoff (1972), Wasow (1972), and Lasnik (1976), noting the marginal coreference in examples like (8a) and the good coreference in those like (8b), proposed that both S and NP count as bounding nodes; this has been called "kommand" or "K-Command" or "govern" (Solan 1978, 1981).

(8) a. *His* mother loves *John*.   (his = John; rare in texts)
    b. After *his* election, *John* announced . . .   (his = John)

To handle (8ab) in a simple surface model, we would need to adopt the K-Command definition of bounding node.

This simple surface Precede/K-Command model gives the right results for (1–4, 8): We get forwards coreference in (1a, 2a, 3a, 4a), because the statement of (6) permits forwards coreference regardless of structure. We get the contrast between the good backwards in (3b, 4b, 8ab) and the blocked backwards in (1b, 2b), because the pronoun both precedes and K-Commands the potential antecedent in (1b, 2b), thus preventing coreference, while the pronoun precedes the antecedent in (3b, 4b, 8ab), but does not K-Command it.

Example (5), however, appears as a major embarrassment for this model. The Precede/Command condition predicts that forwards coreference will always be possible, but the forwards coreference in (5a) is blocked. The pronoun *him* in (5b) both precedes and K-Commands *John*, so that (6) predicts that coreference should be blocked; but coreference is possible. Precede/Command predicts exactly the opposite of the actual coreference pattern.

Crucially, (5ab) have the same coreference pattern as the corresponding examples where the PP is not preposed:

(9) a. **He** saw a snake near *John*.   (He ≠ John)
    b. *John* saw a snake near *him*.   (John = him)

If we can set up our model so that the relevant coreference rule does not apply to the surface form of (5ab), but to an abstract structure with the essential properties of (9ab), we will get the right result. Rather different models with this basic approach have been proposed by Lakoff (1968) and Kuno (1975).

For example, within a Standard-Theory model, or a classical generative or interpretive semantics model, we would get the right result by letting the relevant coreference rule apply before the Adverb Preposing rule. In the derivation of (5a), for example, coreference would be determined on an abstract structure essentially like (9a), fixing *he* a non-coreferent with *John.*[3] Adverb Preposing would then apply to produce the surface form (5a).

This straightforward proposal runs into immediate trouble with (4a). If there is a general Adverb Preposing rule, and coreference is determined before preposing, or if, more generally, coreference is determined on some abstract, unpreposed structure, then we must predict that (4a) should show the same coreference pattern as the corresponding unpreposed structure (2b). But coreference is blocked in (2b), and permitted in (4b). Some further complication is required, as both Lakoff and Kuno saw: We need to set up a model that will treat the preposed time adverbial clause in (4a) differently from the preposed locative PP in (5a).

The adverbials in (4a) and (5a) differ on several dimensions, so there will be several possible approaches. Following Kuno, and anticipating some upcoming evidence, I will outline an analysis that builds on the fact the the potentially coreferent NPs are clausemates in (5, 9), but not in (2, 4).

Any model for coreference will have to treat coreference in "reflexive environments" differently from ordinary coreference:

(10) a. *John* shot **him.**   (John $\neq$ him)
     b. *John* shot *himself.*   (John $=$ himself)
(11) a. Bill talked to John about himself.   (himself $=$ J or B)
     b. Bill talked about John to himself.   (himself $=$ B, $\neq$ J)
     c. Bill talked about himself to John.   (himself $=$ B, $\neq$ J)
(12) a. Bill told John the truth about himself.   (himself $=$ B or J)
     b. Bill told John that Harry liked himself.   (himself $=$ H, $\neq$ B, J)

The required Reflexive rule will have to specify an appropriate domain, roughly the simplex clause (12a vs 12b), define a set of relevant potential antecedents, roughly subjects (10, 11, 12), objects, and indirect objects (11a, 12a), but excluding typical OPs (*himself* ≠ *John* in (11b)), and (at least for these cases) require the reflexive pronoun to follow its antecedent in linear order (11a vs 11c). This rule, whether we state it interpretively or generatively, will have to have the effect of assigning coreference for reflexives and blocking coreference for certain non-reflexive pronouns (10a).

Kuno's approach to blocked forwards coreference requires two moves, both motivated primarily by the blocked-forwards examples themselves: (1) State the domain of Reflexive so that it assigns coreference to the non-reflexive pronouns in examples like (9b): A literal application of a clausemate condition will have this effect, but we will need to state the rule so that reflexive morphology is optional on OPs like that in (9b), but obligatory for coreference with DOs, Datives, etc. (10, 11, 12). I'll call this version of Reflexive "Extended Reflexive" (ER), to emphasize that alternative treatments of the coreference in (9b) are imaginable. (2) Order ER to apply before adverb preposing; for example, the classical analysis in which ER is cyclic[4] and Adverb Preposing is post-cyclic would give the right result. We could get similar effects in other models, for example by extensions of trace theory, or by appealing to "reconstruction" rules in the Logical Form component.

We can call this approach the "Abstract Model," since (in contrast to the Reinhart-type "Surface Model" to be discussed in section 2.3) it requires that at least one coreference rule (ER) apply to an abstract structure distinct from surface structure.[5] The Abstract Model will give derivations like (13), (14), and (15) for our problem cases (5a), (5b), and (4a):

(13) a. He saw a snake near John ⟹ (ER applies)
    b. He_i saw a snake near $John_{j \neq i}$ ⟹ (Adverb Preposing)
    c. Near $John_{j \neq i}$, he_i saw a snake.

(14) a. John saw a snake near him ⟹ (ER applies)
    b. $John_i$ saw a snake near him_i ⟹ (Adverb Preposing)
    c. Near him_i, $John_i$ saw a snake.

(15) a. He went to school after John finished breakfast ⟹ (ER applies without effect)
    b. He went to school after John finished breakfast ⟹ (Adverb Preposing)
    c. After John finished breakfast, he went to school ⟹ (regular coreference)
    d. After $John_i$ finished breakfast, he_i went to school.

The Abstract Model generates the data, but no one could call it elegant. We will consider an alternative approach in section 2.3, and some additional adult data in 2.4; but for the moment our main interest is the predictions the Abstract Model appears to make about the sequence of acquisition.

From the point of view of the Abstract Model or any model based on the Precede/Command apparent generalization, the blocked forwards coreference in (5a) is a major anomaly. The possibility of backwards coreference in (5b) is also a problem, but a lesser one, since an adjustment in the definition of bounding node would handle the problem (at least for the examples we have been considering). The blocked-forwards case, however, requires the analyst, and thus the language learner, if the analysis is correct, to posit an abstract structure and to apply to that abstract structure an extension of the Reflexive rule, which at first glance seems to apply to a rather different range of cases.

To learn the contrast between good backwards (3b, 4b) and bad backwards (1b, 2b), the learner needs to master a single constraint (6), and work out the appropriate definition of bounding node. Both the constraint and the general notion of command are plausible candidates for universals (to the extent that we can say anything abut universals from the present rather thin data base), while the definition of bounding node is relatively insensitive for the range of examples we have considered so far, so that several different settings would give apparently correct results.

To learn the contrast between good forwards (1a, 2a, 3a, 4a) and blocked forwards (5a), given a Precede/Command type of model, the child has to learn an exception to the overall pattern, and set up messy machinery along the lines of my Abstract Model to handle the exception.

The Precede/Command approach in general, and the Abstract Model in particular, thus appear to predict that the backwards contrast should be markedly easier to learn than the forwards contrast.

2.3 Reinhart's Surface Model

As we have just seen, the blocked-forwards cases (5a) must be treated as exceptional in models based on developments of the Langacker/Ross Precede/Command condition. Reinhart, in her 1976 thesis, proposed an alternative model in which the blocked-forwards cases are not exceptional at all. This analysis has been widely accepted, and is assumed in most work in the Government-Binding framework. For example, (16) is essentially equivalent to Condition C of Chomsky's Binding Theory (1981, p. 188; 1982, p. 20).

Reinhart's basic claim is that, contrary to earlier proposals, linear order is actually irrelevant to the examples we have been discussing: "The linear order of the NPs plays no role in the sentence-level anaphora restrictions." (Reinhart 1981, p. 605) She demonstrates that, given an appropriate definition of bounding node, and suitable assumptions about the tree structures involved, the whole basic paradigm (1–5, 8) will follow from the very simple structural condition (16):

> (16)   The Order-Irrelevant C-Command Condition: A pronoun must not C-Command its antecedent.
>
> (17)   Definition: Node X "C-Commands" node Y iff the branching node most immediately dominating X also dominates Y.[6] (In our earlier definition (7), this is equivalent to saying that all branching nodes count as bounding nodes.)

For most of the cases we have discussed, (16) makes the same (correct) predictions as the Precede/K-Command condition (6); the interesting examples for comparing the models involve preposed adverbials (4, 5) and the blocked-forwards contrast. To see how (16) works, consider the following trees for (5b) and (5a):

> (5b)   Near *him, John* saw a snake.   (him = John)
> (5b′)

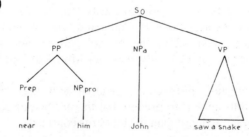

In (5b), the first branching node above NP_{pro} is the PP. NP_{pro} will therefore C-Command only material dominated by the PP; in particular, it will not C-Command NP_a. (16) therefore correctly predicts that coreference will be possible in (5b), looking solely at the given surface structure. If we had used S-Command or K-Command instead of C-Command, then the relevant bounding node would have been the S, and we would have incorrectly predicted that coreference was impossible. Recall that this difficulty was part of the evidence that forced us to the more complex abstract analysis in section 2.2.

(5a) Near *John,* **he** saw a snake. (John ≠ he)

(5a′)

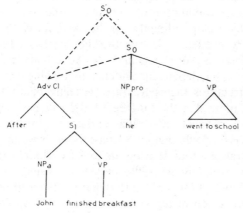

In (5a), the first branching node above NP_{pro} is the S, which in turn dominates the PP. NP_{pro} therefore C-Commands NP_a. (16) therefore correctly blocks coreference, again working directly on the given surface structure. Note that this analysis makes the claim that exactly the same mechanism (16) blocks the blocked forwards in (5a) and the blocked backwards in (1b, 2b): In both types the pronoun in subject position C-Commands the potential antecedent, and the linear order is simply irrelevant.

As with the Abstract Model, the contrast between the good forwards in (4a) and the blocked forwards in (5a) causes some trouble:

(4a) After *John* finished breakfast, *he* went to school. (John = he)

(4a′)

If the preposed adverbial clause in (4a) hangs in the same structural position as the preposed PP in (5a), then (16) will predict that they act alike for purposes of coreference: If the Adverbial Clause hangs from S_0 (dashed line), then NP_{pro} will C-Command the Adverbial Clause, in particular it will C-Command NP_a, and coreference will be blocked. Since coreference is possible in (4a), something needs to be done. Reinhart's proposal is to specify a different surface structure: She notes that the adverbial clause in (4) is, on standard analyses, a sentence adverbial, while the PP in (5) is a VP adverbial. She suggests that, when preposed, S-Adverbials hang one node higher up the tree than VP-Adverbials. Thus if the PP in (5a) hangs from S_0, the Adverbial clause in (4a) will hang from S_0', as indicated by the dotted lines.

If we apply (16) to this structure, we now get the right results: The first branching node above NP_{pro} is S_0, but in the dotted-line structure S_0 does not dominate the Adverbial Clause. Thus NP_{pro} does not C-Command NP_a, and coreference is correctly predicted to be possible; again (16) can apply directly to the surface structure. Since (16) can handle all the given data looking only at a single level, the surface structure, a point of potential theoretical significance,[7] I will call it the "Surface Model," in contrast to the Abstract Model discussed in section 2.2.

It should be clear that Reinhart's Surface Model is a marked advance over the Abstract Model for the data we have been considering. While the Abstract Model was forced to treat the blocked-forwards cases as exceptional, and set up some reasonably complex machinery to handle them, Reinhart showed − an observation that could fairly be called brilliant − that a single condition (16), actually simpler than the earlier condition (6), could account directly for blocked forwards with no additional machinery needed. It is true that her proposal for distinct structures for preposed S-Adverbials and VP-Adverbials is ad hoc in the sense that there is no independent evidence motivating the structural contrast, but the structures themselves are perfectly plausible. In the next section I will argue that the Surface Model will have difficulties when we consider a somewhat wider range of data; but for the examples of section 2.1, there is no doubt that the Surface Model is winning.

The crucial generalization underlying the Surface Model is the claim that linear order is irrelevant to (sentence-level) coreference, and, in particular, that the blocked forwards in (5a) and the blocked backwards in (1b, 2b) show the action of the same constraint (16) applied in the same way.

The claim in turn makes a prediction about the sequence of acquisition: If blocked forwards (5a) and blocked backwards (1b, 2b) simply
reflect the action of a single mechanism, then (other things being equal),
when a child gets the blocked-backwards contrast, he should also get the
blocked-forwards contrast.[8] There might be the usual sort of gradual
development, whereby a rule or process spreads from one construction
to another, but if so the blocked-forwards cases should fall randomly
among the constructions where backwards is blocked. The Surface
Model and the Abstract Model therefore make sharply different prima
facie predictions about the sequence of acquisition: As we saw in section
2.2, the Abstract Model predicts that the blocked-backwards contrast
should be substantially easier to learn than the blocked-forwards
contrast, and so that the blocked-backwards contrast should be learned
first, while the Surface Model predicts that the two contrasts should be
learned at essentially the same time.

2.4. *Considering a Wider Range of (Adult) Data: Evidence for the Abstract Model*

So long as we limit our attention to the basic paradigm discussed in the
preceding sections, the Surface Model seems markedly superior to the
Abstract Model. When we consider a somewhat wider range of data,
however, I would argue that we find good evidence that the more
complex Abstract Model is right after all. I outline some of the relevant
arguments below (cf. Carden 1981).

2.4.1 *Evidence for the Role of Linear Order*

(18) a. Penelope cursed *Peter* and slandered *him*.   (Peter = him)
     b. Penelope cursed *him* and slandered **Peter**.   (him ≠ Peter)

Langacker (1969) used (18) and other examples to show that
backwards coreference is blocked across a coordinate conjunction
regardless of the command relationships: note that *him* will not
C-Command *Peter* in (18b). These examples might be handled by
assigning some special status to coordinates;[9] but Solan (1978, 1981)
points out that parallel problems arise within the VP:[10]

(20) a. Mary showed *John*'s picture to *him*.   (John = him)
     b. Mary spoke to *him* in **Ben**'s office.   (him ≠ Ben)

If dative PPs count as bounding nodes, the Surface Model will correctly permit the coreference in (20a), but incorrectly also permit coreference in (20b). If dative PPs do not count as bounding nodes, as Reinhart suggests (1981, p. 631f), then the coreference in (20b) is correctly blocked, but we incorrectly block the coreference in (20a). The only way for a command-type model to handle this contrast is to mention linear order directly: Note that the Precede/K-Command condition of the Abstract Model makes the right prediction here.

2.4.2 *Evidence that a Clausemate Condition will be Relevant*

(21)   In the ivory box that *Ben* brought from China, *he* put his cigars.   (Ben = he; Reinhart 1981)

(22) a. Next to the woman *John* was courting, *he* put a rose.

(John = he)

   b. Next to *the woman John was counting,* **she** put a rose.

(woman ≠ she)

Lakoff (1968) and Reinhart (1976, p. 160ff; 1981, p. 632f) note that forwards coreference is possible in examples like (21, 22). This contrast, where coreference is blocked between clausemates (22b) but permitted between non-clausemates (21, 22a), is of course what the Abstract Model predicts.

How could a Surface Model handle this data? Minimal pairs like (22) show that it will not help to hang "heavy" PPs higher up the tree as Reinhart proposed for the time-adverbial clauses. Reinhart suggests that the relevant anaphora rule obeys Subjacency, so that it would fail to mark non-coreference on the NPs in the subordinate clauses in (21, 22a). However, as Reinhart observes, this subjacency restriction by itself incorrectly predicts that coreference will be possible in the un-preposed versions of (21, 22a):

(22) a′. He put a rose next to the woman John was courting.

(He ≠ John)

To handle the contrast between (22a) and (22a′), further machinery will be needed, setting up an exception to the subjacency condition. Without attempting to evaluate the particular proposal Reinhart makes (1981, p. 633), it is clear that the simplicity advantage of the Surface Model has largely disappeared.

2.4.3 *Evidence that the Rule Applies to an Abstract Structure*

(23) a. It was near *John* that **he** saw the snake. (John ≠ he)
     b. It was after *John* finished that *he* went to school. (John = he)
(24) a. Near *John* was where **he** saw the snake. (John ≠ he)
     b. After *John* finished was when *he* went to school. (John = he)

The familiar blocked-forwards contrast between locative PPs (23a, 24a) and time-adverbial clauses (23b, 24b) appears also in *it*-clefts and *wh*-clefts. A purely surface model cannot handle this data, since the pronouns in (23a, 24a) are buried inside surface subordinate clauses: *he* cannot C-Command, K-Command, or S-Command *John* in the surface structures of (23a, 24a).[12]

On the other hand, the Abstract Model seems to lead smoothly to an analysis: If we assume that the derivation for clefts will include, somewhere in the abstract syntactic or semantic structure, a stage with an unclefted structure, and if the relevant coreference rule (ER) applies to that abstract structure, we will then get the right result.[13]

2.4.4 *The Surface/Abstract Debate: The Role of Acquisition Evidence*

The Surface Model can fairly be described as the current standard approach to coreference (cf. Wasow, this volume). On the other hand, I would argue that the examples listed in the preceding subsections, and others discussed by Carden (1981), Carden and Dietrich (1981), and McCawley (1984), make a good case that the Abstract Model is in fact a better account of the adult data. Recall that the Abstract and Surface models made sharply different prima facie predictions about the sequence of language acquisition. In the following sections I will be arguing that the available acquisition data, on balance, confirms the prediction of the Abstract Model. This result should be no surprise, if I am right in my analysis of the adult data: The acquisition data and the adult data both support the Abstract Model against the Surface Model.

3. EVIDENCE FROM ACQUISITION STUDIES

3.1 *The Blocked-Backwards Contrast*

A number of studies have investigated the acquisition of backwards coreference; in general[14] these studies show good agreement on two points: (a) Forwards coreference is preferred to backwards coreference, even in structures where adults permit backwards coreference. This is no great surprise, given the far greater frequenccy of forwards coreference in speech and in texts.[15] (b) While forwards coreference remains favored, the contrast between good backwards (4b, 5b) and blocked backwards (1b, 2b) is established at the latest by age six or seven (C. Chomsky 1969), and, for many subjects, apparently considerably earlier (Lust et al. 1980; Ingram and Shaw 1981).

As a sample, I give below data from studies by C. Chomsky (1969), Solan (1978), Lust et al. (1980), and Ingram and Shaw (1981). These studies used different methodologies and present their data in different formats, so that a fair amount of interpretation is needed to compare their results; my analyses and interpretations do not necessarily agree with those of the authors. The Lust et al. study, which will play an important role in our later discussion, presents special difficulties of interpretation. First, Lust et al. collected data under two conditions, with and without a "pragmatic lead" (+PL and −PL),[16] with the −PL condition more comparable to the other studies. Second, under Lust et al.'s coding criteria, a substantial proportion of the responses were not coded either as coreferent or non-coreferent. They report the coreferent responses directly, but the number non-coreferent and the number not coded for coreference ("other") can only be estimated by a calculation starting from the reported "correct" figure.[17] I report here per cent coreferent, plus my best estimates of per cent non-coreferent and "other". For the other studies, all or essentially all responses were coded for coreference, so I report only the per cent coreferent.

Good Forwards Coreference (1a, 2a):

(25) a. Pluto thinks he knows everything.
      (C. Chomsky, age 5;10−6;10, 85% coref)
   b. The horse told the sheep that he would run around.
      (Solan, group mean ages 5;65−7;69, 91% coref)
   c. Oscar bumped the wall when he found the penny.
      (Lust et al.; age 3;5−7;5; −PL 91% coref, 2% non-coref, 7% other; +PL 72% coref, 7% non-coref, 21% other)
   d. Donald thinks he is the fastest runner.
      (Ingram & Shaw, age 3;0−7;11, 78% coref)

Good Backwards Coreference (preposed adverbial clause, 4b):

(26) a. After he got the candy, Mickey left.
              (Chomsky, 20% coref)
       b. After he ran around, the horse hit the sheep.
              (Solan, 36% coref)
       c. When he closed the box, Cookie Monster lay down.
              (Lust et al.; −PL 24% coref, 41% non-coref, 34% other;
                           +PL 59% coref, 20% non-coref, 21% other)
       d. When he went to the store, Mickey fell down.
              (Ingram & Shaw, 53% coref)

Blocked Backwards Coreference (1b, 2b):

(27) a. He didn't know why Pluto felt so sad.
              (Chomsky, 3% coref)
       b. He told the horse that the sheep would run around.
              (Solan, 11% coref)
       c. He turned around when Snuffles found the penny.
              (Lust et al.; −PL 15% coref, 66% non-coref, 19% other;
                           +PL 36% coref, 42% non-coref, 22% other)
       d. He is sad that Mickey is leaving.
       d'. He cried when Mickey got lost.
              (Ingram and Shaw, mean coref 24%)

The numbers in (25−27) show substantial differences in raw per cent
coreferent. Comparing the numbers within each study, however, we find
a consistent pattern: High coreference for good forwards (25), substantially less coreference for good backwards (26), and still less
coreference for blocked backwards (27). This data establishes a preference for forwards over backwards and, within backwards, a significant
contrast between good backwards and blocked backwards.

The group data above shows only that the blocked-backwards contrast is established within the age range covered, 3;0 through 7;11; it is
harder to establish when in this period the blocked-backwards contrast
typically comes in, and what the sequence of development is, both
points of considerable importance for our theoretical issue.

C. Chomsky (1969) observed a sharp contrast between her 5-year-
old and 6-year-old subjects, and concluded:

If our small sample is representative, this [the blocked-backwards contrast – GC] seems to be a fact about his language that a child learns with considerable regularity at about age 5 or 6. (p. 109)

Solan's youngest group (mean age 5.65) showed a sharp blocked-backwards contrast, suggesting that the contrast may be learned somewhat sooner than Chomsky thought. Studies with younger subjects (Lust et al., Ingram & Shaw) produce data suggesting that a fair proportion of the subjects master the constraint considerably earlier. The Ingram & Shaw study has the unusual merit of analyzing the individual-subject response patterns. Their analysis (Ingram & Shaw 1981, Figure 1) shows that 30% of the subjects from 3;0 through 5;11 have the full adult blocked-backwards contrast (their pattern IV), while another 15% have one part of the blocked-backwards contrast (their pattern II). 60% of the subjects from 6;0 through 7;11 show the full blocked-backwards contrast (IV), while pattern II essentially disappears. The fairly sharp jump in the data at about age 6 is consistent with Chomsky's results. However, Chomsky's youngest group (5-year-olds) showed no contrast between good backwards and blocked backwards, which contrasts with Ingram & Shaw's report that 30% of their 60 subjects from 3;0 through 5;11 had the blocked-backwards contrast. Lust et al. (1980) provide only group data; their four youngest groups (42 subjects, age 3;5 through 5;5) show a substantial blocked-backwards contrast:[18]

Good backwards (26c): −PL: 30% coref, 30% non-coref, 40% other;
                                    +PL: 65% coref, 7% non-coref, 30% other.
Blocked backwards (27c): −PL: 14% coref, 60% non-coref, 26% other;
                                    +PL: 43% coref, 23% non-coref, 31% other.

Combining the Lust et al. and Ingram & Shaw data, it seems likely that the 8 subjects in Chomsky's youngest group were not representative of the whole population, and that in fact a substantial proportion of children (e.g. Ingram & Shaw's 30%) master the blocked-backwards contrast before age 6.

Data about the stages by which the children reach the blocked-backwards contrast is thin. Lust et al. (1980) found no significant interactions of Developmental Level (age) with the structural factors involved in the blocked-backwards contrast (1980, p. 379, 381).[19] Ingram & Shaw (1981) also found no significant effects of age in their group data, but they deduce a developmental sequence from an analysis of the individual-subject data. They find five main response patterns, covering 86 of their 100 subjects. Analyzing the age distribution of these patterns, Ingram and Shaw argue that the most likely developmental sequence shows the child beginning with no constraint on backwards or forwards coreference (their pattern I), developing a constraint that blocks all backwards coreference (pattern II developing into pattern III), and finally developing an exception to that constraint that permits the good backwards cases while blocking the bad backwards cases (patterns IV and V). The data is admittedly thin, with only five responses per subject for each structural type; and the age distribution of the response patterns could sometimes be given altenative interpretations. Obviously it would be good to have a substantial longitudinal study, or another large cross-sectional study with more data points for the individual structural types. Still, the Ingram and Shaw study is the best data available on the sequence of acquisition, and they make a strong case for their interpretation. In my theoretical discussion, I will assume that they are basically correct.

Summing up, we find a marked preference for forwards coreference throughout the age range 3−8. What is theoretically more interesting, we find that the children show a contrast between good backwards coreference and blocked backwards coreference, at least by age 5 or 6, but for some subjects considerably younger. To account for this data, we must postulate somewhere in their linguistic systems (syntax, semantics, or pragmatics) machinery that is sensitive both to linear order and to structural relations, apparently to some type of command condition.

3.2 The Blocked-Forwards Contrast

Data bearing on the blocked-forwards contrast has been collected using three different tasks: Lust et al. (1980) and Lust and Clifford (this volume) used elicited-imitation and act-out tasks; and Ingram and Shaw (1981) and Taylor-Browne (1983) used a question-answering task. These studies do not show the same overall agreement we saw for the blocked-backwards contrast: At least at first glance, it seems that different tasks give different results; and there is some controversy about how these results should be interpreted.

In my opinion, the available elicited-imitation data does not provide significant evidence bearing on the choice between the Abstract and Surface Models: It shows a preference for forwards over backwards, but little effect of structure within a given linear order; in addition, there are more general difficulties of interpretation. I will therefore discuss only the data from the other tasks.

The question-answering and act-out tasks do provide evidence that bears on our theoretical issue; but the individual studies appear to point toward different conclusions. I will discuss this data in some detail, and argue that the weight of evidence shows that the blocked-forwards contrast is learned substantially later than the blocked-backwards contrast. These results thus tend to support the Abstract Model against the Surface Model.

3.2.1   Question-Answering Interpretation Tasks

Ingram & Shaw (1981) and Taylor-Browne (1983) report data from a question-answering task (28): The experimenter read a sentence, and then asked a question to test how the child interpreted the pronoun.

(28)   Near Donald he could see a rabbit.
         Question: Who could see a rabbit?

The possible range of referents was established by making a set of dolls available to the children. This proved a relatively easy task, and all of Ingram & Shaw's responses and the great majority of Taylor-Browne's responses could be coded as coreferent or non-coreferent. Ingram & Shaw report data from 100 children from 3;0 through 7;11 and from 20 adults; Taylor-Browne reports data from 27 children from 6;2 through 10;5, from 6 older children 11;6 through 12;2, and from 10 adults. I give group data from all of Ingram & Shaw's children and from Taylor-Browne's younger group below; Table I gives a partial break-down by age.

Good Forwards:
Pronoun in complement clause:

(29) a. Mickey is afraid that he might fall down.
              (Ingram & Shaw: 78% coref)
     b. Ken's mother said that he was sick.
              (Taylor-Browne: 96% coref, 0 non-coref, 4% other)

Antecedent in preposed adverbial clause:

    (29) c. Before Mickey went to school, he fed the dog.
              (Ingram & Shaw: 80% coref)

Blocked Forwards:

    (30) a. Under Mickey he found a penny.
              (Ingram & Shaw: 78% coref)
        b. Near Barbie, she dropped the earring.[20]
              (Taylor-Browne: 76% coref, 24% non-coref)

Good Backwards:
Preposed adverbial clause:

    (31) a. When he broke the dish, Donald was sad.
              (Ingram & Shaw: 53% coref)

Object of preposition in preposed PP:

    (31) b. Near him, Wayne found the programme.[20]
              (Taylor-Browne: 69% coref, 30% non-coref, 2% other)

Blocked Backwards:

    (32) a. He was glad that Donald got the candy.
              (Ingram & Shaw: 24% coref)
        b. He was glad that Wayne was coming.
              (Taylor-Browne: 13% coref, 78% non-coref, 9% other)

If we look at this group data, the younger group (Ingram & Shaw) shows essentially the same results for blocked forwards (78% coref) as for good forwards (78%, 80% coref). The older group (Taylor-Browne's 6;2−10;5 group) shows substantially less coreference for blocked forwards (76%) than for good forwards (96%), but blocked forwards still shows slightly more coreference than good backwards (69%), and much more than blocked backwards (14%, omitting the "other" responses).

This evidence for a relatively late development of whatever machinery blocks Blocked Forwards is confirmed when we look at the individual-subject data: Nine of Ingram & Shaw's 100 subjects have fewer than 3 coreferent responses to their five blocked-forwards examples.[21] One of the nine is age 3;5; the other 8 range from 6;3 to 7;8. If we follow Ingram & Shaw in taking this relatively weak criterion for mastering the

Blocked-Forwards constraint, 1 of the 60 subjects under six meets the criterion, and 8 of the 40 subjects from six to eight meet it. Six of Taylor-Browne's 27 subjects from 6;2 to 10;5 meet this criterion, and four of her six subjects from 11;6 to 12;2.

These individual-subject results for Blocked Forwards contrast with the results for Blocked Backwards. Ingram and Shaw reported that 30% of their subjects under six have the adult Blocked-Backwards contrast, and 60% of the subjects from six to eight have it. Using a similar criterion, Taylor-Browne reports that 81% of her subjects from 6;2 to 10;5 have the Blocked-Backwards contrast, and all the six subjects from 11;6 to 12;2.

This data implies that children typically learn the Blocked-Forwards contrast substantially later than the Blocked-Backwards contrast: Blocked Backwards seems to be typically learned around six, and Blocked Forwards around eleven or twelve.

3.2.2 Act-Out Interpretation Tasks

Lust et al. (1980) and Lust and Clifford (this volume) report data from an interpretation task in which the child is required to act out the test sentence using dolls and other props. These studies present some difficulties of interpretation, and I will be arguing for an interpretation that differs in important respects from that of Lust and her associates. In particular, I will argue that a correct interpretation of the Lust et al. data agrees with the Ingram and Shaw and the Taylor-Browne results in implying that children master Blocked Backwards before they master Blocked Forwards, while the Lust and Clifford data stands alone in seeming to imply that Blocked Forwards and Blocked Backwards are mastered at about the same age.

These difficulties of interpretation arise in part because of the nature of the act-out task. The objective is to discover whether the child is interpreting the pronoun in the test sentence as coreferent (+CR) or non-coreferent (−CR) with the proper name in the sentence. However, Lust and her associates correctly point out that it would not be appropriate to code a response for + or − CR unless the child was reasonably successful in acting out the whole test sentence. They developed detailed criteria for coding, and found that a very substantial number of responses could not appropriately be coded for + or − CR. For example, Lust and Clifford's Table VI shows that only 41% of the responses were coded for + or − CR, leaving 59% "other" responses.

Lust and Clifford report both + and − CR, so that "other" can be calculated directly. Lust et al. report only "coreferent" and "correct," but the proportion of non-coreferent responses can be estimated by the method given in Note 17. As discussed in section 3.1, Lust et al. had two experimental conditions, with and without a "pragmatic lead"; the −PL condition is the one comparable to Lust and Clifford's data.

I give these results below, including my estimates for "non-coref" and "other" in the Lust et al. study. For comparison, I repeat the relevant data from section 3.1.

Good Forwards:

(33)   Oscar bumped the wall when he found the penny.
            (Lust et al. −PL: 91% coref, 2% non-coref, 7% other;
                    +PL: 72% coref, 7% non-coref, 21% other)
        (Lust & Clifford: 66% coref[22])

Blocked Forwards:

(34) a. In Cookie Monster's mouth, he put a candy.
            (Lust et al. −PL: 23% coref, 7% non-coref, 70% other;
                    +PL: 60% coref, 12% non-coref, 27% other)
    b. On Cookie Monster, he quickly dropped the choo-choo train.
            (Lust & Clifford: 18% coref, 19% non-coref, 63% other)

Good Backwards:
Preposed Adverbial Clause:

(35) a. When he closed the box, Cookie Monster lay down.
            (Lust et al. −PL: 24% coref, 41% non-coref, 34% other;
                    +PL: 59% coref, 20% non-coref, 21% other)
        (Lust & Clifford: 18% coref[22])

Preposed PP:

(35) b. Under him, Big Bird quietly pushed the choo-choo train.
            (Lust & Clifford: 23% coref, 22% non-coref, 55% other)

Blocked Backwards:

(36)   He turned around when Snuffles found the penny.
            (Lust et al. −PL: 15% coref, 66% non-coref, 19% other;
                    +PL: 36% coref, 42% non-coref, 22% other)

How should we interpret this data? Lust and Clifford note that the contrast between blocked forwards (18% coreferent) and the corresponding good-backwards structures (23% coreferent) is significant at the .01 level, and concude that the children have mastered the blocked-forwards contrast. This argument could be strengthened by noting the contrast (presumably significant) between the good forwards (66% coref) and the blocked forwards (23% coref).

While I admit the force of Lust and Clifford's argument, I am not convinced. My doubts come in part from a comparison with other studies and in part from what I see as potential internal problems with the Lust and Clifford data.

Consider first data from other studies, beginning with Lust et al. If we look simply at raw per cent coreferent for the blocked-forwards examples, and compare Lust et al. with Lust and Clifford, we seem to have a close replication. However, when we look at the non-coref responses as well, a substantially different picture emerges: Lust and Clifford show a roughly equal number of coref and non-coref responses (18% vs 19%), while Lust et al. show many more coreferent than non-coref responses (23% vs 7%).[23] Suppose we calculate an adjusted per cent coreferent, counting only those responses that the experimenters coded for + or − CR:

(A)   Adjusted % coref = number coref/(number coref + number non-coref)

We get the following results: Blocked Forwards: Lust & Clifford 49% Adj. coref, Lust et al. −PL 77% Adj. coref; Good Backwards: Lust & Clifford 51% Adj. coref, Lust et al. −PL 37% Adj. coref.

The Lust et al. data therefore shows little evidence that the children have mastered the blocked-forwards contrast, once we focus attention on the responses that could be coded for coreference. The question-answering studies reported in section 3.2.1 agree with Lust et al. in showing a high proportion of coreferent responses to the blocked-forwards structure, and fewer coreferent responses to the good-backwards structure: Ingram and Shaw (1981): Blocked Forwards 78% coref, Good Backwards 53%; Taylor-Browne (1983): Blocked Forwards 88%, Good Backwards 79% (age 6;2−7;3). The Lust and Clifford study therefore seems to stand alone in finding significantly more coreference for good backwards than for blocked forwards in children under 8.

When we look at the Lust and Clifford data in detail, three problems appear that might make us worry about the authors' conclusion, independent of the replication problem. (1) The fact that only a minority of the responses could be coded for + or − CR in itself casts doubt on the data: When less than half the responses can be coded for the crucial variable, we must ask whether the experimenters would not have been wiser to choose some other task, e.g. picture choice or question-answering.

It could be argued, of course, that failure to produce a codable response is itself a datum, evidence that the child had difficulty processing the sentence. Even if we grant this, and assume that the difficulty involved the child's processing of the input sentence, rather than the act-out task itself, we are still not much further forward in testing for the existence of the blocked-forwards contrast: There is no a priori reason to expect processing difficulties to correlate with assignment of coreference, and in fact the blocked-backwards examples in Lust et al. are intermediate in per cent "other" between the good backwards and the good forwards. Similarly, the Lust and Clifford data shows 55% "other" for good backwards and 63% "other" for blocked forwards, suggesting that most of the putative processing difficulty would have to be blamed on the preposed-PP construction itself, independent of the adult coreference assignments.

(2) A second problem involves the interpretation of the contrast in per cent coref between good backwards and blocked forwards. Good backwards (35b) shows 23% coref and 22% non-coref; blocked forwards (34b) shows 18% coref and 19% non-coref. Lust and Clifford use the significant (.01) contrast between 23% and 18% coref to argue that coreference is better with good backwards than with blocked forwards. We might almost as well use the contrast between 22% and 19% *non*-coref to argue that coreference is worse with good backwards than with blocked forwards. Lust and Clifford point out that the 22%−19% contrast fails to reach significance (p = .08), but the difference between the contrasts remains a small one. With the blocked-forward type showing 18% coref and 19% non-coref, and the good-backwards type showing 23% coref and 22% non-coref, we cannot rule out the possibility that the subjects were treating the two types alike for coreference, with the only difference being that slightly fewer of the responses to the blocked-forwards examples could be coded for coreference (63% "other" vs 55%). As I argued in (1) above, there is no reason to suppose

that the proportion of "other" responses in itself gives evidence about the coreference assigned by the child.

(3) A third problem involves the development with increasing age. Lust and Clifford's ANOVA did not show a significant effect of Development (age) on coreference for these structures, but they point out that the two youngest groups (ages 3;5—4;4) show the sharpest contrast (14% coref forwards vs 25% coref backwards), while the two oldest groups (age 7;0—7;11) show essentially no contrast (forwards and backwards both 29% coref). This is suspicious, since there is no obvious reason that the youngest children should show an adult contrast that the older ones seem to have lost. It is worth noting that this developmental anomaly goes away if we adopt a suggestion by William O'Grady (p.c.) and score Lust and Clifford's "self as agent" responses (their Table 7) as coreferent, taking the child as acting **for** the doll he is manipulating, as O'Grady has observed in a similar act-out task with reflexives. Under this revised coding, the two youngest groups would show 84% coreferent for blocked forwards, against 68% for good backwards, and the two oldest groups 53% against 55%, with a coherent development for the intermediate groups. This revised coding would bring Lust and Clifford's results much closer to the results of the other studies, but must of course be regarded as speculative lacking further information about these "self as agent" responses.

3.2.3 Comparison and Evaluation

The preceding subsections summarize data from four studies on the acquisition of the Blocked-Forwards contrast. The results differ substantially, and further experimentation will be needed before we can have full confidence in our conclusions. Still, when we put all the data together, a reasonably clear pattern seems to emerge. To facilitate the needed comparison, I list the results next to each other in Table I.[24]

Comparing the results, Lust et al. (1980), Ingram and Shaw (1981), and Taylor-Browne (1983) all seem to point in the same direction. Lust et al.'s act-out task shows a high proportion of "other" responses, but if we focus on the cases where the subject produced a response that was coded for + or − coref, the proportion of coref to non-coref is essentially the same as in Ingram and Shaw. Taylor-Browne's youngest group overlaps with Ingram and Shaw's older subjects, and provides a close replication. This match-up is confirmed by the close agreement in the

TABLE I
Acquisition Studies: Act-Out and Question-Answering Tasks

Task:	Act-Out		Question-Answering						
Study:	Lust et al.	Lust & Clifford	Ingram & Shaw	Taylor-Browne				adults	Ingram & Shaw adults
Age range:	3;5–7;5	3;5–7;11	3;0–7;11	6;2–7;3	8;1–8;9	10;0–10;5	11;6–12;2	adults	adults
Number of subjects:	82	94	100	10	8	9	6	10	10
	% coref[a]	% coref[a]	% coref	% coref[a]	% coref	%coref	% coref	% coref	% coref
Sentence type									
Good Forwards									
– Pragmatic lead	100%		79%	100%	100%	100%	100%	100%	93%
+ Pragmatic lead	91%								
Blocked Forwards (PP)									
– Pragmatic lead	76%	49%[b]	78%	88%	65%	73%	30%	16%	14%
+ Pragmatic Lead	83%								
Good Backwards									
– Pragmatic lead									
Subordinate Clause	37%								
PP		51%[b]	53%	79%	69%	61%	42%	60%	92%
+ Pragmatic lead									
Subordinate Clause	75%								
Blocked Backwards									
– Pragmatic lead	18%	24%	24%	27%	6%	11%	0	0	3%
+ Pragmatic lead	46%								

[a] Percentages calculated counting only responses coded as coreferent or non-coreferent.
[b] Combines + and – Depth.

individual-subject data for the two studies that report individual-subject data, Ingram and Shaw and Taylor-Browne. Taken together, these three studies make a strong case that most children master the Blocked-Backwards contrast by age five or six, but that the Blocked-Forwards contrast shows a slower and more gradual development, with most children mastering Blocked Forwards as late as age ten or twelve.

The results from Lust and clifford (this volume) seem to point in the opposite direction: Their act-out data shows more coreference for Good Backwards (51% coref) than for Blocked Forwards (49% coref), a difference that is significant at the .01 level. Lust and Clifford interpret these results as showing that their subjects have mastered what I have been calling the Blocked-Forwards contrast.

How can we resolve this conflict of evidence? Based solely on the data we have been discussing, I believe that we would be justified in setting aside the Lust and Clifford data, and accepting the results of the other three studies. This conclusion is not based solely on the principle that majority rules, but also takes into account the possible alternative interpretations of the Lust and Clifford data discussed in section 3.2.2.

In addition, we now have some new evidence suggesting that group data parallel to that of Lust and Clifford can turn out on closer inspection to be quite compatible with the implications of the other studies. Jennifer Hsu and Helen Cairns have kindly let me see the results of a recent study of theirs (Hsu et al. in preparation), which provides act-out data from 81 children from three to eight. If we adopt a coding like that of Lust and Clifford, Hsu et al.'s group data closely replicates Lust and Clifford's Blocked Forwards results: 18% coref, 24% non-coref, 58% other. However, when we look at the coreference implied in the "other" responses, at the implied sequence of development, and at the individual-subject data, a good case can be made that the actual behavior of the subjects is the same as that found by Ingram and Shaw, Taylor-Browne, and Lust et al. For example, suppose we look at the individual-subject data, and adopt a plausible coding to determine whether a given subject clearly has a particular constraint, clearly lacks it, or whether he produced too many "other" responses for us to be certain. Consider now the 16 subjects of Hsu et al.'s oldest group (mean age 7.6): For Blocked Backwards, 12 clearly have the constraint, 1 clearly lacks it, and 3 are uncertain. For Blocked Forwards, 4 clearly have the constraint, 4 clearly lack it, and 8 are uncertain. This data merits further analysis and discussion, but we can already see the familiar pattern where Blocked Backwards is mastered earlier than Blocked Forwards. We do not have a similar breakdown for the Lust and Clifford data; but it seems reasonable to hope that their data would also turn out, on closer inspection, to be compatible with the results of the other studies.

In summary, the available acquisition data is complex, and there is room for disagreement about its interpretation. Certainly we can all agree that further data collection is highly desirable. On the existing evidence, however, I believe that our theoretical interpretation should be based on the four studies that converge to imply that Blocked Forward is learned substantially later than the Blocked-Backwards contrast. I take that conclusion as the basic datum we need to explain.

4. THEORETICAL IMPLICATIONS OF THE ACQUISITION DATA

4.1 *The Abstract Model*

According to the Abstract Model, the machinery involved in blocking coreference in the Blocked-Forwards construction is substantially more complex than the machinery involved in the structural condition on backwards coreference. Other things being equal, the Abstract Model therefore predicts that children will master the constraints on backwards coreference before they master Blocked Forwards. As we have just seen, this prediction appears to be correct.

Looking at the available evidence about the whole sequence of acquisition, the Abstract Model appears to permit what we could call a gradualist account of the acquisition process, where the child's grammar at each stage is built on the grammar of the preceding stage, with no need for global restructurings. I list below the major stages implied by my analysis of the acquisition evidence, with a sketch of how each stage would be analyzed within the Abstract Model:

I. No constraint on either forwards or backwards coreference.

II. Forwards only. In actual discourses, the overwhelming majority of within-sentence coreference goes forwards (cf. Carden 1982). The child responds to this data by setting up a sentence-grammar constraint "A pronoun shall not precede its antecedent."

III. Forwards plus structurally-restricted backwards. The child notes that backwards coreference (and other types of backwards anaphora) can occur, and sets up an exception to the previously established forwards-only rule: "A pronoun shall not precede its antecedent unless the pronoun is in a subordinate structure."[25]

IV. Adult System: Constraints on both forwards and backwards. The child produces the adult Blocked-Forwards contrast with a minimum change in the stage-III analysis of the other coreference data, but by giving a more abstract treatment to the relevant preposed PP structures, thus producing the adult Abstract Model.

This analysis of the developmental sequence is, of course, seriously incomplete. Most important, it fails to address the question of what triggers the change from the less-restrictive system at stage III to the more-restrictive system at stage IV. Must we postulate that the child learns by indirect negative evidence that coreference is blocked in the Blocked Forwards structures? Such a requirement for indirect negative evidence might be suggested as itself an explanation for the lateness with which the Blocked-Forwards contrast is learned. But one could also put forward proposals under which the learning of Blocked Forwards was triggered by superficially unrelated evidence: For example, learning that the (Extended) Reflexive rule was cyclic might suffice to trigger Blocked Forwards, and the lateness might follow from the need to process multi-clause input to determine the cyclicity.

At present we lack data to fill these gaps and find what evidence triggers the various changes. Such data will obviously be crucial to choosing among models for coreference. On the available data, however, I have argued that the sequence of acquisition supports the Abstract Model over the Surface Model on two counts: (1) My analysis of the acquisition data implies a primary role for linear order, consistent with the Abstract Model but not with the Surface Model. (2) My analysis of the acquisition data shows that the blocked-backwards constraint is acquired substantially before Blocked Forwards, again as predicted by the Abstract Model, but not by the Surface Model.

4.2 The Surface Model

According to the Surface Model, exactly the same machinery is involved in Blocked Forwards and Blocked Backwards: "the linear order of the NPs plays no role" (Reinhart 1981, p. 605). The Surface Model therefore predicts, assuming the simplest sequence of development, that when the child learns the contrast between good backwards and blocked backwards, he will set up the simple rule "a pronoun must not C-command its antecedent," rather than a more complex rule mentioning order. This rule will block coreference in the blocked backwards and blocked forwards structures equally. The Surface Model thus predicts, other things being equal, that Blocked Forwards and Blocked Backwards should be learned at the same time.

As I have argued, the weight of evidence from section 3 shows that in fact Blocked Forwards is learned substantially later than Blocked Backwards. The most natural prediction of the Surface Model therefore is incorrect.

In the typical case, a model cannot be overthrown by a single piece of evidence: It will usually be possible to make some adjustments to accomodate the new data. In the following subsections I discuss some moves that could be made to handle the acquisition data within the Surface Model, and suggest some further experiments to test these moves.

4.2.1 *Large-Scale Restructuring*

How much restructuring takes place in language acquisition, and at what stages? The coreference data we have been discussing brings this issue sharply into focus.

The Abstract Model permits an account of the acquisition data in which the adult system develops gradually, by a series of additions that leave the Precede condition playing a crucial role from age 3 or 4 onwards, and require only local restructurings. The Surface Model appears to force us to posit a large-scale restructuring after age 10: The acquisition data shows that linear order plays a crucial role, with a Precede condition at stage II and essentially the Abstract Model's Precede/Command condition at stage III. To reach the Surface Model for the adult system from stage III, the child must abandon his precede condition for the whole relevant domain, and adopt a new model in which linear order "plays no role."

I have argued that the necessity of positing this sequence of development is evidence against the Surface Model; but it is clear that my argument turns on an unexamined assumption, the assumption that the type of large-scale restructuring apparently required by the Surface Model does not occur in normal first-language acquisition. If we are to use acquisition evidence to test models for the adult coreference system, or, more generally, if we are to use acquisition evidence to test models for any aspect of adult language, we will need to find independent evidence about how much restructuring occurs, and at what stages. Lacking such evidence, my argument for the Abstract Model depends on the untested claim that we should prefer a gradualist acquisition model that permits an account of the sequence of acquisition without large-scale restructurings.

4.2.2 *A Reinterpretation of the Data, with a Modular Model*

While I argued in section 3 that the weight of the data showed that children learned the backwards condition substantially earlier than they learned Blocked Forwards, there is a possible reinterpretation of the data that requires consideration. Notice that, across all the studies that provide a comparison, the blocked-forwards examples come out less coreferent than the good forwards. The effect sometimes fails to reach statistical significance, as in Ingram & Shaw's (1981) question-answering task, but it is always there. A defender of the Surface Model might then argue that the child's grammar proper, syntax or logical-form component, was treating blocked forwards and blocked backwards alike, inhibiting coreference in both cases, but that this inhibition was largely overcome in the blocked-forwards case by a massive, non-grammatical preference for forwards coreference. One might then go further to argue that only the act-out task, as refined by Lust & Clifford (this volume), was sensitive enough to detect the underlying grammatical effects.

Of course it is always possible to propose this type of modular analysis, in which you retain a simple model for the grammar proper, while appealing to some other module of the system to account for the data that the simple model fails to handle. Such analyses are not good or bad a priori; testing them requires looking for evidence about whether or not two independent mechanisms are involved.

To make the necessary test, I will propose an explicit modular version of the Surface Model, along the lines suggested by various people in conversation. In the grammar proper, the child learns essentially the adult constraint (16) of the Surface Model at stage III, and no further development takes place at stage IV. Outside the grammar, in a separate module X, there is a constraint CX giving a strong preference to forwards coreference in both comprehension and production. CX appears at stage II, remains through stage III, but is markedly weakened in comprehension (though perhaps not in production, considering the rarity of backwards anaphora in speech) at stage IV. The weakening of CX at stage IV gives the impression that the child is only then learning Blocked Forwards, even though in fact he has had the relevant constraint in his grammar since stage III.

Such a simple modular model, at first glance, appears to account adequately for the general outlines of the acquisition data we have seen. It fails, however, when we look at the data in more quantitative terms: If (16) and CX act independently, as the modular model requires, then we can make predictions about the magnitude of their effects: Subject to ceiling effects and such, a violation of (16) should inhibit coreference equally forwards or backwards. Similarly, a shift from forwards to backwards in violation of CX should inhibit coreference equally whether the examples violate (16) ("blocked coreference") or obey (16) ("good coreference"). Table II gives the necessary comparisons.

The data in Table II shows that a simple modular model fails this quantitative test. Four studies allow the necessary comparison with an interpretation task, and in three of the four a violation of (16) has a substantially greater effect on backwards coreference than on forwards. The exception is Lust et al.'s −PL condition, but even there the proportionate effect is far greater on backwards: A violation of (16)

TABLE II
Test of a Modular Analysis

Study	Per Cent Coreferent Forwards			Backwards		
	good	blocked	difference	good	blocked	difference
Ingram & Shaw	79%	78%	1%	53%	24%	29%
Taylor-Browne[a] (age 6;2−10;5)	100%	76%	24%	69%	14%	55%
Lust et al. (Act-out[a])						
+ pragmatic lead	91%	83%	8%	75%	46%	29%
− pragmatic lead	100%	76%	24%	37%	18%	19%

[a] Percentages calculated counting only responses coded as coreferent or non-coreferent.

moves forwards from 100% coref to 76%, a reduction of about a quarter, while a violation of (16) moves backwards from 37% coref to 18%, a reduction of about a half.

These results are not consistent with a simple modular model, in which the effects of linear order (CX) and a structural violation (16) should be independent. Any model that allowed for the necessary interaction, to make a violation of (16) more severe in the backwards direction, would involve a serious weakening of the Surface Model claim that Blocked Forwards and Blocked Backwards were handled by a single structural mechanism, in which linear order "plays no role."[26] On the other hand, the results are consistent with the sequence of development assumed by the Abstract Model, where this group data would represent a stage where most of the subjects have mastered the Blocked-Backwards contrast, but fewer than 25% have mastered Blocked Forwards.

4.2.3 *A Change in Tree Structure*

For a defender of the Surface Model, the most appealing way to bring his model in line with the acquisition data is to postulate a change in the tree structure that the child assigns to preposed PPs. Recall that the Surface Model handled the contrast between good forwards with preposed time adverbial clauses (4a) and blocked forwards with preposed locative PPs by postulating that the preposed time adverbial hung one node higher in the tree. Suppose now that the child at stage III has the adult Surface Model constraint (16), but the wrong structure for the preposed PPs: If the child hangs the PP where the adult hangs the time adverbial, then (16) would predict that forwards coreference would not be blocked. On this analysis, the child would not need to learn anything about coreference per se to move from stage III to IV: As soon as he learned the adult structure for preposed PPs, the forwards coreference in (5a) would automatically be blocked.

Unfortunately, there is no obvious way to test this proposal within English:[27] Just as there was no evidence independent of coreference for postulating the different structures for preposed time adverbials and locatives, so there will be no direct test we can make (independent of coreference) to see whether the child has the postulated difference in structure. The best hope would be to look for correlations between the time when Blocked Forwards is learned and possible triggers for reanalyzing the structure of the preposed PPs. There, the small amount of evidence that is available tells against the hypothesis: One obvious possible trigger for re-analysis of the PPs would be learning that certain verbs like *put* require an obligatory locative. This sub-categorization rule would require (on standard analyses) that the locative be part of the VP, and so could trigger Reinhart's S-Adverbial/VP-Adverbial distinction. This in turn could trigger the different structures for the preposed adverbials, and so yield blocked forwards coreference. However, Solan and Roeper (1978) show that children age 4–6 already have the relevant strict subcategorization for *put*, much too soon to be the trigger for the appearance of blocked forwards at age 11–12.[28]

In addition to these empirical problems, it is important to note that this tree-structure proposal for the acquisition data depends crucially on the correctness of Reinhart's original tree-structure proposal for the adult contrast between (4a) and (5a), and that the adult proposal is difficult to maintain in the face of the data from sections 2.4.2 and 2.4.3.

5. CONCLUSION

Section 2 outlines two competing approaches to the analysis of coreference in English, the Abstract Model and the Surface Model. When we apply these models to language acquisition, they make sharply distinct predictions about the order in which certain coreference constraints should be learned. In the Abstract Model, the mechanisms involved in blocked forwards coreference are substantially more complex than those involved in controlling good backwards coreference; other things being equal, the backwards constraint should therefore be learned before blocked forwards. In the Surface Model, exactly the same mechanism controls blocked forwards and good backwards coreference; other things being equal, blocked forwards should therefore be learned at the same time as the backwards constraint.

I have argued that the weight of the acquisition evidence discussed in section 3 shows that the backwards constraint is learned substantially earlier than blocked forwards. For example, we find that 60% of Ingram and Shaw's (1981) subjects from age 6 to 8 control the backwards constraint, as do 88% of Taylor-Browne's subjects from 8 to 10, while less than 25% of the same subjects control blocked forwards. To find a majority of subjects controlling blocked forwards, we have to go to Taylor-Browne's 11–12 year old group.

The acquisition data therefore agrees with the prediction of the Abstract Model, but not with the natural prediction of the Surface Model. This result, I suggest, should not be a great surprise. While the Surface Model has been widely accepted, the data and references of section 2.4 show that the Surface Model is not descriptively adequate in its simple form, and that the modifications needed to reach descriptive adequacy would result in an overall model that was inferior to the Abstract Model. If the Abstract Model is in fact the correct analysis of the adult data, we would expect to find that it also made the correct predictions about acquisition.

The adult and acquisition data thus work together to support the Abstract Model against the Surface Model. This conclusion is of some theoretical interest, since the Abstract Model is not compatible with Chomsky's (1981, 1982) hypothesis that a single level of S-Structure is the sole input to Logical Form and semantics.

NOTES

* I am grateful for useful comments and criticism on various parts of this paper from Elan Dresher, Lynn Gordon, Nobuko Hasegawa, Carolyn Johnson, Susumu Kuno, William O'Grady, Janet Randall, Michael Rochemont, Larry Solan, Donca Steriade, Vicki Sudhalter, Jindra Toman, and Greer Watson. Barbara Lust provided exceedingly helpful detailed comments on an earlier version of this paper, leading to substantial revisions. I am especially grateful to Helen Cairns, Jennifer Hsu, David Ingram, and Karen Taylor-Browne, both for their advice and for their letting me report some of their unpublished results. Of course the people who have helped me do not necessarily agree with my conclusions; and I believe that in fact some of them would disagree very strongly.

[1] O'Grady (1983ab) makes some very interesting proposals that are different in character from both the Abstract and Surface models.

[2] Langacker's statement was slightly more complex, since it also covered the coordinate cases discussed in section 2.4.1.

[3] This wording seems to imply an interpretive treatment of coreference, but in fact the rule statements for the present data would be essentially equivalent using any of the familiar mechanisms: A classical pronominalization rule, Jackendoff-type coreference tables, a generative-semantics variable-replacement rule, a Lasnik-type disjoint reference rule, or a GB-type coindexing would work equally well.

[4] Carden and Gordon (1982) give an independent argument for a cyclic treatment of Reflexive, even in a model with trace theory.

[5] Within a Government-Binding model, one might attempt to define the (relatively abstract) level of S-Structure as the input to Adverb Preposing, so that ER could apply to S-Structure. This would not help with the theoretical problem for this model, however: The Abstract Model crucially depends on having ER apply to an un-preposed

structure, and regular coreference to a preposed structure. Whichever level a GB analysis selected as S-Structure, it would still need input to Logical Form from the other level. The best that could be done without a major change in the GB model would be to have a reconstruction rule or an extended trace theory that would make information from the second level available within the LF component.

[6] Actually, Reinhart proposes a slightly more complex definition, together with slightly more complex tree structures. Following Reinhart's practice (1981, p. 612), I will use the simplified definition and structures here.

[7] In Chomsky's Binding Theory, the relevant level is S-Structure. On standard analyses, S-Structure and surface structure would be the same in the relevant respects for the examples we are discussing.

[8] Reinhart (this volume) would make the same prediction, to judge from her very brief discussion of the issue. I should point out, however, that she is skeptical that it will be possible to collect useful experimental data on the sort of coreference that is involved in most of our examples, which she would now analyze as "pragmatic coreference."

[9] Reinhart is aware of these examples, but would apparently wish to treat them as "really" coreferent, and provide a special non-syntactic constraint (Reinhart 1976, p. 141).

[10] I am grateful to Greer Watson for drawing my attention to these PP examples.

[11] I am grateful to Nobuko Hasegawa for drawing my attention to the relevance of clefts.

[12] I assume that no defender of the Surface Model or of GB is likely to propose that (23, 24) should be derived from un-clefted S-Structures. See also note 5.

[13] McCawley (1984) gives cleft examples implying that the required cyclic rule could not have the clausemate condition proposed by Kuno (1975) and Carden (1981). Instead, he argues that the rule will need to apply to an abstract level with the property that the rule's domain can include complement clauses while excluding modifier clauses. I will not attempt to deal with McCawley's data here, but it can be seen that his analysis offers no comfort to defenders of the Surface Model.

[14] Goodluck (to appear) appears to be an exception to the general pattern; Tavakolian (1978) does not provide the particular comparisons we are interested in.

[15] Carden (1982) provides some data bearing on the frequency of backwards coreference and backwards anaphora in general.

[16] In the +PL condition, the test sentence was introduced by "Now I am going to tell you a little story about _ ," where the name in the test sentence appeared for "_"; in the −PL condition, the test sentence was presented with no introduction.

[17] The per cent coreferent can be calculated directly from Lust et al.'s Table 6. I have estimated the per cent non-coreferent from Table 5, "Mean Number of Items Correct." "Correct" for this act-out task was defined by refined scoring criteria: Lust informs me (p.c.) that the coding of "Correct" and "Coreferent" was in part linked and in part independent: For a response to be coded "Correct," it must have been coded + or − for "Coreferent", and the coreference value assigned must correspond to a possible adult reading of the test sentence. In addition, the response must meet other criteria for accuracy and completeness. For a response to be assigned any coding (+ or −) for coreference, the child must have "acted out the two clauses with reasonable success in achieving the grammatical relations, with correct lexical content, etc." (Lust, p.c.). Thus, in order to be coded + or − for "Coreferent," a response had to meet most, but not all,

of the accuracy and completeness criteria for "Correct." These coding criteria suggest that it is likely that it was relatively uncommon for a response to have been coded with a correct (adult-like) value for + or − "Coreferent" without also having been coded as "Correct." In my calculations below, I have omitted such (presumably uncommon) cases, and used number "Correct" as an estimate of the number of responses showing a correct "Coreference" judgement.

Given this assumption, we can estimate the number of non-coreferent responses as follows: For blocked backwards and blocked forwards, where the adult judgement is − coref, number "Correct" should approximately equal number non-coreferent. For good forwards and good backwards, where either + or − coref would be a possible adult judgement, number "Correct" should be approximately the sum of number + coref added to number − coref. Number non-coreferent should then equal number "Correct" minus number "Coreferent."

We can similarly estimate the number of responses not coded as either + or − coref ("other" responses) as the total number of responses minus the sum of (number "Coreferent" plus our estimate of number non-coreferent).

This estimate of the number of non-coreferent and "other" responses will become crucial in our discussion of the blocked-forwards cases (section 3.2.2), where the number of "other" responses becomes so high that small errors in the estimation might have a major effect on our interpretation of the proportion of coreferent to non-coreferent. I regret that I have not been able to obtain more exact figures for the Lust et al. study.

[18] The interaction with the PL manipulation is complex for this data: The two youngest groups show a significant blocked-backwards contrast for +PL, but not for −PL, while the next two groups (III, IV) show a significant contrast for −PL, but not for +PL. The four groups combined show a significant contrast for both + and − PL.

[19] Lust et al. did find that the effect of Pragmatic Lead decreased with advancing age in just those constructions where coreference was blocked for adults, giving evidence of progress toward the adult system.

[20] Taylor-Browne's paradigm included a range of types of preposed PPs. For the simplest comparison with Ingram & Shaw's results, I report data only for the plain object-of-locative-preposition type illustrated in (30b, 31b), corresponding to her types (1) and (8).

[21] I report here the nine subjects listed in Ingram & Shaw's Tables 12 and 13. In addition, one subject (age 6;6) gave only non-coreferent responses to all sentences, and some of the six "isolated" cases that did not fit any of Ingram & Shaw's patterns may have given fewer than three coreferent judgements for Blocked Forwards.

[22] This data was provided by Lust (p.c.); I regret that I do not have the corresponding figures for "non-coref" and "other."

[23] It should be recalled that the number of non-coref responses was estimated from Lust et al.'s "correct" figure, and that this estimate will understate the number non-coref to the extent that there were responses accurate enough to be coded as "non-coref," but not accurate enough to be coded as "correct." The Lust and Clifford data suggests that, for the blocked-forwards structure, this effect was probably minor: They reported 19% non-coref for blocked forwards (Table VII), and also 19% correct (calculated from Table VI). My estimating technique would therefore have produced exactly the correct result,

applied to this Lust and Clifford data. I should mention, however, that my estimate would not have been so accurate for the Lust and Clifford good-backwards examples, where a susbtantial number of examples (15%) were coded for + or − CR, but not coded as "correct." I have no explanation for this asymmetry between the structural types in the Lust and Clifford data.

[24] To facilitate a comparison across studies with widely differing numbers of "other" responses, Table I gives an adjusted per cent coreferent, calculated by the method described in section 3.2.2 and notes 17 and 23. In the Lust and Clifford data, the figures for Good Forwards (41) and Good Backwards/Subordinate Clause (43a) are omitted, since I have only the raw per cent coreferent, with no information on per cent non-coreferent and "other," and so no way to calculate an adjusted figure comparable to the data from the other studies.

[25] I am disregarding the important question of whether the child's grammar's definition of "subordinate structure" is the same as the adult's. Additional evidence, primarily from Solan (1978, 1981) and Taylor-Browne (1983), suggests that the child does not have the adult definition of "bounding node" until about the age where the Blocked-Forwards constraint is also being mastered. It is natural to speculate that these two developments are linked, with one being the trigger for the other.

[26] We could obtain a further test for a modular hypothesis by comparing acquisition data for our blocked-forwards construction with equivalent data for two structurally distinct types where forwards coreference is also blocked, Postal's (1971) Cross-Over examples and Ross's (1967) backwards Equi examples.

[27] Jindra Toman points out (p.c.) that the required independent test is available in Czech, where clitic placement is sensitive to where a preposed adverbial hangs.

[28] However, Dollighan (1981) gives evidence from a grammaticality judgement and correction task implying that strict subcategorization violations are first clearly detected around age 10, a result difficult to reconcile with Solan and Roeper (1978).

REFERENCES

Carden, G.: 1981, 'Blocked forwards coreference', paper presented at the Linguistic Society of America Winter Meeting, New York.

Carden, G.: 1982, 'Backwards anaphora in discourse context', *Journal of Linguistics* **18**, 361–387.

Carden, G. and T. Dietrich: 1981, 'Introspection, observation and experiment: An example where experiment pays off', in P. D. Asquith and R. N. Giere (eds.), *Proceedings of the 1980 Biennial Meeting of the Philosophy of Science Association*, 2, East Lansing, Mich., pp. 583–597.

Carden, G. and L. Gordon: 1982, 'S-structure coreference assignment will require both reconstruction and extended trace theory: Evidence from English and Fijian', unpublished paper, Harvard University.

Chomsky, C.: 1969, *The Acquisition of Syntax in Children from 5 to 10*, MIT Press, Cambridge, Mass.

Chomsky, N.: 1981, *Lectures on Government and Binding*, Foris, Dordrecht.

Chomsky, N.: 1982, *Some Concepts and Consequences of the Theory of Government and Binding*, MIT Press, Cambridge, Mass.

Dollaghan, C. A.: 1981, *Developmental Changes in Children's Awareness of Some Verb Propositional Schemata*, unpublished doctoral dissertation, University of Wisconsin — Madison.

Goodluck, H.: to appear, 'Children's interpretation of pronouns and null NPs: An alternative view', in Lust, B. (ed.), *Studies in the Acquisition of Anaphora*: (Volume 2), *Applying the Constraints*, D. Reidel, Dordrecht.

Hsu, J., H. Cairns, S. Eisenberg, and G. Schlisselberg: in preparation, 'Children's interpretation of coreference', unpublished paper, City University of New York.

Ingram, D. and C. Shaw: 1981, 'The comprehension of pronominal reference in children', unpublished paper, The University of British Columbia.

Jackendoff, R.: 1972, *Semantic Interpretation in Generative Grammar*, MIT Press, Cambridge, Mass.

Kuno, S.: 1975, 'Three perspectives in the functional approach to syntax', *Papers from the Parasession on Functionalism*, Chicago Linguistic Society, 276—336.

Lakoff, G.: 1968, 'Pronouns and reference', Indiana University Linguistic Club.

Langacker, R. W.: 1969, 'Pronominalization and the chain of command', in D. Reibel and S. Schane (eds.), *Modern Studies in English*, Prentice-Hall, Englewood Cliffs, N.J., pp. 160—186.

Lasnik, H.: 1976, 'Remarks on coreference', *Linguistic Analysis* 2, 1—22.

Lust, B., K. Loveland, and R. Kornet: 1980, 'The development of anaphora in first language: Syntactic and pragmatic constraints', *Linguistic Analysis* 6, 359—391.

McCawley, J. D.: 1984, 'Anaphora and notions of command', in *Proceedings of the Tenth Annual Meeting of the Berkeley Linguistic Society*, University of California at Berkeley.

O'Grady, W.: 1983a, 'A computational approach to anaphora', *Journal of Linguistic Research* 2, 81—101.

O'Grady, W.: 1983b, 'Anaphoric relations in the clause and the NP', *Papers from the Nineteenth Regional Meeting*, Chicago Linguistic Society, Chicago, pp. 317—328.

Postal, P.: 1971, *Cross-Over Phenomena*, Holt, Reinhart and Winston, New York.

Reinhart, T.: 1976, *The Syntactic Domain of Anaphora*, unpublished doctoral dissertation, MIT. Cambridge, Massachusetts.

Reinhart, T.: 1981, 'Definite NP anaphora and c-command domains', *Linguistic Inquiry* 12, 605—636.

Reinhart, T.: 1983a, *Anaphora and Semantic Interpretation*, Croom Helm, London.

Reinhart, T.: 1983b, 'Coreference and bound anaphora: A restatement of the anaphora questions', *Linguistics and Philosophy* 6, 47—88.

Ross, J.: 1967, 'On the cyclic nature of English pronominalization', in *To Honor Roman Jacobson*, Mouton, The Hague, 1669—1682, and reprinted in 1969 in D. Reibel and S. Schane (eds.), *Modern Studies in English*, Prentice-Hall, Englewood Cliffs, N.J., 187—200.

Solan, L.: 1978, *Anaphora in Child Languge*, unpublished doctoral dissertation, University of Massachusetts.

Solan, L.: 1981, 'The acquisition of structural restrictions on anaphora', in S. Tavakolian (ed.), *Language Acquisition and Linguistic Theory*, MIT Press, Cambridge, Mass., pp. 59—73.

Solan, L. and Roeper, T.: 1978, 'Children's use of syntactic structure in interpreting relative clauses', in H. Goodluck and L. Solan (eds.), *Papers in the Structure and Development of Child Language*, Occasional Papers in Linguistic, 4, University of Massachusettss, Amherst, pp. 105–126.

Tavakolian, S.: 1978, 'Children's comprehension of pronominal subjects and missing subjects in complicated sentences', in H. Goodluck and L. Solan (eds.), *Papers in the Structure and Development of Child Language*, Occasional Papers in Linguistics, 4, Univesity of Massachusetts, Amherst, pp. 145–152.

Taylor-Browne, K.: 1983, 'Acquiring restrictions on forwards anaphora: A pilot study', *Calgary Working Papers in Linguistics* 9, 75–99.

Wasow, T.: 1972, *Anaphoric Relations in English*, unpublished doctoral dissertation, MIT.

LIST OF CONTRIBUTORS

Guy Carden
University of British Columbia
Vancouver, British Columbia, Canada

Terri Clifford
Cornell University
Ithaca, New York

Catherine Cross
Carolina Population Center
Chapel Hill, N.C.

Suzanne Flynn
Massachusetts Institute of Technology
Cambridge, MA

Robert Freidin
Princeton University
Princeton, New Jersey 08540

Barbara Lust
Cornell University
Ithaca, N.Y.

Tanya Reinhart
Tel Aviv University
Tel Aviv, Israel

Thomas Roeper
University of Massachusetts
Amherst, MA

Elaine Schuetz
Cornell University
Ithaca, N.Y.

Janet Cohen Sherman
Massachusetts Institute of Technology
Cambridge, MA

Larry Solan
208 8th Street
Hoboken, New Jersey

Henk van Riemsdijk
Tilburg University
Tilburg, The Netherlands

Thomas Wasow
Stanford University
Stanford, CA

TABLE OF CONTENTS
VOLUME II: APPLYING THE CONSTRAINTS

361

INDEX OF NAMES

INDEX OF SUBJECTS